TWO
EAST ANGLIAN
DIARIES
1641–1729

ISAAC ARCHER
and
WILLIAM COE

Mildenhall Church: aquatint by James Scales of the exterior, *c*.1825 (*above*); and lithograph after C.J. Greenwood, *c*.1840, of the 'preaching box' interior, much as Archer and Coe knew it (*below*).

TWO
EAST ANGLIAN
DIARIES
1641–1729

ISAAC ARCHER
and
WILLIAM COE

Edited by
MATTHEW STOREY

General Editor
DAVID DYMOND

The Boydell Press

Suffolk Records Society
VOLUME XXXVI

A Suffolk Records Society publication
First published 1994 by The Boydell Press, Woodbridge

ISBN 0 85115 564 2

Issued to subscribing members
for the year 1993–94

The Boydell Press is an imprint of Boydell & Brewer Ltd
PO Box 9, Woodbridge, Suffolk IP12 3DF, UK
and of Boydell & Brewer Inc.
PO Box 41026, Rochester, NY 14604–4126, USA

British Library Cataloguing-in-Publication Data
A catalogue record for this book is available
from the British Library

This book is printed on acid-free paper

Printed in Great Britain by
St Edmundsbury Press Ltd, Bury St Edmunds, Suffolk

Contents

List of Illustrations

Acknowledgements

As with any project which has taken a long time to complete, there are always many people to thank. I began work on Isaac Archer's diary as part of a PhD dissertation; I am therefore indebted to Dr Margaret Spufford for first encouraging me to undertake research on the diary, and for her guidance and friendship as a supervisor. I trust that this volume may serve as a token of my thanks. I also owe very many thanks to Professor Patrick Collinson, who kindly agreed to act as my supervisor at a critical stage, and whose timely suggestions and immense learning directed my studies along many fruitful paths. More recently, this volume has benefited from the expertise and generosity of Dr Elisabeth Leedham-Green.

I was first enabled to come to Cambridge to study by way of a British Academy Research Studentship. Without that generous support, the project which has ended with this volume could not even have begun.

Transcribing the diaries and researching their historical background has taken me to a number of record collections around the country; to the staff of the following repositories I offer my sincere thanks for their kind assistance: Cambridgeshire Record Office, Cambridge; Suffolk Record Office, Bury St Edmunds; the Manuscripts and Rare Books collections of the Cambridge University Library; Public Records Office, Chancery Lane, London.

Many people showed early interest in the publication of the diaries which appear in this volume, and it is to them that I owe special thanks for bringing this project to completion. Dr F.G. Emmison first gave me the idea of seeking a publisher for Archer's diary, after he sold the work to the Cambridge University Library. Dr Philip Saunders of the Cambridgeshire Records Society gave much helpful advice following my approach to that society with a view to publishing Archer's diary. However, the Suffolk Records Society seemed to offer the best prospects for early publication of both Coe and Archer, who surely belong together in a single volume. My very sincere thanks must therefore go to Norman Scarfe, Peter Northeast, and especially to David Dymond for their expert advice, persistent encouragement, and constant assistance in ensuring that the volume was accurate and complete. I have gained much pleasure in working with, and learning from, them. I hope that they will derive as much satisfaction as I will from the completed volume. I also owe deep gratitude to the following for so generously supplying information on the family background of William Coe, which has so dramatically improved that section of the Introduction: Dr Colin Dring, Jean Lock, Ray Lock and Dr John Blatchly. Phillip Judge drew two valuable maps.

I reserve my profoundest thanks until last. During the course of a long research project, there have been some to whom I will always be indebted for their unwavering friendship and loyalty. To my parents and sister, I owe thanks for their extraordinary support, emotional and financial, which throughout has been quite beyond the call of duty. My father, in particular, has shown avid interest in all aspects of the volume and I am grateful for his extraordinary efforts to help bring this work to completion: he has driven me throughout Cambridgeshire and Suffolk to take the photographs for my thesis, has produced family trees for the Archer diary, and has improved my ideas for maps. Finally, I wish to thank those whom I have met whilst at Cambridge who have shown, by their steady and quiet loyalty, the true meaning of friendship: Alison Booker, Lisa Chamberlain, Alice Coudreau, James Cormick, Dr Claire Fitz patrick, Professor David F. Ford, Dr Ian Gray, Steven J.R. Hartley, Matthew Jacobsen, Rabbi Seth Kunin, Rev. Michael Morton, Henrik Rasmussen, Dr Mark Rudnicki, Ian Selby, Marcus Stewart, Stephen Teichgraeber and Ian Thomas. This volume is dedicated to them.

NOTE: The two diaries in this volume are reproduced by kind permission of the Syndics of Cambridge University Library.

Introduction

ISAAC ARCHER: HIS EARLY LIFE AND EDUCATION

Archer was born in north Suffolk in 1641, probably in the parish of South Elmham St Margaret (though the baptism register does not survive for the crucial period). Suffolk was the home of several of his maternal relatives, while his father's family came from Essex. It was to the latter county that William Archer moved his family only a few years after Isaac's birth. Although too young to be profoundly influenced by the bloodshed of the Civil Wars, the diarist gratefully recounts his family's escape from rampaging royalist soldiers during the siege of Colchester in 1648. Archer makes much of the fact that his father providentially found shelter in a field, and escaped the swords of the King's troops by the closest of margins. He had been pursued because of his deep commitment to the religious struggles in Essex, and his preaching against the royalist cause. Later, in 1649, he approved of the King's execution.[1] Readers of the diary cannot fail to be struck by the enormous importance which Archer attaches to three factors: the relationship with his father, the decisive influence of that relationship upon all his thoughts (ranging from pastoral matters to his choice of spouse), and the deep regret and guilt which lingered in his conscience after his father's death in 1670.

When Archer was only eight years old, his mother Mary died. This sad event threw him into full dependence upon his father, and partly explains why William Archer features so strongly in the diary.[2] The sense of loss was compounded by the deaths of his brother William and sister Elizabeth, only weeks later. Another sister, Mary, survived during his adolescence, but died in 1664, leaving Archer as the only survivor of five children born to his father's first marriage.[3]

Personal loss was doubtless exacerbated by loneliness, when in 1653 his father insensitively decided to board him at Halstead school. Leaving home so

---

1 Diary, 1653–54, pp. 13–14. A recent work devoted specifically to the religious justification of regicide, is N.H. Mayfield, *Puritans and Regicide: Presbyterian-Independent Differences over the trial and execution of Charles (I) Stuart* (New York and London, 1988). Mayfield tries to show, using somewhat confused and perhaps simplistic categories, how it was expectation of Christ's earthly rule, and not liturgical or ecclesiological disputes, which motivated those who desired the King's execution. That Mayfield's categories are simplistic is illustrated by the case of William Archer himself who, although doubtless an Independent, does not seem to have shared the morphography of conversion propounded by Independents such as Thomas Goodwin.

2 Archer, commenting on the crucial question of his mother's spirituality, records that she was 'remarkable for her piety and prudence'. Oliver Heywood reports a similar opinion of his mother; see J. Horsfall Turner (ed.), *The Rev. Oliver Heywood, B.A., 1630–1702; his Autobiography, Diaries, Anecdote and Event Books*, I (1882), 51.

3 Diary, 1648–9, p. 9.

suddenly and unexpectedly left a strong mark on Isaac's personal development, further confusing the emotional relationship with his father. While at Halstead Archer's consciousness of his spiritual pedigree[4] was reinforced by his master, Mr Covill, who drew his attention to the outstanding godly example of his family, in an attempt to persuade him to think more seriously about the welfare of his soul.[5]

During Isaac's years as a boarder, a pattern emerged which was to characterize the relationship with his father for as long as he was dependent upon him. William Archer's material provision for his son, throughout his school and university years, was meagre and inadequate in the extreme.[6] His parsimony does not seem, initially at least, to have been the result of financial difficulties, for the diary states that the Colchester lectureship was worth the substantial sum of £100 a year, in addition to which William Archer took as his second wife 'a rich, religious and a well-bred gentlewoman'.[7] However, following her death in 1657, after seven years of marriage, William was sufficiently grieved to leave Colchester and his lectureship there, and that may have caused his financial position to deteriorate.

In spite of his father's attempts to subject him to punitive discipline, Archer proved a somewhat mischievous boarder and was particularly prone to petty theft, an activity which must have been encouraged by his meagre allowance. Significantly, however, these educational and familial disciplines did bear fruit in one important area: his wrongdoings provoked within him the profoundest sense of guilt and fear of judgement.[8]

Religious discipline in the family home revolved around the reading of scripture and reciting of sermons, but they proved onerous chores indeed to the young Archer. This was partly due to a speech impediment which prevented him from reading aloud with fluency, and must have later contributed to his dislike of the set and repetitive liturgical forms contained in the Book of Common Prayer. It is not surprising that the reintroduction of that book after the Restoration aroused the strongest antipathy in William Archer.

Financial considerations seem to have provoked William Archer's opposition to his son's further education at university, and initially dashed Isaac's hopes of becoming a scholar at Cambridge. William defended his decision by insisting that Isaac would be unfit as a minister of the gospel because of his stammering speech, and because he lacked the requisite seriousness in spiritual matters. He was also fearful that the broadly-based and tolerant religious policies of the Interregnum would not survive the restoration of the monarchy.

Consequently Isaac was sent to be apprenticed to a linen draper in London, on the grounds that his best hope of financial independence lay in learning a trade. A predictable series of events ensued which, however, worked distinctly to Isaac's advantage. His father terminated the apprenticeship because of the expense involved, once more illustrating his strange unwillingness to support

---

[4] Oliver Heywood was also keen to emphasize that his own father was godly, and came from a family noted for their godliness; J. Horsfall Turner, I (1882), 77.

[5] Diary, 1655–6, p. 16.

[6] Diary, 1652–4, p. 14.

[7] Diary, 1650–2, p. 11.

[8] Diary, 1652–6, pp. 14–15.

his first-born and only surviving son. Opposition and neglect of this magnitude required a 'speciall providence', if Isaac's aspirations were in any sense to be realized. Such a providence was forthcoming when Henry Dearsly, an acquaintance and Fellow of Trinity College, Cambridge, persuaded William Archer finally to agree to a university education for his son.

Archer increasingly realized that the fluid and uncertain intellectual and religious environment of Cambridge University on the eve of the Restoration, afforded him freedom to explore and pursue many new ideas and opinions which were not allowed him in the closed and narrowly defined world of family and school.[9] The embracing of 'contrary' views at Cambridge was an experience which he later repented. He promised his father that he would give up the company of 'inexperienced' and 'frivolous' people who were allegedly responsible for encouraging such laxity.[10] However, he had difficulty in finding sober and serious company, and was drawn towards the less reputable elements of college society. They encouraged him in 'erroneous opinions', which in turn he was tempted to espouse as a way of securing such companions.[11] Apart from the spiritual turmoil in the diary at this period, the reader may also be struck by the depth of understanding which several of the senior Fellows of Trinity College showed towards Archer, as he struggled after 1660 to come to terms with the implications of the Restoration and church settlement. Henry Dearsly features as particularly sympathetic, offering him spiritual and practical advice, gaining him the favour of the Master, Henry Ferne, and acting in loco parentis when William Archer cast off his son and refused him further maintenance.

Archer also records the profound impact of hearing sermons and religious lectures, and the relative benefits which they brought to his spiritual welfare. A popular resort of the diarist, apart from a wide selection of college chapels, was the parish church of Holy Trinity in Cambridge, home of a famous puritan lectureship held by such eminent divines as John Preston and Richard Sibbes (both were there before Archer came up to the university). At Holy Trinity, Archer consciously began to associate himself with this puritan tradition by diligently learning the art of note-taking at sermons, a task which had proved so taxing to him as a young boarder in Essex.

Little mention is made of day-to-day life at university, and the inward-looking concerns of the diary at this time reflect a period of intense psychological turmoil and concentrated self-reflection. In the university environment Archer felt uncertain and threatened, principally because of political and religious changes following Charles II's return. Yet, in earlier and more certain times, Archer had viewed the prospect of attending university with the greatest enthusiasm. He looked forward to quiet study and serene meditation, which would enable him to consider his 'soule's estate'. In the event, Archer

---

9 On the character and potential challenges of university life for those of a puritan disposition, see J.T. Cliffe, The Puritan Gentry (1984), pp. 83–103.

10 Significantly, when Archer reasoned with his father that he must conform in order to obey the King (to whom they were both equally bound), William Archer replied that 'he must be obeyed rather, for magistracy is founded upon family government'; Diary, 19 Aug. 1662, p. 71.

11 On discipline and vice at the universities, see Cliffe, op. cit., pp. 83–5.

THE ARCHER FAMILY

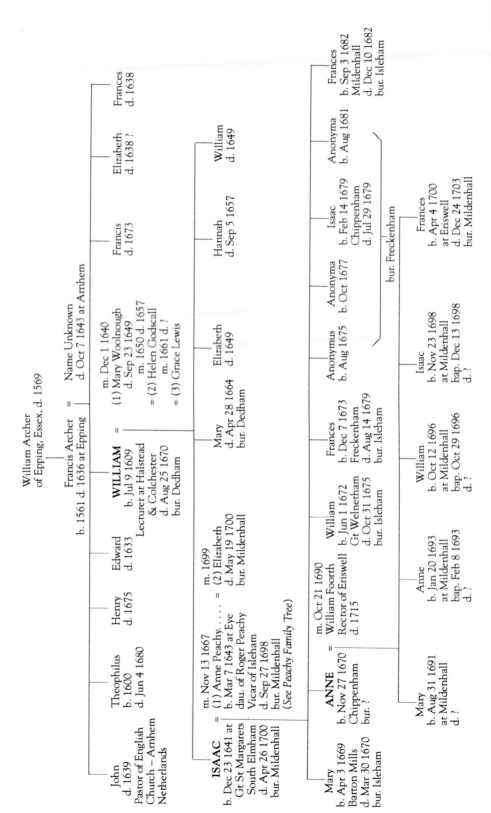

William Archer
of Epping, Essex, d. 1569

Francis Archer = Name Unknown
b. 1561 d. 1636 at Epping   d. Oct 7 1643 at Arnhem

John
d. 1639
Pastor of English
Church – Arnhem
Netherlands

Theophilus
b. 1600
d. Jun 4 1680

Henry
d. 1675

Edward
d. 1633

WILLIAM =
b. Jul 9 1609
Lecturer at Halstead
& Colchester
d. Aug 25 1670
bur. Dedham

m. Dec 1 1640
(1) Mary Woolnough
    d. Sep 23 1649
= (2) Helen Godscall
    m. 1650 d. 1657
= (3) Grace Lewis
    m. 1661 d. ?

Francis
d. 1673

Elizabeth
d. 1638 ?

Frances
d. 1638

ISAAC =
b. Dec 23 1641 at
Gt St Margarets
South Elmham
d. Apr 26 1700
bur. Mildenhall

m. Nov 13 1667
(1) Anne Peachy.....
b. Mar 7 1643 at Eye
dau. of Roger Peachy
Vicar of Isleham
d. Sep 27 1698
bur. Mildenhall
(See Peachy Family Tree)

= (2) Elizabeth
    d. May 19 1700
    bur. Mildenhall

Mary
d. Apr 28 1664
bur. Dedham

Elizabeth
d. 1649

Hannah
d. Sep 5 1657

William
d. 1649

Mary
b. Apr 3 1669
Barton Mills
d. Mar 30 1670
bur. Isleham

ANNE =
b. Nov 27 1670
Chippenham
bur. ?

m. Oct 21 1690
William Foorth
Rector of Eriswell
d. 1715

William
b. Jun 1 1672
Gt Welnetham
d. Oct 31 1675
bur. Isleham

Frances
b. Dec 7 1673
Freckenham
d. Aug 14 1679
bur. Isleham

Anonymus
b. Aug 1675

Anonyma
b. Oct 1677

Isaac
b. Feb 14 1679
Chippenham
d. Jul 29 1679

Anonyma
b. Aug 1681

Frances
b. Sep 3 1682
Mildenhall
d. Dec 10 1682
bur. Isleham

bur. Freckenham

Mary
b. Aug 31 1691
at Mildenhall
d. ?

Anne
b. Jan 20 1693
at Mildenhall
bap. Feb 8 1693
d. ?

William
b. Oct 12 1696
at Mildenhall
bap. Oct 29 1696
d. ?

Isaac
b. Nov 23 1698
at Mildenhall
bap. Dec 13 1698
d. ?

Frances
b. Apr 4 1700
at Eriswell
d. Dec 24 1703
bur. Mildenhall

found few companions as single-minded as himself. However, the undoubted generosity shown to him by Trinity College endeared Cambridge to him, and he was naturally reluctant to return home, knowing that his father would treat him censoriously and meanly. These potent factors persuaded him to take holy orders in the Church of England, in direct opposition to his father's express command to reject conformity.

THE DIARY OF ISAAC ARCHER

This diary is in the manuscript collection of Cambridge University Library, and bears the class mark Add. MS 8499. It was sold to the library in 1985 by the then owner, the eminent Essex historian Dr F.G. Emmison, on condition that it be published at the earliest opportunity.

The manuscript is a small volume bound in brown leather; the front cover is now loose. Its pages measure approximately 95mm by 155mm. They are all in a good state of preservation with few visible signs of deterioration beyond occasional fraying. Some 228 written pages were numbered by the diarist himself, and throughout the book entries occur on both sides of the paper. At the end about one third of the pages remain blank. Inside the back cover are a family tree and other notes pertaining to Archer's children, along with a valediction to his grandfather. The diarist's hand is not by any means an elegant one and exhibits many idiosyncrasies of style. However, largely owing to Archer's method of composing the diary, of which more will be said below, most of the text is clearly decipherable. Nevertheless, his hand steadily deteriorated in the 1690s so that the last few pages do raise palaeographical problems.

In terms of the sheer number of words, Archer's diary is shorter than, for example, both Oliver Heywood's diaries and notebooks and Ralph Josselin's autobiography. The text extends to about 82,000 words, less than a third of the length of Josselin's diary which Alan Macfarlane calculated at 290,000 words.[12] Similarly, Archer's entries tend to be somewhat less frequent than those of his counterpart at Earls Colne. Perhaps only one half of the entries are clearly dated in any way, and after 1688 the frequency of dated entries declines dramatically. While the first twelve years of his parochial ministry occupy ninety-five pages, the last twelve years of his life are dealt with in just sixteen pages. Thus, the bulk of entries in Archer's diary concern his life as a student at Cambridge University and his next twenty years as a clergyman.

When Archer's diary is compared with others of the period, several differences of composition become evident. Although many comparable diarists wrote retrospectively of their childhood and upbringing, it seems that Archer throughout his life retained the habit of writing about events some time after they had happened. Thus, although the diary covers the whole of Archer's life, from 1641–1700, he revealed that he did not begin to keep a diary of any description until 1659.[13] Furthermore, it is clear from internal evidence that

12 Alan Macfarlane, *The Diary of Ralph Josselin, 1616–1689*, Records of Social and Economic History, new series 3 (1976).
13 Diary, 1641, p. 1.

THE PEACHY FAMILY

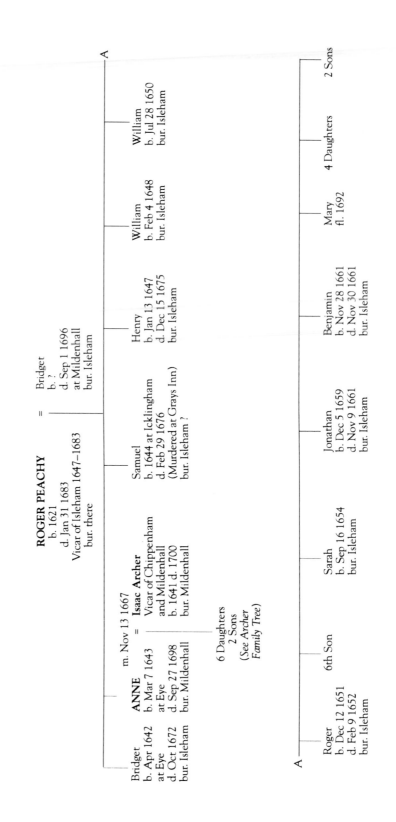

ROGER PEACHY
b. 1621
d. Jan 31 1683
Vicar of Isleham 1647–1683
bur. there

=

Bridget
b. ?
d. Sep 1 1696
at Mildenhall
bur. Isleham

m. Nov 13 1667

ANNE
b. Mar 7 1643
at Eye
d. Sep 27 1698
bur. Mildenhall

=

Isaac Archer
Vicar of Chippenham
and Mildenhall
b. 1641 d. 1700
bur. Mildenhall

6 Daughters
2 Sons
(*See Archer
Family Tree*)

Bridget
b. Apr 1642
at Eye
d. Oct 1672
bur. Isleham

Samuel
b. 1644 at Icklingham
d. Feb 29 1676
(Murdered at Grays Inn)
bur. Isleham ?

Henry
b. Jan 13 1647
d. Dec 15 1675
bur. Isleham

William
b. Feb 4 1648
bur. Isleham

William
b. Jul 28 1650
bur. Isleham

A

Roger
b. Dec 12 1651
d. Feb 9 1652
bur. Isleham

6th Son

Sarah
b. Sep 16 1654
bur. Isleham

Jonathan
b. Dec 5 1659
d. Nov 9 1661
bur. Isleham

Benjamin
b. Nov 28 1661
d. Nov 30 1661
bur. Isleham

Mary
fl. 1692

4 Daughters

2 Sons

A

the work we now possess is not that begun in 1659. An inscription inside the front cover reads 'I. Archer's book 1665 July 15', which strongly suggests that the manuscript is a later version of earlier drafts, made while he was at university, which were then written up after he had embarked upon his ministry.

We can be sure that the habit of keeping 'an even account with God' was inculcated by exchanging correspondence with his father, which was at its most intense in the years 1659–60. At precisely this point, Archer was also engaged in a profound struggle of conscience concerning both the veracity of his own conversion and the ethics of conforming to the Anglican church and its Book of Common Prayer. These significant upheavals, in which his father was deeply, if sometimes vicariously, involved, are most likely to have prompted Archer to record the nature of God's dealings towards him. This traumatic period in Archer's life first prompted him to attempt a spiritualized interpretation of his life. For this reason, it is clear that at many points Archer shaped his account of certain key events in the light of more recent and considered reflection. It is conceivable, then, that Archer had kept a book of experiences while at university and during the earliest years of his ministry, which served as a reminder of such key events and his initial responses to them. This book may then have served as the basis for the diary we now possess, which in turn marks a more advanced and considered stage of a interpretative process. The habit of reworking or reinterpreting material did not cease after he began to keep this diary, and many entries suggest that Archer frequently recorded the details of certain events, and his reaction to them, several days or weeks after they had occurred.

This structural feature is indicated by the fact that sometimes large blocks of text were committed to paper in a single sitting, often with no breaks or paragraphs. For ease of reading as well as for aesthetic reasons, the transcript produced here has been divided into more manageable paragraphs, instead of reproducing pages of unbroken text. By contrast, periods which Archer regarded as particularly eventful are covered by more frequent entries which, even if not precisely dated, can be distinguished from surrounding material either by a change of ink or by size of script. A good example of this more conventional method of diary-keeping may be found in the period 1665–6, one of the more detailed sections of the diary, where nine changes of ink occur in five pages. Even here, in at least three places, Archer writes retrospectively of events which had occurred several days or even weeks before.[14]

What therefore are the motives which impelled Archer to keep his diary, and which dictated its overall form? Any answer is complicated by the fact that, in spite of certain thematic threads running through the book, it divides into fairly distinct sections. Furthermore, there are a number of significant silences which also require explanation.

Although Archer includes occasional details about natural events, they are entirely incidental to other concerns and cannot be compared with the wonderfully vivid reports of the climate, seemingly recorded for their own sake, in Ralph Josselin's diary.[15] When Archer records anything which does not

14 See Diary, pp. 115–19.
15 See for example the entry for Feb. 1644, in Alan Macfarlane (1976), p. 35.

THE RUSSELL FAMILY

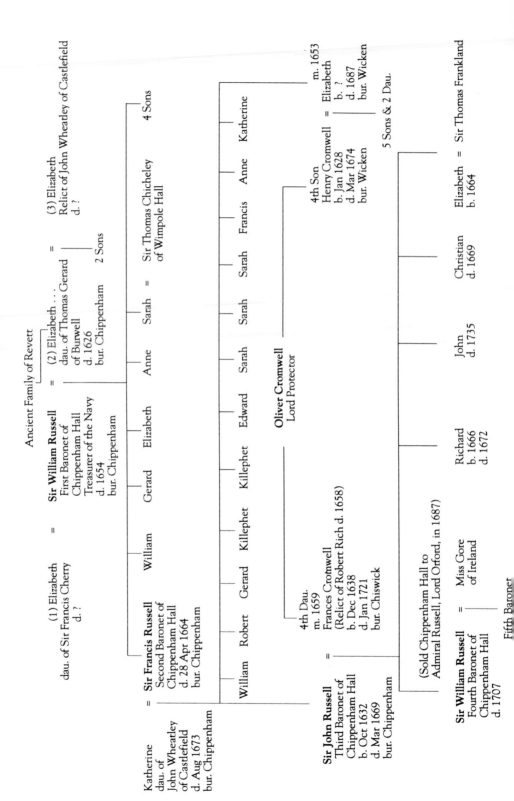

Ancient Family of Revett

Katherine dau. of John Wheatley of Castlefield d. Aug 1673 bur. Chippenham

(1) Elizabeth dau. of Sir Francis Cherry d. ? = **Sir William Russell** First Baronet of Chippenham Hall Treasurer of the Navy d. 1654 bur. Chippenham = (2) Elizabeth . . . dau. of Thomas Gerard of Burwell d. 1626 bur. Chippenham = (3) Elizabeth Relict of John Wheatley of Castlefield d. ?

2 Sons

4 Sons

= **Sir Francis Russell** Second Baronet of Chippenham Hall d. 28 Apr 1664 bur. Chippenham

William · Gerard · Elizabeth · Anne · Sarah = Sir Thomas Chicheley of Wimpole Hall

William · Robert · Gerard · Killephet · Killephet · Edward · Sarah · Sarah · Francis · Anne · Katherine

Oliver Cromwell Lord Protector

4th Dau. m. 1659 = Frances Cromwell (Relict of Robert Rich d. 1658) b. Dec 1638 d. Jan 1721 bur. Chiswick

4th Son Henry Cromwell b. Jan 1628 d. Mar 1674 bur. Wicken = m. 1653 Elizabeth b. ? d. 1687 bur. Wicken

5 Sons & 2 Dau.

Sir John Russell Third Baronet of Chippenham Hall b. Oct 1632 d. Mar 1669 bur. Chippenham

(Sold Chippenham Hall to Admiral Russell, Lord Orford, in 1687)

Sir William Russell Fourth Baronet of Chippenham Hall d. 1707 = Miss Gore of Ireland

Richard b. 1666 d. 1672 · John d. 1735 · Christian d. 1669 · Elizabeth b. 1664 = Sir Thomas Frankland

Fifth Baronet

immediately touch upon his own life, he seems to be guided by a desire to understand the workings of providence; both the mundane and the remarkable are deployed to serve this interpretative task. If Archer does not share Josselin's wide interest in local and national events, outside his personal ministry, neither does he share Oliver Heywood's habit of precisely quantifying his ministerial efforts and achievements. While Heywood keenly enumerated the sermons he preached, the fast days he kept and the feasts he attended, Archer gives the clear impression that his sociability was very much more circumscribed. He frequently expresses a weariness of worldly cares and economic concerns.[16] For example, unlike Josselin, he never records in detail the value or condition of his estate. These features of the diary, which mark it out from other comparable accounts, largely result from the uses for which Archer intended his diary.

Archer notes that the decision to keep a diary was first and foremost the result of his father's prompting, itself a significant admission and one which suggests that William Archer may have kept such a book himself. Indeed, after his father's death in 1670 Archer relates that he had acquired many of his father's letters and other papers, the contents of which he sometimes reveals. Since some of these writings greatly surprised his son, it seems reasonable to speculate that William had also kept 'an account of his life in writing', and that perhaps the form of Isaac Archer's diary was influenced by reading his father's. Isaac's awareness of the dangers caused by such personal disclosures could have made him wary of committing everything to paper.

In a deliberate and consistent way, Archer refrained from referring to his parishioners by name. It is informative to compare this habit to Ralph Josselin's treatment of his flock at Earls Colne. Josselin chose to record the names of many of his ordinary parishioners, and did not scruple to mention their personal misdemeanours when he considered them worthy of note. Alan Macfarlane complains that Josselin 'only referred directly or indirectly to between two and three hundred of these [parishioners]. He mentioned by name approximately one-twentieth of his congregation in any context'.[17] This is a strikingly high figure when compared with the coverage in Archer's diary, even if references to unnamed parishioners are included. Only members of the Russell family, the lords of Chippenham manor, are mentioned by name during the entire period of Archer's incumbency there, while other persons named in the diary were almost exclusively visitors to Chippenham Hall or friends who offered Archer prospects of ministerial preferment or change.

One possible explanation of this strange absence of named parishioners is that Archer may have envisaged that his diary would one day be read by others. An entry made in 1676 seems to presuppose at least the possibility of a wider readership, when Archer is at pains to set several disputed facts straight once and for all. The entry concerns the very important and sensitive issue of the true reasons for his choice of spouse. Six years after his father's death and following his success in regaining much of his lost estate, Archer writes almost with a larger public in mind, to correct the notion that his marriage was the cause of

---

16 Diary, 19 October 1664, p. 95; cf. J. Horsfall Turner, III (1883), pp. 238, 285.
17 Macfarlane (1976), xxi.

his father's anger: 'To satisfy the world that my father's giving the estate from mee was for my conforming, and the consequences of it, and not at all in respect of my marriage, as he would have it thought, I have two things to say . . .'[18]

Archer's account of his ministry at Chippenham is punctuated by mentions of very close pastoral contact with a number of distressed parishioners, despite the fact that he appears as a marginal figure, in some ways, in parish life there. He does not appear as a scribe or witness in any local wills, notwithstanding his close involvement with some parishioners who were very near to death. He also distanced himself from life at Chippenham Hall for fear of being compromised in his ministerial duties, and because he profoundly distrusted its moral influence on the village. The afflictions of his parishioners ranged from psychological torment and physical distress, which often had a suspected spiritual cause, to various moral failings. Archer discusses these disorders and conditions, and the assistance which he was able to offer, but remains silent as to the identity of the individuals concerned. He must have felt that the highly personal nature of the pastoral problems with which he dealt, entailed a sort of professional confidentiality, even within the confines of his own diary.

The diary incorporates subject matter of a fairly wide range; it includes for example mundane comments on the weather and local farming. However, there are undoubtedly three issues which predominate: family relationships, the performance of ministerial duties, and personal spiritual endeavour. Notwithstanding the diversity of concerns common to all diaries, Archer's account possesses quite clear subdivisions of interest which give it a distinct flavour, and which can be demarcated chronologically. Thus, at the risk of appearing arbitrary, it seems reasonable to divide the diary into certain fairly distinct sections. Of course, each section overlaps to a certain degree with those that precede and follow it, so that the time-periods chosen here mark the approximate, but main, boundaries of Archer's changing concerns.

In the first section, covering the years 1641–1659, Archer notes that he did not begin to make a record until the end of the period. Therefore the first eighteen years of his life are described entirely retrospectively. Many of his recollections, particularly of his earliest years, are by his own admission 'weake', while much is based on family tradition and hearsay. However, the account of his days at school and at Cambridge University is marked by a spontaneity and freshness, born of clearer recollection. Archer's selection of autobiographical material rests largely upon two considerations: experiences of providence considered significant, and an overbearing sense of his own moral and spiritual 'fallenness'. Indeed, these two themes commonly intersect in Archer's interpretation of events in his youth, producing a tension in his notion of providentialism at this time. While one instance of providence might remind Archer of his precarious spiritual position, another might remind him of his privileged, if unworthy, position as heir to a lively spiritual heritage, nurtured by his family's zealous espousal of godliness. The diary thus bears witness to Archer's intense psychological struggle with, and attempt to resolve, these two conflicting possibilities. The interaction of expectation and responsibility is underwritten by

[18] Diary, 1 Nov. 1676, p. 179.

Archer's acute awareness of the futility of his own attempts to attain salvation. This fact clearly shapes his experience of conversion.

The second section, covering the years 1659–1669, is mainly focussed on two highly personal issues. First, Archer expresses agonising doubts about the reality of his own conversion,[19] and secondly, in his conscience he wrestles with the strong temptation exerted upon him by his college to conform to the Church of England in order to secure a livelihood. The central influence of his father is evoked in some detail, especially his vehement condemnation of the formalism and ritualism which he warned would flavour the re-established church. The whole episode illustrates the young diarist's predicament as he is caught between the Scylla of conformity to the national church in order to gain financial independence, and the Charybdis of being rid of a troubled religious conscience yet dependent on his father's 'arbitrary allowance'. After his painful decision to conform, the diary is taken up with the practicalities of parish ministry although, as a kind of sub-text, he still expressed doubts concerning the lawfulness of the 'new ceremonies'. Thus, much of the diary in the critical years 1664–6 details practical measures whereby Archer contrived to lessen the sting of full conformity. Indeed, Archer is brought to the brink of resigning the Anglican ministry altogether, but financial concerns, along with the new incentive of a potential marriage partner close to hand, conspire to hold him in the Church of England and away from Essex, in spite of his father's repeated solicitations to have him return home.

The third section, from 1669–1672, details events leading up to his father's death in 1670, the subsequent and momentous proving of his will, and the discovery of his father's private papers. The enormous financial and emotional implications of his father's decision to disinherit Archer of much of his rightful estate are dealt with in considerable detail, almost to the exclusion of any other aspect of Archer's life. It would appear that Archer used the diary as an effective medium for coming to terms with his father's devastating decision. Archer reviews their relationship in detail and includes a lengthy analysis of their sometimes passionate correspondence, most of which passed between them while Archer was at university and afterwards, in the early part of his ministry, at Chippenham. Archer effectively supplies a spiritual valediction to his father, which mixes a somewhat idealized assessment of his father's life and personal qualities with a rather pessimistic view of his own role in their relationship. Not surprisingly, much is written about the legal tussle which ensued to regain Archer's alienated estate, providing details of the legal personnel he sought and the advice they gave, along with fragmentary information reflecting upon his step-mother's character and her role in their apparently troubled relationship. Archer's diary also supplies details of the gradual settlement of his father's estate, which supplements the information contained in William Archer's will,[20] and gives some insight into the workings of kinship as he sought the advice and support of family members in his protracted legal quest.

The fourth section of the diary may be identified as covering the period

---

[19] Diary, 1657–9, pp. 28–40.
[20] See Appendix 1 (p. 185) for William Archer's will.

1669–83. This section is overwhelmingly concerned with events surrounding the establishment of a new nuclear family, following the diarist's marriage in 1667. While this preoccupation with childbirth is unsurprising, the diary perhaps contains more detail relating to these family events than any other comparable account, owing to the exceptional misfortune which the Archers experienced in their attempts to build a family. Archer attached great importance to the notion of a sacred covenant, which in turn made the birth of children a significant spiritual event. However, the tragic deaths of several of his children inevitably challenged Archer's theological presuppositions, and helped to shape his views of the workings of providence. Many entries in the diary reveal his reactions to the suffering of his children and, in the case of his older surviving offspring, the nature of the relationship he enjoyed with them. The trauma induced by almost overwhelming personal tragedy leads Archer into radical self-questioning. His litany of domestic suffering is consequently interspersed by introverted and deeply emotional reflections on the possible reasons for such losses. At the same time, the diary affords a retrospective view of Archer's struggle with the implications of certain long-held doctrinal opinions, and their subsequent modification as a direct result of personal tragedy. Most prominent is the connection he believed to exist between personal sin and ill-health.

The final section of the diary runs from 1683–1700. Once Ann Archer's childbearing days are over, and the diarist's hope of a son 'to stand in my stead' have evaporated, Archer's attention in the diary switches back to problems associated with his continued ministry in Chippenham. He records increasingly frequent inquiries into the possibility of securing a new and stable living in the Church of England, not just poorly paid curacies. This development appears to have been the result of growing tensions between Archer and his patrons at Chippenham Hall. After six or so years of disappointed searching, the diary describes Archer's negotiations for the advowson or patronage of Mildenhall, and his subsequent move to become minister of that parish in 1688. This move coincided with the sale of Chippenham Hall and uncertainty caused by the departure of the Russell family.

A new feature of the diary in this period is Archer's growing interest in national politics, especially the events surrounding the accession of James II in 1685. He expresses his deep anxieties about the survival of Protestantism in England, and about his own security as a minister of the established church. With evident relief Archer expresses a cautious welcome to William of Orange, but following the apparent success of the Prince's assumption of the throne, the diary falls silent on matters political and theological.

The remainder of the diary, in which the number of entries declines considerably as time passes, refers to the last decade of Archer's life. It considers the marriage of his sole surviving daughter, a matter which was clearly of some importance in the light of the traumas which had surrounded his own match. His daughter's marriage, however, was to be blighted by her husband's bankruptcy; the diary supplies illuminating details of Archer's extraordinary financial and emotional support for the couple. The diarist is increasingly aware of the approach of death and of the preparation necessary for it. He gives a moving account of the last illness and death of his wife Ann, and a *post-mortem*

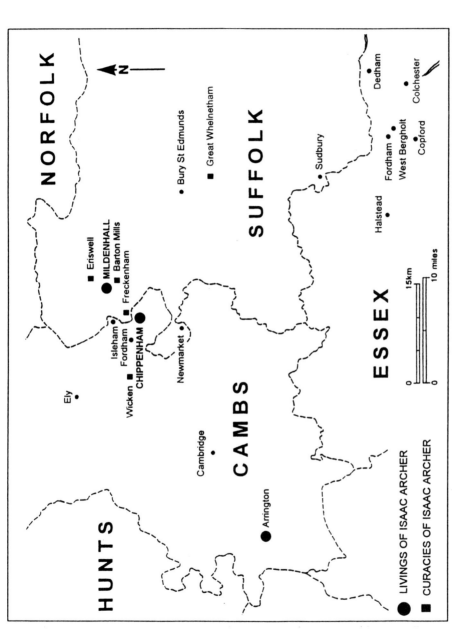

Map 1: Principal locations mentioned in the Diary of Isaac Archer (1641–1700)

assessment of her life and qualities. However, in 1699 Archer took a young woman, probably from neighbouring Eriswell, as his second wife. Being infirm and increasingly troubled by illness, he revealed that he needed her as a nurse and as a serious religious companion. The diary's last entry, which tells of the happy occasion of the birth of a granddaughter, is dated just a few weeks prior to Archer's own death in May 1700.

The periodic structure of the diary means that different sections were composed in different ways, and that consequently the material included by Archer has been worked-over and interpreted in varying degrees. Much of the diary for the years before 1665 is thus characterized by hindsight and a more considered interpretational style. This is so, even when events are re-told as if they had occurred recently. For example, Archer describes his many efforts to secure another living, after being asked by Sir Thomas Chicheley to resign his first curacy at Arrington, in a way which shows that he pondered over the story for some time. The strongly narrative style belies Archer's method of sifting disparate experiences and reworking them into a larger and more connected whole, especially as a means of imbuing the events with a providential coherence and significance. Another feature of the diary in this early period is that there are very few dated entries, a fact which further betrays the studied autobiographical style of Archer's account of life before 1665.

However, even after 1665 Archer frequently retains his habit of recording certain events with hindsight. Most noteworthy are his deeply considered reflections upon the death of his father in 1670, and on the nature of their troubled relationship, which are allotted almost fifteen pages. He is particularly concerned with the final ten years of that relationship, when father and son were increasingly torn apart by the ecclesiological and liturgical issues which were to divide so many after the Restoration. Archer's detailed review of their correspondence is clearly an attempt to come to terms with their disagreements, apportioning almost all blame to himself. His version of events reads as though an audience is envisaged, and it certainly true that he intended his diary as an honest record which would in turn be examined by 'the court of heaven'. Psychologically, his belief in God's omniscience enabled him to soothe his troubled conscience by re-telling and reinterpreting the story of his life.

THE GEOGRAPHY OF ARCHER'S MINISTRY

The principal part of Isaac Archer's ministry was exercised in the Deanery of Fordham, a sub-jurisdiction of the Diocese of Norwich which straddled the county boundary between Cambridgeshire and Suffolk.[21] Archer's most noteworthy achievement, at a time when he desperately sought financial independence from his father, was his ordination at the age of only twenty,[22] a favour which he owed to several fellows of Trinity College who were sympathetic to

[21] See Map 1 (p. 13) and Table 1 (p. 17).

[22] The minimum age required for ordination as deacon was 23; see Diary, 1662, p. 72.

his predicament. In September 1662 he was made a priest of the diocese of Ely by that well-known Laudian and formalist bishop, Matthew Wren. Although Wren might have been expected to display a renewed zeal for ceremony, Archer notes that his own deliberate omission of bowing to the altar, in contrast to his more complying fellow-ordinands, failed to attract suspicion or rebuke.[23]

Archer's first parochial appointment followed soon after, when he was presented to Arrington in west Cambridgeshire, a living in the gift of his college. Archer reports that the living was a very poor one, and that the fabric of the church was dilapidated and in need of immediate repair.[24] After residing there for only four months, Archer was petitioned by the local knight, Sir Thomas Chicheley of Wimpole, to resign as incumbent and to place himself once again at the disposal of Trinity College.

Shortly afterwards, a fortunate series of events allowed Archer to preach at Chippenham in the south-east of the county, and close to the Suffolk town of Newmarket. Richard Parr, chaplain to the resident patron Sir Francis Russell, indicated his willingness to resign the living and Archer was invited to succeed him. His acceptance marked the beginning of a long, but often troubled, relationship with the parish and its manorial lords which lasted for over a quarter of a century.[25]

The disillusionment and disquiet which Archer periodically experienced as the parish's minister, coupled with intense paternal pressure to resign from his profession altogether (at least while it was exercised under episcopalian administration), often persuaded the diarist to seek rewards in other livings where he could enjoy greater freedom from the constraints of religious formalism. Many of these projects were not fully realized, but Archer regularly served and preached at neighbouring cures, sometimes moving away from Chippenham altogether to take up temporary residence in a parish which seemed to offer him better prospects of success.

The fact that Archer rarely felt settled in his parishes and, in consequence, was regularly looking for alternatives, means that it is difficult to delineate the exact itinerary of his ministry. Confusion arising from the fact that the diary often gives no clear date when a post is either taken up or effectively resigned, is compounded by Archer's patterns of residence: he often served a cure while living outside the parish boundary. At one point in the 1670s he even seems to have held the title of more than one living. I shall attempt to describe Archer's complicated movements, with the help of a table and a map (Table 1, p. 17; Map 1, p. 13).

The first venture which appeared to satisfy his need for a godly patron who would interpret liberally the requirements of the Act of Uniformity, and allay

---

23 Josselin also refused to show reverence to the altar, Macfarlane (1976), p. 8; Diary, 20 March, 1664/5, p. 100.

24 Diary, 26 and 28 Sept. 1662, p. 74. Cf. CUL Ely Diocesan Records, H1/1 and B2/59. The living was valued at only £40 a year as late as 1728, B8/1.

25 Diary, 14 Jan. 1662/3, p. 79. Calamy gives Parr as ejected, Cal. Rev., 381. CUL: MS Add. 41, f. 262 cites the incumbent before Archer as George Warren, presented to the living on 22 April, 1642.

his father's fears concerning the corrupting influence of the 'new ceremonies', took place in 1664. He was invited by Colonel Henry Cromwell, fourth son of the former Lord Protector, to serve at Wicken, a parish in Cambridgeshire lying to the north of Chippenham. Nevertheless, in response to Sir John Russell's anxieties concerning the supply of Chippenham, Archer returned to preach there every Sunday afternoon.[26]

In spite of evident success in his ministry at Wicken, Archer was persuaded by his father to forsake his profession in the Church of England altogether and, unofficially at least, resign from both Wicken and Chippenham.[27] But the stress of renewed financial dependence upon his father ensured that Archer's departure from the ministry was but a short one. Cromwell shortly afterwards approached Archer again, evidently under pressure from the parishioners of Wicken, to invite him to serve that cure very nearly in the capacity of a 'lecturer', an arrangement which even pleased the usually implacable William Archer. Even the relative isolation of this fenland parish could not wholly protect Archer from the threat of suspension by ecclesiastical courts, and he eventually felt it expedient to leave the company at Spinney Abbey, the Cromwells' house in Wicken.[28] Determined to support himself, Archer prevailed upon Sir John Russell to allow him to return to Chippenham 'upon such termes as I offered at Spinney', and there he employed a relative, James Goodwin, as his permanent reader of services from the Book of Common Prayer.[29]

In December 1667, at the invitation of the incumbent John Lillyman, Archer ventured to Barton Mills, which lay to the north-east of Chippenham and in the county of Suffolk. Once again, the diary clearly indicates that Archer continued to serve Chippenham in some capacity, and was occupied by many pastoral concerns there in this period. His ministry at Barton was cut short in 1670 by Lillyman's selfishness in taking a new living. Next he tried to move to All Saints' parish in the Suffolk town of Sudbury but, ironically, found the considerable nonconformist element in the town distinctly unwelcoming. Unsuccessful in that attempt, Archer returned to live at Chippenham, not least because Sir John Russell had recently died and 'now there would be no [spiritual] discouragements as formerly.'[30]

The prolonged business of challenging and executing the particulars of his father's will after 1670, may have distracted Archer's mind from any immediate thoughts of moving from Chippenham. Nevertheless, a chance meeting with William Herbert, rector of Great Whelnetham in Suffolk, gave Archer the opportunity of serving the cure there, and the additional prospect of eventually purchasing the advowson or patronage.[31] Great Whelnetham lay to the south of Bury St Edmunds and in the Deanery of Thedwastre, and although Archer

---

[26] Diary, 11 Aug. 1664, p. 94.
[27] Diary, 25 March 1665, pp. 100–01.
[28] Diary, 30 May 1665, p. 103. However, Archer plainly continued to perform some preaching duties at Wicken, for want of a settled incumbent, for an unspecified period from April 1667.
[29] Diary, 30 May 1665, p. 104.
[30] Diary, 24 June 1670, p. 130.
[31] Diary, 29 Sept. 1671, pp. 150 –51.

initially relished the prospect of uninterrupted tranquility which it promised, he spent two somewhat lonely years there. Feeling distanced from his relatives-in-law at Isleham, he seized the opportunity in 1673 of serving at Freckenham in Suffolk, which abuts Chippenham.

At this time Archer's ministerial duties were at their most complicated, for he continued to supply readers at Great Whelnetham, the advowson of which he held until late 1677, and at Chippenham (occasionally returning to each himself), while preaching at Freckenham.[32] Indeed, such was the balancing act which he had to perform that he was on at least one occasion suspected of pluralism, recording that 'my supplying 2 places raised a clamour . . . I putt of my reader, and the maintenance of Chipnam is now setled, and the occasion of murmuring is taken away, and I doe not in the least remitt of my paines.'[33] The illnesses and deaths which beset his family during their residence at Freckenham rectory convinced Archer that he had to move away, so in 1680 he retired to nearby Mildenhall, also in Suffolk, yet continued to preach at Chippenham on Sunday mornings.[34]

TABLE 4

DETAILS OF ISAAC ARCHER'S MINISTRY, 1662–1700

Parish	Patron	Incumbency, dates	Residence, dates
Arrington (Cambs.)	Trinity College, Cambridge	Sept. 1662–Jan. 1663	Sept. 1662–Jan. 1663
Chippenham (Cambs.)	Sir Francis Russell	Jan. 1663–Apr. 1664	Jan. 1663–Aug. 1664
"	Sir John Russell	Apr. 1664–Mar. 1670	Jun. 1665–Feb. 1668
"	Sir William Russell	Mar. 1670–Mar. 1688	Jul. 1670–? Sept. 1671
Wicken (Cambs.)	Henry Cromwell		Aug. 1664–Jun. 1665
Barton Mills (Suff.)			Feb. 1668–Jun. 1670
Gt Whelnetham (Suff.)	John Gipps		Sept. 1671–Sept. 1673
Freckenham (Suff.)			Sept. 1673–Sept. 1680?
Mildenhall (Suff.)	Edmund Colman and John Gipps	Mar. 1688–Apr.1700	Sept. 1680–Apr. 1700
Eriswell (Suff.)	Thomas Smith	(Sequestration, Dec. 1693– Apr. 1700)	

After 1673 the diary provides only limited details of Archers' commitment to Chippenham, and does not make clear what his ministerial duties were after the dismissal of James Goodwin as reader in 1674.[35] It is, however, significant that Goodwin was removed because he 'was so violent against Nonconformists',

---

32 The balancing act sometimes became even more complicated, as when Erasmus Warren tried to force him to take the vicarage of Freckenham, only to try to place his own choice there; Diary, 1672, p. 160. This should be compared with later arrangements when Archer had come to an agreement with Warren; Diary 1 Jan. 1674/5, p. 171. Cf. also the problems which arose when a reader decided suddenly to leave; e.g. Diary, 20 Nov. 1675, p. 177.

33 Diary, 20 Nov. 1675, p. 177.

34 Diary, 1 Sept. 1680, p. 194.

35 Diary, 13 Sept. 1674, pp. 169–70.

and because Archer had agreed to lease his house at Chippenham to the nonconformists Samuel Fairclough and a Mr Sheriffe, 'whose son should offici- ate', presumably as reader. The sudden collapse of this arrangement drew Archer back to Chippenham, where he seems to have ministered regularly again . . . 'and so God opened mee a way, and I thinke it his will that I should doe him service at Chipnam; it being the 3d time I have bin strangely brought thither.'[36] Renewed uncertainties about the Russells staying as owners of the Chippenham estate, and therefore of his own position as minister, prompted Archer in 1687 to negotiate for the purchase of the advowson of the nearby town of Mildenhall. Once that was secured, he remained there as incumbent until his death in 1700. His only other ministerial excursions between 1693 and 1696 were to neighbouring Eriswell, the sequestrated living of his impecu- nious son-in-law, William Foorth.[37]

ARCHER'S MARRIED LIFE

The diary contains very scanty references to Archer's courtship of the woman who became his wife, only later mentioning her origins in the parish of Isleham, which bordered Chippenham to the north. The circumstances are obscure, but it seems most likely that Isaac Archer and Anne Peachy met as a result of ministerial contact between Archer and her father, Roger Peachy, vicar of Isleham. Roger Peachy was a minister of like disposition,[38] and they may well have shared similar scruples about the post-Restoration church settle- ment, although Peachy obtained his living before the King's return. There is some indication that his title was in dispute, even though he does not appear as an ejected minister, while Archer himself described his father-in-law as a 'non-conformist'.[39] Nevertheless, the diarist provides a list, useful to historians of the family, of the wifely qualities which attracted him to Anne Peachy and which persuaded him of her suitability as a spouse. The reasons for selecting a spouse were probably much the same as they are today but, significantly, they were given different priorities.[40]

Physical attraction ranks high on the list but is not deemed sufficient, taken alone, to convince Archer of her compatibility. As one might expect, he ranked moral and spiritual considerations very highly, but not to the exclusion of another critical virtue: her practical ability in the management of household affairs.[41] He does not mention financial considerations, quite probably because

---

[36] Diary, 13 Sept. 1674, p. 170.

[37] Mildenhall parish registers indicate that Archer's ministerial involvement there may have begun as early as October 1686. From that time several entries appear in Archer's hand. For the Forth family, see also p. 12.

[38] Cf. Oliver Heywood's delight that his first wife, Elizabeth, was a godly minister's daughter; J. Horsfall Turner, I (1882), 170.

[39] The Isleham parish registers suggest much quarrelling as to who ought to make official entries. The register has considerable lacunae, possibly as a result of this lack of certainty; the register of births and deaths is empty for most of Peachy's post-Restoration incumbency of 1662–83.

[40] Diary, 1670, p. 139.

[41] See R.A. Houlbrooke, The English Family, 1450–1700 (1984), 75–6.

he felt that the jointure was a matter over which the respective fathers had ultimate control. He may also have foreseen few financial difficulties, since his intended was the daughter of a clergyman and therefore likely to have family resources similar to his own.

Although Archer keenly sought and reverentially regarded his father's advice on marriage, they soon disagreed on the question of a suitable jointure.[42] Financial considerations began to interfere with the course of personal affection and love, and caused conflict between the two families. William Archer regarded the Peachys as slow in dispatching their business, and also suspected them of wishing to seize his estate after the marriage.[43]

Once they were married, Isaac and Anne seem to have lived together in a close relationship. Archer records that only once in his entire married life had he been away from his wife for more than eight days. Nevertheless, he was at times worried by critical comments about his spouse's role in their marriage, and was forced on more than one occasion to seek God's forgiveness for his own deportment.[44] The Archer's relationship stabilized over time and appears to have become more tender as well as more mature.[45] The early troubles which marred their union were short-lived and, following the final settlement of William Archer's estate in the mid-1670s, their married life trod a happier course.

Indeed, their last years together were in many respects the most happy and fulfilled. By the late 1680s, Anne had lost her sight and was unable to perform the normal domestic duties which were regarded as so important in a wife's role, but this disability in no way soured their relationship. Isaac showed great tenderness and devotion to his wife, performing religious duties with her, reading to her from the scriptures, and leading her to church as a 'friend'. When eventually she was unable to leave her bed, he nursed her until she died on 25 September 1698. In his diary Archer records the following eulogy, expressing the very real closeness which they enjoyed, and bearing witness to her accommodating and encouraging nature: 'She had the ornament of a quiet spirit! suitable to mee, and bearing with mee, and hiding my failings . . . she had a deepe sense of religion, and gott good at my ministry, as she owned.'[46]

---

42 Archer was convinced that his father had given implicit approval for the marriage, provided he could secure a safe living; Diary, 29 Sept. 1667, p. 119. He was also promised a good reward in his father's will, if he married Anne Peachy. This is the first indication that he was disinherited, not for his marriage contract, but for his religious conformity.

43 Diary, 1670, p. 133.

44 Diary, 3 Apr. 1681, p. 195.

45 Oliver Heywood liberally recorded his affection for his wife Elizabeth, believing himself bound to her 'by many invincible bands of cordial love'; J. Horsfall Turner, I (1882), 170. Cf. the more reserved, but no less genuine, affection he reserved for his second wife Abigail; J. Horsfall Turner, III (1883), 270.

46 Diary, 25 Sept. 1698, p. 224. Anne Archer's disposition should be compared to that of Elizabeth Heywood, who was extremely knowledgeable in the scriptures, and regularly sought her husband's advice and learning on the problems she encountered in her studies; J. Horsfall Turner, I (1882), 58–59.

ARCHER'S FAMILY LIFE

Archer and his wife suffered extraordinary tragedy in their attempts to build a family, losing eight of their nine children in infancy. These dreadful experiences challenged the coherence of Archer's views of the workings of providence. He was accustomed, like most contemporaries, to explain even the most ordinary occurrences as providential – that is, according to the will of an omniscient and omnipotent God. Inevitably therefore, he saw the sufferings and deaths of his own dear children as the judgement of God, and in great mental torment tried desperately to understand why his marriage and family were deprived of God's blessing. Indeed, under such dreadful and recurrent pressures, the whole fabric of Archer's theological faith threatened to collapse. However, although providentialism permeated every aspect of his life, it did not follow that the sufferings of his children were accepted passively or fatalistically. The principal dynamic of providentialism was that it allowed men not only to read but also to influence God's action in the world, by altering personal behaviour. Repentance meant a 'changing of mind' for the individual believer, but it might also lead to an alteration in the intentions of God himself.

Archer prayed for the 'blessing of the wombe', the natural fruit of a productive union,[47] and also desired that each of his offspring would grow up to become part of 'the household of faith'. As soon as his wife noticed signs of 'quickening', Archer expectantly awaited 'a son of prayer'. In this he deliberately imitated his father's reaction to his (Isaac's) conception, and in so doing consciously affirmed his place in a highly prized tradition of godliness which he hoped would continue with his own children.[48] His awareness of belonging to a family 'eminent for piety' may have influenced his overwhelming desire for a son, for a male heir would carry the Archer name into the next generation, and with it, it was hoped, the spiritual renown attached to it. Although the diary contains little evidence to suggest that Archer thought less of his daughters, or that he gave them less attention, it is clear that the gift of a son was deemed to be more significant of God's approval than any other temporal blessing.

However, the experience of sickness and frequent mortality amongst his children forced Archer to reconsider this simple genealogical attitude to procreation. When in 1678 his two surviving daughters contracted fevers, he reversed his judgement that children were an unreserved blessing, and equated his fortunes to those of King David, whose own children 'were chastnings sent by God.'[49]

For much of the time Archer was convinced that the health of his children was intrinsically bound up with his own obedience to God.[50] In spite of the cruel dealings of providence, which struck indiscriminately like 'poyson darts',

---

[47] Some writers thought such fruit necessary for a proper marriage, including William Perkins in *Christian oeconomie or a short survey of the right manner of ordering a familie, according to the Scriptures* (London, 1609).
[48] Diary, 10 June 1677, p. 181.
[49] Diary, 10 Aug. 1678, p. 184.
[50] E.g. Diary, 10 Aug. 1678, pp. 183–4.

the path to abundant blessings was seen to lie entirely in personal reform and 'better obedience'. In other words, suffering served as a reminder both of man's imperfection and frailty, and God's unchanging nature and sovereignty. Paradoxically perhaps, suffering operated as a spur to more vigorous religious commitment, rather than as a significant disincentive from it.[51]

It would be unjust to seventeenth-century parents, and an inaccuracy, to suggest that the higher incidence of infant mortality which distinguished that period from our own, produced a kind of emotional sclerosis. Archer's diary, along with numerous others, provides significant evidence to the contrary, demonstrating that deep personal attachment quickly developed between parents and children. Of course, if a child died, its age to a large extent dictated the intensity of the emotional loss and bereavement experienced by parents. However, Archer occasionally describes in luminous detail the tender feelings which he shared with his children, and thus helps to contradict the assumption that parent-child relationships in early modern England were authoritarian and unchanging.[52] The most striking portrait of family love in the diary is Archer's account of the last dying moments of his six year-old daughter Frances, whose humanity and intelligence are beautifully evoked.[53]

ARCHER'S MINISTRY: RELATIONSHIP TO NONCONFORMITY

In the 1660s, as half a century before, the debate surrounding the issue of separating from any state-imposed church was crucial to nonconformity. To this extent at least, Isaac Archer and his father faced a common problem in their response to the Church of England. But there were important differences between them. Having ministered almost wholly during the Interregnum, William Archer held quite determined and inflexible views on episcopal authority and liturgical formalism, both of which were reintroduced after 1662. By contrast Isaac Archer, living in an ideological melting-pot at Cambridge before and after 1662, had to face the thorny question of whether or not he could bring himself to accept the Book of Common Prayer. Thus, the fact that William Archer had retired from the ministry before the great ejections of St Bartholomew's Day, and that his son was just at this time seriously considering entering the profession, meant that their practical experience of ministry was to be wholly different. According to William Archer the root of his son's troubles as a minister lay in the sin of 'bowing the knee to Baal', in even contemplating collusion with an episcopalian church which was bound to be as impure and idolatrous as Israel's golden calf.

---

[51] Diary, 10 Dec. 1682, p. 200; cf. Diary, 19 Apr. 1685, p. 207: 'I begged . . . a child, though I deserve to be bereaved wholly.'

[52] The classic statement of this argument is L. Stone, *The Family, Sex and Marriage in England, 1500–1800* (1977).

[53] Diary, 1 Aug. 1679, pp. 189–91. This incident should be compared with John Angier's spiritual questioning of his daughter as she died: see Ernest Axon, *Life of John Angier*, Chetham Society, n.s., Vol. xcvii (1937), 126–7.

While the diary does not attach a specific denominational label to William Archer's zealous protestantism, other sources suggest that he held strong Independent sympathies, and was in all probability a Congregationalist. In a review of his early childhood in Essex, Archer noted that his father refused the ordinary maintenance of ministers by tithes, drawing instead upon the voluntary contributions of his congregation.[54] The diary is punctuated with references to his father's adamant opposition to what he saw as the liturgical restrictiveness and downright erroneousness of the Book of Common Prayer. William Archer evidently belonged to a closely-defined religious world which was underpinned by a network of ministerial support. It is no surprise, therefore, that references in Archer's diary to his father's friends and allies who were 'lecturers' and 'silenced ministers', read as a short list of Essex and Suffolk Independents.[55]

By far the most contentious issue affecting Isaac Archer's ministry in the restored Church of England was the newly re-imposed adherence to the Book of Common Prayer and its rubrics. The prospect that Archer's ministry would, of necessity, be circumscribed by structures instituted by human reason, rather than based on scripture, fuelled his father's consistent opposition to the liturgy. Archer's first mention of direct conflict with his father on the matter of liturgical formalism came in his last year at Cambridge, when he was still significantly influenced by the intellectual ferment caused in the university by the return of Charles II. Archer's telling account of his father's opposition to Common Prayer indicates the true depth of his hatred for man-made traditions which, unacceptably, took precedence over and restricted the preaching of the Word.

The ferocity of his father's language against formalism is striking and, as if to justify such a tirade, is replete with Biblical allusions condemning idolatry. 'He wrote mee word that he never thought that one sprung from his loynes would plead for Baal; and that if he thought I adored those abominable idols, and danced to that molten calf etc., he would come and stampe it to powder, and make mee drinke it etc . . . he said 'twas vomit which the nation cast out 20 yeares agoe, and ask't if it were indifferent to play the dogg or the sow . . .'[56] All that his father had consistently struggled for, and even endangered his life for, was threatened and put at risk by the return of Charles II in 1660. It was the highest possible insult to his most deeply treasured principles that his own son should write to him 'in defence of the common prayer'.

Archer succinctly records the reasoning behind his father's rejection of the revived liturgy. 'He looked upon thees ceremonies as superstitious, idolatrous, and so atheisticall . . . they were bad because humane inventions, which could not be done out of faith and so were sinfull Romans 14: last. They could not be

---

[54] Diary, 1649, p. 7.

[55] On lecturing generally, see Christopher Hill, *Society and Puritanism in Pre-Revolutionary England* (1964), 78–120. P. Seaver, *The Puritan Lectureships: The Politics of Religious Dissent 1560–1662* (Stanford, 1970), 15–54. On early Congregationalism, see G.F. Nuttall, *Visible Saints: The Congregational Way, 1640–1660* (1957). For the Congregationalists' dilemma regarding separatism, see M.R. Watts, *The Dissenters: From the Reformation to the French Revolution* (1978), 94–105.

[56] Diary, 1661, p. 54.

done out of faith because they had no ground in God's word.'[57] Thus, there was a two-fold justification for rejecting Common Prayer which was of critical importance in defining the puritan tradition itself: the liturgy lacked a fully substantiated basis in scripture, and being fixed and repetitive it excluded the exercise of faith. To support the Book of Common Prayer was to make human initiatives and sentiments as important to salvation and worship as the Word itself. And because the rubric largely prevented spontaneous prayer, its words were condemned as hollow and without the life-giving marrow of faith.

In spite of this early antagonism between Archer and his father concerning the observation of the Prayer Book, Archer demonstrates after 1662 his own antipathy to much that would count as liturgical formality. A telling critique of formalism is offered by Archer himself in the context of his own conversion. In 1659, in spite of several years of sermon-tasting, self-examination, and consultation with several of Cambridge's most eminent divines, Archer still laments that he is 'tossed to and fro', unable to find peace. He realized that 'duties' (regular prayers and other religious exercises) were essential in finding an assured salvation, but he was also aware of the extent to which these prayers and petitions might themselves become a snare, especially in the set and repetitive forms of Common Prayer. 'Many times in prayer evill thoughts would arise, and many callings of would happen; but yet I would, as I thought, make it up, and as it were make God amends another time; yet then would I suspect my selfe of hypocrisy, whose propertye it is to give prayers by number and not by weight, by tale and not by strength and syncerity. Thus was I afraid of formality, and customarines in God's service'.[58]

Yet the diarist's first experience of a Prayer Book service did not seem to bear out the harshness of his father's censure. Forced to attend Trinity College chapel by the necessity of entering the ministry and as a mark of his goodwill towards the senior fellows, Archer unexpectedly 'found none of those things we had at our ordinary service sinfull, or contrary to God's word . . .'[59]

Archer's unfortunate speech impediment was another reason for his turning away from set forms of prayer and worship. So disabling was this infirmity that on occasions it prevented him from performing the most extempore of duties. During a trial period as incumbent of All Saints, Sudbury, Archer was forced to conclude that the largeness of the church was too much for his weak constitution. 'But what they pretended, I found reall: that is, though I spoke loud enough for that great church, yet it spent mee too much, and would soon have killed mee.'[60] Periodically in his ministry Archer was unable to secure the services of a reader, and on these occasions his battle to read Common Prayer placed a great strain upon both his body and conscience. He was unable, and probably unwilling, to read extensively from the Prayer Book, and that made him liable to prosecution in ecclesiastical courts. It was a matter of considerable relief when Archer successfully obtained a reader, and he noted the security it brought. For example at Great Whelnetham in 1672, he remarks: 'I tooke a

[57] Diary, 1661, p. 60.
[58] Diary, 1659, p. 32.
[59] Diary, 30 March 1662, p. 68.
[60] Diary, 1670, p. 129.

young schollar to read service for mee. I found my selfe unfit, and was much discouraged in God's service by reason of it. 'Tis a great ease and comfort to mee, if God enable mee to maintaine it, and it may take away all exceptions against mee etc.'[61]

The persistence of Archer's speech impediment makes it harder to gauge how far his attitude to the Prayer Book may have changed during his ministry, for whenever he is without a reader he refers to the physical difficulty of publicly reciting set forms, rather than to any conscientious scruples that he has. Indeed, to balance what had already been noted, Archer sometimes seems to imply that he might be willing to read service if by force of circumstance he had no other option: 'I had from Easter last til Michaelmas an assistant to read . . . but his friends, being for more maintenance, take him away at Easter. I shall have the former man, with whom the parish was pleased, *in case I should not doe all*; and so is to reside there, read and preach once a day' (my italics).[62] By the time Archer becomes vicar of Mildenhall, he clearly indicates that he is publicly reading Common Prayer. He reveals very little about his feelings on the matter but, by practising the daily office, is able to report an improvement in his speech: 'This yeare I went on in my worke of the ministry; but at Midsummer my reader left mee, and the whole burden lies on mee. By use I find it easier, and my speaking much better.'[63]

What can safely be said is that Archer did not relish the prospect of reading Common Prayer, and only read it out of bare necessity, in the absence of an assistant, to prevent prosecution or suspension. That he continued to have doubts about the Prayer Book is shown by the lengths to which he went to secure the services of a reader. The most notable example of this, and one which illustrates the great advantage of having a flexibly-minded bishop, is the occasion when Archer employs an unordained reader at Mildenhall for a short time: 'My reader went away; but I had another offered mee; the bishop would not ordaine him, being not old enough; but winkes at his reading service for a time.'[64]

Because he was persistently ambiguous in his attitude to conformity, Archer found himself the natural ally of many moderate nonconformists, who were themselves struggling with the implications of the Restoration church settlement. The first post-Restoration sacrament which he celebrated at Chippenham was used as an opportunity to spread peace and unity amongst fellow communicants, and to attempt to incorporate those who had scruples concerning the Book of Common Prayer. Archer's preaching ministry was both evangelical and moral; these qualities won him many keen hearers as well as harsh critics. His hearers were frequently those of a nonconformist disposition, who often came from other parishes to hear him, in spite of the threat of prosecution for forsaking their own minister.

In spite of Archer's moderate yet committed ministry, he did not always meet with the favour of all nonconformists, nor did he approve of everything they

---

61 Diary, 1672, p. 157.
62 Diary, 5 March 1680/1, p. 195.
63 Diary, 1689–90, p. 214.
64 Diary, Aug. 1696, p. 221.

did. Although known as an opponent of strict formalism, he was treated frostily by the nonconformists of Sudbury, where in 1670 he had been invited for a trial period as minister of All Saints. Holding the balance of power in a parish which still elected its minister through the corporation, the nonconformists strongly opposed Archer because they 'cared not to have a man setled, least their meetings should be interrupted'.[65] Further, he found most of the nonconformists there 'rich and of great sway' and, interestingly, found the extent of religious division in the parish inimical to the exercise of his ministry.[66]

Perhaps the most striking example of Archer's relationship with nonconformity, and one which he chose not to record in his diary, was his response to the Declaration of Indulgence proclaimed by Charles II in 1672. For a short period this gave dissenters liberty to worship in their own way, providing their places of worship were properly licensed. Under this dispensation, Archer obtained a licence to hold a Presbyterian meeting at his house in Chippenham. Meanwhile, he retained his cousin, James Goodwin, as reader in the parish church, and Goodwin certainly lived in the vicarage. The licence of 1672 merely states that the Presbyterian meeting was held in 'I. Archer's house': this could refer to the vicarage, or to the farm and house which he had in Chippenham, and later intended to lease to Samuel Fairclough.[67] Any attempt to explain Archer's motives in taking out the licence, must also include the fact that he was not even resident in Chippenham at the time. Having taken charge of Great Whelnetham in 1671, he had made arrangements for Chippenham to be supplied with a reader; the diary is unclear as to whether Archer returned there on a regular basis.

In taking out a licence for a Presbyterian meeting, Archer at least availed himself of the chance of holding 'official' meetings in his home, in order to practise spiritual exercises and 'duties' with the more 'godly' members of Chippenham society. The Indulgence seems to have made no difference to patterns of attendance at church, so it is possible that Archer's main supporters merely welcomed the freedom to join together informally, in an act of worship unrestricted by liturgical formality.

That Archer had a registered meeting place did not, in turn, indicate a whole-hearted desire to leave the Church of England. Indeed in his diary he specifically disavows any intention of doing so.[68] Rather, he was taking full advantage of legislation which allowed the spiritually zealous to meet informally; such meetings had always been a feature of the religious tradition to which he belonged.[69] Archer was not alone in this conviction. Other diarists of the period, Adam Martindale for example, firmly refused to accept that such extraordinary meetings could in any sense be regarded as heretical or seditious.[70]

---

[65] Diary, 1670, p. 129. Nonconformists worshipped in the church of All Saints, Sudbury, while there was no settled minister: see R.L. Greaves, *Enemies under his Feet* (Stanford, Calif.), p. 157.

[66] Diary, 23 Apr. 1670, pp. 128–9.

[67] G. Lyon Turner, *Original Records of Early Nonconformity under Persecution and Indulgence* (1911–14), vol. 2, p. 862.

[68] 'I am more satisfied in the Church of England then ever', Diary, 30 March 1673, p. 161.

[69] See P. Collinson, *The Elizabethan Puritan Movement* (1967), pp. 333–84.

[70] Adam Martindale, *The Life of Adam Martindale, Written by Himself*, ed. Richard Parkinson, Chetham Society, Vol. 4 (1845), pp. 194–5.

Thus, while expressing his contentment as a member of the national church, he could simultaneously encourage his parishioners to meet privately for devotions under his supervision. He saw nothing in this practice which could be regarded as contrary or detrimental to the established church, so long as people continued to uphold public worship in their parish church. His greatest fears about the future of the Church of England centred on the possibility that its government might rest too greatly in the hands of bishops, that as a consequence the government of parishes would be effectively removed from individual incumbents, and that a damaging uniformity would be placed upon all worshippers.

As time progresses, the diary is less often punctuated by Archer's concern for freedom from conformity. Its focus is redirected to issues like Christian unity, and preserving protestantism within the kingdom. The national upheaval caused by the departure of James II came at the point when Archer had secured the living and advowson of Mildenhall. In the diary he expresses an overwhelming desire for peace and unity. The uncertain days which followed the arrival of William of Orange prompted him to record his anxieties about the state of the nation's spiritual life: 'Besides what I used to aske at the sacrament, as pardon, and strength, and growth etc., I begged a settlement in church, and state, a continuance of us in the ministry; and that God would keepe my people in the unity of the faith, now seducers are let loose upon us, and give mee wisdome to carry my selfe, in my place, as I ought to all.'[71] Clearly, Archer's principal preoccupation after the 'Glorious Revolution' was to ensure that his own ministry was freely exercised, and that heretical (especially popish) doctrines were exposed. The passage of the Act of Toleration may have made Archer's position in, and commitment to, the Church of England clearer than at any time during his whole ministry. This, coupled with the continued threat of foreign and, by implication, Catholic domination during William III's European wars, persuaded Archer of the necessity of remaining firmly within the Church of England and striving for unity therein.

The diary is disappointingly silent as to the nature of Archer's ministry at Mildenhall. However, a lengthy literary war which was fought between the local anti-Quaker polemicist, Francis Bugg, and the national leader of the Friends, George Whitehead, records the extent of Archer's involvement in a debate which raged in the town for many years. It is a testimony to Archer's moderate and peaceable temper that he confined himself to strictly doctrinal issues. Legally he wished that the Quakers might continue to enjoy liberty under the provisions of the 1689 Toleration Act, even though he felt them to be in error. Specifically, according to Bugg and Whitehead, Archer confronted the Quakers publicly on their system of church government, and on their doctrine of the Incarnation. Bugg reports that Archer compared Quaker teaching on the Incarnation to that of several notorious heresies, Sabellianism, Arianism and Socinianism. He was clearly prepared to defend orthodox doctrine, as promulgated by the Church of England, against the wiles and subleties

[71] Diary, 2 Sept. 1689, p. 213.

of a dissenting group, a fact which illustrates the clear limits of Archer's adherence to the nonconformist tradition from which he was descended.

WILLIAM COE: HIS LIFE AND BACKGROUND

Our second diarist was born in 1662 in the parish of Mildenhall, Suffolk, and died there at the age of 67 in 1729. He lived in a house called the 'Brewhouse', described as close to the Ferry Inn, in the large straggling hamlet of West Row which lies on the north bank of the River Lark about two miles west of the 'High Town' of Mildenhall. Contemporaries regarded William Coe as a gentleman, and he was so described on his gravestone. Wealth and status were inherited from his father and grandfather, both of whom had also lived in Mildenhall. He held several parochial offices including that of churchwarden for West Row in 1693,[72] and frequently mixed with the leaders of local society, such as Sir Thomas Hanmer.[73] He was also cited by the polemicist Francis Bugg as one of the leading men of the town opposed to the presence of Quakerism there in the 1690s.[74] In general his was a leisurely life which involved regular travelling[75] and much drinking and gaming in private houses and local alehouses. On the other hand, it is equally obvious that he was also a practical farmer and producer of malt. For example, he occupied around 100 acres of land in the local manors of Mildenhall and Aspalls, had a corn-chamber and malt-chamber at West Row, and mentioned 'his malt' at Royston in Hertfordshire.

The history of the Coe family, so far as it can be reconstructed, is summarized in the family tree on pp. 28–29. William was the name given to the eldest son in at least four successive generations living in the parish of Mildenhall: the diarist is third in the sequence. The first known William, and Charles, probably his brother, paid Ship Money in 1640 on their holdings in West Row. At his death in 1661, this William was immensely wealthy. He left over £1000 in legacies, and the total value of his probate inventory was £4892, of which £3230 were debts owing to him. Significantly described as a clothier, he left in his house and outbuildings no fewer than 464 todds of raw wool worth £586.[76] It therefore appears that the wealth inherited by William II and William III, both ranked as gentlemen, had its origin in the Suffolk cloth trade. William I was not born, it seems, in Mildenhall, and probably came from the south of Suffolk where families of the name of Coe (or Coo) had flourished for generations. It cannot be accidental that he left to his wife land in Clare worth £30 a year.

---

[72] SRO(B), E18/425/3.

[73] E.g. Diary, ff. 18r, 36r. Sir Thomas Hanmer (1677–1746) married the Dowager Duchess of Grafton in 1698; he was briefly Speaker of the House of Commons in 1714, and produced a six-volumed edition of Shakespeare in 1743–44 (DNB).

[74] Francis Bugg, One Blow More at New Rome (1691).

[75] Coe mentioned a number of horses which he kept, and referred to the covered coach which his family was privileged to own.

[76] Will of William Coe I, SRO(B), E18/452/66; his inventory, PRO, PROB 4 12614. Mary, wife of William I, was the grandmother from whom Coe admitted stealing money, and lying about it.

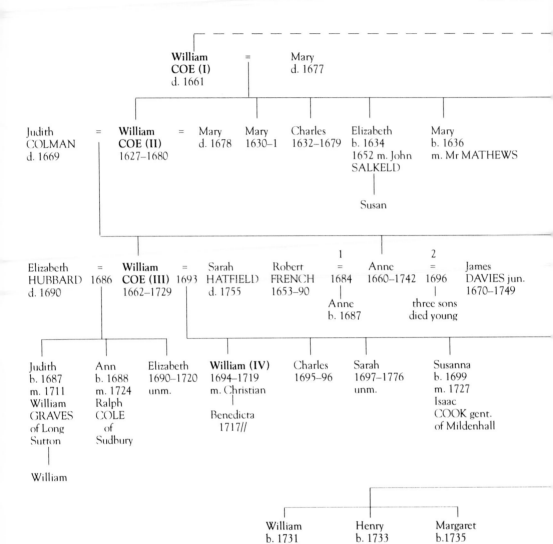

William COE (I) = **Mary**
d. 1661 / d. 1677

Judith COLMAN d. 1669 = **William COE (II)** 1627–1680 = Mary d. 1678 / Mary 1630–1 / Charles 1632–1679 / Elizabeth b. 1634 1652 m. John SALKELD / Mary b. 1636 m. Mr MATHEWS

Susan

Elizabeth HUBBARD d. 1690 1686 = **William COE (III)** 1662–1729 1693 = Sarah HATFIELD d. 1755 / Robert FRENCH 1653–90 = 1684 Anne 1660–1742 = 1696 James DAVIES jun. 1670–1749

Anne b. 1687 / three sons died young

Judith b. 1687 m. 1711 William GRAVES of Long Sutton

William

Ann b. 1688 m. 1724 Ralph COLE of Sudbury

Elizabeth 1690–1720 unm.

William (IV) 1694–1719 m. Christian

Benedicta 1717//

Charles 1695–96

Sarah 1697–1776 unm.

Susanna b. 1699 m. 1727 Isaac COOK gent. of Mildenhall

William b. 1731 / Henry b. 1733 / Margaret b.1735

FAMILY

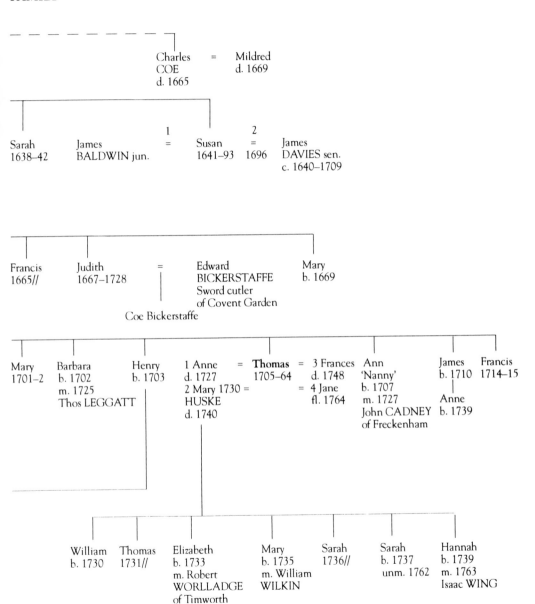

Charles = Mildred
COE d. 1669
d. 1665

Sarah James 1 2
1638–42 BALDWIN jun. = Susan = James
    1641–93 1696 DAVIES sen.
      c. 1640–1709

Francis Judith = Edward Mary
1665// 1667–1728 BICKERSTAFFE b. 1669
    Sword cutler
    of Covent Garden
  Coe Bickerstaffe

Mary Barbara Henry 1 Anne = **Thomas** = 3 Frances Ann James Francis
1701–2 b. 1702 b. 1703 d. 1727 1705–64 d. 1748 'Nanny' b. 1710 1714–15
  m. 1725 2 Mary 1730 = = 4 Jane b. 1707
  Thos LEGGATT HUSKE fl. 1764 m. 1727 Anne
    d. 1740 John CADNEY b. 1739
      of Freckenham

William Thomas Elizabeth Mary Sarah Sarah Hannah
b. 1730 1731// b. 1733 b. 1735 1736// b. 1737 b. 1739
   m. Robert m. William unm. 1762 m. 1763
   WORLLADGE WILKIN   Isaac WING
   of Timworth

Through his father William II, the diarist derived several interesting connections with families of local clergy. First, in 1652 William II's sister Elizabeth had married the well-known Presbyterian minister John Salkeld, who in 1662 was ejected from his living of Worlington. William II himself made a very good match when in 1659 he married Judith Colman of Bardwell. Her father William Colman, gent., of Bardwell and Bury St Edmunds, was 'register' to the archdeaconry of Sudbury and the town of Bury; while her mother was Judith, daughter of Thomas Muriell, archdeacon of Norfolk, also of Bardwell (see family tree, p. 33). The next year, Elizabeth, another daughter of William and Judith Colman, married Arthur Heron, rector of Bardwell from 1631. This gave the Coes two strong links with a parish fifteen miles to the east of Mildenhall. It is therefore not surprising that William III, born in 1662, was sent to school there.[77]

No licensed schoolmaster is listed for Bardwell, but there could have been no objection to Heron, a former fellow of St John's College, Cambridge, teaching a nephew with other local lads. One indication that William III received a good early education is his handwriting, which is elegant and better than that of Isaac Archer. He also quoted a wide range of authors, and knew how to write in Greek and Hebrew characters.[78] But Heron died in 1676 when William Coe was only fourteen. The latter stated in his diary that he was still a schoolboy in 1680; the implication is that he was then at Bury. When the Heron boys reached school age, their mother chose Bury grammar school for Arthur and Charterhouse for John; both proceeded to their father's college in Cambridge and were subsequently ordained. William Heron, destined for humbler things than his brothers, appears in the diary as 'cos. W. Heron', and was a boon drinking companion of the author.

In 1674 William Coe II paid for 8 hearths at West Row: this implies a fairly substantial house which was no doubt passed on to the next generation. He had lost his first wife Judith, the diarist's mother, in 1669 and remarried in 1678.[79] He died in 1681, leaving all his lands to his son and £1200 to his two surviving daughters.[80]

William Coe III's diary is not much concerned with family life, and is thus significantly different from Archer's. Nevertheless, his two marriages and families can be reconstructed from a variety of other sources. His first marriage in 1686 was to Elizabeth, daughter of George Hubbard (or Hubbart) of Southery near Downham Market, Norfolk. Coe was 24 and his wife about 20, but after bearing him three daughters, all of whom lived into adulthood, Elizabeth died in 1690. Three years later, William married Sarah Hatfield, who was the daughter of Ann Hatfield, widow of a wealthy grocer of King's Lynn. She bore him eleven children, eight of whom survived infancy. After his second marriage in 1693, perhaps as a New Year intention on April 1st 1694, William Coe started keeping his diary in earnest. His first and second families, his friends and relations, all gain frequent mention.

---

[77] Diary, f. 2r.
[78] No evidence has been found to suggest that William Coe went to university.
[79] The first name of William II's second wife was Mary; maiden name unknown.
[80] William Coe II's will, 1681; SRO(B), E18/452/66.

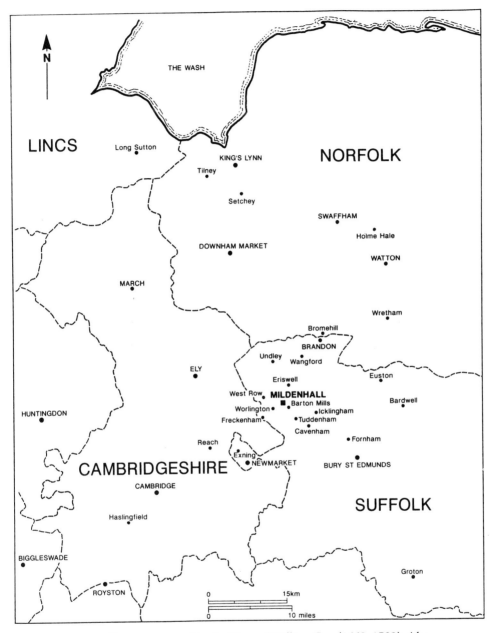

N

THE WASH

LINCS

Long Sutton

KING'S LYNN

Tilney

NORFOLK

Setchey

SWAFFHAM

Holme Hale

DOWNHAM MARKET

WATTON

MARCH

Wretham

Bromehill

BRANDON

Undley
Wangford

ELY

Eriswell

Euston

West Row   **MILDENHALL**

HUNTINGDON

Worlington   Barton Mills

Bardwell

Freckenham   Icklingham

Tuddenham

Cavenham

Reach

Fornham

Exning

CAMBRIDGESHIRE

NEWMARKET

BURY ST EDMUNDS

CAMBRIDGE

SUFFOLK

Haslingfield

BIGGLESWADE

Groton

0   15km

0   10 miles

ROYSTON

Map 2: Places mentioned in the Diary of William Coe (1662–1729). Also mentioned but not shown are Beccles, Leicester and London.

William III led a gentleman's life, but he probably had more financial anxieties than his father. For example, out of income from his inherited lands, he had to pay his two sisters substantial legacies of £600 each. He also had to provide the Brewhouse and 68 acres of land as jointure for his first wife Elizabeth, a decision which was the subject of an action in the Court of Common Pleas by his sister Anne and her husband surnamed French. It was not until 1728, shortly before his death, that William Coe signed a covenant with William French junior, to settle 'doubts and scruples' as to whether he had 'a clear and full power' to execute the marriage settlement of 1686.[81]

William Coe's marriage to Sarah Hatfield forged a complicated connection with a clerical family named Davies (see details, p. 33). James Davies, father and son, held between them the livings of four parishes near Mildenhall.[82] The elder James married three times: his second wife had been William Coe's aunt Susan, and in 1696 he married Sarah's widowed mother Anne. At about the same time the younger James probably married William's sister Anne, who thus became the 'sister Davies' of the diary; she had previously been married to Robert French. William's 'Sister Bickerstaffe' was Judith, five years his junior; she married Edward Bickerstaffe, sword-cutler of Covent Garden in London. Her son was named Coe Bickerstaffe and seems to have emigrated to Jamaica. 'Uncle Chambers' was Joseph Chambers, gent. of London, who married Marian Colman, a younger sister of William Coe's mother. 'Uncle St Gens' (probably St John) may have been the husband of Coe's aunt Mary.

Marriage took two of the three daughters of Coe's first marriage north and south of Mildenhall. Judith married William Graves of Long Sutton in Lincolnshire, while Ann married Ralph Cole of Sudbury in southern Suffolk. Their unmarried sister Elizabeth died in 1720, leaving £500 to her 'dear and loving father' as well as legacies to her two sisters and benefits to her step-brothers and step-sisters, all from the lands and jointure inherited from her mother.

From Coe's second marriage, the first-born William arrived promptly in 1694. He was subsequently apprenticed to Mr Bangor, apothecary of Wisbech in Cambridgeshire, but died in his mid-twenties leaving a widow called Christian. Susanna married Isaac Cook, gentleman of Mildenhall. All three of Coe's other surviving sons had families, but it was Thomas Coe, maltster and gentleman, four times married, who maintained the family's profile in the area after the diarist's death in 1729. Although all William Coe's land was sold by the terms of his will, Mary Huske, soon to be Thomas Coe's second wife, purchased the Brewhouse from William's estate. But a few weeks before he died in 1764, Thomas and his third wife Jane disposed of the old family home, the Brewhouse, and some 200 acres of land to Sir William Bunbury for £860.

Several friends and acquaintances named in the diary can also be identified. Sir Henry Bunbury, 3rd Bt, and Sir Thomas Hanmer, 4th Bt, were brothers-in-law through Susanna, Sir Henry's wife and Sir Thomas' sister. The presence of William Coe at the funeral of the Duchess of Grafton at Euston in

---

[81] SRO(B), E18/452/66, Bundle 2/2.
[82] Barton Mills, Cavenham, Culford and Tuddenham; all of which feature in Coe's diary (see Map 2, p. 31).

JAMES DAVIES, senior and junior, ministers

JAMES DAVIES senior, MA and Fellow of Jesus College, Oxford c. 1640–1709, Rector of Barton Mills from 1670 and of Culford from 1683.

married 1. Elinor ——, who bore him 5 sons and 2 daughters between 1670 and 1681: JAMES DAVIES junior (see below), William, Edward, Ann, Richard, Francis and Mary. She died 1681/2.

married 2. in 1682, Susan, sister of William Coe (II) and widow of James Baldwin junior. She died in 1693.

married 3. in 1696, Ann née Brown widow of William Hatfield grocer of King's Lynn, whom she married at St Nicholas there in 1662. She died in 1700.

JAMES DAVIES junior, Westminster and Trinity College, Cambridge, BA, Ord. Norwich 1693. 1670–1749, Rector of Tuddenham and Vicar of Cavenham,

married in 1696, Anne Coe (1660–1742) sister of William Coe (III), and widow of Robert French (1653–1690), who bore him three shortlived sons: Edward 1697–8, James 1698–9 and William 1700–1.

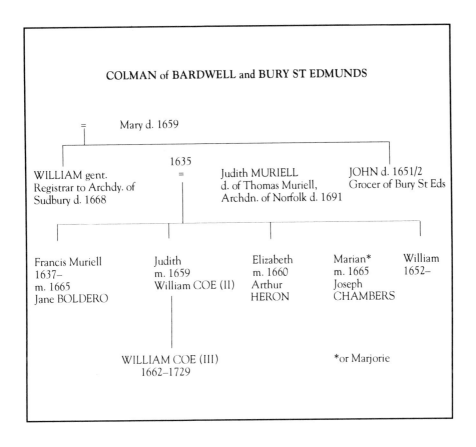

COLMAN of BARDWELL and BURY ST EDMUNDS

= Mary d. 1659

1635

WILLIAM gent.
Registrar to Archdy. of
Sudbury d. 1668

= Judith MURIELL
d. of Thomas Muriell,
Archdn. of Norfolk d. 1691

JOHN d. 1651/2
Grocer of Bury St Eds

Francis Muriell
1637–
m. 1665
Jane BOLDERO

Judith
m. 1659
William COE (II)

Elizabeth
m. 1660
Arthur
HERON

Marian*
m. 1665
Joseph
CHAMBERS

William
1652–

WILLIAM COE (III)
1662–1729

*or Marjorie

February 1723 is explained by the fact that she, the Dowager of the first Duke and Countess of Arlington in her own right, had married Sir Thomas Hanmer in 1698. The Hanmers lived at the Manor House in the centre of Mildenhall town. The Foorths, often mentioned, were William, rector of Eriswell from 1683 until his death in 1715, and Ann, daughter of diarist Isaac Archer, whom he married in 1690 at Mildenhall. The strangely named Mr Meillabars (or Mallabar) succeeded James Davies senior as rector of Barton Mills, when the latter died in 1709. William Glascock, Esq., senior and junior, were prominent in the affairs of Barton Mills. The Seyliards (or Sulyards) were another well-to-do family; Thomas Seyliard, gent., also lived in West Row. The Coes also visited other friends or relations who lived at a place called Holme; Canon Raven is probably right in identifying this as Holme Hale near Swaffham in Norfolk.[83] Three ministers who preached at Mildenhall and were noted in the diary, were Samuel Newson, rector of Great Waldingfield 1657–1693, James Paine, vicar of Mildenhall 1700–1712 and John Badcock, vicar of Godmanchester 1651–1691.

THE DIARY OF WILLIAM COE

This diary is also in the manuscript collection of Cambridge University Library, having been presented in 1935 by Mr G.O. Read, and bears the class mark Add. MS 6843. Considerably shorter than Archer's diary, it contains about 35,000 words. It is a small, leather-bound volume containing 111 folios which measure 142 by 88 mm. Its condition is good, except that the spine has been replaced. The book seems to have been adopted by Coe, for it originally belonged to his first wife's brother, Jonas Hubbart, who had begun to use it for his accounts in 1688 but made only a single entry.

The diary mentions nothing about William Coe's early life, but concentrates on his final thirty-six years from 1693 to 1729. Broadly, the diary seems to have been used for two main purposes: firstly, to record his own sins, failings and 'resolutions of ammendment', and secondly to register important 'providential' mercies to him and his family.[84] This is reflected in the arrangement of the book, for Coe usually chose to record his two sets of concerns on separate pages. For example, a list of 'mercyes received' is often recorded on one side of a folio and is continued on the corresponding side of the next folio, while confessions and resolutions appear on the intervening sides. However, this is not always consistently followed.

This diary is a fascinating revelation of the inner struggles of a strongly Anglican layman and parishioner. Coe's genuine religious instincts were constantly warring with temptations of earthly indulgence, made possible by his considerable wealth and leisure. Excessive drinking and habitual gambling, often well into the early hours of the morning, were the sins which he was for ever confessing and repenting. So frequently does Coe record his bibulous

---

[83] J.J. Raven, A History of Suffolk (1895), p. 236.

[84] Among the most common 'mercies received' were falling off horses without injury and avoiding the swallowing of pins in food. See Diary, ff. 43v, 82v.

time-wasting, and his corresponding resolutions of reform, that the reader is commonly left frustrated or even infuriated by the constant and apparently unavailing repetition!

Another less frequent sin, but clearly one which greatly troubled Coe's tender conscience, is registered in the diary cryptically. He records what were evidently sexual transgressions or temptations by using a special symbol, represented in this edition by an asterisk, frequently followed by dates indicating night-time, and by abbreviated Latin phrases (see facsimile, p. 228). Unfortunately, these entries are not always decipherable, since Coe later thought better of recording his more embarrassing secrets, and scored through them heavily. However, some of the more legible entries include the abbreviated words 'unnat. poll.', which probably mean 'unnatural defilement'. This phrase certainly suggests a sexual activity, but of what kind we can only guess. There is no reason to suspect that a second party was involved.

One other feature of the diary deserves discussion. Among the people of Mildenhall and area, William Coe is still remembered as 'Squire Coe' who in 1700 commissioned a new wig to be made from the hair of his three eldest daughters. This affectionate tradition is based on two published sources: alleged extracts from Coe's diary which were published in The Athenaeum of 1869; and a poem of Mortimer Collins which appeared in the journal All the Year Round for April 1871.[85] Both pieces of writing were stimulated by an event which took place at Bury St Edmunds in 1869. This was the annual meeting of the Royal Archaeological Institute, at which a 'temporary Museum' was organized for members. One of many exhibits was the diary of William Coe, then owned by Mr James Read, solicitor of Mildenhall.[86] The two entries relating to Coe's wig, purporting to come from his diary, were published again in 1892, this time by A.E. Simpson in his History of Mildenhall. Yet, in a very different vein, Canon Raven wrote in 1895 that he could find no trace of these extracts, and they certainly do not feature in a transcription of the diary published by Evelyn White in the East Anglian of 1906–07.[87] By 1945, the editor of the East Anglian Miscellany was convinced that the story of the wig was 'spurious'.[88]

So, is this story a genuine but lost part of the diary, or is it a picturesque hoax? In fact, the likely answer has always been apparent in the original manuscript. Between folios 10 and 11, a single page has been cut out which relates to the years 1701–02. This is the only excision visible in the volume, and the missing sheet must surely have carried the entries about Coe's wig, as well as other revelations about his breaking of the 6th to 8th Commandments. We have no clue as to who cut out the page, or for what reason, but the deed was probably done in the early 1890s: after Simpson made his extracts in about 1892 and before Raven vainly searched the manuscript in 1895. The missing entries, which have caused so much speculation, run as follows:

85 The Athenaeum, 31 July 1869, p. 152; All the Year Round, n.s. 5, 15 Apr. 1871, 468–69. Mortimer Collins (1827–76), prolific journalist, novelist and poet (DNB).
86 Archaeological Journal, XXVI (1869), p. 407.
87 J.J. Raven, op. cit. (1895), p. 234; East Anglian, or Notes and Queries, Vol. XI (1906–07), pp. 310, 339.
88 East Anglian Miscellany, Jan.–June 1945, p. 12 (No. 11271).

1700 [sic], Feb. 14. Mr Eldred of Bury cutt off my girls' hair, (viz.) Judith, Anne and Elizabeth, to make me a wigg, ten ounces bare weight.

May 7. Received a wigg made of my girls' hair as abovesaid, weighing eight and a half ounces bare weight, cost 8s. making.[89]

FORMER USES OF THE DIARY

As will be known to many readers, this edition of William Coe's diary is not the first to appear in print. A transcript of the diary originally appeared in *East Anglian, or Notes and Queries*, published in 1906–07. A new version in 1994 can be justified by the fact that the transcript in the *East Anglian* is not easy to read with its reproduction of original abbreviation marks and, moreover, contains a number of faults and omissions. It includes some significant misreadings, fails to record accurately some of Coe's original spelling and, most significantly of all, does not print all the original manuscript. The lengthy devotional passages which Coe includes alongside more personal prayers, themselves significant guides to his religious commitment, were omitted. However, omissions were not confined to these 'appendixes', as some entries in the main body of the diary have also been excised. Coe's cryptic references to his sexual failings, which are discussed above (pp. 34–35), also found no place in the first edition.[90]

In the edition which appears here, Coe's own system of numbering pages has not been followed, for the simple reason that it is confusing and switches between pagination and foliation. Consequently, the foliation supplied by a later owner of the diary, which is consistent throughout, has been preferred. For the purposes of accuracy and comparison with the original, a 'conversion table' has been included (p. 279) to indicate the correlation between Coe's own numbers and those chosen for this edition.

COMPARISON OF THE TWO DIARIES

In spite of very great differences between the two diaries, in both content and style, they bear comparison in a number of ways. In addition to their common geographical background, both diaries record the spiritual endeavours of their authors, and attempt to interpret God's actions and interventions in everyday life. In this sense, they both possess a distinctive theological flavour, and thus it is possible to compare the spiritual priorities and motivations of Archer and Coe. Archer emerges as a meticulous, thorough-going yet moderate puritan; Coe as a frequently wayward, but no less committed stalwart of the established

---

[89] From *The Athenaeum*, 31 July 1869, p. 152; almost certainly the year should be 1702. Simpson's extracts from the diary also contain errors of transcription, particularly where dates are concerned.

[90] One significant omission is Coe's reference to his unsettling disagreement with a neighbour, who had allegedly fathered a bastard child (Diary, 12 June 1709, f. 37r).

church. Both men courageously and persistently battle with their own peculiar faults and failings, in an attempt to establish 'peace with God'. Coe, in spite of his obvious infection with worldliness, is no less preoccupied with eternal issues than the more withdrawn and sober Archer. Coe frequently, and as plainly as Archer, affirms the reality of divine judgement which awaits every man and woman. Although Coe does not share Archer's concern for a puritan-style conversion, he is as convinced as Archer that righteousness can only be obtained through complete resignation to Christ's meritorious work. It is perhaps Coe's affirmation of his own intrinsic human weakness which throws him so fully upon reliance on Christ.

In terms of their practical spirituality, the two diarists agree strongly in their approach to, and treatment of, the Lord's Supper. Both men viewed the sacrament as an opportunity for a wide variety of spiritual exercises, ranging from the confession of sin, prayer for sick relatives, hope for spiritual renewal and, most importantly in Coe, resolutions of 'better obedience' to God. As a committed adherent of the Church of England, Coe may be expected to have had a more acute sacramental awareness than the more nonconformist Archer. However, Archer's diary amply demonstrates how reverently the sacrament could be treated by a moderate puritan, and the very profound emotional and spiritual significance it could possess. Therefore the two men's approaches to the Lord's Supper show a striking convergence of sentiment, in spite of important differences in their background and churchmanship. Finally, because they knew each other[91] and each left an absorbing diary, it is perhaps not inappropriate that today they lie within a few feet of each other. Archer rests in a now unmarked grave in the chancel of Mildenhall church, and Coe under an inscribed slab in the vestry.[92]

---

91 See Coe's diary, 12 Feb. 1696/7, f. 18r: 'Causlessly thought ill of Mr Archer, my minister'.

92 The badly worn inscription over Coe's grave reads: 'Here lyeth the body of William Coe, gent., who dyed Aug. 31, 1729, age 67 years . . .'

Editorial Method

The following editorial conventions have been used in this volume:

Insertions in the manuscript are shown by oblique lines, thus	\ /
Deletions, still readable, are shown in angled brackets, thus	< >
All editorial insertions are in italic type within square brackets, thus	[*sic*]
Illegible words or sections are shown thus	[*illeg.*]
Deleted and unreadable sections of the manuscript are shown thus	[*deletion*]
Damaged and unreadable sections of the manuscript are shown thus	[*damaged*]
A reading open to question is followed by an italicised question-mark in square brackets, thus	[*?*]

In order to preserve the full flavour of their writing, the original spellings of Isaac Archer and William Coe have been retained throughout. This includes a number of idiosyncrasies which may, at first sight, appear to be misreadings. For example, Archer frequently uses 'of' to mean 'off', and 'then' for 'than'.

Obvious abbreviations have been extended without comment. Thus, 'Xt' is rendered as 'Christ', 'Mr' and 'Mrs' as 'master' and 'mistress', and 'Dr' as 'doctor'. Similarly, the ampersand (&), liberally used by both authors, has been changed to 'and', and '&c' to 'etc.' However, 'viz.' (Latin, *videlicet* meaning 'namely') has been left in its contracted form as it is in common use today. Again, as an aid to readers, all scriptural references have been given in full where frequently in the original they were contracted. All dates have been expanded, to make the chronological structure of the diaries as clear as possible. (See below for monetary abbreviations.)

The Anglo-Saxon character known as the thorn has in all cases been re-placed by 'th'. Thus 'þe' becomes 'the', and 'þt' becomes 'that'. All Latin and Greek entries have been reproduced in italic type, and where possible an English translation is given in a footnote.

As an aid to readers, punctuation has been modernized. In most cases, this has meant the insertion of new punctuation marks, particularly commas, where none existed before. However, no punctuation has been introduced where there is a danger of imposing one reading in preference to another. Less fre-quently, original punctuation has been changed, for example to substitute full-stops for semi-colons, or to remove commas placed in misleading or incor-rect positions. A feature which has not been 'corrected' is Archer's use of 'it's' where today we would use 'its'.

New paragraph breaks have been introduced to divide solid blocks of text, particularly in Archer's diary. Whenever either diarist begins an entry with a full date, this has been indented as a new paragraph.

The use of capital letters has also been modernized, by deleting those used unnecessarily by the diarists, and by inserting capitals at the beginning of each sentence and for all personal and place names. Where the title of a book is cited, the title has been italicized and key words capitalised: for example, 'Sibbe's bruised reed' becomes 'Sibbe's *Bruised Reed*'. Ecclesiastical offices are begun with lower-case letters, for example bishop, dean, vicar, etc. Upper-case letters are only used for the titles of named individuals, such as Bishop Wren.

Money
Whenever sums of money are mentioned, the abbreviation 'li' used to represent the pound, has been modernized as '£'. The abbreviations 's' for shilling, and 'd' for pence, have been retained.

Old-style and new-style dates
Under the old Julian calendar, the new year began on Lady Day, 25 March. Under the new Gregorian calendar, becoming popular in England from the late seventeenth century onwards but not formalised until 1752, the new year began on 1 Jan. In the late seventeenth and early eighteenth centuries therefore, it became common for writers such as Archer and Coe to record dates between 1 Jan. and 25 March in both ways. For example, 20 March 1665 by the modern calendar was represented as 20 March 1664/5. The split dates are retained in this edition.

Abbreviations Used in Footnotes

Al. Cantab.	*Alumni Cantabrigienses*, eds J. & J.A. Venn, Part 1 (1922–27)
BDBR	*Biographical Dictionary of British Radicals in the 17th Cent.*, eds R. Greaves & R. Zaller (3 vols, 1982–84)
Cal. Rev.	*Calamy Revised*, ed. A. Matthews (OUP, 1934, 1988)
CRO	Cambridgeshire Record Office
DNB	*Dictionary of National Biography*
Foster	J. Foster, *The Register of Admissions to Gray's Inn, 1521–1889* (1889)
PRO	Public Record Office, London
SRO(B)	Suffolk Record Office (Bury St Edmunds)
VCH	*Victoria County History, Cambridgeshire*

THE DIARY OF
ISAAC ARCHER
1641–1700

Cambridge University Library
Additional Manuscript 8499

A recta conscientia latum unquem in tota vita non oportet
quenquam recedere.

sic fere Cicero ad Atticum[1]

[Inscription]

Συν Θεω/pret. [damaged][2]

I. Archer's Book
1665
July 15.

Haec olim meminisse iuvabit!
Ἀκριβωσ περιπατειτε![3]

[Preamble]

A faithfull account, and register of God's dealings both to bodye and soule, to
his glory, and my owne peace!

O Lord God, the searcher of hearts, I thy unworthy servant humbly beg thine
assisting grace that I may record and write what thou hast done for mee, as to
soule or bodye; and that I may conceale nothing that may make for thy glory,
though it be for my owne shame! Grant this, holy God, for the sake alone of
Jesus Christ, my Lord and Saviour. Amen!

1

Anno Domini 1641

Forasmuch as all my thoughts, words, and actions, with every sin and debt of
mine, [deletion] are recorded in heaven, and the whole series of my life perfectly
knowne to God, I thinke it expedient, being counselled therto by my good
father (whose words, when my heart was tender, I look't upon as oracles) to

---

1 Thus, approximately, Cicero to Atticus. The actual quotation is *Atque hoc 'in omni vita sua
   quemque a recta conscientia traversum unquam non oportet discedere' vide quam φιλοσοφωσ*: 'And
   see what deep philosophy there is in this other sentiment of mine, "In all of one's life one
   ought not to stray a nail's breadth from the straight path of conscience" ', Cicero, *Epistularum ad Atticum*, XIII, 20.
2 Συν Θεω: 'with God'. *Pretio*, the price which Archer paid for the book is lost through
   fraying.
3 *Haec olim meminisse iuvabit*: 'it will be a pleasure to look back on these things', Vergil, *Aeneid*,
   I, 203. Ἀκριβωσ περιπατειτε is taken from Ephesians 5:15 and translates as 'walk circumspectly'.

keep my accounts as even as I can with those in the court of heaven, that through faith in Christ Jesus, that sure covert till the indignation be ov[er] past, I may not feare the face of my judge, as knowing him a mercifull father. And God grant that I may rip up the sores of my heart heer, in order to the healing of them, that they may never rise up in judgment against mee in the other world to my confusion!

I began to take an account of my life in writing but in the yeare 1659: Oh that I had begun sooner! Therfore I must be the shorter in the years of my infancy, youth, and inadvertency, and heedlesnes.

2/1641

Some things I write from tradition, others from weake recollections, and the rest from attentive observation and watch, viz. from the years of discretion and so onwards as God shall spare my life.

I was borne in Christmas week,[4] as I have heard, in the yeare 1641 of good parents. My father, Mr William Archer, was borne at Epping in Essex, where his ancestours had enjoyed an estate more then 200 yeares but *vix ea nostra voco* etc.[5] My grandfather and grandmother were eminent for piety in their gener-ations; and God granted him this blessing, that on his death-bed, with tears of joy, he said he had lived to see grace in all his children, wherof he[6] then had 7, as his father had 30 *Quaere*/[7] by two wives; my father was the 5th[8] sonne; his eldest brother John was famous at London, Hartford and Arnhem in Gelderland where he dyed;[9] my father was Lecturer at Halsted in Essex, and Colchester many yeares and was more

3/1641

eminent then I may modestly speake. My mother was Mistress Mary Wool-nough of good parents, and a good woman as could be found usually in those dayes; she was remarkable for her piety and prudence, chiefly for heer meek and quiet spirit of so great price with God, as 'tis 1 Peter 3:4. The place of my birth was Great St Margarets in High Suffolk, one of the 9 parishes so called,[10] at the house of my mother's parents. My name was Isaac because I was a son of many

---

4 Margin: 'December 23'.
5 The full quotation, which puts Archer's remarks in context, is *Nam genus et proavus et quae non fecimus ipsi, vix ea nostra voco*: 'For as to race and ancestry and the deeds that others have done, I call those in no true sense our own', Ovid, *Metamorphoses*, XIII, 140–1.
6 Margin: 'Edward died afore'.
7 *Quaere*: to check or query. Inserted here later by Archer, showing doubt about the figure.
8 '5th' has been corrected later from '4th'.
9 John Archer, pastor of the English Church at Arnhem, Netherlands, where he went into exile. He was firstly lecturer at Allhallows, Lombard Street, and St Antholins, London, from 1627–30, when he was suspended by the strongly anti-puritan bishop of London, William Laud. He wrote two books, *The Personall Reigne of Jesus Christ upon Earth* (1642), and *Comfort for Beleevers* (1645), both published posthumously, BDBR, I, 18.
10 Almost certainly St Margaret's, South Elmham, the parish registers of which do not survive for the period before 1679.

prayers;[11] and I hope what a bishop[12] said to Monica concerning Austin her son will be true heer, *fieri non potest ut filius istarum lachrymarum pereat*; Austin's *Confessions lib. 3, cap. 12, ad fin.*[13]

And thus was I borne in sin, and conceived in iniquitye as well as others, as much a child of wrath as any else, yet I blesse God that I was borne of good parents, for the promise was to them and their children after them, if they kept themselves in the love and favour of God,[14] which God grant I may doe to my live's end!

4/1642–5

When I was halfe a yeare old I was brought to Halsted in Essex, whither my father was unanimously invited to be Lecturer. My infancy was spent in sin and vanitye, even as 'tis in all before they know their maker; the Lord pardon the sinns of my tendernes and infancy! Then I was stubborne, and selfe willed, and Oh how have those sinns stuck close ever since! Then I was a crosse to my parents, and Oh what little amendment hath there bin! But the good Lord passe \by/ those sinns of ignorance, wherby I posted to hell and knew nothing of it! I can remember little of what I did then, only believe I was as bad as any, by knowing somthing of my selfe, by God's goodnes, since.

This I remember that God was good to mee in preserving mee, as from all manner of dangers so, especially from drowning severall times. For instance, once I used to hang by the hands at the end of a cart that went through the river, neer which our house stood. The man had warned mee in vaine, and one time let mee alone till I was in the midst of the river, and then whip't mee and forced mee to let goe,

5/1646

and by consequence to fall into the river. The rude man took no care of mee, but my God, whom I then knew not, did, to whom I give the glory of all. Another time the schollars were leaping from the arch of the bridge, which stood hanging somthing over the water, and by a slight they would leape on one side on to the banke without danger: this I minded not, but leap't directly into the river, and sunk twice; at last one of the lads took mee out. Though then I could not look to 2d causes, yet now I desire to magnify God who saved mee from death.

I remember also one of our neighbour's children, being at play with mee in the field, fell into a pond and I was lying over the brinke, in great danger, and reaching my arme to helpe him out; so by endeavouring to save another my owne life might have gone: but God ordered it so that my sister seing mee in that case cryed out, and my mother hearing it, ran hastily to my helpe, leaving the infant she had in her armes upon the grasse, and thus both were rescued.

---

11 Isaac means laughter or mockery in Hebrew because Sarai laughed when told she would bear a child at ninety years of age. However, the fact that she had waited so long meant that Isaac was certainly 'a son of many prayers'.

12 'Ambrose' is here crossed out and replaced by 'a bishop'.

13 *Fieri non potest ut filius istarum lachrymarum pereat*: 'It is not possible that the son of these tears should perish', Augustine, *Confessions*, III, 12:20.

14 Mention of 'the promise' harks back to the story of Isaac. See especially Genesis 17:7.

6/1647–8

I had also a dangerous fall from an horse, and might have bin killed but that God saved mee from that also, whose name be praised for ever more!

In the yeare <47> '48, during the warre betwixt the King and his Parliament, some of the King's partye came to Halsted (taking it in their way to Colchester, where they caused that grievous siege)[15] and threatned, if they could find my father, to chop him as small as herbs for the pot; so that he and another townsman fled and lay in a field under some faggotts all night; yea (as I heard since) though they came into the field, and over the very faggotts, yet God preserved him from their bloody hands. My mother, in the meane time, and her 5 children, 2 sonns and 3 daughters, fled to a green a mile and halfe from the towne, where we were till day-breake and then we fled on foot, to Coggeshall, 5 mile of, where, as I thinke, was a garrison of the Parliament's side. During this, the greedy Cavaliers, as they called them, came and searched for us, and not finding us they brake my father's study open, and missing him, when wee expected they should

7/1648–9

have done us mischiefe, they were restrained by the good hand of our God; yea though my father had purposely left, on the shelfe, money for them that they might spare his books, yet they saw it not, only took away some farthings we used to play withall; and thus did God preserve us.

In '49, my father, by the importunitye of the Mayour and Aldermen and the failing of his maintenance at Halsted, where they had contributed beyond their abilityes, and yet because he medled not with the living they were brought to straits; went to Colchester the summer after the siege, and was Lecturer, and had £100 per annum out of the towne stock, without burdening any man; this was according to his mind, for he was against the ordinary maintenance of tithes, though my mother was not for that remoove, nor scarce any of his friends at Halsted where he was very much beloved.

We had not bin there long, but I fell into rude company, who easily gulled mee, being but a child, and perswaded \mee/ to give them money, and steale more from my father; thus for toyes would they gett anything of mee; yea they would carry mee to the taverne at my owne cost, and gett money from mee

8/1648–9

in exchange for trifles, or brasse money, and by many such cheats brought mee to that passe that my father was justly angry and deservedly corrected mee for it; and as I now thanke him for nipping mee so in the bud, only I wish it had bin more seveer, so I desire my God not to remember the sinns and extravagances of my childhood.

---

[15] A reference to the Parliamentarian siege of Colchester, from June to August 1648. The Royalist forces were compelled to surrender unconditionally owing to starvation and disease. The Royalist commanders, Sir George Lisle and Sir Charles Lucas, were executed afterwards by the victorious Sir Thomas Fairfax. An old but thorough treatment of the incident may be found in Philip Morant's, *The History and Antiquities of the most Ancient Town and Borough of Colchester* (London, 1748; new edition reprinted, 1970), 57–65.

It happened that one of Halsted came to see us, and under colour of going only to visitt my old acquaintance my father sent mee to boord at Halsted with Mr Covill; thus was I by this fetch, weaned from my friends, wheras otherwise such was my stubborne wilfulnes, I should scarce have bin drawne away.

When I found my selfe thus catch't, and in this manner drawne from my sinfull yet beloved company, Oh how did I frett, and fume! How oft did I attempt to run away! But my schoolmaster had a strict hand over mee, for which now I blesse God. I was very bad, and unlucky beyond the rest, and kept my filching tricks now I was kept bare of money, and strictly to my book; I went on ignorantly, and rashly, yet somtimes my conscience did check mee and dogg mee, though young, so as I was scarce at rest, and yet would stifle all!

9/1648–9

The good Lord lay not this to my charge! but teach mee to hate the memory of it!

September. Soon after this, it pleased God to take away my deare mother of a feaver, and it seems after miscarrying;[16] within lesse then a month after, my 2d sister dyed; and that one griefe might follow another, in the neck of that comes the death of my brother, the youngest of us all. This treble losse so grieved my father that he could take no rest at home, nor preach, but rode up and downe to find comfort; and this aggravated it much, when some did not stick to say that God's hand went out against him because he went from his beloved and loving people at Halsted; taking upon them to interpret God's actions, whose judgments are in the great deep, and his wayes past our searching. It would have grieved mee surely, had I bin at the years of discretion; but alas! I was but a child and was more pleased with the cakes my mistress,[17] who was with her when she dyed, brought mee, then grieved for so unspeakable a losse, which since, by the want, I have found it.

10/1649–50

I had an impediment in my speech, I know not how I came by it, but I have heard I was not borne so, neither was it naturall so much as acquired, though now I thinke it was naturall, for the organs of speech are not so well framed as in others; and I believe will continue so to my dying day: it may be God laid this upon mee to teach mee to bridle my tongue, wherwith since I have offended God and man, friend and foe; for I had a kind of sagacity in speaking and replying bitingly and smartly as others have told mee; yea, so provoking was I that my master would say that in Ovid, *lingua fuit damno* etc.[18] would be true of mee; but yet I hope, through God's grace, he will proove a false prophet.

Whilst I was at home, I remember, my father would make mee read the Bible; which, through an eager desire of play, and that inbred corruption wherby I hated all things that were good, I cared not for; this unwillingnes to

---

16 See also the entry of 10 October, 1698 (p. 226) which supplies more details on her death and its consequences.

17 Presumably his schoolmistress at Halstead, wife of Mr Covill.

18 *Lingua fuit damno*: 'his tongue was his undoing', Ovid, *Metamorphoses* II: 540.

read, and stammering when I did read did tire out his patience, so he would let mee leave of; thinking withall that I stammered on purpose to be from my book, though in that he was mistaken for I never could helpe it, and would give much that I were

11/1650–2

free from it, for it hath bin, for sometime, a griefe and burden to mee so as to hinder mee in my studyes, and to dampe laudable and ingenious enterprises and attempts; but God still sees it good for mee, and so I submitt; though I blesse his name 'tis somwhat better with mee now I am growne up in years. My tongue was cutt 2 or 3 times, but I gott no good; at last there came a man that pretended he would cure mee, and thrust his fingers into my mouth, and broke or bruised the strings of my tongue, and thus instead of doing mee good he did mee hurt.

I thinke in the yeare 1650 my father, by reason of his melancholy, wherby he could not be alone, and that he might have a consort to helpe him in his sicknes and infirmityes and other reasons, married an antient widow Mrs Godscall, who was rich, religious and a well bred gentlewoman, and so might suit my father, and bring up my sisters vertuously. With her my father lived very contentedly, and peaceably, for both minded heaven.

In the meane time I run on furiously in sin, vanitye and vice; not knowing any thing of God, though I had good and godly education, had I understood my selfe or else minded the instructions, and examples of my master and mistress, and some pious youths in that family who would pray etc.

12/1651–3

by themselves; though I would be sorry that I could not doe so, when they lovingly gott mee amongst them. Although I had such examples yet my heart was corrupt, and the relicks of my Colchester sinns staid with mee; hence it was that I would steale as occasion served, and robb orchards (which St Austin took notice of)[19] and with the other boyes be rude, saucy, lascivious; also, how often did I profane the Lord's day though I was made to goe to church, and repeat what I could remember of the sermon. And Oh, what fruit have I of thees sinns wherof now I \am/ ashamed! How foolish and sinfull was I, O Lord, yea even as a beast in thy sight! Psalm 73:22. I am vexed at the thoughts of that wickednes, and those abominations which I furiously commited at school, without feare of God, or man; and I desire God would never bring them in judgment against mee! By observing school-boyes since, I thinke we were worse then any; and all this was hid from our Master's knowledge; yet then I had checks of conscience, though I stifled them, and would not hearken to the voyce of God's Holy Spirit striving with mee.

13/1651–3

Yet, Oh Lord, thou wert good to mee all this while that knew nothing of thee! I must confesse, with shame for my ingratitude, that thou didst still deliver mee

[19] Augustine, *Confessions*, II: 4.

48

from many dangers. To instance, one of our boorders by night threw a flint stone at a dog, and just then I came out, so that it smote mee in the forepart of the head and brake my skull as is to be felt now, so as the blood came running downe to the feare of those that were by; but, by God's providence, my mistress was in the way, who had skill in chirurgery and cured it in some time, though the skarre and hole will goe to the grave with mee. Thus how good was God to mee a sinner! How forbearing and long-suffering! My soule, forget not thou thees mercyes though others passe them by as common.

I went home to see my mother in law[20] and spent my time idly enough; one mis-chance I remember hapned through my meanes; my brother in law used to clothe pictures with iznigglasse,[21] and silke etc. There was the King's picture, who was beheaded in 1648; and my father, I know not why, with a knife, cutt out his head in the picture; this I told in Colchester and it made some wonder,

14/1652–4

for I told them my father cutt off the King's head; this at first was not understood, but afterwards they knew the mistake. The Lord forgive mee that I should be instrumentall in defaming my father!

Yet God delivered mee from dangers; for we were playing at 9 pins, and one of the boyes cast the boule into the aire and 'twas my unhappines to come just under the boule, so as it fell full upon my head, and sanke mee; but, blessed be God, I was well againe. And Oh, that by thees warnings I had broke of my sinns, and turned to God! but I knew not God.

I remember when I went to schoole my father kept mee bare of clothes, and as for money I had none as the rest had; it was my hap to find a silver seale upon one of the beds, which drop't out of the pocket of some body in the house; this was soon missed, and I was conscious who had it. There was a maid who had stollen things from the same party, and was putt away, so as the seale was charged upon her who had it not, though the sending to her for that, caused her to send back some other things she had stollen; this I kept secret a good while, but

15/1654–6

such is the power of conscience, even in children, that I was not at rest, my heart condemned mee, my conscience was awakned, and dogged mee wherever I went; I acknowledge and confesse this to God's glory that I was afraid even of my owne shadow, and how oft did I wish it had never bin done! How oft at prayer did my heart accuse mee in that extremity that I was ready to cry out guilty before all!

The party that lost it gott mee to write to London for a new one, which I did and had one, but my mind was not at rest. I dared not to keep it, but laid it up in an hole of a post on the house top almost, and it was covered with cobwebbs; yet I thought it not safe, and feared a discovery, and went to see it in the night somtimes, though I was afraid the devill should appeare, and bring it to light; at

---

20 Mother-in-law is frequently used to denote step-mother, in this case his father's second wife, Mrs Godscall.
21 Iznigglasse: isinglass; a form of gelatin, got from the viscera of some fish, used in making glue.

49

last I remooved it to a neighbour's house, and laid it in a place more secret; but if any look't thereabouts I thought it was for that; thus was I tormented daily and knew not what to doe; sell it I dared not, keep it I was unwilling to, restore it I would, but was very much ashamed; my conscience had such powerfull workings that it was a perpetuall torment to mee; at last I was resolved to be rid of it, though I made no gaine of it; and one day going by the river's side, I threw it in; thus the feare of being found out

16/1655–6

ceased, but the guilt remaynes, and must so till the blood of sprinkling be applyed; but I hope God will pardon this with all the rest, and blessed be his name that I was convinced thus, and made to know there was a God though I had not had a Bible.

In the year 1655 I began to have some serious thoughts God-wards, and concerning the welfare of my soule; some convictions I had before, and long-ings, after I had heard a sermon, that I were so or so as the minister said, that I might goe to heaven, though as to the way I was ignorant enough. I would somtimes gett by my selfe, and read or pray, or see if I could inlarge my selfe upon any scripture so as to understand the sense fully. When I did amisse my master and mistress would tell mee how good my parents and relations were, that they knew none of my family but were godly; and if I prooved naught it would be a disgrace, and a great sin in mee, yea far greater then if my friends had bin bad etc. They would tell mee of Josiah, who sought God betimes (though secretly I thought I was not so old as he was when he began, and so I might putt it of awhile)[22] and some of our

17/1655–6

boyes were religious far beyond mee, whose example they would sett before mee.

Now all this together did somthing affect mee; and the worst of our boorders were gone, so that I was left alone as to old acquaintance; hence then I began to be more serious, and would pray by my selfe somtimes, though fearfull least others should know it, and laugh at mee, for I was ashamed to owne that which then, I thinke, I had a love for. God was pleased to worke a secret willingnes in mee for the good of my soule, and then began I seriously to hearken to the good counsell of others.

Once, I remember, upon the Lord's day, I was at prayer by the bed's side, and was taken in that posture of kneeling by some of the boyes who came in on the suddaine; now there stood a boxe under the bed, out of which somthing was lost, and they doubted not to charge mee with stealing it, because that formerly I was given to it; though I never broke open a box or trunk in my life for that end; this thou knowest, Oh my God, that I was unjustly charged with it; however it was but according to my deserts! They suspected mee also because I was ashamed to tell them what I was doing by the bed's side; I hope heerafter I shall openly and couragiouslye owne the wayes of God!

---

[22] The reference to Josiah is 2 Chronicles 34:1–3. Josiah sought the Lord when he was sixteen, hence Isaac's excuse since he was only fourteen at the time.

18/1655–6

It was the custome of our lads to pray together, and they would not allow mee to be of their number, or observe my course, because my speech was stammering, and they said God would not heare mee; I know God would not have heard mee, as a sinner, but Moses was heard for all his slownes of speech,[23] and so might I without doubt. Therfore would I gett by my selfe, and doe that according to my weaknes, which they did by themselves: moreover when we had some lads, whose friends had learned them formes of prayer, that would say their prayers every night, I would make up the want of a forme as well as I could; but they were soon laught out of their open and constant devotion, and I with them; although secretly, somtimes, I kept up my prayers, and hope the same of them too. Yea, when on sabbath dayes others would be at play, I would be by my selfe, praying, or reading, or looking over my notes of the sermon I was to repeat to my master; thus had I some liking to dutyes, but did not look at Christ the fountaine of them, and the acceptance they find with God; I rested upon them, and thought the better of my selfe, though I never had seen the worst of my heart.

19/1656

Thees things I write, not to boast of any thing I had or did, for 'twas all from God, or out of pride of spirit but, to be evidences upon record that God was mercifull to mee whilst young; and when I look back upon my life past, it may shame mee that my heart, which was so tender then, should be hard, and not so pliable to good counsell now! And Oh that I might by this also gett good to my soule!

But this, to God's glory, I confesse; that all this while, though I had strong motions to that which was good, I saw so many hindrances of piety and devotion (or at least as I apprehended it) by reason of the ill company of others; which I began now to be weary of though before I had loved it; that I putt of my good resolutions till I went to Cambridge; for from a child I eagerly desired to be a schollar, where I thought I might serve God more and better, having time and a study to my selfe, and no ill companions to hinder mee in minding my soule's good, which now I made my maine busines, and by God's goodnes was very frequently in my mind, though I kept all this to my selfe; thus I pleased my selfe with the thoughts of that happy life I was to lead at Cambridge; though I begg that God would pardon my deferring my conversion!

20/1656

Though I was so desirous of being a schollar, yet my father was unwilling; as thinking mee unfitt for the ministry because of my stammering, also not knowing how long those times of libertye might last, and withall considering that a trade would be more profitable in respect of gaine: so that he had mee up to London to be bound to a linnen draper, but, as God ordered it, he found fault with mee that I was not big or strong enough, and besides demanded more then my father was willing to part with; and 'twas well I was not bound for the man broke soon after.

[23] See, for example, Exodus 4:17.

This I can say, that my eagernes of learning and the ministry, and my aversenes from a trade was because I would serve God better, it being my generall and particular calling to mind heavenly things, and because that I was afraid of plunging my selfe into the affaires of the world (and I am of the same mind now) as thinking they would steale away my heart from God, and that I could not be able to keep my desires within the bounds God allowes in that case; and not for pride or lazines, as God knowes.

Heer I must acknowledge, as a special providence of God, that my father was made willing by this meanes. There was one Mr Dearsly, fellow of Trinitye Colledge in Cambridge,[24] and acquainted

21/1656–7

with my father; his mother lived at Colchester and coming to see her (because he had bin from the colledge, at Newcastle, 2 yeares or more and was newly setled in his fellowship againe), he visited my father also just at the time that I had sent him a Latine epistle to desire him once more that I might be a schollar; Mr Dearsly liked the letter so well that he perswaded my father to send mee to the universitye, which then he yielded to. And heer I blesse my God, who by his wise providence brought that to passe which I almost despaired of.

I went then to be admitted at Trinitye Colledge October 29 where, after much conversing in Latine and Greek, I was entred under Mr John Templer,[25] though Mr Dearsly did take the care of mee wholly, except in lectures and such like exercises. My friends thought it convenient I should not continue for a while, so I came back, and was, as it were, my Master's usher till April 20 1657 when I went to continue at Cambridge.

When I was newly come, either through my naturall melancholick temper, lack of suitable acquaintance (for idle ones I might have had abundantly, but then I hated such) or the absence from my friends, I was very sad and pensive; this, and keeping alone did very much dispose mee to piety, and devotion, and 'twas, by God's blessing, a meanes to settle mee in a course of dutyes

22/1657

and serving God, though but weakly; but it was a beginning and foundation to that which by his assistance I have kept up since, and doe still.

Just before my going to continue at the colledge, my mother dyed, which was a griefe to my father in that kind that he had little or no joy to live in Colchester, yea he laid downe his lecture not long after.

Now it was that I called to mind my actions which had not bin good, and recollected that good counsell which before I had despised; now I liked and loved such things as before I had no esteem for; now I was very serious, and too pensive, which although it had naturall causes yet was by God blessed to a better end then I could have thought of; now I found my whole man so changed, my understanding, will and affections bent another way, so much was

---

[24] Henry Dearsly, Fellow of Trinity College, 1649; vicar of Enfield, Middx., 1664–72, *Al. Cantab.*

[25] Archer was admitted as a subsizar and matriculated the following year, W.W. Rouse Ball and J.A. Venn (eds), *Admissions to Trinity College, Cambridge* (5 vols., London, 1913), II, 439.

I unlike my selfe at school that I might have said, with that noble convert, *ego non sum ego;*[26] truly I wonder at it now, though then I was confused and knew not what to make of it, and though I dare not say that this was an orderly conversion, yet I thinke since that God had an hand in it, and shall blesse him for it while I live.

23/1657

And as 'tis a refreshment to remember how content and humble, how submissive to God and my superiours, how studious and consciencious, yea how much changed I was to the better: so 'tis my shame that now I should be so to seek for that holy flame, and that innocence, and content, that meeknes and quietnes that I then enjoyed.

I saw all was not well with my soule and therfore resolved to sett upon a course of duty, and service of God, resting upon them when I should have stayed my selfe upon the fountayne of them Jesus Christ. We had many sermons, and common places, and good prayers and reading every morning in the chappell where I would very constantly be, not *formidine poenae*[27] but as I thought *pietatis amore;*[28] especially because I saw goodnes encouraged, and vice discouraged.

Thees things ran so in my mind, and I was so taken up with my soule-affaires, that one lecture day at Trinity church[29] I heard Mr Dearsly preach, and was so affected with some things that I had no rest in my soule till I went to him for advice for my soule's health. He referred mee to that James 1:5. This I liked, though too generall for my case; and accordingly I prayed more fervently then ever I had done, and expected what I prayed for; but this heat soon abated by my acquaintance who were civill but not so holy as I could have wished them.

24/1657

Neither could I have the confidence to aske Mr Dearsly any more about it, because he was not so free, or thought I spoke out of a melancholick humour, and because I was ashamed of such serious things, seing them so little minded as I did in the colledge, except it were in a superficiall way. Yea I could find none, but God, to tell my mind to though it was full fraught, and wanted a vent; I therfore kept all this to my selfe, neither could any man tell my case.

Finding none that I could be plaine with, and being burdened with cares about my soule's state, I resolved to acquaint my father, as a most experienced Christian, and one that naturally would care for mee as to body and soule, and desire his directions what course to take in serving God, and working out my owne salvation; as also for my studyes: this I did accordingly and he was overjoyed to heare of such a change in mee, and wrott mee severall savoury, humbling and yet comfortable letters, which I read with such attention and

---

26 *Ego non sum ego:* 'I am not I'. Author unknown.
27 *Formidine poenae:* 'for fear of punishment.'
28 *Pietatis amore:* 'for love of piety.'
29 Referring to Holy Trinity church, Cambridge, which had a famous lectureship in the early seventeenth century. It attracted such important divines as Richard Sibbes, lecturer from 1610–15, and vicar from 1633–5, and John Preston, lecturer from 1625–28.

reverence almost as if they had bin God's word; thees did mee so much and so apparent good that I went on cheerfully in a course of dutyes and of serving God.

25/1657

My father in his letters grounded mee in practicall divinity; and when by dutyes I strived to worke out salvation, and by strict observing God's law, and the sabbath day I thought to please God, he beat mee of from a resting in any thing I did, and sent mee higher then all such performances.

I strived indeed to make God's wayes pleasant, and his day my delight, but I found in my heart a grudging when that day came, and thought much to be abridged of my studies; so eager was I of my book, though I might well have spared one day to study my owne heart in, if God had not required it. Yet thus farre, through God's goodnes, I prevailed with my evill heart, which envied God his owne, that when any of my acquaintance that were not religious in good earnest, came to see mee on that day, I would not open to them; or, if I did, I would entertaine them with such discourse as pleased them not, and so gott the ill will of some of them, though I knew that my God could make up all, and be to mee instead of many friends.

When I had bin there almost a yeare, I was not of so pensive a spirit as formerly, but by degrees came of from that morosenes, and severity which was observed in mee, wherby to please God, as I thought, I would shunne the company of men.

26/1657

In December, at the end of it, it pleased God to visit mee with the small poxe, which made mee look about mee, for I thought verily I should have dyed, and gone to hell. I knew not what course to take, for my tutour was out of the colledge, I had none to look after mee but my bed-maker, who was none of the skilfullest; therfore, notwithstanding the violence of my disease and my many indispositions which had some influence upon my mind, I used to pray secretly, and make strong resolutions that, if God would be pleased to raise mee up, I would feare him more faithfully, and conscienciously; indeed God's goodnes was such that, after 9 or ten dayes, he raised mee up, but I have bin much wanting in performing my promises.

But one remarkable providence I hope I shall never forgett, that is this: when I was sick at first, not thinking it was the small poxe (though 2 days before in the Petty-Cury[30] I mett with a girle who had newly had them, of whom it seems I catch't them) at midnight I was very thirsty, and rose in my shirt, and went into the coale-hole a little out of the chamber, and drank a black pott full of cold water; which desperate course struck the poxe in againe which came out the evening before, as they told mee when the danger was over. Now Oh my God how good wert

---

[30] Petty Cury, a street in central Cambridge.

27/1657

thou to mee when I knew not the danger my selfe! Let mee never forgett this mercye! Thou deliveredst mee from the jawes of death, let mee praise thee for it, with joyfull lipps in the land of the living, Oh God my God!

My father, nor scarce my tutour, for I called Mr Dearsly so, knew nothing of my sicknes till I was well againe. Then I wrote him a letter how I had bin sick, and how gracious God had bin in raising mee up againe; he wrote to mee expressing his thanks to God for my recovery, and promised to supply mee with necessaryes, which also he did. When I was past the worst of my sicknes I would be almost continually reading the Bible or other books; and though my tutour, who came often to see mee, after his returne to the colledge, told mee in that case God would have mercy and not sacrifice,[31] yet would I studye hard to gett up what I had lost in the reading the Bible, stinting my selfe to many chapters a day according to Mr Bifield's book,[32] or in other studyes, that I might be equall to the rest of my yeare; though I thinke it was not very good for my eyesight.

My recovery, to the wonder of others, made mee sensible of God's love, and that (as my father wrote) he gave mee a new life to the end that I might spend it to his glory; this was in a great measure fixed on my heart then, and was a spurre to mee in devotion, and I hope it will be so to my dying day.

28/1657

Though I had thus resolved upon serving God, yet many inconveniences and letts I mett with, and many temptations from without, and from within: the devill would suggest to mee that I could doe God no service heerafter because I stammered and had not the perfect use of my speech; hence I was discouraged from my studyes, and chiefly from divinitye, as considering how useles I should be in my generation; such thoughts as thees lay upon my spirit a long while, and I would daily pray to God, and that earnestly and with teares, that he would give mee perfectnes of speech; yet in the meane time knew not whether I sinned or no in so doing: at last I propounded the case to some others, in the person of another, that I might keep it secret; they told mee miracles were ceased, and 'twould be a miracle to restore speech to a stammerer, as Mark 7:32, therfore it was not to be prayed for; neither doe we find a promise to give any thing of that nature; thus was I satisfyed, and left desiring it of God. And in many other scruples, which would arise, I would aske others in the name of a 3d person, or upon supposition; and had satisfaction either from them or by reading Dr Ame's cases of conscience.[33]

But still I observed that Satan would be busy, and putt vaine thoughts into mee and cloud my understanding with darknes; he would disturbe mee at my devotions and somtimes try to make mee leave

29/1657-8

of all manner of serving God, and all face of religion, because I saw no difference betwixt godly and ungodly in outward things, but that all things fell

[31] See Hosea 6:6.
[32] Nicholas Byfield, *Directions for the private reading of the Scriptures* (1618).
[33] William Ames, *Conscience with the power of cases thereof* (3 parts, 1639).

alike to all, Ecclesiastes 9: 1, 2. This I acquainted my father with, and he bid mee as he had another in the same case, leave of prayer, reading, meditation etc. if I could, or if I dared; meaning that my conscience would not let mee: yet this I can say, that at any time when Satan cast drowzines, or any other temptation upon mee to keep mee from serving God in prayer, or the like dutyes; I would most of all watch, and performe dutyes reverently then, if it were but to crosse the devil; and so I thought I should please God. Thus was I beat of from trusting to, or resting in dutyes, for I was out of conceit with any thing I did; only I dared not leave of because all are bound to pray, though the prayer of the wicked is abominable; and of the 2 evils I would take the least; and moreover I knew that I was in a way of God's appointing and if I perished it should be in his way.

All this while I kept thees things secret; and though I liked not my dutyes, looking at and longing for somthing higher, yet I would often cast forth ejaculations, and desire God's assistance and blessing in every thing I went about; this I continued in though I observed others to thrive and fare better who never minded any thing of that nature, and I hope such providences shall not discourage mee in my dutyes.

30/1658

When I was to goe a journey, or to doe any publick exercise, as declaime, dispute, or sitt for any preferment, I would pray for God's assistance and had it to that degree that at such a time I found my speech farr better, and little or no haesitation in publick performances, and so I have found God's helpe in preaching since, for which I blesse his name.

Mr Charles Robotham,[34] whose proper sizar I was, left the colledge; but God's care over mee was such that Mr Scot,[35] who succeeded him, took mee for his sizar, though I lost seniority by it.

In the midst of all God's gracious dealings towards mee, I must confesse I carried my selfe unworthily. For being by nature given to quarrelling (though God be thanked 'tis in some measure mortifyed since) and reviling, and speaking evill of others; I had well nigh bin mett withall soundly by being complained of to the master and seniour fellowes; and gott the ill will and hatred of some deservedly. But when the greatest dangers were imminent I would with prayer and weeping apply my selfe to the throne of grace, and beseech God to turne the hearts of my enemyes for good towards mee, and to turne away their rage and fury, and keep mee from offending for the future; and in 4 or 5 cases God delivered mee from the very jawes of danger, for which I must ever praise his glorious name.

31/1658–9

I found I was still very subject to backbiting, and slaundering and busying my selfe with things not belonging to mee; this I earnestly prayed against, and read

[34] Charles Robotham, Fellow of Trinity College, 1645 and rector of Fakenham, Norfolk, 1655–1700, Al. Cantab., I, 3, 476.
[35] Probably Robert Scott, Fellow of Trinity College, 1649, and Dean, 1659–60, 1674–7 and 1691–2, Al. Cantab., I, 4, 32.

in the Proverbs, and in the 3d of James about the mischiefe of an unruly tongue; I strived also to leave of such tatling courses, and by degrees did mend, for which I blesse my good God.[36]

At Easter in 1659 wee had a sitting for schollarships, and God moved the hearts of the master and seniours towards mee that I gott one, which was not only honour but profit to mee. I took notice of this as if God did prosper my endeavours, and crowne my wishes for this end that I might be wonne to himselfe, and as if he gave mee thees blessings to lead mee to repentance; wherfore, I often resolved to set my heart seriously to seek him, but I was hindred by many businesses, and callings of, so that I was grieved at the very heart: this also troubled mee that I could not keep my heart in so good a frame as God required, and as I desired; and though I strived to keep vaine thoughts from lodging within mee, yet they would come by reason of my weaknes to resist the temptations of the adversary. Thus did I struggle, and strive to bring my heart into such a mould as would be fitt for the service of God which I aimed at; and to gett the better of my lusts, vices, and corruptions which did warre against my soule; but I ought to have sought strength elsewhere.

32/1659

Somtimes I thought I could pray heartily and with teares in God's sight, but at most times I was dull and languid, frigid and senseles, so as I could not bring my heart to bend, or fashion it as I would have had it. Many times in prayer evill thoughts would arise, and many callings of would happen; but yet I would, as I thought, make it up, and as it were make God amends another time; yet then would I suspect my selfe of hypocrisy, whose propertye it is to give prayers by number and not by weight, by tale and not by strength and syncerity. Thus was I afraid of formality, and customarines in God's service.

In this manner I continued tossed to and fro, and could not find rest; yet I dared not speake peace to my soule before God did it, neither could I find my heart any softer but wholly out of order and unsetled. I found and perceived in my selfe good thoughts, and motions, which, for ought I knew, were from the spirit of God, wherfore I endeavoured to cherish them what I could, neither willingly would I grieve the good spirit of God. Somtimes I had secret desires of taking Christ upon his owne termes, and I thought I could doe it, and was, as I thought, very willing to it; but alas! when I came to try, I found no strength at all; wherfore I prayed for strength for a long time and yet found none, neither would my heart willingly give way to any such things; I resolved however to wait upon God in his ordinances, and see

33/1659

whether God would meet mee in his owne wayes and when I remembred him, if he would prevent mee with his loving kindnes; and thus I went on.

But my heart was so deceitfull that I soon forgate my watch: for see how I was overtaken with a lie; my chamberfellow and I would rise betimes in the morn-ing, and walke into the field or walks to study Divinity and Metaphysicks

---

36 On the unruliness of the tongue, see Proverbs 21:23; 25:23; 26:28; James 3:1–12.

together; he bad mee tell no body of what we did, but I told one that spake of it to him againe, and when he asked mee if I had told any body, I wickedly, and against my conscience said no; but my heart smote mee for this, and I besought God to pardon this sin to mee, and wash it away with the blood of sprinkling.

This summer I went to see my father who was very desirous to see, and speake with mee after I had from time to time acquainted him with my soule's estate. I was bashfull, and very fearfull least my father should find mee worse in discourse then in writing; I was almost ashamed to owne or speake of those things I had found in my heart before; and therfore, though I longed for more soule-counsell, omitted speaking to him; but he, good man, found an opportunitye of speaking to mee, and asked mee if I were reall in what I wrote all along to him; I told him yes; and made him understand the depth of my heart as well as I could for weeping, for my heart was tender; he was exceedingly glad, and comforted mee, but my soule

34/1659

refused comfort, I could find no peace, scarce hope for my soule; all that he could say was not sufficient to make mee thinke my condition safe, or my state good.

However in my darkest houers it was a great encouragement, and support to mee that my father, by my letters and speaking with mee, judged well of my case. I have some letters of his, which refresh mee when ever I read them, wherin he told mee that he did not doubt but God had begun a good and saving work in my soule, and that he would goe on with it, if those impressions did not weare of by my negligence and carelesnes. He feared I would have bin spiritually proud, but I wrote him word of that grievous evill heart, and tongue set on fire from hell, and such like experiences; that he judged God let mee see so much to keep mee humble and preserved mee from selfe-confidence; and he let mee see no more yet, or at once for feare of despaire and being overwhelmed; he told mee that it was no good argument I had used, to gather there is no grace because so much sin and corruption appeares, for grace discovers sin; and that should make mee see the more need of God's spirit to vanquish sin in mee, yea that God left mee to see what was in my heart, but all that could not hinder free grace to appeare, and grow up in my soule. He exhorted mee to be found constant in dutyes, whether God spoke peace or no, and what

35/1659

though I waited long? Others had done so, and had at last peace spoken; as Mr Throckmorton that waited 36 years in an exact course of dutyes, and yet he found no peace, scarce hope; and what though I should have no peace at all?[37] 'Twas but my duty to wait on God, and 'twas good being found so doing. He comforted mee with that of Sampson's mother, Judges 13:23, that God would not destroy mee in that he had showne mee such things. He confidently told

[37] Job Throckmorton (1545–1601), the puritan controversialist of Haseley, Warwicks., who assisted with the publication of the Marprelate Tracts in 1588–9. 'It is said that for thirty-seven years he sought in vain a comfortable assurance of his salvation, but secured it within an hour of his death', DNB.

mee I could not perish in the way which I went in, and that God would manifest his love at the last; he told mee my despairing, and distrust of my heart and salvation was the safer way of perishing, but I needed not to feare that; yet all this could not comfort mee, or make mee thinke there were hopes of mercy for mee.

In July thees things chiefly happened, and then also had I dismall thoughts of death, hell, and judgment: I feared to be taken away before my peace was made with God; to this my experienced father answered, that if God in his wisdome should take mee away without peace sensibly spoken to my selfe, my eternity did not turne upon that hinge; yet I did well in being in continuall expectation of that houre, and that afterward I should find all that I had sowne in prayer and other dutyes should be returned, and that it was but laid up in store for mee; and that God heard the prayers of his whilst unconverted, and knowes what he drawes from them in prayer though they thinke they pray not in faith etc. He judged that after I had bin

36/1659

troubled about my condition I would make out for comfort and peace, and so I did; 'twas so with him, and others; some God went so farre with, and when they mett with a temptation they would goe back to their assurance and peace, and there would stay; this he thought a fine way, but his brother putt him upon a way of faith, and recumbency rather then sensible assurance; and told him this relying, and hanging upon God's bare word of promise did most of all glorifye him; my father was much addicted to that sensible way till God took him of; and wish't mee to goe on in a way of faith, and leave it to God whether he would give peace or not, being found in a way of waiting etc.

I thanke God thees thoughts of death, and the last judgment were a meanes to keepe mee from secret sinns, or doing any thing in secret which I would be ashamed the world should know, for there was a day coming wherin the thoughts of heart should be made manifest. It kept mee from wronging others by fraud or pilfering, which at school I was addicted to, so that when many splendid opportunityes were offered mee, and the devil tempted mee, I would not consent, and so resolve to keep my selfe.

I found in prayer, and other dutyes my heart so hard and dull that I had no sense of sin, especially originall sin; neither could I feel my sin as a burden too heavy for mee, nor found I strength to lay my burden upon the shoulders of Christ Jesus. In this was I most miserable that I knew not my owne misery and wretchednes.

37/1659

I prayed to have sense of sin, and my lost estate by nature, but I found no answer; neither could I pray rightly for want of God's Spirit, without which I could doe nothing acceptably. Neither would any sermon stay long with mee, but the watchfull enemy would sow his tares among the good wheate of the word; neither could I at any time practise any thing I had heard in a right manner, for I had not that new principle to act from: this I was sensible of, though I in no wise could helpe my selfe; I saw I could not please God, though I strived to please him; I had no spirituall hungrings or thirstings after righteousnes, but thought I had need of nothing; whereas I needed all things; because I had not a sense of my owne wants: now though I was thus hard and insensible, yet for ever blessed be my God that gave mee a sense of my owne senselesnes!

By reason of my weake constitution, and the quality of those meats wee had in commons, by the rising of vapours out of my stomach, my head would ake; and this hindred mee both from my studyes on week dayes, and from giving such good attention at church on the Lord's dayes as I would, and as God did require at my hands. My head would ake every Lord's day, though I had eaten sparingly, I thinke for this reason: I went to sermon soon after I had dined, and usually stood a good while e're they began; and all the while standing and writing, leaning my head downe, and giving attention would make my head \ake/. Thus was I indisposed, to my griefe, and was somtimes forced to goe to bed without praying to God as I used to doe; only some short ejaculations in my bed

38/1659

I would putt up to God, being really grieved for my indispositions, and could scarce be satisfyed with that; I \will/ have mercye and not sacrifice,[38] but still would be eager of dutyes, and doing somthing for the good of my soule, which indeed is very naturall. I thought much to be saved for nothing, and was willing to doe my worke before I had my wages; but, if God intends mercy for mee, I must be brought to him by faith in another, and be made to believe in him that justifyeth the ungodly, who have no good workes to boast of, and plead in their owne defence: and blessed be God that I see any thing of this nature, for my owne good!

When I was well I prayed that my meat might give mee such nourishment as would fitt mee for God's service: I was more fat and fleshy before I came to the colledge then since, in so much that some wondred how I did to subsist; much lesse able was I to labour, or take bodily paines; I verily thinke I impaired my health by overmuch and unseasonable study, which I would not intermit, both because of that love I ever had to learning, and feare least others should outstrip mee.

I observed that in reading God's word I could not frame my heart aright, and as I would, nor could I meditate on it, as was my duty, by reason of many idle and evill thoughts which came in, but were very unwelcome. However I was diligent in reading the scriptures every day, and read them once through in a yeare for the 3 first yeares according to Mr Bifield's directions;[39] yet gate I not much good for want of due meditation. I took notes also out of the Bible and putt it under such heads as might \suit/ any state

39/1659

of life what so ever. I read Dr Wilkins of prayer,[40] and in reading the Bible observed and wrote downe in a book notes for matter, method and expression;

---

[38] Hosea 6:6.
[39] See note 32, above.
[40] John Wilkins, A *discourse concerning the gift of prayer* (1651).

and although by such industrious wayes I had a gift of prayer, I knew that except the spirit of God helped my infirmityes with groanes unutterable, Romans 8:26, I could not pray in such a manner as to please God. I found it much better to use scripture phrase, on all occasions, then to trust to parts, and pray at random.

I must heer take notice of a providence of God towards mee. Once I had spoken evill of a lad's father behind his back (though it was what I had heard, yet I should have concealed such things which I knew not the truth of). This was on the Satterday, and on the next day by God's providence I went to a sermon, which was taken out of the Proverbs, so directly against my sin of slaundering and backbiting, that I thought verily God directed the preacher to speake particularly to my case, and it [deletion] stuck so by mee that after that I was carefull to avoid that sin.

At our ordinary prayers in the chappell, where the conducts were holy men, I found I could not joyne with them so attentively and fervently as I desired, and as I should have done; vaine thoughts would lodge in my soule whether I would or no, so weake was I to resist the least temptations of Satan. This by the goodnes of God I can say, that I was much displeased and vexed at my selfe, and took no delight in them, but would check my selfe for them; and though I knew that all strength must be drawne from Christ Jesus, in order to the vanquishing such temptations, yet I found no heart to pray for strength; I might have ventured, considering that God was more willing to give then I was to aske,[41] but alas I was stupid, and knew it not!

40/1659

I heard Mr Shelton[42] preach out of that Lamentations 3:39, and learned not to murmure or complaine; for all my afflictions were for my sinns; and if my life were given mee 'twas rich mercy; therfore, when I mett with any sort of afflictions, I concluded it was that I should amend, and indeavour to please God more.

In November I heard Mr Perrot of Sydney Colledge[43] preach about living in love and peace with all men; I was much affected with it, because I looked on it as a cure to mee who lived often in strife with, and hatred of others; he said that those things which hindred us from living in love and peace were thees, viz. an evill, suspicious and surmising head, a proud heart, and an unruly tongue; this was very suitable to mee for I knew my selfe to be suspicious by nature and proud in heart and of an high spirit, which is an abomination to the Lord; but above all to have an unruly tongue, which I had prayed against a long time, and strove against, but could scarcely [deletion] be rid of it but offended either by vaine words, or medling with others; which indeed is that sin which doth so easily beset mee[44], and which yet I pray to be delivered from. But when I read

41 Cf. Luke 11:13.
42 William Shelton, Fellow of Jesus College, 1655–63, vicar of various Essex parishes including St James', Colchester, 1670–99, and Stisted, 1691–9, Al. Cantab., I, 4, 58.
43 Perhaps Richard Perrott, admitted to Sidney Sussex College in 1645. He was a canon of York, and preacher at York Minster, before being ejected in 1662, Al. Cantab.
44 See Hebrews 12:1.

that James 3:2, how almost impossible it is in this fraile state not to offend in word, I am ready to despaire of getting the mastery of it; yet I hope I shall not give over fighting, and resisting unto blood as long as I live. Those things that helped to peace and living in love and unity, were to beare with the constitutions and tempers of men, to take every thing and word in the best sense, and as candidly as I could, and to mind my owne affaires and let others alone.

41/1659

I desired to practise thees truths, but could not of my selfe; I desired to be rid of that corrupt nature which \was/ so strong in mee, for in part I saw (and Oh, that I could see it more) how sad a case I was in since the fall, which is so hard to know.

I was perplexed so about dutyes, that I knew not what to doe; I kept with a chamberfellow and dared not doe any good dutyes in his audience, for feare it should be imputed to hypocrisye in mee, but considering that this might be a kind of disowning Christ, and being ashamed of his wayes before men, and a profession of the gospell openly; I thought it my duty, as occasion served, to owne all such things; thus was I hurried in my thoughts, and abused by Satan, from whom I desired a deliverance in God's time which is best. Yet in the midst of all thees disquietments I kept on in my course of secret dutyes, though often interrupted by company; for so bashfull was I in the affaires of God that, rather then others should know what I was doing, I would breake of my dutyes, though I made them up another time.

I wrote to my father about being troubled with vaine thoughts in prayer, and hearing the word; and somtimes through weaknes of my body, I would sleep at prayers in my tutour's chamber; wherupon he wrote mee word that I must watch Satan, and that was the way to weaken him, and drive thees fowles away which would eat up my sacrifice, as Abraham did, Genesis 15:11, and that I should goe on cheerfully, as knowing I could not be freed from them in this life, though they should be my burden.

42/1659

I heard a sermon on 1 Samuel 30:6, wherin I learned that 'twas no new or strange thing for God's Davids to be afflicted, also the grounds and reasons of it, and my duty to encourage my selfe in God in the greatest straits. This was a great comfort that I had a refuge to goe to in my greatest straits and necessityes, and God grant that in all occasions I may use it!

The next lecture-day I was incouraged to be zealous for the cause of God, notwithstanding the opposition it hath in the world, and the reproach that good men mett with, for those that will live godly must suffer persecution of the tongue at least;[45] this I found very hard to doe and irksome to flesh and blood, but I desired the assistance of God's Spirit to carry mee through so as I might have a tender respect for the name of God, that it be not evill spoken of for my sake.[46]

December 14. One of our fellowes made a common place in the chappell, and proposed to us thees 4 queryes. 1: Whether we did ever seriously look back

---

[45] Cf. 2 Timothy 3:12.
[46] Cf. Romans 2:24.

into our lives past, and commune with our hearts, and upon that search. 2: Whether we did really choose the way of God and Christ before any other way in the world? 3: Whether we were willing to take the yoake of Christ on us though never so burdensome to flesh and blood? and if we were willing to live under Christ's discipline, and observe those rules which he commanded his disciples to follow, as the schollars of the ancient philosophers subjected themselves to the rules of their sect? Then 4: whether we were cleansed from the pollutions of the world? If we found thees within us, he said we were in

43/1659

a state of regeneration, otherwise not. Thees things much affected me, and I resolved to venture upon a search of my wayes; and that I would choose Christ for my leader whose rules I would follow; but thou, Oh Lord, knowest how deficient I was in thees things, and how I imagined them easier then indeed they are! To choose Christ is the almighty worke of faith with power, which of my selfe I cannot attaine to; Oh doe thou give it mee!

In January this yeare a providence happened which I shall relate. A seniour Bachelour, one Sir Croyden,[47] was led away by ill company, so that being overtaken with wine he was found dead in the morning; this young man was poor, and would make others sport that he might drinke with them etc., though of himselfe he was civill, and once made a profession of being converted, being scared, it should seem, by the devil who represented his sinns before him, but thees things soon wrought of. I am sure this startled mee, and made mee shy of such occasions of sin, though I gott an ill name among some, because I would not joyne with others, or goe on with them in the same excesse of riot, and drunkennes.

My chamberfellow left the colledge, and now, because I kept alone, was I free both for study and devotion. I constantly heard Mr Shelton of Jesus, who preached at Allhallowes;[48] he was a good man, and spoke plainly and home to the consciences of his hearers. I diligently wrote his sermons, and read them by my selfe, chiefly about the worth of the soule, the great danger of loosing it, the little profit, and the irrecoverable losse etc. from Matthew 16:26, also those of making sure of that enduring substance, Hebrews 10:34.

44/1659–60

Once he had a passage which I took notice of in a sermon about the difficulty of being saved, viz. that when we sinned we did our owne actions, and that being so naturall to sin we could not easily be brought of from it; and therfore conversion was a going against our evill nature.

Though I might have had chamberfellows enough, yet I refused (though it was cheaper to have kept with one) because I could find none that I could open my mind to, or joyne with in religious dutyes, which was my aime and end. Thus I denyed my selfe some outward comforts, and putt my father upon the greater charge, that I might have the greater freedome of serving God.

47 Edward Croyden of Somerset, admitted sizar at Trinity College, 1653, *Al. Cantab.*
48 Another name for All Saints Day, November 1.

In the beginning of the yeare 1660 I went home to Colchester; and my father was displeased with mee because of my opinions which I had suck't in by conversing with others at the colledge, viz. about monarchy, and church government. After the King came in May 29, it was bruited abroad that we should have the service book, as indeed it was read at one church then, and I was much troubled because of what my father and others said of it when I was with them. This I resolved on, that I would the more narrowly look after my owne private prayers, when, as I thought, we had not publick ones so good as we used to have.

I heard Mr Shelton preach about repentance, and his sermons much affected mee, and mooved mee to search and examine my owne heart. I wrote them out for a farther perusall, and I desire that God would blesse all such meanes! I read also Dr Taylour[49] of practicall repentance, and Dr Preston of faith,[50] and found good by them.

45/1660

We had a private meeting of some pious lads of our colledge, but this was generally spoken against, not only because good in it selfe but, because of the failings, yea grosse sinns, of some who were discovered, and brought to light. One especially, who had by chance killed another and instead of being softned he grew more hard; was prevailed with by Satan to give himselfe to stealing, and grievous swearing, which was a great scandall to that meeting, as usually wicked men say, so heer they judged all alike; though some were good.

At length some of my neer acquaintance joyned them selves to that meeting, which when I saw it troubled mee much, neither knew I which way to goe; I was convinced that their doings for substance were good, but whether 'twas required as a duty I doubted; besides evill report and losse of credit which they branded such withall did keep mee from joyning with them (although since I wish I had done it); in the midst of thees uncertainties I had my father's advice, and he weighed some circumstances and thought it not best for the present to joyne with them. But the chiefe thing that beat me of was this, I feared I should not live up to that strictnes which they pretended, and which was by others expected from them; and indeed if so be they fell short, they were scandalized by the profane lads of the colledge; now I thought if I could live as strictly as they it would be better, and if I had any failings, I should not be scandalized, because it was not expected I should be better.

I remember one Mr Kenyon,[51] a good man, preached about repentance, and one marke of a true sorrow was this, when we could be as sorry that such a sin was \done/ as we were glad, and took pleasure in the commission of it. This seemed hard to mee, and past my strength, therfore I desired that God would open mine eyes, and heart! but this

---

[49] Jeremy Taylor, D.D. (1613–67), bishop of Down and Conor; a strong opponent of Catholicism, he keenly supported the return of Charles II in 1660. He was a prolific theological author, particularly of sermons, DNB.

[50] John Preston, The breast-plate of faith and love (1643).

[51] Probably Roger Kenyon (or Kenion), of St John's College, who was afterwards ejected from Ripponden, Yorks., in 1662, Al. Cantab.

46/1660

he told us; that, least we should be discouraged at the difficulty of repentance, and that irksomenes that was in it, if we would not believe his experience, we might aske any Christian, and we should find this to be the common experience of good men, that there is as much comfort, and sweetnes, and pleasure in repentance as is in the commission of sin; and if so, how much comfort will the fruits of repentance bring? Surely more every way.

I went to a meeting in the towne where only Masters of Art exercised; there I heard what a dangerous thing it was to be ashamed of God's wayes, and religion, and confessing God with those that were good, and to refuse their company when occasion served. He exhorted mee not to be ashamed of the meetings of God's people, neither to gaine the honour and applause of men to dishonour God in the least. I was convinced that one great reason why I did not joyne with those in the colledge was for feare of loosing my credit with others, or of dulling my parts. For I observed that some of them (I knew not the reason of it) did degenerate in learning from what they were formerly before they took that course, which I wondred at. Yet I hoped that God would be found of mee in my clozet-duties when I sought him, and that he would give mee Christian fortitude to stand for the truth, if ever a day of triall should come upon mee, which I feared might be if the bishops did gett the upperhand.[52]

During thees convictions Mr Stockton haply came to towne, and preached about walking with God as Enoch did;[53] which sermons did convince mee that I ought to keep closer to God, and his people, and not to conforme my selfe to all companyes, but to walk in the narrow paths of Christianity with my whole heart, and this I desired God to bring mee to, if it were his will.

47/1660

A little before the King's returne, I was overtaken with evill talking of such things as belonged to him, so that they took notice of mee as one of a factious spirit (though I did it meerly for discourse, and to maintaine an argument, but my subtle adversaries made an advantage of my freedome, and took all in the worst sense). This I was sorry for by my selfe, and prayed against it, that God would keep my tongue from evill, and my lipps from speaking perverse things. And, I blesse God, in some measure I watch't over my selfe in that kind, neither was I so free of speaking among such captious and urging people as we had then, and who would informe the seniours of all, and so I hope I shall continue, and rather offend by my silence (though *nulli tacuisse nocet*)[54] then rash and unadvised speaking about things too high for mee.

July 8. Mr Seniour of our colledge,[55] a good man, preached about sanctifica-

---

52 Archer refers to the possibility, eventually realized, that an uncompromising form of episcopalianism would be established as the official policy of the Church of England.

53 Owen Stockton, lecturer at St Andrew's, Cambridge, 1656, and town lecturer at Colchester, 1657, *Cal. Rev.*, 464. On Enoch, see Genesis 5:24.

54 *Nulli tacuisse nocet*: 'It is harmful to no one to have been silent', Dionysius Cato, *Disticha de Moribus*, i, 12.

55 Thomas Seniour, Fellow of Trinity College, ejected October 19th 1660 for nonconformity; lecturer at Holy Trinity, Cambridge and ejected in 1662; afterwards a nonconformist preacher at Hackney, *Al. Cantab.*

tion and gave some markes of it (which, as he said, was the best way of preaching). By this I was something comforted, and thought well of my selfe, and my soule's case, which I dared not doe before that. His marks were thees: if there was a reall sense of originall sin, this I found hard to have in mee, though I was convinced of it by the sad effects and fruits of it, yet not, as I feare, in a due manner, and a due measure. Another was, if there was a tender heart, and an awakened conscience after sin committed, especially grosse sins, which consisted in a suddain reflexion upon our selves, and also an hearty sorrow for that sin committed, and a firme resolution, by God's grace, to be overtaken no more in that kind. This signe I partly found in my selfe for which I blesse God, that I had, in some measure, a tender conscience, for when I was overtaken with a sin in the day time, I would be sure

48/1660

of night to reflect upon it in my study, and to grieve for it, and pray against it as well as I was able. Another marke was, when \wee/ were holy by our selves, in our private devotions when no eye of men saw us. This, I blesse God, I found in some measure, viz. that I took more care to approve my selfe sinceer in God's sight in private, then in publick; yea I took such care least I should fall into hypocrisy, that I did what I could to keep it unknowne that I did any dutyes in private, and when I removed into any chamber, I would choose a study remote from the rest, where freely I might poure out my prayers to God, upon all occasions.

Another signe was, when there was an even frame in all conditions whatsoever, and at all times. This I could not find in my selfe in any measure, for in prosperity I was apt to be slack in God's service, in adversitie not so, neither did I keep so holy a frame of spirit in all companyes as I should have done, but rather did conforme my selfe to them too much. The last marke was if we could truly love the brethren, and heer I found my selfe very defective (though since 'tis otherwise in some measure by God's grace) and yet I prayed that love might be shed abroad in my heart by the Holy Ghost. Then I found a secret rising in my heart against those that were good, and if they were overtaken with a fault I had so wretched a heart as secretly to be glad of it. I wished my selfe free from so ugly a nature which rendred mee odious both to God and men; yea I found that men by moralitye, and without speciall grace and piety, might maintaine friendship with others, which I could scarcely doe with any. This I impute to my corrupt nature which sheweth it selfe, and also to my

49/1660

being transported by my passions, from the violence of which I desired God to deliver mee, and must say amen to it as long as I live in this world.

I was, I thinke, about 2 yeares in suspence betwixt 2 opinions, whether I should goe to the meetings in the towne and colledge, or not. Somtimes I went into the towne, and was convinced of the lawfulnes of them, so that my conscience told mee they would doe mee good. Yet to keep my good name, as I called it, I did still abstaine because that way was evill spoken of, but after I saw some of my acquaintance, whom I thought no more then civill, turne to that way, I thought much, and wondred at it. I knew they were turned by going to one of their meetings by chance, and would discourse with them about it, and my conscience would make mee almost yield somtimes, yet to keep my credit in the colledge I refrained still. And when the common prayer was forced, and the other ceremonies, I thought to leave the colledge, and in the country with my father, I intended to goe to such meetings, for there they were in credit and esteem.

But October 19. Mr Seniour, who was turned out of his fellowship for Nonconformity, convinced mee by his sermon about being hated of the wicked world in that manner, that I was about going to him to thanke him that he had setled mee in that which I doubted of before. Upon this I resolved to goe to those meetings and grow acquainted with such as went. In his sermon he dealt so plainly, and spake so home to my conscience that I was convinced of my duty. He said the people of God were hated universally, irreconcilably by all wicked men, but chiefly by the profane, and morall men, and also, and that worst of all, by those that stood so much upon the formall way of worshiping God. This I found true in the colledge, for all Nonconformists were

50/1660

hated by such most who were most zealous for the ceremonies. He told us that if wicked men did love us, it was because they saw in us something that was bad, which pleased them, quoting Bishop Hall,[56] who bids us examine our selves especially when wicked men loved us, or spake well of us, for the wicked hate the godly as such, and loved them only so far as they were like them.

When thus I considered that it was the portion of God's people to be hated heer, I thought that I would venture my credit and all for the sake of Christ and the gospell. And accordingly I sett to it, and went to their meetinge, in which I desired I might find peace, and was sensible of that favour wherby God had so signally showne mee what I should doe to be one of his servants. Moreover when I considered that those that had bin so changed by one of their meetings used to speake against them before, and be against them more then I was, I thought I would venture as they had done before mee.

But this did not hold long, for no sooner had I begun almost to frequent those meetings, but some fell away from them, which did much startle mee. Yea, I gave way to many occasions that seemed to hinder mee from going to their meetings, as studying for my degree, and such like. Yet did I stand for them, and defend them against such as were against them; but when I saw my selfe deceived by one of them, I did not putt such confidence in them as formerly.

And in December, by reason of the rising of many 5th monarchy men under the conduct of one Venner who was afterwards hanged etc.,[57] the king straitly forbade all manner of meetings upon

---

56 Joseph Hall, bishop of Exeter, 1627–41, and bishop of Norwich, 1641–56; a renowned theological author, *DNB*.

57 Thomas Venner who, with his Fifth Monarchy men, attempted to overthrow the government in January, 1661; he was hanged on 19th January, *DNB*.

51/1660

any pretence what so ever; yea, after some had mett and were putt in prison, and made to take the Oath of Allegiance,[58] I wholly forbore going, yet continued my acquaintance with them, and used private duties more then before.

In January, in order to our going out Bachelours of Art, the subscription to the 3 articles was urged,[59] and I resolved against it, being warned against it by my father. I thought indeed by reason of the king's declaration from Breda,[60] where he promised sufficient liberty of conscience, they would not have imposed it, but they did. At the 1st all the lads of our colledge, but two, refused to subscribe, and one of those two had protested against it a little before, and upon this all of us, but those two, were stopped in the Regent House,[61] upon which they all but my selfe, went and subscribed (for we had bin before a meeting of the master, Dr Ferne,[62] and the seniour fellowes, who were angry at my refusing, and had chid all of us sharply). Yet after a fortnight's stopping they were admitted, and by God's providence, and the industry of my father, as they call him,[63] though there were some Masters of Art who opposed mee, and after presentation would not have suffered mee to be admitted, yea though they had given mee their *placet*,[64] and were searching for my name in the book where they subscribed during my admission, I only of the Non-subscribers was admitted as soon as the rest.

I am much bound to Dr Ferne, the vice-chancelour that yeare, and the father for their care, the one for defending mee against Dr Martin and others, and for sending the Bedle with word that he was satisfyed concerning mee, when I was bid to goe out of the Regent-House by some among them; the other for fetching mee up, when I had timerously withdrawne, and bringing mee to admission.

52/1660–1

And thus God gave mee favour in the eyes of some from whom I could not expect it, and defeated for mee the designes of my adversaries, for which I blesse his name, for I had not deserved it from him.

When I was 19 yeares old, by reason of my age and heat, I was haunted with

---

[58] The Oath of Allegiance bound a person not to take up arms against the reigning monarch.

[59] The three articles were to accept the Act of Supremacy, the Thirty-Nine Articles and the Book of Common Prayer in full.

[60] Charles II's Declaration of Breda was issued on April 4, 1660. In it he promised liberty to all Protestant dissenters of peaceable and moderate intent. The text is reproduced in S.R. Gardiner, *Constitutional Documents of the Puritan Revolution 1625–1660* (Oxford, 1927 edn), 465–7.

[61] The Regent House was the assembly of teaching Masters, the chief legislative body of Cambridge University.

[62] Henry Ferne, Master of Trinity College, 1660–2, vice-chancellor, 1660–1, bishop of Chester, 1661–2, *Al. Cantab.*, 1, 2, 132. Ferne was a Royalist during the Civil War, but at the Restoration he readmitted all who had been made Fellows of Trinity during the Commonwealth, *DNB*.

[63] Archer here refers to Henry Dearsly who had been so effective in gaining Archer exemptions from certain strict religious requirements. Dearsly had become so closely associated with Archer's plight, especially his struggle with his own father, that he must, in some sense, have been seen as acting *in loco parentis*.

[64] *Placet*: 'it pleases', an affirmative vote in a university assembly.

lascivious, and vaine thoughts, and very often yielded to them, not considering that thoughts ought to be restrained, for feare they breake out into words, and actions. Yea when I did strive against them most, they were suggested most, so that I was distracted in my studyes; and was vexed with my selfe, though I knew if I disallowed of them, and diverted them, and saw the evill of them, they were Satan's sinns, and not mine. But in March Mr Stockton preached about grieving the Holy Spirit, and among other sinns which grieved him, he named lasciviousnes, and that not only actuall but speculative, which I knew my selfe guilty of. I blesse God that I was convinced of it, by his ministry, and I resolved to pray against it, and resist my naturall sinfull inclination to such thoughts, and did desire God's assistance for that purpose.

In Aprill 1661 I went to Dedham where now my father lived, having newly married the widow Lewis whom I went to see. I had promised my father I would not conforme, meaning throughly (for I only heard service, neither medled I with the surplisse etc.). Now there came 2 men to Colchester from Cambridge, who had taken a note of all the Non-conformists in the university, and my name was not there, though I was counted one in the colledge, and wished there had bin no such thing. This note Mr Stockton of Colchester saw, and told my father that my name was wanting; when therfore I came home, my father asked mee if I did conforme.

53/1661

I answered somwhat dubiously and fraudulently (which I desire God would not remember against mee), that I did not. He suspected somwhat, and after a while examined mee more strictly about it, and I told him the truth that I had heard common prayer somtimes. Though this I confesse, that my intentions at first were wholly to abstaine, and I did so a while, thinking that my friend Mr Dearsly, being Deane that yeare, would, according to my understanding of his promise, save mee harmles (though, it seems, he meant only in regard of the surplisse, and so my father should understand his promise, though neither he at all, nor I at first took it so) but he bid mee goe to chappell. So that he who was the cause of my going to Cambridge, was the occasion of that unhappy breach betwixt my father and mee, the flame wherof, through my pride, and undutifull carriage with all my rashnes and unadvisednes, and his impatient and cholerick temper, is scarce yet quenched, though I blesse God very much abated.

At that answer of mine my father was so angry that I had deceived him (though I sawcily defended my aequivocation) in not meaning as he did, that he brake out into many passionate words. And yet withall he told mee that if, for the future, I would promise him not to conforme at all, he would maintaine mee as formerly. I promised this, but the same day that I came from Dedham, after some provocations on my side (though I remember not what they were) he told mee he would not owne mee notwithstanding what I had promised (though I was faithfull in that, however in the 1st I had disappointed him). By this I was so vexed, that I could not speake to him, such was my unruly temper. He told mee also that I should not see his face till I had humbled my selfe for my disobedience to him, and sin against God. Now for the former of thees, I was told by my friends at the colledge that it was not disobedience in such things which a parent could not reach, viz. religious worship,

52   1660.   1661.

And thus god gave mee favour in ye eyes of some
from whom I could not expect it, & defeated for
mee ye designes of my adversaries; for wch I blesse
his name, for I had not deserved it from him.

        when I was 19 yeares old, by reason of my age
& heat, I was haunted with lascivious, & vaine
thoughts, & very often yielded to them, not con:
sidering yt thoughts ought to be restrained, for feare
they breake out into words, & actions. yea when
I did strive against them most, they were suggested
the most, so yt I was distracted in my studies;
& was vexed with my selfe, though I knew if I
disallowed of them, & divided them, & saw ye evill
of them, they were Satans sinns, & not mine. But
in March mr Stockton preached about grieving
ye holy spirit, & among other sinns wch grieved
him, he named lasciviousnes, & yt not only actuall
but speculative, wch I knew my selfe guilty of;
I blest god yt I was convinced of it, by his mi:
nistry, & I resolved to pray against it, & resist my
naturall sinfull inclination to such thoughts, & did
desire gods assistance for yt purpose.

        In Aprill 1661 I went to Dedham where now
my father lived, having newly married ye widow
Jenis whom I went to see. I had promised my
father I would not conforme, meaning throughly
(for I only heard service, neither meddled I with ye
surplisse &) now there came 2 men to Colchester
from Cambridge, who had taken a note of all ye
Non conformists in ye university, & my name was
not there; though I was counted one in ye col:
ledge, & wished father had bin no such thing;
this next mr Stockton of Colchester saw, & told
my father yt my name was wanting; whereon
therefore I came home, my father asked
mee if I did conforme, my father asked ...

I answered somewhat dubiously, & fraudulently (w^{th}
I desire god would not remember against mee) y^t I
did not; he suspected somewhat, & after a while examined mee most strictly about it, & I told him, ye tru:
th y^t I had heard common prayer sometimes; though
this I confesse y^t my intentions at first were wholly
to abstaine, & I did so a while, thinking y^t my fri:
end Mr Dearsly being Deane y^t yeare, would accor:
ding to my understanding of his promise, faire mee
harmles (though, it seems, he meant only in regard of
ye surplice, & so my father should understand his pro:
mise, though ntithelse he of all, nor I at first took it
so) but he did nett goe to chappell; so y^t he who was
ye cause of my going to Cambridge, was ye occasion of
y^t unhappy breach betwixt my father & mee, ye flame
whereof, through my pride, & undutifull carriage, withall
my rashnes & undiscreet, & his impatient & cholerick
temper, is scarce yet quenched, though, I blesse god,
very much abated. At that answer, I blesse god,
was so angry y^t I had desired him (wherein my father
by defended my aequivocation) in not meaning as he did,
y^t he brake out into many passionate words. And y^t
withall he told mee y^t if, for ye future, I would pro:
mise him not to conforme at all, he would pro:
mise as formerly; I promised this; but ye same day
y^t I came from Dedham, after some provocations on
my side (though I remember not w^t they were) he told
mee he would not owne mee notwithstanding w^t I had
promised (though I was faithfull in y^t) howsoever in y^t, I had
could not speake to him. By this I was so vexed, y^t I
He told mee also, y^t such was my unruly tempter,
I had humbled my selfe for my disobedience to him
& sin against god &; how far ye formes of this, I was
told by my friends at ye colledge y^t it was not diso:
bedience in such things wch religious worship parent could not diso:
not weake, wch religious worship parent could not diso:

54/1661

and we had examples of some in the colledge, who crossed their parents in such things; and as for the latter I only heard the service, which I thought no sin, only I sinned in the non-attention, as in other parts of God's worship, which I pray God forgive. Yea, if it were not disobedience, it was no sin, for my father meant that by offending him, I sinned against God.

I must confesse, conversing with green heads, and being back't by others, I wrote sawcily enough to my father in defence of the common prayer, and he as sharply wrote against it. He wrote mee word that he never thought that one sprung from his loynes would plead for Baal; and that if he thought I adored those abominable idols, and danced to that molten calfe etc. he would come and stampe it to powder, and make mee drinke it etc., and that he had rather make mee an ostler to weare a frock, then a schollar to weare a surplisse but once etc., and said he wished he had followed mee to my grave when he let mee goe to Cambridge last from him, to learne such things as I did. He said 'twas vomit which the nation cast out 20 yeares agoe, and ask't if it were indifferent to play the dogg or the sow,[65] and said he did loath them the more because, when young, he did them and was caught in that snare. He said this because I used that as an argument why I might doe the same. Yet in the midst of all this he wrote mee good counsell as to follow good dutyes, mind faith and repentance, and heart worke, so as I am beholding to him for that good foundation, which, I hope, is laid in my soule.

I am ashamed to thinke how sawcily I wrote to him that I had so honoured before; it had bin better that I had never heard a word of common prayer then to make my father my enemy by it. It was the love of a colledge life that transported mee beyond religion, yea and

55/1661

morality too in that manner of writing to a father, so as he might well bid mee study ethicks, and the 5th commandment better; so as now I am sorry for it, yea I blush at the remembrance of what passed, and Oh that God would not lay any of those sinns to my charge! I was very foolish, arrogant, and conceited, and by thees practises the worke of grace, I thinke, was damped in mee.

My father, though by his authority he might command, for love's sake did intreat mee not to breake his heart, or goe against his mind. This did melt mee, and many struglings I had, yet my desire of living in the colledge, and distrust of my father's competent maintaining mee elsewhere did gett the upper hand. I had a promise from Mr Dearsly that I should not have any damage if I went not to chappell, which my father look't upon as a providence, and was willing I should stay upon such termes, and pardoned all that had bin amisse in my writing to him. When I could be no longer there without going to chappell, I was willing to leave the colledge and wrote to my father to provide a place for mee in a Nonconformist's house, which much rejoyced him, and I was reall in it, though he could not bring it about; and yet he wished mee to keep my

---

[65] 2 Peter 2:22: 'A dog returns to his own vomit and a sow, having washed, to her wallowing in the mire.'

schollarship till they put mee out of it, and this also was the advice of my uncles at London, or, in case I was putt out, to take a chamber in the towne etc.

After I had so rudely taken my leave of my father in the Spring, it much troubled mee that I had so angred him, and the workings of my conscience were great, and strong, yet would not my proud stomach come downe or yield. I was heartily sorry for what had passed then, and much more now that I understand more, and am not so conceited, which is indeed the way to wisdome. I wished all was well, and had a mind to goe back to him, and aske him pardon, but my heart would not. Yea, it was a great and terrible storme that day I went, so that my guilty conscience told mee

56/1661

that the heavens seemed to disallow of what I had done.

And see how one sin followes another! As I came in the road betwixt Colne and Halsted, some that were mending the high wayes asked mee to give them somwhat (now 3 dayes before I had given an almes to some that were mending the wayes not far from that place) and when they came to take hold of my horse, I of a suddaine, being putt to it, told them I gave them somewhat the other day; they could not contradict mee, and so I escaped. But my conscience smote mee, as soon as I was past them, for telling a lie so needlessly, wheras all liars should have their portion in the burning lake: yet the devill suggested to mee that it was no lye, for I had given before to them, that is to men of their profession, and for aught I knew they were the very same, but it troubled mee still. When I came to Cambridge I heard that one of my neer acquaintance, that I had kept withall, was lately dead: then I reflected upon what I had done, and was afraid least God should take mee away also, for he was as young as I, and in order of standing I was next him. I thought God's judgment might as well reach mee as any for my late sinns.

On the Lord's day I heard Mr Shelton preach concerning a willingnes to dye; he said if we had any guilt on our consciences we should not be willing, and so could not answer that which God required; and the way to be willing to dye was, by a particular repentance, to make our peace with God, who would cleanse our hearts for us. So I was grieved for what I had done, and desired God to wash it away with the blood of Christ; and because repentance was a turning from sin to God, I resolved for the future, to speake the truth to all men, and not to lye through covetousnes, or any other sin, which God grant I may performe!

57/1661

I mused on what my father had said last, that he would not owne mee etc., whether I conformed or not, and thought my selfe compelled to conforme to get a livelihood, especially in that he said if any one else would maintaine mee, well and good. Upon such termes he seemed to give me leave, though he threatned to disinherit mee, as Mr Gurdin had served one of his sonns upon the same account. On the other side I saw how high things were like to be carried, and was afraid to engage that way, so as I knew not what to doe; I advised with Mr Dearsly, who hearing what had passed betwixt us advised mee to sell my things and goe home rather then to hazard all by conforming without his leave.

July 12th. I went from the colledge on the suddaine and had not sold halfe my goods; now by reason of buying mee clothes I was in debt about £6 10s 0d, also because I had stayed 3 weeks onwards of a new quarter, and yet my father had not allowed mee for that (though in former quarters I had gone beyond my allowance, so that he resolved to keep mee short). This debt I desired him to pay, but he would not, but said the selling my thinges would answer all, though in that he was mistaken.

I staid at home above 6 weeks, and found that leaving the colledge had made mee more solid and staid, though by reason of want of company I lived but sadly, and could not study so well. However, I performed my dutyes Godward the rather because incited by the good example of my father; I spent also some time in meditation, and had not so many occasions of sin and vice as at the colledge. I had promised to send Mr Dearsly some money the next week after I went, not doubting but my father would have paid it, but he would not, and so I was forced to breake my word through his meanes. I wrote to Mr Dearsly, very perplexed as I was, in that manner that he took it all well from mee, but blamed my father's ingratitude much, that he should forget all former offices for one supposed fault etc.

58/1661

During my being at home, my father sought out places for mee, but could get none; he sent to Dr Owen,[66] with whom I should have lived, and he promised to come but did not. At last he putt mee upon this, that I must thinke of some way of life heerafter; he told mee 2 or 3 times that I might conforme if I would, but he dared not maintaine mee in it, for feare of being accessory to my sin. I told him I would not by that meanes, loose his favour, but be at his allowance still, and would thinke of a way wherby I might live heerafter.

I was startled to thinke of what my father now thought of mee, in respect of my soule's case Godward. He wrote mee word that first convictions did worke too sleightly, and that God must goe over againe, that I was not brought of from selfe; yet he hoped that God did this to try what was in my heart when I was left to my selfe, and told mee withall that all was out of true soule-love to mee that had passed. And indeed I was brought up from him, and was out of government, and thought much to be controlled, or crossed in my will, and Oh that I had a child-like and humble spirit! as Matthew 18:3. He check't mee for my talking too much, and said taciturnitas was a vertue in ethicks and divinity too; and though I pretended it was only *disputandi gratia*[67] that I defended those things, he judged I was for them in heart only abstained to please him; though [deletion] I never \much/ loved any of those things, yet out of a spirit of contradiction, and crossegrained humour I would be defending of them. And now I am sorry for that also, and heartily desire that I may governe my tongue well, and know how *cum ratione tacere*;[68] I wish for a calme, peaceable, and

---

[66] John Owen, the leading Congregationalist divine; lecturer at Coggeshall in 1646; at Colchester in 1648, *Cal. Rev.*, 376–7.

[67] *Disputandi gratia*: 'for the sake of argument'.

[68] *Cum ratione tacere*: 'with reason to be silent'.

quiet temper, but I cannot hope grace will change my naturall temper, only qualifie it! Amen.

59/1661

I considered with my selfe that it would be no advantage to mee to follow the ministry, séing things so high as they were, and I could have no place without conforming; wherupon I pitched upon the study of Physick, in order to which I thought it most convenient to live in Cambridge, because of many helpes that were not elsewhere, and acquaintance which I had, and, as I thought, to be in a capacity of serving Mr Dearsly, of whose favours towards mee I had a very gratefull sense. I propounded this to my father, who before was willing enough to it (though just before I went to Cambridge, he was so much against it that he would not let mee have Physicall books) and he granted my request, that I might boord in the towne so that I would not conforme. This I was willing to observe, as having then a certaine [*deletion*] dislike to those things, though I did not expresse it; thus both agreing we waited only for my going.

I observed then, and have done all along since, that when I have insensibly, as it were, lived in any sin, it hath hapned that for some cause or other I have taken a distast either at the persons or things which have bin the occasions of it, and so left it out of a passionate and peevish humour. Though this way be somthing indirect, yet I blesse God that I leave sin any way, and the rather ought I to be humbled that I did not leave sin of my selfe. I saw such corruption in my heart that as long as there was pleasure in the sin I did it, but when any crosses came then I left it, not as sin but as a thing full of crosses. Thus have I cause to blesse God for crosses, because they drive mee neerer to him; and I desire that God would this, or some better way, still bring mee out of love with every sinfull course, and false way, that I may please him by walking in the way that is called holy.

60/1661

Whilst I was at Dedham Mr Newcomin[69] had a passage in his sermon about Franciscus Junius,[70] who, by being acquainted with a professed atheist at the university, became one himselfe; upon which his father sent for him home, where he had bin well brought up, and gave him severall books to read, and among the rest the Bible, and by reading the 1st of John he was converted. Now wheras the lecture before he had made it cleare that idolatry and superstion [*sic*] were atheisme; my father thought this concerned him, and one day took mee aside and told mee this (which I also had minded) and applied the story to my case; for he looked upon thees ceremonies as superstitious, idolatrous, and so atheisticall, and thought it his duty to take mee away from the colledge where I had learned them. This did somthing worke upon my spirit, and I admired at his care of mee who had suck't in such wrong and false opinions at Cambridge; they were bad because humane inventions which could

---

69 Matthew Newcomen, lecturer at Dedham, after suceeding John Rogers in 1636; after ejection he became the pastor of the English church at Leiden, Netherlands, where he died in 1669, *Cal. Rev.*, 363.

70 Probably Francis Junius, or Du Jon (1545–1602), the Protestant theologian, *DNB*.

not be done out of faith and so were sinfull, Romans 14: last. They could not be done out of faith because they had no ground in God's word. He wished mee the same successe with Junius, and this affected mee much, so that I resolved to obey, love and honour him more, which God grant for Christ's sake!

My sister in law was sick, and was made worse by my owne sister's carriage, who was melancholick, and not able to endure talking, or cheerfulnes, but said it was a sin to laugh or be merry, and that she could never laugh or be merry but her conscience would check her, and she was the worse for it afterwards. She was of few words, and would say 'little said is soon amended.' I laboured to perswade her out of her pensivenes, and told her it was a temptation to some

61/1661

to be too tender and scrupulous; one told my father that it was a sanctified humour, because it disposed to seriousnes, and so to holines, but others from experience have said that it was the shop and bath of the devill, and that those who were most tempted were such: however I tooke notice of her words, and (though by nature I was of the same temper, yet by education among those of contrary tempers had overcome it, and was, I feare, gone too far on the other hand, though others thought mee melancholick) resolved to be more serious, yet reserved a place for joy in the Lord, and honest mirth and recreation; and Sir West,[71] my intimate friend and fellow collegian, would tell mee that singing of psalmes was the only singing allowed of, how then shall I answer for my vaine singing, and foolish talking? The Lord pardon this in his servant!

August 28. I spoke to my father of going to Cambridge, and he would have mee goe then because of sending back my goods at Sturbridge faire, in case I could not gett a place in the towne. He told mee he would, as formerly, allow mee £20 per annum; though before I had diet for nothing, and now that would be all for diet and all, yet seing I could not perswade him to allow mee more I would try how I could make a shift with that.

So August 31 I came to Cambridge, where they were sickly, which was some discouragement to mee, yet was not the season so very sickly as was reported in the country. When I acquainted Mr Dearsly with my designe of living in the towne he told mee he was for my stay in the colledge, and promised when the master, Dr Ferne, came home he would get mee a dispensation, if he could, from conforming. So I entred into commons, and waited the master's coming home, that I might know what might be done concerning mee.

September 6. It pleased God to visit mee with an ague, which took mee violently in the night so that I could not sleep; then I thought of my former evill wayes, and sought to God to take his

62/1661

hand of from mee, and that I might heare the rod, and him that sent it, and search what sins they were that God punished mee for, as knowing that afflictions came not out of the dust, but for some cause.

---

[71] Benjamin West, who was admitted to Trinity the same year as Archer. See *Admissions to Trinity College, Cambridge*, II, 439.

September 8. Mr Seniour preached from Deuteronomy 7:15 and shewed mee that sin was the cause of sicknes; this was seasonable for that time, and I took notice of it as if it had bin spoken to mee chiefly. He told mee the reasons why God punished sin were that he might shew his indignation against it, and the heinous nature of it, to restraine it for the present, and prevent it for the future. The uses were to teach us what great hurt wicked men doe in the world, who by their sins bring God's judgments upon themselves, and others that live by, and with them; to reprove those that impute sicknes to second causes, which opinion proceeds from atheisme, or misunderstanding God's word, and because they are afraid of God, and dare not look him in the face who is their judge, and enemy. From hence also I might learn patience under sicknes, and by present repentance and turning to God I might prevent future sicknes.

He told us God seemed to punish us for thees sins: our opposition to the power of godlines by being against zealous prayer and preaching or sharp correptions [sic], and reproofs for our sins; our hating good men, though it be for their sakes we were not worse, for they stood in the gap; or by our sinfull compliance to things either unlawfull in themselves, or unlawfull to us though, it may be, not to others. About the middle of the sermon my ague came upon mee, and I thought it the better because it came not on mee whilst I was doing any sin, but doing my duty, wheras also in sermons we should observe such things as we can apply to our selves. I thought this suitable to mee.

63/1661

September 10. I had another fitt worse then either of the former, and I be-sought God not to take mee away in my sins but spare my life if it might seem good in his sight, yet did not I limit him what to doe but resolved to submitt to his holy will. When I could take no rest I thought of my disingenuous carriage to my father, and againe resolved to honour him more then I had done for-merly; I desired that God would make it a time of love, and passe by mee in my blood, and say to mee live; and that in the latter end I might have cause to say that 'twas good for mee I was afflicted.

September 12. I had a most grievous fitt, which held mee all day long; the apothecary told mee I should have no more but that, and such credit gave I to his words, and my imagination was so possessed with it that, next to God, it was a meanes that I had my ague no more. In my paine and anguish I called upon God, and desired that he would deale favourably with mee, least the soule that he had made should faile before him. Thus it pleased God to remove his hand, and I was very thankfull, outwardly at least, and desired that I might shew my thankfulnes by obedience to his commands all my life long; I desired that I might prize health more, and in it provide for sicknes, and in time for eternity. Amen!

September 22. I heard a sermon about the new birth, and Mr Huff,[72] for he preached, shew mee that the substance of the soule was not changed, but only the old soule had a new bias, and inclination; neither as to the constitution of the body was there any change, but only by grace a man was inabled not to

---

[72] Presumably Edmund Hough of Jesus College, *Al. Cantab.*

follow the evill inclinations of such a temper and constitution. He said this principle was reall and new, and incited us to duty, and kept us from knowne sins. This comforted mee, for I found in my selfe a principle putting mee on to dutyes, and keeping mee from sin

64/1661

which, at least, argueth an awakened, and enlightned conscience, for which I blessed God, and desired that new principle, from which I might act so as to please him.

September 30. Mr Dearsley had spoken with the master and had gotten liberty for mee to continue in the colledge without conforming in the least, and of his owne accord, without asking, ordered that I should not be punished. This I took as a great favour from him, and a good providence of God who sett the hearts of my enemies towards mee; and I desired that I might carry my selfe worthy of such a favour both to the master, and others of my new-acquired friends.

October 11. There was in the towne a lad killed by a spirit in the likenes of a woman, which had haunted him for 8 years. Some of my friends saw the print of her hand on his face which was black with the stroake. This troubled mee, and made mee question God's speciall providence over mee, because I knew not whether I belonged to him or not, and it was also a meanes to make mee more religious, and carefull of sin, and I desired that God would sanctify every such providence to my good. Amen!

November 24. Mr Shelton had bin long preaching about repentance, and I delighted to heare him concerning such points. At last he exhorted mee to the practise of it, and gave directions which were,

1: to doe all I could in order to it, for though it be God's gift yet 'tis our act, and God would not worke without our meanes. I must call to mind all the sins I could thinke of by a strict search into my life past, and that not in generall but in a particular manner. I must doe this orderly by dividing the severall stages of my life, and viewing the sinns of each, as of childhood, youth etc.,

65/1661

or by considering the severall callings, and conditions of life I had bin, and how I had behaved my selfe in them, and what sins I had bin guilty of in each of them, so in my relations, and my actions, thoughts and words; but the best way was to compare my life spent with the rule by which I ought to walke, and by which I must be judged, and so to run over all the commandments, and see how I had broken them all. I must also, he said, aggravate those sins, and not let the consideration of them goe of my mind till I were seriously convinced of them, and the punishment due to them.

2: When I was come thus far, I was to pray to God to give mee a true sorrow of heart, and amendment of life, which was his worke and part in this great duty. This sermon did very much affect mee, and because I had not so strictly examined my selfe (though in the generall I had) I set about it one day, and called my sins to remembrance, and condemned my selfe for them. Yet I feare it was not done in a right manner, or measure deep enough because as yet I cannot perceive God hath wrought a godly sorrow in mee. The Lord in mercy carry on his worke so distinctly that I may not only have grace, but know that I have it! Amen!

After my recovery from my ague, my father wrote mee good counsell; now God had spared mee the 2d time, he bid mee amend or else beware the 3d time. He thought I was not brought of from selfe, and that the plaister of contrition was too soon taken of, and that I needed initiall repentance, though I might thinke my selfe to need none, as Luke 15:7, and he thought 'twas harder to convince mee throughly then those that were more loose. This made mee look about me and I began to mind the practise of repentance more then formerly; but it must be God that can give a soft heart, and successe to the weake endeavours of his servant, and I desire him that true repentance may not be hid from mine eyes!

66/1661

Because my father kept mee bare in money, although now I thinke 'twas large allowance, but I wanted discretion to lay it out, I talked broadly and unbeseemingly of him, neither minding what, or to whom I spoke, and he heard of it and justly blamed mee for it. He thought I carried my selfe in a displeasing manner to him at home because he should be weary of mee, and send mee to Cambridge, and the rather because it was my policie, when a little one, to weary him with my company, and then to tell of it: but I had no such designe in my being at home last, nor, that I remember, in my childhood. He thought I ran an high desperate course, and indeed I was discontented at his allowance, and ungratefull, for which now I am sorry, and I knew not what I did, so rash and inconsiderate was I in speaking and acting; yea I am ashamed to thinke of many things that passed then.

December 12. He taxed mee in his letter with ill habits, conceitednes, and vanity, which I could not at that time discerne in my selfe, yea mine enemies did not cast such vices in my dish; but since I have observed it, and bewailed it, so that my father knew mee better then my selfe. He now putt mee upon looking out a way of living of my selfe, and he said after the yeare was out he would putt mee upon shifting for my selfe; or if I would not he would putt mee to boord, and look to mee, and hold mee closer to it, in respect of allowance, as I thought.

Now this filled mee with dread, for I knew his parsimonious temper would keep mee bare as to every thing, neither dared I venture my selfe to be at his allowance, nor can I to

67/1661–2

this day bring my selfe to it, but am for a fixed allowance to dispose of as I will, and dare not be at his arbitrary allowance as to cloths, diet, money etc. In that letter he taxed mee with childish behaviour, and vanity, and frothy discourse, which, though I saw it not then, I was guilty of; and blessed be God who hath showne mee any thing of my selfe, and brought mee of from pride and conceitednes in some measure! I desire him to shew mee the worst of my selfe to humble mee.

In a letter [of] January 29 my father, for my base and lavish speeches of him, and carriage towards him, threatned that I should have little of him, though I reckoned all mine (which yet I did not) and that he would in my portion sett of what I spent now, and had used that verse in Ovid, *filius ante diem patrios inquirit in annos*,[73] though to this day I know not what estate he hath. And againe putt mee upon shifting for my selfe as soon as the yeare was out, and that I should not always live upon him, and if I would not doe so, or could not live by my learning he would now, when I was 5 years standing at Cambridge, bind mee apprentice to some trade I might live by. If I would not give eare to that, and my conscience would lett mee after all he had written, he bid mee conforme, and take my course, and see how I could keep my selfe, and how my idoll would maintaine mee, for he thought that my heart was that way, and that I forbore meerly to please him. He told mee he would let mee alone, as Hosea 4:17, and saw little spiritualnes upon my heart now of late, which once I had, as he hoped, and thought I would make little use of his spirituall experiences, and so he should loose his aime; but yet he would daily pray that God would turne my heart to himselfe, to which I say Amen!

68/1662

March 30. When I had received my last money, and, conforme or not conforme, he would allow mee no more, I went to chappell againe by the advice of Mr Dearsly, who said he would provide mee some place or other which might maintaine mee without the helpe of my father. Thus was I involved, as it were, in a necessity of conforming, but yet I examined things as well as I could, and found none of those things we had at our ordinary service sinfull, or contrary to God's word, though even then I had rather not have done any of such things.

After I had taken this course, I wrote to my father a valedictory letter, for I thought he had cast mee of quite, which much displeased him, and I heartily now wish I had not wrote so to him, and am ashamed when I read his answer. The Lord in mercy forgive my unnaturall carriage to a good father who mourned over my sinfull behaviour! and I desire to make amends for the future. Amen!

I began to conforme the week before Easter, and Mr Dearsly earnestly and importunately desired mee to take the sacrament (thinking that a sufficient pledge of my conforming, and that it would make way for my livelihood by taking a place) which I did. Now though, by reason of the short warning, being Satterday night, I could not so throughly examine my selfe, so as to be prepared according to the preparation of the sanctuary, yet I did my endeavour, and the more fervent was I because of my short warning. It was so solemnly done that never any thing moved my affections as that did, in so much as I could not forbeare weeping at the receiving of it. Now I thought [*deletion*] my selfe bound in a more especiall manner then before, for this was the 1st time that

69/1662

ever I took it, to live holily, and strictly in God's sight, and was glad that I had such obligations upon mee, and engagements to serve God, and live better; and

---

[73] *Filius ante diem patrios inquirit in annos*: 'the son inquires into his father's years before his time', Ovid, *Metamorphoses*, I, 148.

I desired that God in mercy would grant mee a growth in every grace, and that I might have cause to blesse him for what I had done.

May 16. I had a letter from my father, who charged mee with contradicting my selfe, and told mee that he never knew any one of such a temper and spirit. Now he thought mee in a far worse posture then before, and thought mee snared with self confidence in spirituall things, and that former convictions were wrought of, or fought against; and wished mee to see my selfe lost, that Christ might find mee, which I desire heartily for Christ's sake! Yet I thinke I was not guilty of selfe-sufficiency, for to this day I cannot find any strength of my owne.

June 11. My father continued in the same mind, and I conformed, and began seriously to give my selfe up to that interest from which I was to subsist; and though I had troublesome thoughts about provoking my father, I kept up my heart as well as I could, neither found I any decay as to any thing that was good, but was as much given to private prayer as before. And I resolved to doe what I did out of sincerity and conscience Godward (yet prayed I to God to shew mee the sin of my conformity, if there were any) and so I went on cheerfully, neither did my conscience accuse mee for it then.

August 14. My father reading the Act of Uniformity,[74] and finding what was required of those that took any place upon them, he sent for mee home, and offered now to maintain mee if I would live where he pleased, and be at his allowance. Now though I dared not venture to be at his arbitrary allowance, yet there was another reason why I did not hearken to him in that, viz. my engagements to the colledge were so deep now that I could not leave it.

70/1662

The master and fellowes had taken mee into their tuition and undertaken to provide for mee when they heard that my father would not; and those threatnings which he had used to keep mee bare etc. made mee afraid, and moreover I was so bare of clothes that, had I bin willing, it was not fitting to goe in such a case, for he had not sent any money, no not to beare my charges. He desired not a full stay, but to advise with my uncles, who were to come but came not, about my settling, and then to leave it to my choice to goe to the colledge; but want of clothes, and money, and a remembring that he \wished he/ had not let mee goe when he had mee with him etc., hindred mee from satisfying his will in that letter also. But I wrote him word that I would come at Christmas, when I should be furnished with necessaries, and doe him any service.

My letter provoked him exceedingly, so that he would beare my sawcy writing (as indeed it was) no longer. He said his putting mee upon maintaining my selfe was no disowning mee, and that I misunderstood him, and that he never refused to maintaine mee; he told mee he was more to mee then all the world. [deletion of three lines] I confesse I was sorry he was so angry, but did not feare his forcing mee home, because he was at such a distance from mee. The Lord humble mee for my undutifull carriage towards him!

August 19. About this time I had some convictions for sin, and I wrote to my

---

74 The Act of Uniformity of 1662 made the newly re-established Church of England the official religion of the nation, thus outlawing dissent.

father about it, and he answered then surely I would be convinced that disobedience to him was

71/1662

against the letter of the 5th commandment; and wheras I pleaded the power and command of the King, whom we both should obey, he told mee he must be obeyed rather, for magistracy is founded upon family-governement. He wished mee to see that rising in my nature against controule and reproofe, and told mee he had not knowne any so young vent so much [deletion] as I had done, or discover such heart sins which were more the devil's sins then fleshly outward sinns. He said moreover that one day I should find this true, and love his memory for hinting it now, and I blesse God I have seen more heart sinns since then ever, and doe love him the better now for dealing so plainly.

August 23. My father sent a man for mee, but I went not because he had but one horse, if I had bin willing, and because of my engagements to the colledge, and still I was afraid to be at his allowance, and could not trust to him for outward things, though for my soule I could more then any one in the world. I confesse I wrote to him at a strange rate, very sawcily and unadvisedly, which I begg the Lord would pardon for Christ's sake! and I am ready to weep when I thinke of it, or reade his answer which is by mee as a witnesse against mee, and I feare he can show mine, which I wish were burnt. He intreated mee to come, when his commands would not doe, and yet I would not. I think verily God left mee to my selfe, to see what was in mee, the Lord forgive mee my sins against my deare father! For now I doe thinke he naturally cares for mee, and then did all for my good. When I pleaded conscience, he told mee that mine was pride, and not tendernes, as chancellour Hide told the Parliament.[75] Truly I thinke mine was so, and I was mad against him for denying mee maintenance at Cambridge, and I begg of God to forgive this also to mee!

72/1662

About this time Sir Francis Nethersole, of Kent,[76] gave £50 to be given to 10 schollars whom our master and seniour fellowes should thinke fitt, for their piety, learning, and honesty, to make choice of: God was pleased to give mee favour in their sight, so that I had £5 for which I blessed God, and thanked them. With this I furnished my selfe, and now, beginning to maintaine my selfe, the breach was made wider betwixt my father and mee, so that now I know not whether \he/ made not my table a snare, and that money an occasion of hardning my heart more in my wayes of disobedience.

Some places were offered mee now they saw I was cast of by my father, and that I was resolved to conforme, and the colledge look't upon mee as a pupill and guardian of their owne, and undertook to provide for mee. I was offered a

---

[75] Edward Hyde (1609–74), 1st Earl of Clarendon, perhaps the most famous Royalist of the seventeenth century. He played a major part in the Restoration of Charles II in 1660, and became his chief minister, although he was later impeached, in 1667. He retired to France where he wrote extensively concerning the history of England during his political career.

[76] Sir Francis Nethersole of Wymondeswold, Kent; secretary to the Electress Palatine, 1620–3; died 1659, Al. Cantab.

school at Willingham,[77] another at Ely; I was to have bin a reader at London, the minister of Wate Barray[78] was at mee to teach schoole, and be curate there etc., but I was not old enough for orders, being not 21, and the new book of consecration requires deacons to be 23. But none of them pleased mee, or, if they did, some stopp or other was still in the way, so that I might have read, by God's ordinary providence, that my way towards my father was not good.

September 4. My father was diverted from caring overmuch, or grieving for mee, by the marriage of my sister in law; she married one Mr Richard Williams a packer of Leaden-hall street. I believe also that it hindred him from coming up to Cambridge himselfe, as he had threatned, though such journeys would have done him hurt, and I much desired him not to come. Mr Crossman of Sudbury[79] came to Cambridge, and would faine have had mee to have taught that schoole, and would give mee £20 per annum, and my

73/1662

boord. I liked the man, and those terms, but Mr Dearsly would not consent to it, except I had the schoole to my selfe wholly, which was not in Mr Crossman's power. Mr Samms of Coggeshall[80] came upon the like account, but Mr Dearsly gave him a denyall in my name, for I knew not of it till afterwards.

September 20. Bishop Wren[81] came to consecrate the chappell at Bennet-colledge, which, though built 80 yeares before by Sir Nicholas Bacon,[82] was not yet consecrated; he intended also to give orders. And now I began to putt my hand to the plough, for by the advice of the master and seniours and Mr Dearsly, I was resolved to be ordained. Our master gott this favour that my age was not questioned at all, and perhaps, being tall, they might judge mee more old then I was. Because without orders I could have no considerable place, and that I might be in readines against any fell, I was the more willing to enter upon the ministry.

I had done but very little in the study of Physick, necessity made mee cast of such thoughts, and I wanted meanes now to keep mee during my preparing for the practise of Physick by which I might have lived after some few yeares. I asked God's direction (as in other things so chiefly in so solemne an enterprise) and endeavoured to fitt my selfe for the sacrament (the Lord forgive my want of preparation in a due manner) which was given at such occasions, and so I went to Dr Baldrow[83], one of the Bishop's chaplaines, to be examined. He gave mee

---

[77] The school was endowed with money from a public subscription in 1593, VCH Cambs., IX, 413.

[78] Probably Barway, near Wicken, Cambs.

[79] Samuel Crossman, vicar of All Saints, Sudbury, 1647–60 and later pastor of a Congregational church there, Cal. Rev., 150.

[80] John Sams, vicar of Coggeshall, 1651–61 and a licensed Congregationalist later, in 1672, Cal. Rev., 425.

[81] Matthew Wren, bishop of Ely, 1638–42, when imprisoned in the Tower; restored to his bishopric in 1660, DNB.

[82] Benet College was the former name for Corpus Christi College. Sir Nicholas Bacon, Lord Chancellor in 1559, was a benefactor of the college, Al. Cantab.

[83] Edmund Boldero, D.D. chaplain to Bishop Wren, 1660, and rector of Snailwell, 1663–78, Al. Cantab.

the 39 articles[84] in Latin, and examined mee, after I had rendred some of them into English, about justification and the sufficiency of the scriptures. I told him the witnesse of the Holy Ghost was the best argument to prove that the scriptures were God's word, but he still urged mee to tell him The argument, as he called it; at last I said the authority of the church was a good outward argument, when he

74/1662

told mee it was the best argument, quoting St Austin who said he would not believe the scriptures to be the scriptures except the church had said so.

September 21. Being St Mathew's day, I was ordained a Deacon, and then I took the sacrament. The great reason of my receiving was this, I had lived in a sin almost a yeare, and yet was not convinced it was a sin, by reason of my ignorance in the extent of God's commandments; but at Sturbridge faire[85] last, having by chance looked on Mr Whately, Bishop Andrewes, and Mr Perkins[86] on the commandments (in which I owne a secret hand of God) I was clearly convinced that my former practise was sinfull, and deserved the stroake of God's vengeance. Now having bin troubled for this, and confessed it to God, and promised to doe so no more, I took the sacrament upon it, and desired grace to preserve mee for the future, which he hath done, blessed be his name! And blessed be God that I am at last convinced of any sin, God grant I may know more!

September 24. I owne God in this also, that the bishop himselfe, who hath the name of covetous, gave charge to his secratary that I should have my orders for nothing.

September 26. Being now in orders, I was presented to a small vicaridge by the colledge, whose gift it was, called Arrington 7 miles from Cambridge: and finding delayes, as to other preferments, and being impatient of running into debt, I accepted it with the good liking of the master and seniours, for none had bin there some yeares.

September 28. I went, and read prayers, and preached having never before performed any duties either in a family or in publick. I found the church out of repair, but they were glad to have a minister, and promised a speedy repaire. So I went on Sunday mornings, and came home at nights. When I returned the 1st time, the master and

75/1662

fellowes promised that, wheras the living was worth but £20 per annum, at the renewing the lease, which was almost out, they would so agree with Mr

---

[84] The complete articles of faith to which all members of the Church of England were required to subscribe.

[85] Sturbridge or Stourbridge Fair was founded in Cambridge in 1211 by King John, becoming increasingly important in the three centuries after. A wide variety of commercial goods were to be found there, including rich cloths and foodstuffs. The fair was administered jointly by the town and university after an agreement made in 1589, *VCH Cambs.*, II, 87–8.

[86] William Whately, *A pithie, short and methodicall opening of the ten commandments* (1622). Lancelot Andrewes, *The Moral Law expounded* (1642); William Perkins, *Armilla Aurea, or the Golden Chain* (1598).

Chichely[87] their tenant, that he should pay mee so much as to make it £50 per annum.

October 9. The bishop granted mee a license which the colledge paid for; and so I began to settle in the study of Divinity, and made that my busines which before was a παρεργον.[88] I desired God, in my daily prayers, to teach mee what I should teach others, and found a great desire of doing good to such an ignorant people. The parish was but small, there were but 20 men in their rate, and so very convenient for a young beginner.

I was casting about with my selfe how I should live till the quarter day (for wages must follow my worke) and behold a providence which I did not thinke of! The master and seniours told mee that all the arrears, which were since the death of the last incumbent, were mine by law, only I must substract what they had given to ministers that somtimes supplied the place. I was glad at this, and owned God's hand in it; and when I came to examine the matter, I found, by the churchwarden's bill (who dealt honestly and gave mee an account of the rate, how much every one paid, and how long their minister had bin dead, and what they had given to others) that there was a yeare and <3> a quarter <s> behind, but they had laid out halfe a year's tithes in getting supply, except a marke which I received; so that there was due to mee the whole value of the vicaridge for 3 quarters of a yeare, which I had to the great helpe and incouragement of mee in my beginning the ministry.

December 21. I had come to London, according to the bishop's appointement, and was glad that he would ordaine mee priest before I was

76/1662
at the full age of 21; I must take notice of it the rather because one of the bishop's friends was putt by because he wanted a fortnight of 24 yeares old. Upon St Thomas his day I was made priest at Ely-house, and so was capable of taking any living.

I had almost putt my selfe out of debt with the money I received; I took little up to London because there was £7–15s–0d due to mee from Mr Chichely, who paid mee without shewing any note from the colledge, only my word satisfyed him. He told mee the genius of that parish, and bid mee have a care of them or they would cheat mee of my due; and I found some of them so base as to wish the churchwarden had not given mee an account of what was due. He gave mee little encouragement to stay there, and told mee he had a friend he would faine promote thither, who would teach schoole, which the parish desired of mee. It seems he had spoken with our master, who had promised to give mee another place, and upon those termes I told him I would lay it downe.

Now wheras they spake of making it £50 per annum, at the renewing the lease there was no such thing mentioned, only they told mee it would in time be worth so much, that is when Mr Chichely had enclosed so much ground, which they had given him leave to doe; but he told mee he would not enclose till the next yeare at the soonest. Thus I could not live upon so small mainten-

---

[87] Sir Thomas Chicheley of Wimpole Hall. Chicheley was connected to the Russells of Chippenham by marriage to Sarah, sister to Sir Francis Russell.
[88] Παρεργον: incidental or secondary business.

ance, for the former vicar offered all to Mr Chichely for £15 per annum, and my horse and selfe spent the greater halfe of that, wherfore I thought of taking some other place, but as yet told not the people my mind.

77/1662

I resolved to goe see my father before I went to Cambridge; so meeting with some Essex men, wholly strangers to mee, I went from London with them, and by the way one of the chiefe told mee that he would doe his best to procure Stoke cum Nailand for mee, which living he thought was not yet supplied. This I took well and thank't him for his kind offer to a stranger, and told him I did intend to call at his house, for he lived at Stoke, as I went to Dedham, and so I did, but it was newly disposed of; I still thanked the man, and came to my father. I owned it God's will that I should misse of that place, which I was not fitt for, and quieted my selfe contentedly.

When I came home I was civilly treated, and was glad to find that my sister, who before \was/ so sick, was somthing recovered. During my stay Mr Brewer[89] of Ardleigh told mee of Little Bromley, which was void, and was the gift of the Lady Vere.[90] He wrote to her by mee, and she expressed a sorrow that she could not pleasure mee in it (she having, as I remember, given it away 2 daies before). She well knew my father, and would have done mee good for his sake; she asked mee of what colledge I was, intending, as she hinted, to make mee her chaplaine, if her owne dyed who then lay sick, and is since dead, though I waved any addresses to her for the place, being provided as well, etc.

My father kept his mind still, only (thinking I was not in orders) offered to maintaine mee if I would leave off all. When I asked him if he would take away that £7 per annum, which he had taken up in my name, he was so enraged that in his passion, he called mee such names as he never did before or since. But I am now very sorry that I gave him such occasion, and provoked him to that height of anger, the Lord lay it not to my charge! When I went from him, I concluded that 'twas not God's will I should be yet employed, and therfore resolved to wait till providence should call mee out.

78/1662

I had gotten an habit of writing \sawcily/ to my father, as he [deletion] \told/ mee; and indeed I did not know my place, having bin from the yoake so many yeares, but wrote unhandsomely [as] if he had bin only my elder. He had used that place Hosea 4:17, and I pleaded that from that time he left mee to my selfe, and other cavills I made which now I am ashamed of. I wrote him an acknowledgment, but he thought I would not hold to it, and invited mee to come and make up the difference, and yet share in his estate, but I had gone so far that I could not come of, though my heart was towards him at times, and I wished I had never fallen out with him.

My father wondred at my venturing to preach and yet sent mee good directions which have done mee some good since. He told mee of Luther's 3 helpes,

---

[89] Stephen Brewer, vicar of Ardleigh, Essex, 1662–4, Al. Cantab.

[90] Mary, Lady Vere, sister-in-law of Sir Edward Conway, Secretary of State, 1623–5, and widow of Horace Vere (1581–1671); she was buried at Castle Hedingham, Essex, Complete Peerage.

oratio, meditatio, and *temptatio;*[91] he told mee how I must be brought of from selfe, before God would make use of mee, that I needed much taming, and heart-breaking, and sorrow for what had passed. He wished mee to study heart converting, and experimentall truths, and to see my owne folly, and buitishnes [*sic*] etc., and truly 'twas well I was thus warned, for it was a meanes to keep mee from giving way to pride, and a conceit of my owne parts etc. to which I, as commonly it is with young men, was prone; and this made mee study plainnes, and practicall points in stead of rhetorick, or high expressions.

After I had, in the beginning of January, gathered up all I could gett of my dues at Arrington, I told the people that I was desired to leave them, and that Mr Chichely had provided them another. They were sorry enough, but some of them said if they had thought I would have left them so soon, they would not have paid mee. Our master offered mee a vicaridge, called Grendon, in Northamptonshire worth £30 per annum ready money as they said, they encouraged mee to goe, and paid

79/1662

45s to the bishop for tenths for Arrington, yet would not hinder mee of a better place if I could heare of any.

January 14. Whilst I was musing with my selfe what to doe, and at last had resolved to goe to Grendon, behold a providence of God! It was Friday when I should have gone with Dr Boreman,[92] because I knew not the way, but he was taken with a cold, and could not goe that week, so that this was some disheartning to mee. Our master was prebend of Ely, and 'twas his turne to preach there the next Sunday. He could not goe because he had hurt his legg, he therfore desired Mr Dearsly to goe, who excused himselfe because he was engaged to goe to another place. He then sent for mee, but my youth was my excuse, and I told him how unfitt for a cathedrall, and such a learned auditory, I was. The conclusion was that he must change, Mr Dearsly was to goe to Ely, and I to Chippenham in Cambridgeshire, though in Norwich Diocese.

Thither then I went on the Satterday, where I was made very welcome by Sir Francis Russell[93] the patron of the place, who in this shewed mee a kindnes, not deserved or indeed thought of, viz. he sent Mr Parre[94] his chaplaine, who had laid it downe at Bartholomew, to mee to offer mee the place on the same after noon I came, before I had preached, when I was wholly a stranger (except Mr Dearsly underhand had said any thing, as I found afterwards he did) and they all strangers to mee. Thus he offered mee the place, and withall sent mee word

---

91 *Oratio, meditatio, tentatio:* Archer has here mistakenly recorded *temptatio* for *tentatio.* As an explanation of these terms Luther wrote, '. . . you should meditate, that is, not only in your heart, but by actually repeating and comparing oral speech and literal words of the book, rereading them with diligent attention, so you may see what the Holy Spirit means by them', *Luther's Works,* 34, trans. and ed. Lewis W. Spitz (Philadelphia, 1960), 286.

92 Probably Robert Boreman, D.D. (d.1675), a Royalist theologian and and Fellow of Trinity College; vicar of Blisworth, Northants., 1662, *DNB.*

93 Sir Francis Russell, 2nd Baronet, was Treasurer of the Navy, a colonel in the Parliamentary army and one of Cromwell's lords in 1657, *DNB.*

94 Richard Parr, vicar of Chippenham, 1659–62; afterwards lived with Henry Cromwell at Spinney Abbey, Wicken, *Al. Cantab.*

that he had a great kindnes and respect for mee. The vicaridge was but £28 per annum, or thereabouts, but he offered mee my boord till the cold weather was past, and then, because his house was full, and his eldest son about marrying, I was to lodge and study at the vicaridge, but to have my diet, and the keeping of an horse, and firing (which yet I stood not upon neither had that performed), his favour, and the freedome of the house, etc. Their former ministers had vexed them with ceremonies, and having heard of my indifference, they the rather desired that I would live amongst them. I took this as a good

80/1662–3
providence, and desired the space of a week to advise with my friends about it, and so, having 20s for my paines, I departed to Cambridge. My friends were very willing, and so the next week I came and accepted of it, paying the knight such acknowledgments and thankes as I could.

January 29. Sir Francis sent his cart for my goods, and on the 31 day I went to settle there.

March 13. When the weather was somthing warme I went to ly at the vicaridge, which was but solitary at first to mee, but I used to take occasion to pray, and renew promises of better obedience, and resolved to be content with my portion, and sett my heart at rest upon God.

February 28. I was troubled at my stammering, for I found it somthing worse now, whether upon change of my diet, or any other cause, I know not: but I resolved to beare it patiently, and look upon it as the hand of God upon mee, for abusing my tongue before to his dishonour and the hurt of my selfe, and others.

By reason of this infirmity I had the harder taske in preaching, for I chose words smooth and easy, and in the very act of speaking, when I mett with stoppings in words, I was forced to invent synonimous words etc. which others were not putt to, as also I had but a very small field of expressions to expatiate in, in regard of what would have bin, had I elocution etc., and to adde to my trouble the devill would be tempting mee to leave of the ministry, but that I withstood, and resolved to employ what gifts I had to God's glory, and the good of his church, if he would make use of mee.

April 4. I observed I was more strict, and watchfull over my selfe then when I was at the colledge, either it was for want of such company as I had there, or, as I hope, because by my place I was to be an example to others, for such thoughts were often upon my spirit, and it was the constant subject of my prayers that God would so guide mee by his

81/1663
Spirit that the gospell might not be evill spoken of by reason of my disorderly walking, and unanswerable practise.

This, through grace, I can say, that I found my disposition much altered, for I was now more peaceable, and more ready to beare injuries, and lay aside malice, which was much against my naturall temper; but though the wanting the occasions I had at the colledge might be somwhat, yet there was strength from God against my passions etc. which I must ever owne, and blesse God for. I refrained my tongue more, and gave offence to none willingly; I was very tender of Non-conformists, and had the love of them all; I did not signe with the crosse because it gave offence, and the Bishop, Dr Reynolds,[95] did not require it in his articles; and I did as little as was possible, without incurring danger, and so kept my selfe very moderate, and displeased, I thinke, none by so doing.

April 12. Mr Benjamin West, fellow of our colledge,[96] and one with whom I had maintained a perfect friendship whilst I lived at Cambridge, dyed to my great griefe; for he was an example to mee, and a restraint from many sinns which otherwise I had fallen into: I had bin witnes of his sober and pious life, and by the testimony of all he dyed well and peaceably. I desired to make this use of it, viz. to take God for my friend, now my deare acquaintance was gone, and desired God to supply my wants by the guidance of his Holy Spirit, when the counsells of a friend were wanting.

April 19. There had not bin a sacrament in Chippenham for about 20 yeares last past, and 'twas expected now; wherfore I preached twice about it, laying downe such qualifications as the strictest divines make use of, and went to the houses of such as would receive, to speake with them concerning so weighty a busines. I found them generally honest in their way, but ignorant, wherfore I told them what I could of the grounds of religion, and particularly about the sacrament, and shewing the great dangers they incurred by unworthy receiving. I left it to their owne consciences what to doe.

82/1663

I thought they would take it ill, that so young a man as my selfe should examine them about such things, but I found them very thankfull, and willing to be instructed. The reason of this may be, next to the over ruling providence of God, because I went mildly to worke, and included my selfe in those sinns I spoke against in them. That which moved mee to receive it, was that I reflected upon my undutifull carriage, and unseemly behaviour of late to my father. I was sorry for it, and, intending to leave it of, I prayed that God would enable mee and I took the sacrament upon it, and promised that I would carry my selfe humbly and obediently towards him; and wheras I was apt to uncover his faults, being vexed he would allow mee nothing, I now resolved to hide them, and to speake alwaies well of him, as I ought to doe.

Thus I gave the sacrament, and found the people very serious and reverent, and loving to one another; and I resolved that when any of them fell back into any grosse sin, I would goe to them, and mind them of their solemne engagements, if that might restore them. The wonder was that one man in the towne, who formerly kept up a meeting at his house in the fennes whither more resorted, I believe, then to the publick, was the first that told mee he would, with his wife, take the communion, which they did, and that kneeling too as the rest; it seems they were so much for peace that they conformed to that which others would not have done.[97]

---

95 Edward Reynolds, bishop of Norwich 1661–76; he had been one of the Westminster Assembly in 1643, DNB.
96 See Diary, 1661, p. 61.
97 Archer's theologically radical uncle, John, was strongly opposed to kneeling to receive the sacrament, preferring a seated posture which he argued was indicative of the '[equality] of

This man, with some of his company of other townes that used to come to heare mee, had a kind of feare upon him, and was shy of speaking good things, thinking that I might have brought him into trouble etc. which I was far enough from; yea after sermon, when I used to goe to an house where they were, and to speake of what was preached, and to countenance them in it, yet they were

83/1663

afraid, almost, of owning what they were so zealous for. And indeed since I have found many of that company, which were scattered up and downe when their teacher left of to exercise, and exhorted them to comply, under too slavish a feare of the magistrate, and not willing to suffer, nor to owne and to stand up for seasons and ordinances that they prized so much; which had bin a caution to mee to hold fast in an evill day.

April 22. Dr Sparrow, arch-deacon of Sudbury[98] had a visitation at Newmarket, whither I went and heard Mr Lloyd, vicar of Fordham,[99] make a railing sermon against that which he had so notoriously bin in the late dayes; I was writing his sermon, and he, having occasion to speake to the gentry, said that though they were not there yet they had their notaries to write sermons, chiefly such things as they did not like, and so would come to heare of it. Now none in the church wrote but my selfe, that I could see, and so I guessed he meant that I would tell Sir Francis, to whom he was much engaged for getting an augmentation from the Protectour[100] formerly for him, but now he had forgotten all favours etc. From sermon I went to Cambridge, and so was not present at the calling over my name, which they took so ill that they threatned mee, and had suspended mee, had not Mr Percivall,[101] an honest and religious lawyer who lived with Sir Francis, engaged to pay such money as was due at such seasons; and thus was I informed against, almost as soon as I came, and I feared the worse for that family which was now under a cloud, though I valued not such things.

I preached twice in a day, which was very unusuall in those parts; neither did I observe the holydayes to keep men from their honest labour, in so much that I was informed against to Sir Isaac Thornton, a justice of the peace of Snailewell, and he said I was a knave for not bidding the holy dayes. And March 25 last, finding Sir Francis his ploughs at worke, he made the men goe home, and said that Sir Francis should not thinke to doe as he had done in old Nol's dayes,[102] or plough

---

fellowship which they should have in his [Christ's] Kingdome', *Personall Reigne of Christ upon Earth* (1642), 17.

[98] Anthony Sparrow, archdeacon of Sudbury, 1660, prebend of Ely, 1661–7, bishop of Exeter, 1667–76, and bishop of Norwich, 1676–85, *DNB*.

[99] Hugh Lloyd, vicar of Fordham. Sir Francis Russell's brother, Gerard, had married Lloyd's daughter, Mabel.

[100] A reference to Oliver Cromwell, one of whose titles was Lord Protector.

[101] Probably William Percivall who acted as an attorney for a number of the Russells' land transactions.

[102] 'Old Nol' was a nickname for Oliver Cromwell.

84/1663

under his nose; and thus did my patron and my selfe suffer in the same cause; and though already I was a marke for their malice, and might look for more, yet I desired to discharge my duty in faithfulnes, and by a convincing conversation to putt to silence, and stopp the mouths of sinners.

May 25. I had a mind to goe and see my father, and to make good by some acknowledgment, what I had promised to God at the sacrament; so I went and found him glad to see mee, and better towards mee then formerly; 'twas often in mind to speake to him, and confesse my faulte, but Satan, through strong temptation working upon my proud nature, would not let mee; at last, the night before I came away, I spake to him, confessed that my carriage had bin unbecoming a child, asked his pardon, as I hoped God had forgiven mee and would enable mee to leave it of; and truly I found him full of compassion, and ready to forgive, and willing to forgett any thing of that nature, yea he was glad that I moved him to it, and shewed his love by giving mee severall things then.

I looked at a secret hand of God in all this, and desired grace to performe what I had promised; one thing that putt mee upon submitting my selfe was that I saw in what awe Sir Francis his children were of him, and what great respect they gave him, which shamed mee, so that by degrees my heart was inclined to love and honour my father, especially when, by reading the history of China,[103] I found that they bore more respect to their parents then any nation in the world.

June 14. I had no license, and was threatned by the court with suspension etc., wherfore I went to Norwich with a formall presentation, and took institution, and order for induction when occasion served; by reason of the greedines of the bishop's servants it cost mee

85/1663

more then 'twas worth. The bishop gave mee good counsell, and remitted 10s of his due; I brought a letter from Colonel Henry Cromwell, but the bishop would scarce take any notice of it etc. Perhaps one expression might offend him, viz. that I was so qualified as formerly his lordship would have liked, or to that sense, for he shew mee the letter before I went; and it may be out of prudent caution he was shy of owning those that in the late times he had bin so great with.

August 16. In harvest time I observed that men used to frequent the alehouse on the Lord's day; I asked the constable to assist mee, but he said he should gett the ill will of his neighbours. I asked him if that should hinder him from doing his office etc., but he would not goe, and so I went alone, and found severall there, some went away; but one of my owne parish, for the others were, most, strangers, asked mee if he might not drinke upon the Sunday. I told him he must not fuddle (as I perceived he was in that case) upon any day much lesse upon that; and so inquiring his name, when the hostesse would not, he told it mee himselfe, and I left him at his potts and pipes. When I was gone, he railed on mee for medling where I had nothing to doe (though 'twas one of the

103 Probably the anonymous work, *The Historie of the Kingdom of China* (1588).

bishop's articles to look to the strict observing the Lord's day, and so did belong to mee, if not upon an higher account) and said he could read the Lord's prayer better then I, and that I could not read Common prayer well, meaning because I stammered; and I blessed God that he had no worse to say of mee, then what, *mutatis mutandis*, he might have said to a blind or deafe man, who could not helpe their losses, and were worthy of pity rather then scoffes. The townsmen were sorry for the affront, but I putt it up, and forgave him and prayed God to turne him from his beastly drunkennes, though to this day he goeth on rather at a worse rate then before.

September 13. When I came to Chippenham first I preached twice in a day on different texts, which was a trouble to a beginner.

86/1663

And moreover finding how grossely ignorant most of the people were when I discoursed with them before the taking the sacrament, I thought there was need of a speedy instructing them in the grounds of religion; and so, after some directions for educating their children, I set upon catechizing the youth of the towne in the afternoon, and after that expounded the heads of religion largely, which was like a sermon without a text, and in the deske; I took Bucan's common places[104] for my guide, and joyned prayer for a blessing upon what was said. This I had done for some while, but I found by degrees they did not come to church so well as they were wont, thinking this not so good as if I preached twice; and besides considering that servants, and [*deletion*] \some/ of their dames, came not in the forenoons, and so had no sermons, and that if I preached on two texts they would benefit little by either of them, I resolved to preach twice, and began September 13, and yet for a while, till the dayes were too short, held on expounding and catechizing, endeavouring to serve my generation.

November 23. One in the towne, who came not to heare, had a child to be baptized but would not have godfathers etc. For peace sake, and that the ordinance should not be omitted, and at his request, I yielded to doe it without any sureties but father and mother. At first he was willing to have it done by the service book, but having some scruples upon his conscience he now dared not yield to it. He told mee his objections, which were weake and misapplied, yet I baptized his child, after a solemne promise of the parents to bring it up in the feare of the Lord, which being honest, I thought they would doe. This gave much satisfaction to the Non-conformists of the towne who were present; this man, who now is one of that sect called Quakers, in some things, would faine have had mee preach to them, of his family somtimes privately, but by reason 'twas forbidden by authority, and because it would keep them the more from hearing in publick, I refused to hearken to.

87/1663

My father wrote to mee, and wished mee to study that practicall divinity which no books could teach, yet had I books from him in order to preaching. He

---

[104] This is possibly Gulielmus Bucanus, *Institutions of christian religion, framed out of God's word, and the writings of the best divines* (1606).

required that when I thought of marrying I would acquaint him with it, which was granted by all to be a part of that honour due to a father; and he told mee 'twas requisite in regard of his estate, and the settlement of it. This I promised him, and resolved to stand to, that I would not match my selfe without his consent. He approved of the family where I lived, having heard very well of Sir Francis Russell; he sent mee some of his sermons, being desirous to teach mee that way, when he had mee not with him.

November 29. I had preached very saving truths, and I had the testimony of some choice Christians that I spoke what they had experienced in their owne hearts: this did somwhat encourage mee in my office, and gave mee hopes of doing some good among them. I was much taken up my selfe with searching into those things I pressed others to, and 'twas the great request in my prayer before I went to church, that God would savingly sett on truths and convince mee savingly of my lost condition by nature. I had convictions formerly, but I feare they had wrought of againe, and I did not find my selfe so eager of salvation by Christ as I was 7 years agoe, which did much trouble mee. I was now at a losse what to doe, or thinke of my selfe; I thought I had some beginnings of grace because of what my father so confidently wrote to mee before my unhappy breach with him, and because of what some good people in the towne thought of mee, likewise because of those experiences I had in my soule; but chiefly this did support mee that I could heartily love good people barely as such, without by-respects, and though compassed about with in-firmities, and though they differed from mee in judgment; this made mee thinke I was passing at least from death to life, as 1 John 3:14, yet I wanted the discovery of my case

88/1663
in an orderly manner, and therfore prayed that I might know my state, and have a due sense of sin, and some feelings of his wrath, if nothing else would bring mee to God.

When I discoursed with some that would tell mee their experiences in God's dealings, and feeling the grace of God in their hearts, and their knowing that they had faith etc., it troubled mee that I could not speake so experimentally as they, yet would I not discover my case to them for shame, because I look't upon it as such that I who was their minister, should be outgone by those whom I taught. Though this seemed to savour of spirituall pride, yet it was a spurre to make mee look to my condition Godwards.

I shall not be ashamed to confesse the ground of the former experience. My father gave mee a book in writing of those sermons he first preached at Halsted, which I prized much, and he bid mee read them well which I resolved upon, as those that contained a method of conversion by the precious works of humilia-tion. My chiefe designe in being a minister, next to God's glory, was that I might be more at leisure for the good of my soule by making that both my generall and particular, which others made their generall calling. In order to this I thought I could goe in no better way (both in regard of my being but a beginner, and as being advised to it by Mr Dearsly, and to have more leisure to study theoreticall divinity which, as my father wrote, was a great worke and required much time) then diligently to peruse my father's sermons, and preach upon those texts, and compare his notes, and inlarge or leave out as occasion served.

This then I did at my first coming, though some sermons for afternoons I made by the helpe of books in an ordinary way, as upon Psalm 4:6 which he never preached; and in his texts sometimes I altred the method, sometimes I made whole sermons upon doctrines he had passed by, and added things so that nothing but the text was from him; and indeed he had

89/1663

an excellent method in dealing with soules, so that better texts could not be taken. This also can I say that I spent as much time in composing a sermon from his notes as I did in making one without them. But though this way could not \be/ justly taxed with lazines because the time was the same, yet it was very helpfull, and did mee good in many respects, for my ambition was to imitate my father (which I have done in sermons of my owne since, as an old hearer of my father in former years, and coming casually into thees parts, and hearing mee, told mee) and this was the readiest way. Heerby also I fixed those saving truths in practicall divinity on my owne heart, which I could not meet with in books. In reading his sermons I would admire his goodnes, and repent that ever I slighted him, in that manner as I did of late, who was so precious a man, and so excellent a preacher. I made his zeale and fervency in preaching a patterne to my selfe, so that many wondred and were amazed that such things should come from one so young as I was. I drew teares from some who were tender hearted, and when one thank't mee for my paines, and said she had cause to blesse God that ever I came, and I said I might look after other's vineyards, and yet not keep my owne, she replied that I could not have such care of the soules of others if I had not experience of what danger they were in my selfe; I can say this without pride and to God's glory, that I was much refreshed by the testimony of this good Christian. This now is the ground of their thinking mee so experienced, because I delivered such saving truths, and it putt mee upon an endeavour after them.

I used to be vexed at my hardnes of heart, and that I had so little sense of sin; yet this comforted mee that that sense of hardnes and insensiblenes was a signe that there was somthing alive in mee, and that discovery of darknes was a signe of some light, Ephesians 5:1. As Manoah's wife said, Judges 13:23, if God would have destroyed mee, he would not have shewed mee thees things. Yet did I not rest heer but went on in my requests for a farther discovery of Christ, and his grace in my soule. I resolved to have comfort from no hands but God's, who was able both to kill and also to make alive againe. Amen!

90/1663

November 30. I was reading, and meditating upon what I read in Mr Rogers his book of faith,[105] viz. that there must be legall preparations before faith is wrought in the soule; I examined my selfe, and could not find that orderly proceeding of God with my soule by humiliation, contrition etc. as I desired,

---

[105] Possibly Richard Rogers, *Certain Sermons . . . to establish and settle all such as are converted in faith and repentance* (1612).

and though I knew that there might be a root of faith, though not perceived, yet, because such were not like to have any growth of grace, or knowledge and discovery of their condition, and would want that comfort which others had, I made it my chiefe request in my daily prayer to God that he would give mee a sense of sin, and (if his will were such, and I could not have faith wrought otherwise) some feeling of his wrath, and hell heer rather then heerafter. I desired not to fare well, or have my portion in this world, but in that to come.

When I was at a losse, and thought that God did not love mee, and that I had no portion in Christ, this would comfort mee that I loved such as were good heartily, though otherwise they were inconsiderable; and I persuaded my selfe that this was a good signe.

Besides this, I found that I was vexed and displeased with my selfe when I sinned, or had evill suggestions from Satan, and this was a signe that I did not take delight in sin. And I read in my father's sermons that men should not so curiously judge their state by signes, or marks; for they must flow from faith, and if this ground-worke were not found, all was rotten; wherfore I earnestly desired God to discover to mee (if he thought good, and I was fitt for it) that all sufficient righteousnes of Christ, and give mee faith to make it my owne; and thus I resolved to wait the leisure of God, knowing 'twas good so to doe.

December 3. A young man discontented ran naked about 7 miles, in a frenzy, and was found dead. I saw this sad spectacle, and it gave mee occasion to pray to God not to give mee

91/1663–4

over to my selfe, or suffer Satan to tempt mee to melancholy and discontent (to which I was prone) to hurt my selfe.

My father desired mee to send him a sermon or two of my owne making, that he might judge: so I sent him two sheets, the substance of 4 sermons, upon Hosea 13:9. He told mee he had no reall exception against it, and wish't mee to goe and doe likewise, and teach my selfe what I had taught others. He retorted upon mee one thing in my notes, viz. I had showne that men destroy themselfe by security, rising at a reproof etc., which indeed had bin my case. He wished mee to be more large in application (the very life of preaching) and to urge things home to the consciences of the hearers; which since I have endeavoured according to my abilities.

April 28. Sir Francis Russell, being much troubled with infirmities, resolved to goe to London to have the advice of the doctours; wherfore April 17 he went, and was searched, and they found he had the stone in the bladder, which he had a long time suspected: upon this he resolved to be cutt, which was done, with a great deale of courage and constancy on his part, saying, as he went to be cutt, *porta mortis magis terret quam ipsa mors*;[106] and with successe on the chirurgeon's, who cutt him April 22 and took 2 stones, weighing about 26 dramms, from his bladder;[107] but his body was brought so low by physick, chiefly by

---

[106] *Porta mortis magis terret quam ipsa mors*: 'the gate of death holds more terror than death itself.' *Cf*. Publilius Syrus, *Sententiae*, 54.

[107] 26 dramms is about 1⅝ oz. The fact that Archer was able to obtain such detailed information on Sir Francis' illness may have been because Jeremiah White, Sir Francis' doctor, was

opium which he took to procure sleep, that the wound would not heale, and so April 28 he dyed. This made a change in the family, for he had hired the farme of his son, who was to live elsewhere; the losse was great to all, but himselfe, who was a gainer, I hope, and went from sorrow to joy; I lost a faithfull friend, but there was a greater losse which I knew not of then, for upon the same day my only sister dyed too. She had bin troubled many years with stoppings, but chiefly the last winter; she had a swelling in her face and body, and twiddles arose under the skinn, April 28 she was taken with convulsion fitts, about one of the clock in the morning, and had them every 4th houer, and at the 4th fitt she dyed.

92/1664

I was at home, with a stranger, a woman of Chippenham who had a sister living at Dedham, when my sister had her fitts, and we were both called up at midnight to helpe her; 'twas a piercing sight to see her in that agony, and I cannot expresse how I found my selfe then. By reason of the woman's hast I was forced to goe back on the Thursday, after I had seen 3 fitts, intending to come againe on the Munday next, but she told mee she should never see mee more when I took my leave of her, and so it was for about 3 in the afternoon she dyed.

God knows I suspected no such thing, but prayed for her when she was dead, though I knew it not; on Munday betimes, after the buriall of Sir Francis on Satterday night, I went to Dedham, hoping to find my sister better, and found that she was dead and buried; this was a very suddain griefe, happening upon the death of my honoured friend. My father loved her entirely, and 'twas a great triall to him; and I reflected upon all my unkind behaviour, and words towards my sister in my passion, when I wrongfully thought that she exasperated my father against mee, and I was sorry and ashamed; yet did not I then find the greatnes of my losse so as I have since, but I was like a stock without that sense that naturall affection brings forth in others, neither could I dissemble. It may be my father thought I was not much concerned, for he wrote to mee bitterly that my eye-sore was taken away; but God knowes that since I find it a great losse, and am in passion when I thinke of her dying fitts, and last words.

I desired that I might lay this providence to my heart, and that God would give mee the comforts of his spirit, and support my father, and that I might make up the want of all

93/1664

his children by my dutifull carriage, and make amends for all my former neglect in that behalfe. Amen!

often at Chippenham Hall and so may have told Archer. A letter from Sir Francis to White survives, and runs as follows: 'I must needs confesse I did once despair of ever enjoying so much health as I have done of late, I mean since I stayed your experiment, yet upon any remarkable change of weather I am put in mind that the root of my disease doeth still ly hid within mee: but I hope it will be of good use and a right instruction to my mind and spirit, because some kind of rod or other is needful for us while we are but young or children, for few or none will learne obedience or wisdome without it, and among the weake and ignorant I am one of the chiefest. Chippenham, 30. Sept. 1663.' Cited in R.W. Ramsey, *Henry Cromwell* (London, 1933), 368.

July 5. My time of going out Master of Arts being come, my father having allowed mee £12 towards my degree and other charges, which supply came unexpectedly and so it was the more welcome. I took that degree too; and found my selfe much weaned from the colledge, which I had so much loved. The week after I went to my father's, where I found my uncles, and a kinsman with whom I went to London to see some other friends; I staid but a week there, and after a small time after my coming to Chippenham, it pleased God to make a way for mee more to my content then Chippenham, now Sir Francis was dead; and it was by the death of Mr Russell of Spinney Abbey[108] in Wicken in Cambridgeshire, 6 miles from Chippenham, the reversion wherof came to Colonel Henry Cromwell,[109] who was desirous of my acquaintance, and I more of his; we had agreed, in case the old man dyed, that I should goe and live with him when he left Chippenham; this was designed halfe a yeare before, and now God making a way by the death of Mr Russell and their minister's offer to lay it downe in case I would come, I went to live with him, to the content of his family and my selfe; for he was a patron of piety, and we had experience one of another, having lived together at Chippenham all the while; neither was he and his lady religious only by countenancing religion, which is the most may be expected usually from the gentry, but by their private examples and duties did shame those of their quality round about.

August 11. I went from Chippenham to the grief of all, except they dissembled with mee, for I blesse God I gave some content to all sides; yea, Sir John Russell, my new patron, ask't mee the reason of my leaving him and was very urgent with mee to stay; but when he understood that I was to live with his brother Cromwell he was vexed with him for getting mee from him, till I

94/1664

protested to him that 'twas of my owne doing. Yet at Sir John's desire I came over to preach every Sunday in the afternoon, and so had the profits of both till Michaelmas. My new place was an appropriation, and so I came into it without charges, neither was it so subject to the spirituall court as livings were. I designed only to preach, for I longed to give my father content in leaving of to conforme, but could not gett any to read common prayer as I thought I might: and so I used my liberty and read as little as was possible, and somtimes in the short and cold dayes none at all but the psalmes and lessons; and though they had the ceremonies to the height before, yet there was no murmuring at what I did, for I made it up in preaching twice, which they liked better.

My noble patron allowed mee £30 per annum, besides boord, firing and candle, washing, and the keeping of a horse, and other conveniences; and withall the profits from christnings, marriages, and burialls.

My chiefe aime in going to this more private place was to serve God more closely, having such pious governours of the family, and prayers every evening, which were not regarded at Chippenham. I had contracted much guilt, and filth by living with those at Chippenham Hall, who did not so much mind the

---

108 See Ramsey, Henry Cromwell, 362.
109 Henry Cromwell, Lord Lieutenant of Ireland, fourth son of Oliver, Lord Protector, DNB.

forme of religion as they should; but I resolved now upon a more strict way of life, and conversation, and to serve God faithfully, and constantly.

September 1. My burden for a great while hath bin that I am pestered and plagued with vaine, frivolous and unprofitable thoughts; so foolish and confused have they bin that I have bin ashamed of them, and even weary of my life; uncleane imaginations would steale into my mind, but when I was my selfe I would abhorre them, and flee them,

95/1664

and daily pray to be delivered from them; I begged of God selfe denyall, humility, and the love of others, for if I could not love my brother, how could I love God rightly? I had a little watched over my soule, and blessed be God who shewed mee thees wants; I resolved not to give entertainment to those idle guests, evill thoughts, but that I would disallow of them, and divert them, and so they should not be imputed to mee, to condemne mee, but to Satan who, taking advantage of my constitution, was the authour of them.

September 21. I found my heart, in some measure, brought of from those vanities and follies I minded at Chippenham, and my retirednes more disposed mee to piety and devotion then when I went into much company. I desired God to keep my deceitfull heart for mee, and teach mee with an high hand that I should not goe in the way of the wicked; and that by my diligence now, I might redeem the time I had lost, and my too much neglect of the best things, and hearkning to the allurements of the world. I resolved upon more strictnes, and so to walke as others might be brought to God, if he pleased, by my example. The Lord strengthen thees weake resolutions, and worke all thees things in mee, and for mee for Christ's sake!

October 19. I was reading the preface to Baxter's Rest,[110] where he writes that we should mind our inheritance, and that because God tossed and tumbled us about in this world to make us weary of it. And this have I often experienced, that I meet with crosses, and can find no content from anything in this world, but an unsettlement in the midst of all my enjoyments, and am weary of the world, and doe find the things therof vexation of spirit: yea, God often crosseth mee in that which I desire most, and yet afterwards can say that 'twas really best for mee, and God's way was the wisest. The Lord grant that I may at last enjoy that rest that remaineth (and why then should I look for rest heer) for the people of God! and I am sure I can find no rest heer, but believe 'tis with God, and this rest my soule breatheth after.

96/1664

November 6. I observed for some years last past, that many vaine thoughts would hinder mee in God's service, but now more then ever when I had resolved upon more strictnes; thus Satan sheweth his enmity against mee; when I was at my studies I was distracted by them, and when, as a minister, I was in a capacity of doing good to others, the devill hindred mee by plaguing mee with evill thoughts. However in former years I took not such strict notice

---

[110] Richard Baxter, The Saints Everlasting Rest (1649).

of them, nor disallowed of them as now I doe; God grant that I may drive them away as Abraham did the fowles from the sacrifice![111] and give mee a renewed mind that I may serve him, though I am sold under sin!

November 27. I observed all along in my preaching, that when Satan was most busy with his temptations, and when I had most discouragements from without, then God did stand neerest mee, and I had most strength from him; so when I trusted most to my selfe, in all duties, then was I left by God most; wheras if I used selfdeniall, and a despaire of my owne strength, God was never wanting. Thus I see I must not rely upon an arme of flesh, or be a man pleaser, but the servant of the living God, from whom alone came my strength and salvation.

December 14. I was overtaken with a fault, yet was not convinced it was a sin, till it pleased God that a child reproved mee for it; this stuck upon mee, and I took it to be the voice of God, for the child could not understand what it said to mee; upon this I reformed, and it putt mee in mind of the asse's speaking to Balaam.[112] The Lord make mee ashamed that I cannot leave of my sinns till by such plaine meanes God make mee know and forsake them! and the Lord pardon mee that I left some sins not so much because they displeased God, or were evill in themselves, as because they were not for my credit, and for feare they should be knowne of men, wheras I should have feared the all seing eye of God!

December 19. I wrote to my father that if he would maintaine mee, I would leave of conforming at Easter. This he was glad of, and promised mee to maintaine mee;

97/1664

yet would he not have mee leave of, so as to be without employment, for that was a worse snare then the other; but would have had mee boorded with a silenced minister, who lived in a farme, and he would pay for my boord; but I desired a stated yearly maintenance, not daring to committ my selfe to his discretion as to that, for I thought I should be kept but barely, in respect of what I had allowed my selfe hitherto; so he said I might live of my selfe, and he would allow mee a sufficient maintenance; but rather wish't mee to thinke of changing my condition, which then would be the best way; and expressed now more then ordinary love in his letters.

February 8. My father's putting mee upon marrying, extorted from mee what I thought not to have told him, viz. that there was a Non-Conformist minister's daughter whom I loved well, and by a providence came to know; but because she could have little during her father's life, my father was against it, and proposed another vertuous and rich enough; this vexed him that if he would not yield to the former, I would not thinke of marrying, but, as he called it, settle sullenly in cælibatu.[113] He wished mee to remember that where I was for my owne way against his mind formerly, I had bin weary and come of, which was true I confesse; and accordingly God's providence hath since stopped my designes, so that I am free for one as well as another. He wished mee to call to

---

[111] See Genesis 15:11.
[112] See Numbers 22:22–35.
[113] In cælibatu: 'in a condition of celibacy'.

mind what savoury counsell he gave mee soon after the death of my sister, which were \as/ his last words, when God's stroake was heavy upon him; he wrote that perhaps he might not have an heart to speake or write so savourily as formerly, and wished mee to prize what he had said and written; which I doe; and thinke I shall love him better as I grow wiser, and now see, and am ashamed to thinke how foolish and obstinate I was.

February 25. In the meane time, after my resolutions to leave of at Easter, I was contriving how or where to live; and I found the family of Spinney much grieved for my going away, and the Colonel willing I should stay with him, yet so ingenuous as not to urge mee still to conforme [deletion]; for he was not much for those things; and living with him putt mee

98/1664

upon thoughts of quitting conformity; [deletion] for when I went to prayer with them fervently, I found my heart more affected then in reading the service (what ever others found) and I thought I was to give God the best, and not offer the lame when I had a male in the flock, Malachi 1:14. Now to mee conceived prayer was best, because it followed my affections, and was the language my wants dictated to mee: by this meanes I had a grudge upon mee when I read the service because it affected mee no more.

In November last Sir John Russell and I made this agreement, that he should enter bonds for, and pay the first fruits of Chippenham (for though I was instituted I had neglected the paying them, and putt my selfe out at Midsummer, thinking to escape; but at the last visitation the archdeacon threatned to make mee pay them if I were in the diocese, which was the occasion of our compact) and I should beare the name of the living, and preach once a month which was perpetuall residence, as they told mee.

Now though I had given Sir John a resignation 'twas nothing, for it should have bin done at the court by a notary, and so the living was still mine. That which putt mee upon it was to avoid the first fruits, and he did it because they threatned him if he did not putt in one in my place, that they would send one, and he could gett none upon such termes as I was there; he had also promised to take the living into his owne hands, and beare all charges, and allow the minister £30 per annum de claro; and thus my holding it saved him first fruits for the new incumbent, for they must have bin payed by him as well as mee, and institution money which I had paid my selfe, and induction charges which he bore for mee. So I went and preached, and lay at Chippenham, once a month (the great family then being at London that winter, and a minister in my room, who changed with mee) and this expedient pleased all parties, and was usefull to both of us.

99/1664

March 13. I was tempted to pride by reason of that applause I found in my preaching, but I withstood it, and did blesse God that I saw my danger; I was much followed at Chippenham, and at Wicken more, because, as some of them said, they had scarce heard any savoury preaching. A stranger heard mee, and said I must needs have the Spirit of God or I could never preach so; I looked into my heart, and was grieved I could not sensibly find his words true, however whatever my case \is/ I will not judge it by sense, for that is deceitfull.

When I went first to Wicken they gave great attention as if they had never heard such things before; wherfore I hoped that God would sett some things home upon their hearts, and I thinke God begun to awaken some of them; this I know that some were brought of from some false opinions which they held, the Lord guide them more into the truth! An eminent Christian told mee that he was sure I had a worke of grace upon my heart because I preached such experimentall things, and searched their hearts so, and because of my savoury discourse with him in private: but Oh I feare he was mistaken, for some things I spoke indeed from experience, but many things I took upon the experience of others; neither yet can I find that orderly worke of God's Spirit in my owne soule, that I described to others, but I hope God will in due time bring forth an orderly worke in my soule.

I observed that on the Lord's dayes Satan would be most busy to disturbe mee, and fill my heart with evill thoughts, which I was not so troubled with on other daies, so that when I would doe good, evill was present with mee; from hence I thought that the Lord's day was to be kept holy, for else why did Satan so keep mee from the strict observing of it? The Lord keep mee humble in all my wayes, and grant that by pride I may not fall into the condemnation of Satan! I found much comfort in conversing with 2 Christians, who came to live at Wicken because their minister was so violent against them; I owne that God hath done mee good by them, so that I shall prize the fellowship of saints more heerafter then hitherto I have done.

March 20. I was zealous as far as I knew, and did not act against my conscience by bauking any truths of God to please men; though in the manner and measure of zeale I believe I was wanting. When

100/1664-5

I lived at the colledge I did not bow to the east, or doe any of those supra-canonicall ceremonies which others observed, though I was indangered in respect of my degree; yet God ordered things so that I had as much favour showne mee as others. When I was ordained by Bishop Wren, who is sufficiently for the ceremonies, I did not doe that reverence to the east that all else did; yet I sped as well as the most forward of them. And since in the ministry, though I had temptations to sloth, and bauking the truths of God in favour of great persons, yet, I blesse God, I strove then to be, and was more zealous then usuall, and did not shun to declare what was in my mind without respect of persons; so that when a chiefe Parliament man who was a sufficient enemy to the power of religion, heard mee, I was as free and plaine-dealing as ever, and shunned not to speake the truth, and at last lost nothing by it.

At Wicken I preached about a quarter of a yeare upon Micah 7:8, and spoke so plainly that 'twas told mee by a friend that had I said so much, though true enough too, at London I should almost have bin torne in pieces; yet God kept mee from harme. And still I trust I shall loose nothing by my courage and plaine and impartiall declaring the mind and will of God, as long as I goe against my outward interest by so doing. I found my heart compassionate for the members of Christ, and could heartily rejoyce at their welfare; and doe hope that this is some ground of my being in the favour of God, and have said thus much for the glory of that God who did all for mee, and who, as I trust, will worke all my workes in mee.

March 25. Out of tendernes to my owne conscience, which had never wholly complied [deletion] with some things other ministers did; and to satisfie my father, and the generality of my friends; and because my strength was not sufficient to read and preach twice, because also I had an impediment so as I could not read anything that was sett mee, though words of my owne chusing in prayer and preaching I could speake so well, that some of my enemies thought I dissembled, but God knowes they were mistaken; and lastly because I saw more and more into the evill of some of

101/1665

those things that were enjoyned, and hope that God will farther convince mee as he seeth fitting: for thees reasons, [deletion] I left of conforming, both to the joy and griefe of my friends at Spinney who would have enjoyed mee [deletion]; and so the quarter day falling the day before Easter, I went to my father, and the Colonel procured another to give the sacrament. The towne of Wicken took it so that one of them, whom I never encouraged to say any such thing, yea to my knowledge never spoke to him, was brought before the justice since I left the towne, for saying that he hoped the Dutch would beat us (for there is warre betwixt us still) because then they should have mee againe for their minister; meaning, I suppose, that there would be a toleration in respect of conformity; but too much of that.[114]

I found my mind so eased as if some great burden had bin taken from mee; and though I could not expect so large allowance from my father as I had at Spinney, yet, I blesse God, it was no motive to mee to conforme againe. Thus what my father wished mee to from the beginning, and I opposed, now of my owne accord, by the secret providence of God, I yielded to.

On Easter day I preached at Halsted, where I was brought up, and there was such a congregation as had not bin since Mr Sparrow laid downe at Bartholomew day in 1662;[115] curiosity and novelty 'tis like prevailed with many of them. I perceived how much they of Spinney, as well as those in the towne, were concerned at the newes of my leaving them; they said I might doe as little as I pleased, in respect of the service, and they would warrant mee no hurt should come of it; at last I thought of this expedient, I offered to give my whole £30 per annum to one that should doe all but preach, and I would stay with them still; this was liked, if it could be brought to passe, and I had my father's consent, but when I thought my selfe secure behold a fall! for the Colonel, having advised with others, thought it not convenient either for his safety or mine to keep two to doe what one might doe; and, considering that since he is come into strict bonds etc., and they asked what chaplaine he had (who is

---

114 The churches of the Netherlands enjoyed relative freedom; they proved a popular retreat for many dissenters who fled religious persecution in England in the seventeenth century, including Archer's own uncle, John; see above, note 9.

115 William Sparrow, vicar of Halstead, Essex, 1650–62; a Congregationalist, *Cal. Rev.*, 453.

conformable). If I had lived with him it would have bin a prejudice to us both; he hath done wisely in it, and I could not blame him.

102/1665

And further, if one lived in the towne, as we had designed, he would (if not very ingenuous) have in time sided with the people (who have bin at jarres with Spinney time out of mind) against the Colonel, especially considering how obnoxious he is; and they might reduce that to a setled living which is but a sine-cure; and so that would have bin true, *turpius ejicitur quam non admittitur hospes.*[116] Thus was I more at a losse then ever, for I was disappointed, and, by mee, my father; yet had I no temptations to conforme, neither would they perswade \mee/, though (as they often told mee) it would have bin much for their advantage etc.

April 19. I lived with them till they should have another setled, as they desired mee; and they had one from Cambridge every Lord's day, who preached once; and I once freely. I heard of a poor maid at Chippenham who had bin vaine and foolish enough, and now God had deprived her of the sight of both her eyes. She was in some disquietment of mind, and ready to despaire; I went to give her what comfort I could, because she desired it by others, and said she could meet with none that could give her ease. And truly I found her of a good humble frame of spirit, bewailing how her heart was harder now then before; and that now she could not pray, wheras before she could at every turne poure out her heart to God; and that though she could weep before others, she could not by her selfe. I spoke to her such things as God was pleased to putt into my mind at that time, and doe hope she may prove a good Christian, and that the blindnes of her body may be for the inlightning of her mind. As I went back to Spinney it grieved mee that I could not find so gracious a frame in my owne heart; and that my heart was harder now then when I was younger, or at least I did not understand it so much; the Lord grant that I may understand his providences more for my owne good! and that by all his dealings with mee he may have the glory, though it be with my shame in this world! Amen!

103/1665

May 30. What straits I was putt to upon my quitting conformity may appeare from hence, viz. my father gave mee a mare worth about £7 and yet would reckon £4 of it, viz. so much as I sold my owne horse for, as part of my allowance which he had so often promised; and wheras I had £30 per annum before, now his allowance was but the 3d part of it, £10 a yeare; and so at Midsummer I had but 20s for my charges every way till Michaelmas. This was hard, for I thought he had given mee the mare as an encouragement for my leaving of conformity; but I blesse God I bore up, and made a shift, and lived as sparingly as was possible, neither did this tempt mee to [*deletion*] doe any thing that might make worke for repentance another day; God grant I may hold in this mind! Amen!

About the beginning of May the curate at Chippenham upon some distast

---

116 *Turpius ejicitur quam non admittitur hospes*: 'It is more disgraceful to turn out a guest than not to admit him', Ovid, *Tristia*, V, eleg. 6, 1:13.

gave Sir John Russell warning, and went away; I made use of this providence, and spoke with Sir John concerning my coming to Chippenham againe upon such termes as I offered at Spinney, viz. to find a reader etc., and though some that had a grudge against mee envied mee and endeavoured to hinder by fraud my going thither (yea, like Bellerophon in another case I carried him a letter against my selfe),[117] yet after a pretended promise, it seems, to another who \should/ take the living wholly, and free mee (which I was willing to), and a disappointment in the man, as some say never sought to or knowne (for such wiles were used towards mee because I was too strict and precise to live among them).

Sir John came to Spinney and invited mee to my old place, to the content of the towne, and all that were lovers of sobriety and the feare of God. Indeed in rigour I could not be hindred, for the living was mine; this I urged, either to quitt the title, or to have some convenience of holding it, and perpetually residing which was required by law, and which I was bound to; if I had quitted it, the 1st fruits would have bin paid, and I freed from that tie of bearing the name; and to have a convenience could not be better then by living in the house.

104/1665

For a month then I procured one from Cambridge to performe what I did not my selfe; but he was minded, I know not upon what grounds, for he pretended none, to leave of; and so by him I sent to Sir Goodwin, fellow of Clare hall,[118] and my kinsman, to gett one to read and he should have all the allowance, when he came himselfe and offered his service willingly. This I look't upon as a providence, for he that was a relation would be more faithfull and loving.

June 9. I went to settle at Chippenham-hall, to the honest envy of those at Spinney, as my Lady Cromwell told mee; on the 11th day my cousin came, and so continued to come on Satterdayes till [sic] the wayes were dirty. I confesse I loved Chippenham better then Spinney, that is the place; but the company at Spinney were far more acceptable, and suitable to mee, yet I was the more taken up in secret prayer now we had none publickly in the house. I had all accommodations now that I had at Spinney, and was well content, only I feared 'twould not last long, and that the court would suspend mee, yet I left that to God.

June 13. I gott a blow on my left eye while I was playing with Sir John at rabated rapiers; it was beyond my calling, and I took it as a warning for the future, for *quantillium abfuit!*[119] an inch lower had putt out my eye, and then my folly had marked mee; I understood that this deliverance might mind mee of

---

[117] Bellerophon, in classical literature, was son of Glaucus, King of Ephyre. Being handsome, the King's wife fell in love with him only to find her advances refused. In revenge, she falsely accused him before the King of attempting to seduce her. Consequently, Glaucus sent Bellerophon to his father-in-law, Iobates, with a letter, written against him, which implored Iobates to punish any man who had mistreated his daughter. See Homer, *Iliad*, 6, 156.

[118] James Goodwin, of Teversham, Cambs. After Archer dismissed him in 1674 he was rector of Nowton, Suffolk, 1676–80, *Al. Cantab*. See Diary, 1674, pp. 169–70.

[119] *Quantillium abfuit*: 'but for that tiny amount'.

the leaving of a sin I was intangled with, and had resolved against; the Lord teach mee by his providences! Amen!

I observed in my selfe that after I had bin melancholick, full of anguish and bitternes, then was I in the greatest calme, had most peace, and ravishing joy at my heart; when I was strip't of outward comforts, then the unspeakable comforts of God's Spirit delighted my soule; blessed be God who doth not send burdens too heavy upon mee! for I could not beare up under the frownes of God and the world too; therfore when I had least incouragements from the world I had most from God, who keeps his best things

105/1665

till the last, and till a soule hath absolute need of them.

July 14. I ought to have bin exemplary in all manner of conversation; and when I would venture in things not belonging to mee, I found I was used hardly, and there was a secret hand of God crossing mee. In all anxieties and disquietudes I used prayer, and found it a generall remedy; and in any trouble, after I had made my case knowne to God and humbled my selfe, I found ease, went away, and was sad no more, as Hannah's case was, 1 Samuel 1:18. Thus by prayer I found ease in all my burdens and vexations of spirit, and therfore desire to use it for the future, not only in straits (for then 'tis no wonder to seek God early, Hosea 5: last) but all my life long, though my cup run over. I left of, through the grace of God, some occasions of sin; I found my selfe in the best frame when I was about my studies, and in my calling I found support from Psalm 94:19 and Psalm 142:3,4,5. and doe desire more to study that book of God so full of remedies.

July 22. I observed that I lived in some sin or other, though at first it seemed none (by reason of my love to it, and not searching God's mind in all I did) yet upon conviction I found it a sin, and left it of in a great measure, though my wicked heart would be somtimes starting aside. Yea, Satan was so busie that I was soon overtaken with some other sin of like nature, which, though at first I thought no hurt, at length I found evill. Oh when shall I be free from living in any sin! when shall I see clearly my duty, and doe the same! this I wish for, this state I desire to be brought into for Christ's sake.

July 26. The plague, which had begun the latter end of April, raged at London sadly; there was a monethly fast set apart by authority for the diverting of it; I composed some sermons upon 1 Kings 8:38, wherin my spirit was much let out in a fellow-feeling with my brethren; and my daily prayer was for them, and to thanke God for my health, although I was guilty also in nationall sinns. My father's book afforded the text, and I invented the rest, for now I had learned with much ease to make sermons, and to be large and long enough upon a text, though I had little or no helpe. The Lord sanctifie and increase my gifts to his glory, and the good of others.

106/1665

July 27. I would propose a settlement to my selfe as to religion and studies; when I went to such a place and had such accommodations, and such leisure etc., Oh, how should I serve God, and follow my study! but alwaies I found some inconveniencies or other in the places where I lived, so that, when I had my desire, I could not settle, somthing I would propose farther, and when I had that, I would not settle then; so that I see 'tis best to have a mind setled upon God in my unsetled condition on earth, for heer is no abiding city, for I am from home.

August 1. I have observed all my life hitherto that I never was contented when I was at \an/ wine, or among such merry companions; I had a check upon mee, and thought my selfe out of my way, and blesse God that I never gave over my selfe to such things, or found satisfaction in them. I used my selfe constantly to prayer morning and night, and on the Lord's day oftner; but was not constant in meditation, I was loath to begin, but if I once began I found it so sweet that I could scarce leave of; I read Mr Baxter's *Rest* about meditation, and was much affected with his way; I perused Bishop Hall's book, and that pleased mee; but I found diversions, and I could not fixe my thoughts long upon one subject; I had so many distractions that I was a burden to my selfe.

When I was abroad, or with company that I could not be so free with as to joyne in prayer, I used either to walke out and pray, or pray in bed, or as I went home next day; my conscience would not lett mee wholly omitt that duty, neither have I for many years; yet could I not be so fervent in such occasions, and therfore I kept at home usually, and had the enjoyment of my selfe.

August 4. I observed in preaching that somtimes things that came into my mind without preparation, and were darted in I know not how in the very act, did as much, or more affect the best of my hearers then what I had studied,

107/1665

as they have told mee, yet was not this a temptation to serve God without due preparation, and with what cost mee nothing. I observed also in prayer, that as the company was good or bad where I had bin, so my heart would be disposed to that duty; but when my mind was thus damped, and clouded I strived to gett a better frame, and with Luther, never left till my heart was somwhat softned; God grant that I may have a sense of my miscarriages!

August 23. I went to Feltwell to Colonel Fleetwood's,[120] being invited by Mr Taylour the former minister of Bury,[121] and it was Wednesday which, it seems, that family set apart for fasting and prayer; they asked mee to joyne with them, which I was glad of; the Colonel himselfe prayed in a most heavenly manner, and Mr Taylour preached very notably, and I prayed with them, but was grieved at my owne deadnes, and that I could not pray so meltingly and fluently as others there, though I checked my selfe for this spirituall pride and envy. They were very urgent with mee to stay, but I came home that night, though it were 5 in the afternoon before we ended; I blesse God some good I gott by going, and wish it were nearer that I might goe the oftner; but 'tis 16 miles from Chippenham, which is too far to goe and come in a day.

August 30. Some had contrived mischiefe against mee, and their con-

---

[120] Charles Fleetwood of Feltwell, Norfolk, Commander-in-chief for Ireland 1652–7, Lord Deputy from 1654, *DNB*.

[121] Thomas Taylor, preacher at a Congregationalist meeting which met in the Shire House, Bury St Edmunds; he was never prosecuted as a nonconformist leader, *Cal. Rev.*, 478.

sultations were overheard by a friend of mine who told mee all, and so God defeated their ill intentions, upon whose providence I desire still to wait.

September 6. It was the fast day, and I was grieved to see others so wicked when God's hand was so heavy upon the nation, and thought it a signe of grace to be vexed and concerned at the provocations of others; by this I did not delight in the workers of iniquity, but could weep at the not keeping of God's lawe which others were guilty in. On such occasions of humiliation my heart would be much let out, and after that, or any other performances, my soule would be sad for a while, and I used to be in a serious frame as having somthing sticking upon mee, or that I had done no better, or could gett my heart no humbler, or from a sense of what I had said or heard; wheras

108/1665

others used to be cheerfull just after duties, it may be because they relied more upon God for hearing and answering the requests putt up to him.

I remember at the colledge and since I used to be seveer against sin, and the workers of iniquity; I was full of zeale so as to desire all were good, and I could scarce indure to see any sin, or offend God; and this was reckoned as a fault in mee by some, but I thought it a duty, and desire to continue in the hatred of all sin.

September 19. I remember at my first coming to Chippenham I spake fool-ishly of my father, and told some weaknesses, which was but a defiling the nest, so that now I am sorry for it; I was young, and inconsiderate, not minding to whom I spoke, in so much that some things have bin made worse by the repetition of tatlers. Mr Benton,[122] a minister and my kinsman, told mee faithfully of it, and so I left it, though still I am prone to it, I know not out of what humour, of talking of such follies.

I distrust my owne knowledge the older I grow; and thinke I doe not under-stand many things now, which some yeares since I thought I had, but that was through confidence, and an overweening conceit of my parts, and knowledge, a vice which young men are prone to; but now I thinke my selfe shallow in many things, and my parts not so quick and good as others and my selfe have thought; the Lord grant that by this meanes I may see my selfe a foole in order to my being wise to salvation! as the Apostle saith.[123]

September 21. Mr William Gerard, who was uncle to Sir Francis[124] and lived with us, departed this life; I saw him give up the ghost, and it much affected mee; I was sorry that I had minded him no more of his soule's health whilst he was in health and strength, for I found in his sicknes he was shy of looking back into his life past as I exhorted him; I prayed for him, as he bad mee when I went into my closet, though not with him for he was for the service chiefly and did not desire I should pray with him; I hope God heard mee, and pardoned his

---

122 Possibly John Benton, rector of Great Dunham, Norf., 1660, deprived and reinstated in 1663; or, Thomas Benton, ejected from Stratton St Michael, Norf., 1662, and later a Congregationalist minister at Wattisfield, Suffolk, *Al. Cantab.*
123 See 1 Corinthians 3:18.
124 William Russell, 1st baronet, had married Gerard's sister, Elizabeth, as his second wife.

sinns; the Lord grant I may make a good use of this providence, and know that I am but dust!

109/1665

And I desired that I might make a good use of it, and number my dayes so as to apply my heart to wisdome; and that whilst living I might lay it to heart, when some I saw careles that night!

September 29. I was much plagued with envy, and was sorry at the prosperity of wicked men, and at that favour which flattery (to which I alwaies had an hatred) brought to some; but from morality I learned that if I knew how dearly it cost them as to soule and body, I would not envy them; and from scripture I found that 'twas a worke of the flesh, Galatians 5:21, and that they were sett in slippery places, Psalm 73, and this somthing quieted mee, yea I could reason my selfe into a good frame at any time, especially if I joyned prayer to all this. I had a contention with one in the house, and it hapned to be my course, in reading the scripture, to read Psalm 131 and Psalm 133, where I was convinced of the happines of a lowly mind (for only through pride came contention) and of dwelling together in unity; therfore I declared to the party my hearty forgivenes and that I laid aside all malice, etc.

About the beginning of October the spirituall court had a visitation, but by God's good providence and my care nothing was objected against, or enquired of mee; only I certified them that we had a sacrament. I gave the apparitour some money towards his feast,[125] and he said he would warrant mee that no hurt should come; I would not let him tell a lie for mee, as he would have done (such officers they have) but told him I went to see my father upon the same day, for I heard that the towne where he lived was infected and knew not but he was sick (and heer I told him true), but when I was called for, he confidently told the archdeacon I was gone to see my father who had the plague; which putt a stopp to all the rest. And thus God, out of evill, brought forth good to mee.

October 6. I preached about the forming Christ in the soule, and found some signes of the new creature in my selfe; I thought that the generall bent and inclination of my heart was changed from what it was; and that I was grieved and vexed at the ill nature which I found in my selfe, that I was sorry I was no better, and did strive against sin more and more, though as to the universall and equall hatred of all sin (great and small) I was not so cleare; God grant mee more of thees signes! Amen!

October 15. Mrs Bridgman, an experienced Christian and one that lived at Halsted and was my father's constant hearer, came

110/1665

to Exening to her son's house; they having no sermon in the afternoon, she came to Snailewell, and enquiring where there was a sermon her friend told her of mee; so they both came, and it pleased God that, as she told mee afterwards,

---

[125] On occasions, the clergy attending a visitation might convene afterwards for dinner to discuss some theological or other issue, and it is perhaps this practice to which Archer refers. See Patrick Collinson, *The Religion of Protestants* (Oxford, 1982), 123–4.

my sermon suited her condition; she was troubled at the small degrees of grace that were in her, and I spoke thees words which I had not written (that God's providence might be seen) viz. that a small piece of money, if it had the King's stampe, was as currant as the greatest; and so a little grace might support if it had but God's stampe on it. From hence she took comfort, and this was some incouragement to mee; as also she told mee that when I was a child (for she knew mee all along), many good things would come from mee to the wonder and astonishment of others; the Lord grant that I may grow in grace more and more!

October 31. I carried my selfe foolishly in my acquaintance with one in the house who was a gentle woman of a very cheerfull disposition and so, being sad somtimes, I used to keep her company; though then I saw not so much by her, yet since I thinke she is of a light carriage, and wantonly given, which is all I can say. Some words of mine were overheard, which were foolish enough, and told to some at Spinney who reproved mee, and told mee my danger, and that they knew more of her then I did, or would believe; I thanked them, and took it well, and resolved better, and owned God for the discovery of this. Yet I must confesse, after this warning, I was too farre drawne away by her temptations and allurements, and yet I alwaies guarded my selfe; and saw all the while the subtleties she and her actions discovered, and had a curiosity to let her alone, and see what she drove at, because I could governe my selfe, by God's grace, in the secretest place, and the fittest opportunities that were offered by her.

There was a talke of our marrying, but we both declared openly against that, and that all our kindnes was but friendship; she was an handsome widow, yet poor though her grandfather was a knight but had spent most, and some of my friends thought she had a designe upon mee, because I was heir to some estate, but I believe it not. I saw cleerly through her plotts and contrivances (so that I have bought witt by the meanes) but did not foresee the evill consequences of it in respect of religion, and

111/1665

my selfe, for such familiarity was not fitting for a minister; and they would wonder that one that quitted conformity should give himselfe such liberty; yea, for ought I know, some fomented the matter that I, and so religion, might be scandalized. After that reproof I spoke of before, I thought of that place, where we are bid to shun meanes and occasions of sin, and to take away occasions from such as sought them; and as I came back I called to mind that place of walking circumspectly, Ephesians 5:15, and resolved by degrees to come of from my familiarity with her, which, although then I did not see the evill of yet, I would doe if it were but to satisfy my best friends.

November 5. Mrs Bridgman came againe, and told mee that she had bin much cast downe in her mind by some things I delivered since (for she came every Lord's day as long as she stayed with her son), but yet was revived by other passages in my last sermon; she, with tears, told mee her soule's case, and how God had dealt with her all along. I wrote to my father of her, and he bid mee encourage her from Psalm 42:5 and that he had knowne many in the darke, yet have had light enough before they died; but I have not seen her since.

November 8. I ended that text 1 Kings 8:38, and found that as those sermons affected mee so they did others, for I spoke home, and was searching; but on the last fast day I spoke against some sinns that reigned in the towne; I advised them to find out their peculiar sinns, and shun the occasions and meanes of them; and wished them to flee evill company, as Proverbs 4:14. I came to my study, and went the same way to worke my selfe, and wish I had done it sooner, and better. And I begged of God to root out of mee that pride, envy, some vices of the tongue, vaine and evill thoughts, frothy unsavoury discourse, unseemly carriage which I had bin, and was too much guilty of. I took up a resolution against thees sinns which had caused the gospell to be blasphemed by some, and endeavoured to be more a patterne of good workes; and God grant that I may be a burning and shining light!

November 26. A chiefe man in the towne, who had made a profession of religion, was become a common drunkard; upon a Lord's day, whilst the sermon, perhaps, was fresh in his memory, I went and (after prayer for a blessing) reproved him in a mild and loving way for it, owning what was good in him, and what was of another nature in mee, yea the seeds of that sin too etc., and he took it well, desired I would pray for him,

112/1665

and promised I should see an amendment in him; but I feare he is now rather worse; however my prayers shall returne into mine \owne bosome/,[126] and I have peace in doing my duty.

December 5. After reproof from some of my honest and religious friends at Spinney, I resolved upon a totall quitting my familiarity with that woman mentioned before, only as far as common civility went, and as I was to the rest; and that I might hold to it the better, I made a solemne vow to God to that purpose for a moneth; which, I blesse him, I did not breake. Thus was I, in a great measure, restored; and people had not those occasions to slight mee, or the wayes of God, which, by my heedles behaviour, they took before; for it is usuall to take words etc. in the worst sense, and so they served mee.

December 29. I must owne God's providence in this, that I came to heare of my faults, which I knew not neither observed in my selfe before, in a way of wrath and railing from one that I had obliged formerly; but this startled mee, and I thought God bid them curse, as David said by the ill language of Shimei, 2 Samuel 16:11,12, and hoped he would turne it to good to mee, as indeed he did afterwards. For this was a farther motive to come of from my giving offence, by my words or behaviour, to such as were too apt to take it. God grant that I may leave my faults one way or other, though the reproof be not as it ought to be.

January 1. I complyed with the family, being courted by considerable persons, to play at cards in the Christmas holidayes; which two yeares before I had refused when asked, and told them though that thing might be done lawfully, as I thought, yet I would not shew an ill example, or encourage others who could not keep those bounds I did. And I wish, from the ill consequences, I had bin as wary now; for it gave offence to some sober people, and I found that the men in

---

[126] Psalm 35:13.

the towne were encouraged by my example (though I played innocently enough, and without those oaths, and passions some would have discovered).

Upon this I wholly left it of, to the anger of some great ones, who, as strangers, were there; they urged, and intreated till I was ashamed, and yet would not yield; Mr Chichely

113/1665

urged mee to play, I said 'twas against the canons, as indeed it is, but he told mee, betwixt jest and earnest, that if I was not as conformable in other things as in that, he would stick upon my skirts, and he would be the bishop's chancellour for once. But I resolved to leave all such things to God's providence. I remember my father would not suffer a card in his house; and when I conformed I would not play, and now I left, it was an offence to some, and thus I resolved against it.

January 18. My obstinate refusall to play at cards gave occasion to some to invent lies, and say I was hired to it, and many other slaunders were raised, which I owned as a punishment of my folly, for I was the occasion of them. That woman with whom I had bin so well acquainted seing my behaviour reserved and strange, betraied mee basely, and told the chiefest things I had said to her (though I never told her any secret, for by her telling mee every trifle done in the house I thought she could keep nothing) and this was for my hurt, for she mixed them with lies and mistakes. It seems, whether employed I cannot tell, she would sift things out of me, and goe and tell her Lady to make sport, but her false dealings shall not be examples to mee, neither will I discover the multitude of tales she told mee, for they would kindle dissentions in house and towne; but doe forgive her.

And so being warned severall wayes I wholly kept from familiarity with her, and wish that I had never bin so foolish as I was in maintaining friendship with one so tatling, and so false; blessed be God who, by his providences, good motions, and the counsell of my friends hath opened my eyes, and awakened mee!

February 11. Chippenham was growne worse now of late then when I came first; as long as the guilt of my late oversights was fresh, I had not the heart to reprove them, but now I had reformed my selfe, I took upon mee, after a desire of God's blessing, to endeavour an amendment in the towne; from Jeremiah 13: last, I expostulated with them, and asked when it would once be that they would reforme their alehouses, profaning the Sabbath, and other vices I had seen in the midst of them! neither did I value the being made the song of the drunkard, 'twas David's case, and blessed be God that sermon made an alteration; it was

114/1665

taken well, and it so affected the officers (to whom I spoke in a more especiall manner) that they consulted, of their own accord, together how to redresse thees things; and presently went with mee, and we looked that no children played, and I went to search the alehouses, and frighted them with threatning severly to execute the law against them etc. Thus after a promise from all of them that they would be strict heerafter in their offices I dismissed them; and hope that the whole towne will grow better, for they were \come/ to an height of profanenes, by the ill examples of some at the Hall, and of those that came, somtimes, as strangers thither. I prayed for the cleansing of towne and house, and my owne heart, and God grant that I may doe, and gett some good amongst them! I intend, when I have a fitt season, to tell Sir John of the abuses he hath suffered in his house to the scandall of his friends, and the ill example of others whom I cannot tell of their drunkennes, but they reflect upon him, and what is done, and suffered in his house. I have preached, and witnessed against such things, and they have bin the worse; so I was silent [and] only by my carriage shewed my abhorring their practises; yet I'le try once more with him, for he is sober, only swaied by ill counsellours.

February 19. Having bin to see a neighbouring minister, in my returne I found one of Chippenham going home; the man had bin given to drinking very much, as he thought (for he confessed it to mee) more then any in the towne. I took occasion to speake good things to him by degrees, when behold! of his owne accord he told mee that I had lately said some things in my sermon which cutt him to the heart, and he had wept and mourned, and resolved to reforme his wicked courses; and that he should remember it to his dying day; other things he said of mee which, in modesty, I shall not mention, but only look up to God as the authour of all; I hope the man is in good earnest, and blesse God for such encouragement in my office. The Lord grant that I may be faithfull in admonishing all such as goe astray, if they may obtaine mercy at God's hands! Indeed, because the sin of drunkennes was so rife, I did speake sharply against it, and turned my selfe into all shapes to see if I could reclaime any, and save them from the fire; and told them, from Jeremiah 13:17 of their unwillingnes to hearken to good counsell; the Lord blesse it to all!

115/1665–6

February 27. I went on with my plaine dealing, and told them of their abuses, and how sorry I was for them, and that if yet they would not heare, I would mourne in secret for the pride of their hearts etc. Some that were netled at what I said, took it ill, and would not believe that I was so sorry or could grieve for them as I said 'twas my duty, yet thou knowest, Oh Lord, that it hath bin a griefe and burden to my soule. Thus they scoffed at it, and abused my kindnes, the Lord forgive them! It hath bin the lot of God's word to be a derision daily, Jeremiah 20:8, and others have bin in the same case before mee; the Lord enable mee to performe my duty faithfully, and in meeknes to instruct such as oppose themselves! and cure the hardnes of their hearts! Yet I found some whose hearts were tender, and took all well; the Lord reforme, and purge the towne more and more!

April 20. The woman before mentioned, for base and scurrilous language given to her Lady, was putt away. I was glad of it, and so were my friends; yet, that I might testify I bore her no malice, and that I forgave all, I was civill to her before her departure: 'twas well she went, for such were her insinuations and subtleties that at the last farewell, I was almost overtaken with former faults.

We had now a great family; the Earle of Scarsdale[127] and his lady and children etc. sojourned with us. I feared worse then I found it, for the lord and lady were so sober, and religious (as far as is seen usually in the nobility) that the family was governed better then before. I desire God to make mee the more watchfull, by how much the more temptations encrease; and the Lord doe this for Christ's sake!

April 30. We had a visitation at Newmarket; but God ordered it so that, though I was before the arch deacon, and was questioned about some things yet nothing was done against mee, and the Dr knew not that I had not read service etc., blessed be God!

116/1666

May 2. I had thoughts of marrying one neer at hand; and after asking counsell of God, I went over to my father, who wished mee to enquire what she was likely to have, which I did; and he did not seem against it, but, when I went over againe to see him, gave mee farther instructions. But he objected that there was not portion answerable to his estate, and putt a stopp to it, when I was too far gone in affection.

May 6. I began seriously to read Dr Preston's sermons of faith; and that I might understand them the better, and that they might be fixed in my memory, I preached upon Ephesians 2:8 and made use of many of his notions. So for his sermons of effectuall faith I had that text, 2 James: last, and for his sermons of love[128] I preached upon Luke 7:47, where many things were coincident. I blesse God I found good by them.

August 26. By reading of Bishop Usher's *Body of Divinity*,[129] I was convinced of my sinning against the commandments of God in many cases, which before I had taken no notice of; as by Mr Dod's book I found I had failed in my duty to my father.[130] I found that still the thoughts of my heart were evill; and when will the deliverer come, and free mee from this body of sin? I begg of thee, my God, not only a sight of sin, which will bring sorrow, but power against it! Amen!

September 2. The city of London was burnt downe, which struck mee with amazement; and all good and bad, were much concerned at it.

September 4. I heard of it, which was the monethly fast; and preaching upon Jeremiah 4:18, I emproved it what I could to worke upon the people's affections.

October 10. We had a fast for the fire, and I preacht upon Amos 4:11, endeavouring to worke my own soule, and the hearts of others to a submission to God, and a seeking his face, and imploring his helpe that we might, in this day of our distresse, prepare to meet our God by true repentance, Amen.

---

127 Nicholas Leke, 2nd Earl of Scarsdale. He was a Parliamentarian in the Civil Wars; married Frances, 3rd daughter of Robert, 2nd Earl of Warwick.

128 John Preston, *Five Sermons on the Divine Love* (1640).

129 James Ussher, *A Body of Divinitie* (1645).

130 Probably refers to John Dod and Robert Cleaver, *A Godly Form of Household Government, for the Ordering of Private Families* (1598).

117/1666–7

January 13. Upon occasion of Sir John Russell's selling the estate, and breaking up house, without taking any care of mee, as to those accommodations I had with him, I went to the vicaridge, and lived with my cozin Goodwin (who still read for mee), and because I was in danger of caring too much for a subsistence, I chose that Philipians 4:6 for my owne satisfaction; and that as many as were concerned might reape benefitt. The Lord grant that desired effect both to them, and my selfe! Amen

February 5. Coming from Spinney, upon an hired horse, I was throwne to the ground, and the horse rolled some part of his body upon mee, yet God's care was such that I gott no hurt, blessed be my father who delivers from danger! I wish his goodnes to his creatures, and mee, may affect mee!

April 17. Sir John Russell's estate could not be sold, and he was to come and live at Chippenham againe, but I took my leave of them from that place, Ephesians 6: last. I was afraid of engaging at that house where would be more danger then before, for great persons were to boord in the family which I was not free to engage among. When I was with my father April 1, I found him unsatisfied as to what I had done, for he said hearing service was the same with reading it; and he would have mee conforme more or lesse, to be hott or cold, to doe more or to be altogether as he was, as to his private opinions. This putt mee to a stand: and farther he would not maintayne, or allow mee in part, except I lived with him, which I could not doe, for that solitary life with his deep melancholy would kill mee; or neer him I know not where, which would putt mee out of the ministry, and draw mee from her upon whom (for many reasons) my heart was sett.

There were severall fires in the city since, most of which were thought to be by Popish treachery; as the 1st was proved to be by the witnes of a French man who was executed for it.[131] The King upon that occasion, sett out a proclamation against priests, and recusants, but it did signify little, etc.

118/1667

From the beginning of Aprill I preached at Spinny; they would have mee live there, and teach 2 sons, but that required more time then I could spare. I went every week from Chippenham, and the people were not offended at my not reading service; I expounded that creed etc., and preached twice which pleased them as well. I found them attentive; and strangers came to heare, but I feared least they should tell etc. to my hurt. God grant that some good may be done by all this!

July 20. I had given my heart too much liberty in thinking; my tongue in speaking, and so for sinfull actions; yet my mind was so clouded, that I knew not whether they were so or not; they might be a shame among men (as some things are which wee question not) but I could not see into the evill of them; I thought the harmles intention qualified, and thought that the same things might be done lawfully by one, and not by another; according as the principle

---

[131] The man was Robert Hubert, a French watch-maker, who was later hanged. See Ronald Hutton, *The Restoration* (Oxford, 1985), 249–50.

of action was good or evill. Thus did I flatter my selfe and disputed my selfe into folly; and did many things after some kind of deliberation, and the suggestions of a better spirit then my owne; at last I resolved to abstaine from such dubious actions, (though now I cannot but call them sinfull) for feare religion should suffer on my behalfe. I solemnly acknowledged my faults to God, and confessed how justly he might bring to light enough to shame mee; yet I begged he would not, for feare religion should suffer.

Upon this I heard a sermon, from one that I thought could not have spoken so home; but God directed it. And this, and my owne meditation made mee know that the profession of religion and making provision for the flesh 'εις επιθυμιας [132] (which are desires of the soule, and bad enough before they are brought into act) were inconsistent. I gott alone, and thought of it; and was indeed ashamed of what I had done, and resolved better; though I know my weaknes to performe, yet be pleased, oh God, to strengthen mee with might. Amen.

119/1667

September 29. I went to my father, and found that he was come of from that severity which he had shewed formerly in respect of her that I loved. He gave way that I might take a living, considering that I had no other way to live but by the ministry, and promised that I should fare the worse neither in his love, nor in his estate. He told mee also that my want of a place, and subsistence, was the only reason that he with held his consent; and plainly intimated that could I gett a place, I might marry, for which I thanked him.

November 13. I agreed with the patron of a living, as far as one may trust another, that I might supply the cure, and have the next avoydance. And, by reason that my mistress had a quartane ague ever since August last, and her friends feared it might kill her, shewing that it came from melancholy concerning my father's harshnes etc., and because many said that marrying would cure her (for we had tried all meanes), I married her November 13. Wednesday, being her sick day. I found my mind satisfied, and hope that my father will forgive my pitching upon the day etc., though, I believe, he thought mee married afore.

November 25. My father was angry that we imputed the ague to his severity; and wrote mee a chiding letter which grieved mee. I confessed all my disobedience to God and him, desiring solemnly pardon from both; and earnestly desired that God would not avenge thees things of mee in the same kind, which I much feared. Lord thou knowest that now I resolve upon more obedience to him! and worke my soule to it I pray thee! Amen.

120/1667

December 1. The gentleman, with whom I treated fell of from his promise; he said he could have more for the next avoydance then he had asked of mee; and when I urged his promise that I should have it before any else, he plainly said,

---

[132] *'Εις επιθυμιας*. The phrase occurs in Romans 13:14 with the sense of 'in order to fulfil [the lusts of the flesh]'.

[133] Henry O'Brien (1621–91), 7th Earl of Thomond and Governor of Clare, *DNB*.

to salve all, that his wife would not lett him sell it. Yet all men spoke as if he had sold it to one that served the cure; who went away, as is said, because 'twas mortgaged before for debt, and he could not gett the money ready soon enough. And thus he that supplanted mee was overreacht etc.

December 9. My Lord Thomond[133] took a liking to my preaching at Chipnam now and then; and wrote to Dr Fuller,[134] his chaplaine, who was lately made bishop of Lincolne, an effectuall letter on my behalfe; I went to London, and delivered it; the bishop wrote to my lord, by mee, that he would prefer mee, when he had gratified some friends, to whom he was engaged before my lord wrote, and took directions of mee how to write to mee. My Lord Thomond gave mee the letter to keep; and offered to gett any place that should be void within that diocese, and that as soon as I could heare of it. Thus it pleased God to stirre up friends for mee unexpectedly, and I desire to owne his good hand of providence in it.

December 16. My wive's friends kindly invited mee to live with them till I could provide for my selfe. Yet 'twas somwhat burdensome to my spirit; and prayed daily that I might not be infected with some ill examples there. Besides they had no family duties, the sabbath was not kept strictly, so that I purposely absented my selfe least I might gett hurt; and longed for a settlement in which

121/1667

I and my house might serve the Lord. And God was pleased to heare my prayers, and answer them in kind. There fell a living, called Barton Mills in Suffolke, 4 miles from Isleham and Chippenham; I wrote to Sir John Archer[135] my cozin to gett it of my Lord Keeper Bridgman;[136] my letter miscarried, and 'twas given to a friend of mine, chaplaine to my Lord Scarsdale. I offered to serve the cure for him; he told mee he had employed another, and so it rested. I came downe from London with him, and went to heare him the first time; we understood that the towne would by no means like his curate, so that then he offered mee to preach there till Easter, which I was very glad of, and began on December 22, whilst he was there.

January 30th. I had a letter that I might goe and live there, and that I should have halfe a yeare's warning. I found the people very loving, and far more complying with plaine and searching preaching then I thought etc. I expected oppositions enough (for they are high conformists, and Royalists) but find them now moderate, far beyond what I expected. The Lord give free course to his word which I have, or shall preach among them. I began to informe them, from Joshua 24:19 what religion, and God's service was, and how mistaken they were in laying their stresse on the forme etc., and thought that it would not

---

[134] William Fuller, D.D. (1608–75), who suffered greatly in the Civil War for his loyalty to King Charles I; dean of St Patricks, Dublin; bishop of Lincoln, 1667–75; DNB.

[135] Sir John Archer (1598–1682), of Theydon Bois, Essex, judge of the Common Pleas, 1663–72 when, for unclear reasons, his services were suspended by the Crown, E. Foss, Biographical Dictionary of the Judges of England (London, 1870), 14–15.

[136] Sir Orlando Bridgeman, Lord Keeper of the Great Seal, 1667–72, and Lord Chief Justice of the Common Pleas, 1660–8, died 1674, DNB.

have gone downe; but they were very attentive, and serious, and loved mee the better for [*deletion*] it.

February 9. I began to expound largely on afternoons; for Mr Lylliman[137] (whose the living was) with the advice \of Mr Warren/[138] would not lett mee serve there, except I would promise not to preach on afternoons; because 'twas unusuall; and 'twould be expected from him etc. They were pleased with the paines I took with their children, and were diligent in learning them the Catechisme. The Lord give his blessing! Amen.

122/1667

February 10. By marriage all my former youthfull desires were cured; and extravagant thoughts ceased. I found it a remedy; but cares came on mee, yet without distraction. I found my wife perfectly devoted to please mee; and I blesse God for giving mee one with a meek and quiet spirit; and well disposed and apt to take in the best things. I found she was patient under her sicknes, and willing to heare any instruction from mee. The Lord continue that which is good in her, and teach her more! and let us both drawe in Christ's yoke till death. Amen.

February 24. I went to settle at Barton; and I found welcome, and content enough. I began to read the scriptures, and pray daily in the house, and found my wife very complying with it. I wrote my father word of my marrying, and intentions to settle; and he was very angry, and threatned to reward mee in deeds; I besought God daily to worke his heart, and open his hand to mee in a way of maintenance; and to dispose my soule to obedience, so as to make amends for all my former disobedience; and my burden was heavy; the Lord speake peace, and make up the breach!

March 23. I went to my father; for he had invited mee, and, when through guilt I could not bring my heart to goe, he wrote mee word that except I came he would write no more. God answered my prayers in kind, for his heart was turned to mee so as to give mee an estate, and forgive mee the wrong I had done him; and, I know not how, my heart was enclined to love, and obey him.

123/1668

I found my heart inlarged to praise God, in that, when I despaired of helpe, he should bring things about to my content; so that I desire to blesse God; and to rely on his experienced goodnes still! I engaged at the sacrament March 22, being Easter, to behave my selfe obediently. The Lord continue in mee such an humble frame of spirit, Amen!

April 22. I was at my wive's father's house, and was taken with a tertian ague; they took a great care of mee. I know not how it came about; for I designed it not; in my 1st fitt I spoke much to my wife concerning religion, heaven, the way thither, and many passages concerning my selfe, and my former life, and what comfort I now found, and what joy I should have in case God should take

---

137 John Lillyman, rector of Barton Mills, 1667–9, *Al. Cantab.*, I, 3, 85.
138 Erasmus Warren, rector of Worlington, Suff., 1666–1718; rector of Freckenham, 1672; son of George, formerly vicar of Chippenham, Cambs., 1642–50; *Al. Cantab.*

mee away. I never spoke so seriously before, and hope that God putt it into my heart, for the good of us both, etc.

May 2. After 5 fitts, the ague left mee. It was God's time, and so best; I could have endured it no longer without strength more then ordinary. I prayed God to remove his chastning, and purify mee by this, and he healed mee! blessed be his name! I will praise my God as long as I live!

September 7. My wife and I went to see my father, and found extraordinary kind usage, beyond my expectation; the times were hard, and the tenant to the land that my father gave mee was not able to pay the rent. And so at Michaelmas I took upon mee to teach the towne boyes, and one boorder I had; endeavouring industriously to make a shift to live in the world.

October 29. An old professour at Chipnam died; and, as I had promised him, I went and preached at his funerall from Job 3:17, and 'twas confirmation to mee in my way that so good a man should hold out so comfortably to the last, and die in peace.

124/[1668]

October 30. It was some comfort to mee in my ministry that God was pleased to doe good to the soule of a poor maid who had bin under great temptations to kill her selfe etc., so that she was brought very low in strength, and ready to die; and was judged out of her witts by some; the devil made her believe that she should be so 30 yeares (this was 1647) yet God kept her up; but of late she was at a losse againe, and violently tempted, and God comforted her through the ministry of the word. The Lord convert, and confirme more and more! and give mee that wisdome wherby I may winne soules!

February 1. I went to see my father, and 'twas fully set upon my heart to aske him forgivenes for all my disobedience. And Satan hindred mee oft; but one morning I went into his study, and with teares confessed what I had done, and how unsatisfied I was at my selfe, constantly promising to be so to him no more. And 'twas comfortable to mee to find that I had done what he had required of mee, which he had expressed in a letter, not sent (for my coming prevented it) but then given to mee. The Lord direct his providences for my good; and blessed be that providence that took away all suspicion of my humbling my selfe dissemblingly, which my father had charged mee withall! I wish the same God may provide! Amen.

1669

My wife had not bin with child for halfe a yeare after our marriage; for till about June she had somthing of her ague. But it pleased God she was delivered of a lusty girle, April 3 at 6 at night, after 6 houres paines. I prayed for a boy, but I wrote my father word I would expound God's denying mee, as if it were to take away feare of such a disobedient child as I was to him, and not to requite mee as I had served him, for I considered girles are not so dangerous.

125/[1669]

The Lord be praysed for this love, which God lendeth mee! I desire it may \be/ a vessell of mercy, and in covenant, and friendship with the God of my fathers! Amen, Amen!

April 6. God sent mee a 2d deliverance, which was by delivering us all from a fire in our house, yea in the roome where my wife lay in. We had smelt smoake on the Saterday, when the beame, under the chimny, kindled; and on Munday too, but we thought the wind made the roome smoake. But on Tuesday at 3 in the morning the nurse putt out the candle, or else had not seen the flame breake out under the hangings by the side of the chimny. Feare and surprise made mee doe more then I could have endured otherwise; I went barefoot, in my shirt for water in the yard, and, I blesse my God, I quenched the flames; yet when neighbours were called, which came in abundance, we saw the great beame all on fire, which we beat downe into cinders into a chimny under it; about a yard of it was burnt in sunder, and the boords burnt arch wise, yet were not the reeds toucht etc., blessed be God, who, in that extremity saved my wife, who was not able to helpe her selfe! and the child of her wombe! We desire never to forget this wonder of mercy. Amen.

November 30. At Chippenham was a young man who came from London to change aire; he had a dropsy so dangerously that he was given over by all. His friends sent for mee to pray with him, and instruct him, as desirous to have seen some good signes of grace before his death. He had bin of a sober conversation, but of very few words, and very loath to expresse his mind. I told him (after I had privately begged God's blessing) what I thought of man's nature since the fall etc., what necessity there was of a remedy; that only Christ was a Saviour, and faith the way to Christ, and to salvation, and other things.

126/1669

He was willing I should pray with him; but was unwilling to speake or answere to questions I thought fitt to putt to him dying. For that time I went away; the same day I was sent for againe (though I could not goe) for he, after my going away, was concerned for his soule etc. and was desirous to speake with mee, and tell mee his mind. Soon after I went, and found him in a good mind; complaining of strange temptations, wheras before all was quiet; very inquisitive about faith, knowledge of God, and other needfull points. In short I found great signes of conversion, and great protestations of love to God, and resolutions of obedience. So he died. This did somwhat confirme mee in the truth and reality of what I believed, and preached; so the Lord grant mee more successe in his service!

My child was very sick, we thought it would have died, but we besought God for it, and he spared it. Upon this I gott a cold that disabled mee from preaching etc. I found that when my strength, and patience were even gone, I had some reviving; and at last I was well. The Lord sanctify every little warning! Amen!

December 1. I found my selfe much better in mind since my reconciliation with my father; my heart was more towards him then formerly, and, when provoked, I never since durst let my heart rise against him as before. So that I hope God hath inclined my soule, after much striving with him for such a frame. I found I lived on God's providence every day, and he sensibly delivered mee out of straits; I followed my worke in the ministry as cheerfully as I could; though I have somtimes bin dejected for want of successe, though I knew that was God's.

127/1669–70

February 7. Mr Lillyman, unknowne to mee, exchanged his living for one in Nottinghamshire,[139] and so was I left in the lurch. He had given out that I should doe every thing as if 'twere mine, as it might be when he resigned etc., but he broke word, and articles with mee; and took no order that I should have 6 months warning etc., besides his hard usage of mee in my bargaine etc., but I pray God forgive him.

March 31. On Maunday Thursday my child died at 10 of the clock in the forenoon, in it's mother's lap. It never outgrew it's sicknes in November, when two teeth came; it looked fresh and fat in the face, but it wasted in the body exceedingly. The continuall cheerlines made us thinke 'twould recover, but sure it had a consumption in the lungs (as my father Peachy said) of which, with hard breeding teeth, it died. A fortnight before, 'twas taken with vomiting fitts, which would make it ready to die; and that was our beginning of sorrow.

Oh what griefe was it to mee to heare it groane, to see it's sprightly eyes turne to mee for helpe in vaine! 'twas as pretty, and as knowing a child as they had ever seen that came to see it! but it's beuty is laid in the dust (in the north isle of Isleham church, at the end of it's grandmother's seat). I have resigned to God, I thinke, willingly; though I would have given any thing for it's life. Our griefe was great, but I was more able to beare it then my deare wife; I hope this losse hath done us good! God saw we were unsettled, and so took our babe to settle with himselfe! He saw we loved it too well, and took it away; God knew how much time it stole from mee, which I ought better to have spent, and so hath warned mee of my duty! I thinke of my untimely marriage; and feare my wive's relicks of the ague laid that foundation of that fatall consumption!

128/1670

The Lord pardon former iniquityes for Christ's sake! and send mee a child, who may be Jedidiah![140] and send mee strong consolation! his comforts I hope I will possesse, and delight my soule! Amen!

In the morning I prayed for the pardon of it's originall sin with many teares, and begged it's life, if God pleased, or that God would ridd it out of it's paine, and so he did, blessed be his name!

April 3. On the day when 'twas borne last yeare, Easter fell; I had made a sermon of Abraham's offering his only son etc.,[141] little thinking (as I told my neighbours) how neerly it concerned mee. Reading Exodus 12 I could not refraine teares at the words of v.30.[142] But by degrees I hope to weare of my sorrow; though it be hard, considering how many things we daily see that bring her to mind. The Lord be our comforter, and make up our losse! Amen.

April 23. I had a letter from Sudbury, whither I had bin invited the last

---

[139] He moved to Gamston, Notts., *Al. Cantab.*

[140] The reference to Jedidiah is 2 Samuel 12:25. The name literally means 'beloved of the Lord'.

[141] Abraham's offering of Isaac is recorded in Genesis 22.

[142] Exodus 12:30 reads: 'So Pharaoh rose in the night, he all his servants, and all the Egyptians; and there was a great cry in Egypt, for there was not a house where there was not one dead.'

November, that Mrs Burrell was dead, and her husband,[143] newly chosen, would leave them. I slip't my season, and my cozin Grey helped him thither, who wisht he had knowne my mind sooner: and now God seemed to make way, he offered mee his assistance. I was chosen, after Mr Burrell's patron, upon much importunity by the towne, and himselfe, would not yield he should hold his living, and goe thither (for his wive's death was not pleaded as before, but if his patron would give way; and his obstinate deniall seemed a 2d providence for mee), and upon May day I began.

There were 3 sorts in the towne; the conformists had the government; and those I gained, but they could doe no more then others, because it went by popular vote: the middle sort I did not doubt of; and the Non-Conformists, who were rich and of great sway, I was advised not to seek to, for that it would hinder mee; and privately the chiefe promised mee his assistance. I found my hearers encreased daily, and had encouragement etc.,

129/1670

only they would have mee come till Midsummer upon tryall. This I found inconvenient, for 'twas 20 miles from Barton, and 'twould have bin too much forwardnes to goe thither with my wife: I found the Non-Conformists, who cared not to have a man setled, least their meetings should be interrupted, to be cold towards mee; and the chiefe man, who had recommended mee to the mayour the last yeare, I believe took it ill (being proud, and rich) that I had not sought to him. He, it seems, filled the mayour with notions that my voice was not loud enough, that I was not so fitt for that place (though they could object nothing as to preaching, or conversation, as they told mee). The mayour was a shallow, flexible man; and told mee this as from the other party (as I found) yet wishing mee to continue etc. But what they pretended, I found reall: that is, though I spoke loud enough for that great church, yet it spent mee too much, and would soon have killed mee.

Upon this, and the length of the way, and the divisions, and sects, that there were in that towne etc., I desired a meeting of the 2 parishes after sermon;[144] and the mayour told them I would come no more. This made some of the chiefe say they should not have a setled minister, till the maintenance was setled, for it was a voluntary, uncertaine contribution, and they engaged from quarter to quarter. Thus I came away; and they have sent to Mr Burrell (who pleased them well, so that 'twas a disadvantage to mee, who could not cant, as they loved, and would not humour them, by dissembling etc.). He is to come at Michaelmas, when he resigneth his living. I hope, this providence is for my good; I am sure 'tis for my health, and the more enabling mee to hold out in the ministry.

May 16. The bishop of Lincolne had sent mee word that he would give mee a living void then; so I went to London but 'twas somwhat too late, for he had given it away, 'twas Grantam. But he gave mee 2 sequestrations of vicaridges by

---

[143] Christopher Burrell, rector of All Saints, Sudbury, and afterwards rector of Tivetshall, 1672–1700, *Al. Cantab.*

[144] All Saints and St Gregory's, Sudbury.

Humber, which they said were worth £100 per annum or neer it. I took a curate with mee, and went that great

130/1670

journey of 100 miles. I found both places not worth above halfe what was given out: and so I left that young man to make what he could, and I would but have my charges, which the bishop putt mee to, answered. What the issue will be I know not; only I find that men of high degree are vanity. \I lost my charges too./

June 24. The time was come when the new minister came to Barton, and I went to my wive's friends. Sir John Russell died in March last, and the stock, and the goods were sold: upon this I resolved to settle at Chipnam, now there would be no such discouragements as formerly. I came July 12, the executour, Mr Cromwell,[145] having promised to allow mee as far as the estate would goe, in stead of boord etc. which I used to have: I wish he performe it as well, thus by taking boorders etc., I make good shift to live.

September 2. My father had a designe to live at London as soon as the house could be sold at Dedham. On Tuesday August 15, he was taken with an ague. That day, 10 yeare since, he had his sicknes at Stratford. On the Lords day before, he preached to a company of Mr Asty's (who died some yeares since)[146] out of Matthew 11:28 for 2 houres, and beyond his strength. Others observed he was very much enlarged, and he owned he had not bin so for many yeares. 'Twas his last sermon, and best: for his ague turned to a double tertian, and he was feaverrish too; on Friday the doctor came and said he was a spent man, and had bin hatch't up thees 30 yeares. Thus he continued rising every day; but on Wednesday, August 24 he was forced to goe to bed. Being helped up by my mother and others, and sitting up in a chaire; he on the sodaine sunk downe in a swoone; but the shrieks of my mother fetch't him againe, and he said 'I am better then I was.' They gott him to bed, and so he lay in no paine, very silent, taking no notice of any one; only

131/1670

when one desired to pray with him, he said 'with all my heart.' My mother ask't him if he thought he should recover, and he said 'what the Lord please'; and againe he said 'why dost aske mee this question?' noting his resigning himselfe to God. He was overheard often to say 'Amen', 'twas supposed the conclusion of prayer: thus about 3 a clock on the Thursday morning he breathed his righteous soule out to God, without the least noise or paine, as could be discerned by my cozin John Archer who was only present; only he shutt his teeth together so as to be heard.

He declared nothing on his death bed, as not in the least looking to die; and he used to be silent in sicknes, and to say 'Let the life shew what the man is';[147]

---

[145] Henry Cromwell was named as an executor. See CRO, R55/7/20/4, will of Sir John Russell (1670).

[146] Robert Asty, Congregationalist and rector of Stratford St Mary, Suffolk; died in 1667, *Cal. Rev.*, 18.

[147] *Cf.* Matthew 7:20.

as indeed his holy, strict, upright life did convince all that he was an eminent servant of God. I was sent for that day, and the messenger came to me at 3 in the afternoon; so I sett out, and ridd as long as I could, and gatt thither next morning. I did not thinke it would have so grieved mee; at the newes, 1st I was taken giddy etc. When I came to my mother I was so feeble I could not hold a glasse without spilling, by a strange kind of surprise.

He used to talke of 63 when he must look to himselfe, but he died at the 61st yeare, and almost 2 monthes, having bin borne July 9 1609. He had bin married to this wife above 9 yeares, and reckoned to live as many yeares; but God took him when he was fully ripe, and had served the worke of his generation faithfully. The Lord grant I may, by the sodainnes of his death, prepare every day, and carry my life in my hands, as he did, and then no death can come on the sodaine to those that are prepared. A non conformist should have preached, and there was many good ministers, 4 of which carried him, to wait on the funerall etc., but Mr Shaftoe of Dedham, though money was offered him, would not give way to it.

132/1670

August 28. I went with my mother to a meeting, where my father used to preach: Mr Asty[148] preached from that text 2 Samuel 3:2 last, and spoke much in commendation of my father, and their losse.

August 29. I found my mother had provided for the funerall; I knew on the Monday that by will she was made sole executrix. The 17 of June 1669, he went to Colchester, and Mr Lucas made his will; for he had borrowed about £100 of my mother, and Mr Angier;[149] and having no personall estate considerable, he made a will to secure them of their money. But the will is so strange that it made a great noise to his prejudice, and her's; all pitying mee.

All was pardoned mee over and over; he said I should fare ne're the worse in his love, or estate, see p.119.[150] Yet hath he named a trustee, my mother's 2d son, now apprentise at London, to take the rents of his estate (all but what was mine before) and emprove them for my children, and pay the money to 4 of them (though none yet borne) at 21 yeares of age. If I have none, or they die under age, all goeth to my heir at law; so that it never cometh to mee, neither is there allowance for education of my children when borne. In the meane time my mother hath his best farme for life;[151] and is to pay his debts, that is, what he ought her, and funerall charges: and then her son enters upon his office.

That he should entaile his estate was reasonable. That my children should have it at age, I should not have wondred at, if I had had it for their education; for I am willing to beare his anger for marrying one of a small portion (yet he

---

[148] This cannot be Robert Asty, mentioned above, who had died three years before.

[149] Probably Samuel Angier, who was born at Dedham in 1639 and was the nephew of the Lancashire diarist John Angier of Denton, *Cal. Rev.*, 12.

[150] See entry for 29 September, 1667.

[151] It seems that this was Pooles in Fordham and West Bergholt, Essex, since he is later forced to buy it from her. See below, p. 222. Also the lands bequeathed in the will of Isaac Archer (1700), PRO, PROB 11 fol. 110. See Appendix 2.

could take this woman with nothing, and leave her £30 a yeare etc.) and I am willing to expound his will

133/1670

thus: viz. he buried 4 children, and so (having given mee at least a 5th part of his estate) he bequeathed what should have bin their's to 4 of mine, though one being dead, the next is to have 2 parts. Blessed be God for what I have! and that my children are provided for! I have deserved this from him, who might doe what he would, with his owne, and much more from God, whose hand I see in it! I hope I shall mind eternity the more for my disappointments heer! and use this as physick in regard of my soule's health.

But I thinke, to give it out of my hands, and leave it to one that is not responsible etc. was very hard. I suppose, and hope my mother did not sett him against mee; but surely my losse is her gaine, and 'twas an occasion of ingratiating her selfe by my absence; and the distast which had 3 yeares agoe bin betwixt us. I believe (as she saith) she pleaded for mee; but 2 yeares since she did mee some ill turnes, so as then my father bid mee have nothing to doe with her, <child> or her children for etc.

I believe the reason of all was a jealousy least my wive's friends should ever be the better for what he had; and he would say they gaped for his estate, but he would make it sure etc., and much to that purpose which I will not remember. As for my wife her carriage was so sweet to him, that he shewed all signes of love to her by words, and gifts; she did not deserve to be thus dealt by. Her friends he never saw, nor by writing was ever provoked; only because her father would not settle £10 per annum (which is her portion) for his £16 a yeare (7 pound of which was mine before) which was all he would give, he took such a distast that he not only thought, but said they would cheat mee, and held of upon designe, gaping for his dying etc., and so he never forgat it to his last day, etc.

I confesse my father in law is slow in his owne busines, and failed of his promise to come and treat; and my father being naturally mistrustfull took it worse then 'twas meant; for I can witnesse he offered to settle it immediately, if my father would give £20 per annum for joynture, and he refused. Neither doe I thinke but he will be just, as having a report for honesty, and square dealing of all that know him. I hope my father died in charity, but the world would thinke this revenge. Thus I, and my

134/1670

wife are not like to enjoy what my father was so long gathering: and what a motive to disobedience 'tis to children to thinke they have no dependence on their parents is easy to foresee [sic]. My uncles were much vexed at it, but can not helpe it, only hope, in the end 'twill worke for good, which God grant for Christ's sake. Amen.

November 6. Having my father's books and writings, I found an old written book of experiences of God to him: in which he confesseth some infirmities which he was guilty of; I knew nothing of it till now. And I find Satan gott the better of him in the same sort of sins, as he did of mee, though I was younger. I desire that as sin abounded in both, so grace may abound in <b> mee, as it did in him since, even to the last. Who would thinke that the same vaine, filthy, lewd thoughts should be in both of us! It may be 'tis more generall, but that men conceale them, and my father wrote downe his thoughts. I have confessed them to God, but I dare not make them knowne. The Lord pardon them, as he hath done to my father! I could not have thought that ever such things had bin in his heart, who even before and then was a gracious, sincere Christian; I did not thinke any had bin so bad that way as my selfe; and thinke so still, for though the same was in him, yet he delighted not in them, but mastered them, which I could, or rather would not, a great while. I hope that I shall, as he, take more heed while I live. Amen.

I was much affected with the godly letters which some friends (as Mr Arthur, Mr Fulham etc.)[152] wrote to him. Surely they spent their time at Cambridge much better then I did! I had no such helpes to watch over my soule, only my father was in that *instar omnium*.[153] There was a savoury spirit then; now 'tis lost in great measure; they were full of Jesus Christ! I live in a place barren of such men. I have that maid p.124[154] living with mee, from whom I find helpe sometimes. I keepe her

135/1670

out of love to my deare saviour, as I hope; and she shewed much faith to forsake all to goe with mee. She feareth God, and I hope God will blesse mee and mine for her sake!

My father wrote till 1668 of affaires betwixt him and mee. And he hath written of my disobedience; but much mistakes in that he was apt to thinke I tooke my wife only to crosse him: God knoweth the contrary. For almost 3 yeares he wrote nothing because God had given mee an obedient frame; and had he lived longer, he would have had more comfort of mee. For God knoweth my heart turned to him. Yet I am still sorry for my 8 yeares dis-obedience, as to conformity, and marriage (though only that it displeased him, not of any choyce, who is a blessing to mee etc.), and could wish all had bin to live over againe. The Lord forgive mee for Christ's sake! and doe not reward mee as I deserve, O my God! Amen.

November 27. My wife growing neerer her time was troubled with feares she should die; and I feared it too. She was much taken up, I saw, with such thoughts, and I was glad, because it was an occasion of seeking God, as I know she did. One morning I gott her to tell mee what troubled her; which was in that she could not remember good things as she desired; and that she thought she grew \worse/, but I thought better. The Lord sanctify my instructions to her, and carry on his good \worke/ in her for Christ's sake. This day she was ill, and her reckoning just out; I wish't it might not distract mee (being the Lord's day) and so she did not cry out till about 8 of clock at night; and at 11 was delivered of a girle, fatter, and stronger, otherwise very like my other. Her paines were sharpe, but short; and she bore them without sicknes (not so as

---

[152] Probably William Fulham who matriculated at Emmanuel College in 1624; could have been William Archer's contemporary at the college, *Al. Cantab.*

[153] *Instar omnium*: the phrase is used to indicate the fact that his father occupied that place of being 'worth all' to him. *Cf.* Cicero, *Brutus*, LI, 191.

[154] See Diary, 30 October, 1668, p. 124.

before) and with great courage. It seems the child came with the face upwards, and did not cry till an houre, and more after 'twas borne.

Thus my heart was full of joy, thinking all over; and praysing God for his mercy: but about 1 of clock my wife began to faint, through an overflow of blood, and was without sensible pulse, or colour; we gave her over, and she took leave of mee (which much concerned mee); the women told mee she would loose all her blood etc. I sent to Isleham for blood stones (tying her fingers in the meane time, and burning feathers),[155]

136/[1670]

but God was better then meanes, who stayed the flow,[156] and she began to revive, and by degrees mended so as we had hopes of her. The Lord grant that both of us may never forget the mercy of God in giving mee her, whom I had given to God, as well as I could. I was sick next morning, which seemed worse then 'twas, and God restored mee soon: his loving kindnes is better then life, my lipps shall praise him.[157]

December 5. Now my Father is dead, and so cannot teach mee by writing; I shall briefly recollect the sume of what passed betwixt us by letters; always acknowledging the good I have gotten by his savoury counsells.

When 1st I went to Cambridge being at a losse as to my soule, and studies etc., I wrote to my father, who wrote his first letter marked on the superscription with 2; and that setled mee somwhat. He took it well that I regarded what my mistress told mee, viz. that my grandfather said at his death (or neer it, because since I understand he died, and none knew it, 'twas so easy; and my father not with him, as was my case etc.) that he had lived to see grace in all his children, having 6 sonns, and 2 daughters. And she said she never knew any of our family, but were godly etc., see letter with 3.[158]

He wished mee not to let those small stirrings of God on my spirit worke of; and hoped a sparke would be a flame. [Letter] 4. He wished mee not to quench the impressions I had on my spirit, least the Lord spake no more. Letter 5. He was going then to Fresenfield[159] where my mother had kinred [sic]. He wrote that 'twould grieve him if those seeming stirrings, and workings towards God etc. should weare of. Letter 6. He was much affected with God's delivering mee from the small poxe; and gave mee excellent counsell. Letter 7. He wish't mee to beware of self confidence, trusting in duties etc., noting the difficulty of true faith, and how easy, and generall, self sowne faith was. He thought faith easy, but when he sett to it, he found it very hard. He repented no charge, if God would but follow those impressions that I had; and noteth what choyce company he had at Cambridge and how taken up he was about soule estate etc., shutt up, dead, perplexed, and made to see that snare of resting on duties, and enlargements etc. which we must disowne etc.,

---

[155] Blood stones were precious stones used as amulets to prevent or stop bleeding.
[156] Cf. Matthew 9:20–2.
[157] Psalm 63:3.
[158] Cf. Diary, 1655–6, p. 16.
[159] Fressingfield, Suff.

137/1670

for inlargements are a very uncertaine bottome etc. Letter 8. I wrote to know the nature of faith, repentance, and good works; and complained of an hard heart, and unruly passions, quarrelled with Providence, because, as to outward things, God made no difference betwixt good and bad; I was perplexed in my mind about God's decrees, and desired advice of him etc., in that I was tempted to leave of all dutyes, because I saw others, that did not serve God, prosper in their studies. His letter of December 8, '58 is a full answer, and worth the studying. He instances in one Fulham (whose letter about this I have of my father's copying out) whose resolution was to doe it himselfe, by fasting, crying etc., but was brought to see he could doe nothing; and then God drew his heart. My father was thus strugling, enlarged, then shutt up etc. most of his time at Cambridge, so as he had not power to looke on a booke which he believed would helpe him. So he adviseth not to strive to swimme, but to lay my selfe on the streame of the promise; and to wait till God enables to believe, and be beat of from my selfe, or any thing I am apt to trust to. See page 33, *huius libri*.[160] I wrote of the sinns I was prone to, envy, malice, strife and contention, backbiting and others; and I find by my father's papers that contention, and envy at saints, was his sin at Cambridge. I hope the Lord will let grace abound to me as well as to him; that as the ill nature was alike, so I may be renewed like him, Amen. See letter 12.

I complained of passions reigning, as envy, and anger: he wrote that good men had bin so, and yet, for the maine, good. That I must mourne under such a nature, and apply Christ's death, and his meeknes to cure mee of those passions. Letter 17.

He did not repent my going to Cambridge when the times turned, because of the good I had gotten for my soule; but he wished mee to have a care of subscription. Letter 19.

Hitherto all was well: but the change, and my love to live at Cambridge was an occasion of some breaches. I had not discretion to lay out my allowance, which was sufficient; and so spent over and above (though in no wastfull way) which angred my father. I gave eare to notions, and sucked in opinions about the state, and the church, as I heard others talke; and was vaine, and foolish in speaking what I thought, which vexed him so as almost to repent sending mee to Cambridge.

138/1670

He wrote that to disobey one's Father would be against one, and a sting to the conscience all one's dayes: and I find it a sting indeed, now he is dead: I was young and knew not what I did; surely I should not have done it, had I knowne what I did; not only for feare of loosing an estate; but that I might have peace; and God can give it yet, Amen! I have burnt some letters of mine, and his, as not so fitt to be kept. In September 1663 I wrote seriously to him, what my sense of displeasing him was, and that I could not have any peace till I was reconciled to him, which newly had bin; also how afraid of being snared with

---

160 *Huius libri*: 'of this book'.

the world, and what little content I had in any thing heer below; and how restles I was.

When I left Spinny he would have had mee lived neer him; but I had a love to these parts, and was afraid to be at his allowance, though it would have bin better for mee, and I should have had more peace. I am ashamed either that I should take up resolutions so hastily, or not keepe them, if good. Yet considering the nature of conforming, or not conforming, and the emergencies then happening, it may not be called a change, or ficklenes to use, or not use indifferent things *pro re nata*, etc.[161]

I wish, as I told my uncles, I had spent the last ten yeares other wise then I did; and 'tis not for his will, or depriving mee of an estate, but for conscience that now I say so. I wrote passionately about my wife that now is, I told him the truth, and dealt openly; neither did he at first write harshly, but said he had no desire to crosse mee. When I was with him he bid mee enquire what her father would doe for her: he at 1st offred £10 per annum after the decease of his wife, then offred that I should have it presently, if my father would settle accordingly. Besides an uncle, and aunt (both childles) promised to give all their estate (and both are rich) among the children, and my wife was promised as great a share as any of them.

Whilst this was brought about (which he thought not feisable) and all things likely to accord as to estate, which was the great remove; and I look't upon it as a good providence, that so much was granted; my father sent one of my brothers in law to putt a stopp, and take mee of quite, after giving waye for neer 3 monthes; and that not upon the account of portion, as he wrote, but because I was irregular in setting my mind before I had

139/1670

his final answer. Now those that know may excuse mee if my affections were gone unawares; she not only being very handsome (which alone would not have taken mee) but very sober, discreet, religious, and an excellent house wife. God hath blessed us all this while, and next to his blessing, her frugality hath bin the cause that we have lived so well upon so little. I confesse riches are a sweet enjoyment, but there are unsufferable inconveniences that accompany a fortune, if the woman be not discreet. I could have wished mine had bin rich with her discretion, but of the two, I would still (if it should be my case, *quod absit*)[162] chuse a wife with a little, and discreet; rather then rich without it.

After my father had wrote so, he thought I would stay till he was dead e're I married, and wrote the inconveniences as to mee and her, as hindring my selfe of the comforts of life, living in discontent etc., and told mee I should not have his estate if I did so (which now I take the more notice of, because I see if I had not married till now, all had bin one; and so I cannot so much impute it to that last act, as somwhat before) but that he would take such sure order, that I should repent it too late. So that my children may know (if God please) that for their mother's sake, and because I could not (nor ought not) take my love from her, and would not take a worse, I loose, and they are gainers.

161 *Pro re nata*: 'according to circumstances'.
162 *Quod absit*: 'and may it not be'.

Yet July 9th, he wrote that except my wife's friends would promise, and make sure somwhat heerafter, he would scarce condescend; which noteth that he gave consent to my choyce, only there was not portion answerable to his estate, which is £100 per annum. Yet since they offred to engage that she should have £100 at the decease of her uncle and aunt Havers; provided he would now settle £10 per annum, as joynture, and he would not: and this proved unhappy for my wife, for I have no free estate to settle on her, 'tis given all to my children; but I charge them, if they live to it, to allow their mother liberally, for whom I have lost, and by whom they have gained so much!

August 14. He wrote that he would not give way, except the uncle would ensure some estate to her heerafter. And indeed my friends are to be blamed for not doing so; which might have bin done, had not my father bin very backward in all such affaires, and sloathfull in busines somtimes.

October 9th. He wrote he would condescend to mee in my way; and wrote to my father that he demanded £500 with my wife.

140/1670

After wards he advised mee to try the temper, and disposition of my intended wife, and to take some other's judgment.

December 25, 1666. When the family broke up,[163] my father would not allow mee more then £10 per annum for diet, and all; and said I spent my paines for nothing (for I kept to my word in not reading service, and so another had what I might have had) the labourer was worthy of his wages etc.

January 29. He wrote that he would maintaine mee heer no longer; and would command his purse, though he could not gett mee away from these parts. My heart was bound up, as I wrote, in her I loved; and now (as before upon my leaving Spinny) I was at a losse for maintenance; but my uncle died and left mee £50, and upon that I was forced to live, till God provided farther for mee. This was a good providence, for else I must have bin putt to straits; yet I might have lived with my father, but my affections were so fixed that I could not be so far, so long absent. See in this book p.117,[164] and how I was freed of promise not to conforme, by his denying what he so oft promised mee.

August 13, '67. He wrote savourily to mee about my state Godward; and wished mee to try my owne heart whether I went upon a right bottome, or were rightly bottomed on it. I used, for my owne satisfaction, to propound doubts, and glosses of new divines, about many points; and he wished mee to keepe to the old Puritan books. It troubled, that I affected frolick company, as he called it, and thought that there was no mixture of seriousnes; but I had serious mixtures, in the time of my dwelling at the hall, which I thinke he meant, though I had need of cheerly company, more then others; or else I should have bin sickly, as he was at my yeares. My uncle John, it seems, diverted himselfe oft with chearfulnes, yet a good man as the earth bore in his dayes, as *Apologet. Narrat.* hints.[165] He told mee of a farme of his, and I wrote that with all my

---

163 The Russell family of Chippenham Hall.
164 See the entry for 17 Apr. 1667.
165 Probably Thomas Goodwin, Philip Nye, Sidrach Simpson, Jeremiah Burroughes, and William Bridge, *An Apologeticall Narration, Humbly Submitted to the Honourable Houses of*

heart I would come and live there, if he would let mee marry, and depend upon God's blessing. But he let his farme to another.

My wife was sick of a quartane in August; and my Father was concerned at it; and prayed for her conversion, as he wrote, and that it might be sanctified, as that sicknes of my mother was to her.

141/1670

I shall transcribe somwhat of what I wrote to his of August 13. 'I have prised your writings, and read them with delight. Sometimes I found hopes, then was cast downe; if one marke of faith, another I could not find; and I can say 'twas my griefe I was not so as God would have mee; and now had rather *ruere cum Christo, quam regnare cum Caesare,*[166] this is sweet in the notion, but when it comes to triall, I might forget my selfe. I thinke I have resolvedly, and with counting the cost taken up my profession of Christianity; and what my education brought I embrace from reasons strong, and weighty.

I now, from that principle, despise the riches, honour, and greatnes of the world, because it crosseth my designe for heaven; and since my retirednes, have denied my selfe acquaintance at the hall, because there are some that will dampe any serious heart. When I lived there, they were a burden; now I am free, I goe not among them, but of a bare necessity. Yea in the family that I visit so, there is but one that I would chuse to converse with. I find more worke with my owne heart, then I can, or shall expresse. I thinke as to the world, I could live almost blameles; but my great busines is in striving to conquer sin, and lust, which would, and doe oft captivate, *'et quamvis hoc sentiam, ad resistendum nullas vires invenio; puto quod vivus sum, quia sentio; sed Judas habuit nimium, peccati sensum, et hic haereo. Nunquam tam humilis fui, quam in jis rebus, quae quosdam superbire facerent; et hoc cum magna lucta carnis, quae, si in tali casu non vigilarem, me funditus perderet. Interim nullum unquam officium peregi quod mihi placuit, quanto minus deo sanctissimo! et in hoc sum totus ut magis vilescerem in oculis meis, quod faxit pater misericors deus! Amen. Quamvis animae statum bonum vocare non ardeo, neglectum, et incognitum non possum affirmare, quia sentio varias mutationes, incrementa, ut puto, gratiae ejusdemque decrementa, prout vel resisto, vel cedo satanae laqueis, carnisque illecebris. Hoc etiam sustentat animam meam, quando per peccatum dejicitur, quod populum dei, qua talem, semper, et ubique diligo; peccatum autem in aliis (utinam et in meipso) odio inveterato prosequor. quid plura! hodie spem habeo, cras fortasse nullam; et hoc modo vitam partim miseram, jucundam partim per aliquot annos traxi. Video autem scientiae et sinceritatis fructus*

142/1670

uti spero, meliores quam antehac; sed vereor ne actiones malas pro indifferentibus, in vitae cursu, quandoque sumerem. Sanctus Spiritus arguat me peccati! Amen.'[167]

Parliament (1643). Goodwin and Nye were Archer's co-pastors at the English Church at Arnhem, Netherlands; Simpson, Burroughs and Bridge were ministers of the Rotterdam English Reformed Church. See BDBR.

[166] *Ruere cum Christo, quam regnare cum caesare:* 'fall with Christ than reign with Caesar.'

[167] A translation might be as follows: 'And however much I feel this, I cannot discern any powers of resistance; I think I am alive because I can feel; but Judas had too great a sense of

Thus I wrote in such Latin as came to mind; of this I had no answer that I know of.

I wrote that some thought his severity was indirectly the cause of my wife's sicknes: I know she was sad, and melancholick because she was the occasion of all this last difference betwixt him and mee. When I earnestly besought him to consent he would write neither one way, nor other; and in that intervall (from August 13 to November 19) I married, going upon that which he had told mee, p. 119,[168] which I faithfully told to two friends, before I married, and they judged it an implicite consent. Yet I wish I had staid longer; or let him know it sooner. For soon after I had a sharpe letter; in that he told mee I might marry against his mind, if I would, and he would not molest mee in it.

And he was angry that from thence I told him not the time, neither ac-quainted him with it before, which indeed I should have done. I pleaded his words; he said want of a place was the cause of his not consenting, and I said if I had a place I would understand his words so that I might proceed; and he did not forbid it, I am sure, as the father, that heard the vow should doe, and so I proceeded. This was a wile, and not justifiable; and I did begg his pardon, and promise satisfaction; and truly I was much troubled for a time, and did begg oft with teares that God would not reward mee as I had served him.

My disobedience before did trouble mee most, for I had not such a sense of my last action, for there was some reason, though not enough; and her illnes and feare of dying was that which prevailed with mee to marry so unseasonably. I doe not extenuate the irregularity of my proceeding; but my case was such that I had no power to doe otherwise; I was unsetled, at a losse, and she very sick, and I much in love; what could I doe? But I suffer for this, and other things, and desire to see the hand of God in it, and bemoane my undutifulnes as long as I live; and yet trust in God. Amen.

143/1670

After all this my father received mee, and gave mee severall things; yet kept his mind to himselfe as to his estate. In November '68 I had household stuffe etc. I wrote that I hoped that his dayes would be lengthned (which I prayed for too)

sin, and here I stick. I was never so humble as in those things in which others take pride; and this is with a great wrestling of the flesh, which, if I am not vigilant, will destroy me utterly. Meanwhile, I have performed no duty at all which has pleased me; how much less Holy God! And in this I am wholly such that I grow vile in my own eyes. May God the merciful Father perform it! Amen. Although I do not dare to call the condition of my soul good, I am not able to assert that it is neglected and unknown, because I feel various changes, increases, I think, of his grace, and decreases, either as I resist or yield to the snares of Satan and the enticements of the flesh. This, however, supports my soul, when it is cast down by sin, that the people of God are of the kind that I always and everywhere love. Sin, however, in others (and especially in myself) I pursue with an inveterate hate. What more! Today I have hope, tomorrow perhaps none. And in this fashion, I have got through a partly wretched and partly happy life for a number of years. But I can see the fruits of knowledge and sincerity, thus, I hope, better than before. But I fear that I might some day take up evil actions instead of indifferent ones. The Holy Spirit convinces me of sin! Amen.'

[168] See the entry for 29 September, 1667.

to see the fruits of amendment in mee, for all that was amisse. Now since that time all was well, not the least jarre about anything.

This recollection hath caused much seriousnes in mee, and I have the more earnestly begged pardon of God; and 'twas some comfort that I was fully reconciled to my father, whose memory I shall honour while I live, long before he died. I saw him at London last May, and we were at my uncle's house with a great deale of kindnes. I wish I had gone since, but my wife was about quickning, and I was loath to venture.

December 10. We had tried all meanes to make my child (who had bin baptized December 8, and named Anne) suck of my wife. She would suck greedily of others, but could not lay hold by reason of the short nipples, and the tongue not so long as in some: we had a child older, and that would not fasten; we gott a puppy, and could not make it lay hold, in so much that we despaired of what I had so desired of God, the blessing of the breast as well as that of the wombe; and my wife was resolving to try no more. When she thought not of it, the child took the breast, and so continueth; which we looke on as a remarkable providence of our God! And shall not I live more to that God, who doth so much for mee?

December 25. I preach't on John 13:27, which was judged very suitable to the sacrament. I, having looked over my actions past, resolved upon amendment. And more particularly engaged to watch my heart, and be much in communing with it, which is a thing (I heard) that a formall hypocrite cannot doe. I was affected before, and since, but not much in the act, because I was a minister to others; wheras when I received from another I used to be much affected at the very time. I had preached on Psalm 119:11, which text had run in my mind a great while, and my heart was lett out; and others found it very suitable. The Lord carry on his worke in mee, and doe good by mee! Amen. Old Mr Fairclough[169] gave mee good advice: I was comforted in that he told mee if I could find but one signe of grace in mee, they were all there. Praised be God!

144/1670

I heard him preach on April 11, 1668, which did so affect mee, that I was strongly moved to open my condition to him; yet then watch't a time, and could not gett him alone; and after it was diverted: since which I have told him very many things, and I find his words savoury, and coming to my heart. The Lord grant mee growth in grace by Christian society!

Lately I found a paper of my father's, where he saith a man may be an hypocrite, and not know it; this startled mee, and made mee search, and pray that God would shew mee more of my vile, deceitfull heart, which he alone knoweth. I asked Mr Fairclough about it, and he confirmed it of formall

---

[169] Samuel Fairclough (1594–1677), rector of Kedington, Suff., from 1629. Following the imposition of the Act of Uniformity, to which he could not subscribe, he went to live with his youngest son, Richard, who was rector of Kennett, a parish adjoining Chippenham to the east: hence Archer's acquaintance. His second son, Samuel (1625–91), was rector of Houghton Conquest, Beds., from which he was ejected in 1662. It was he who obtained a licence to teach as a Congregationalist in Chippenham in 1672. See DNB.

hypocrisy, though not of grosse: and told mee that God gave such over in judgment, to be deceived in their condition;[170] and wished mee to secret heart tryall, and there was no great feare of that judgment. Since I have thought of it, and endeavour to judge my selfe; and know that sincerity (as other graces) in the best <are> is imperfect, and some hypocrisy lurketh; the Lord deliver mee from heart deceitfulnes for Christ's sake!

I heare good people complaine of an evill heart, and my father bemoaned his deadnes etc. Surely my heart may be in a good state though indisposed etc., if I allow not such things. By conference I find some comfort, the Lord give more! All that I stick at is I have perceived nothing of that enabling to take Christ (which is faith), nor of that terrour for sin; nor much of that kindly sorrow for sin: yet I thinke there are some signes of grace in mee, but not to keep out doubtings. The Lord cleare my state to mee, and worke orderly in mee! I assent, and consent to Christ, and am willing (as far as I know) to take him as Lord and saviour; and find it hard to believe, but have not found God drawing mee, and giving a power: but I long for it, and cannot take comfort till then.

February 26. Looking over Mr Bifield's book called *The Spirituall Touchstone*,[171] I noted severall signes of a good man, according to which thus I find my selfe for present:

1. An holy thirst after good things I have found; yet more for God's favour, then for full delivery from sin, or for the salvation of others, p.146. 'Tis in my sense somtimes of my affections, but more in my

145/1670–1

judgment. This appetite is somtimes more, and somtimes lesse; 'tis renewed after a languishing, by reason of some sin etc.

2. A love to God's word I have found, and doe find; so that I esteem it above any thing; and owne the threatnings as well as the promises.

3. The spirit of prayer, and the gift have I found; if the spirit of prayer be an hearty motion of my will Godward, and full of desires after spirituall things; and if the gift be a tolerable readines to expresse my wants either alone, or with others, these I have found. And if I find any straitnings, 'tis after sin, or security, or for the want of meditation before hand; I find much variety in my selfe, commonly doing best, when I feare I shall doe worst etc. As Psalm 69:10, I make prayer my refuge, though it be a reproach to call upon God, and few countenance such things.

4. A love to my enemies (and I know of none, except sin maketh them so, or it be upon the common account of holines, and religion) I find so as to desire their conversion, for then they would not be enemies; and dare not in a private way avenge my selfe upon those that injure mee. Yet cannot I but estrange my selfe from such, till satisfaction made; without which my temper will not let mee (for some time) forgett, though I dare not but forgive. I could doe a courtesy, if desired, for the worst of those that ever I had a breach with, which, I thanke God, are very few, p.157.

---

[170] Romans 1:24–6.
[171] Nicholas Byfield, *The Spiritual Touchstone: or, the Signes of a Godly Man* (1619).

5. A longing for Christ's appearance (which is the last marke) I cannot so clearly find; or a desire to die. But truly 'tis because I thinke my selfe unfitt, or feare it; not out of love to the world, for I find no solid contentment heer below. Now though I find it thus with mee, yet I cannot take the comfort of it; but still feare the worst, and would faine have my heart sensibly drawne to Christ, that I may sett to my seale to the word. Amen!

April 19. God visited mee with an ague; it was but gentle, and I feared it would continue. On the 21 day I had a 2d fitt, and I vomited choller. On the 23th was Easter day, and I prayed that God would restraine it, at least till the service of that day was over; and he did so, but I could not serve him with the delight which was required, which the Lord pardon to mee. The fitt came 2 houres after I looked for it; and on the Tuesday next it went away, which did enable mee to take a journey into Essex to make up all kind of differences (if possible) with my mother.

146/1671

August 5. The last Michaelmas I was with my mother to see the will, for before the proving it she would not let me see it, though earnestly intreated.[172] The 1st thing I minded was that the house at Colchester was not bound to pay debts; and so she had no right to meddle with it; and 'tis said that J[ohn] Lewis should take rents of the lands; and this being only a house, I thought it fell to me as heir at law. So my father Peachy thought too. So in December I seized on it, and tooke bond for the rent, and gave bond to beare the tenant harmles.

I thought not of medling with any more of the estate, only made entry on all with my cozin Archer of Stoke. I wrote to my uncle Francis what I had done; he said I might have all the estate as well as that house: upon this I consulted with my father, and he said that the fee simple was in mee, and the land fell to mee because my child was not borne when my father died; or much to that purpose; as concerning the personall estate paying the debts, and the feoffee giving security etc., so we advised with Mr Buller, and he confirmed it, and was clearer in the case. I now began to have some hopes.

God ordered it so that my cousin Sir John Archer came the circuit at Bury assizes, and I was resolved to have his advice; I could not speake with him the 1st night, and his clerke told mee he would not, nor ought to give counsell; and God putt a sodaine thought to goe to Mr North (who now is solicitour generall),[173] so he studied upon the will, and in the morning gave it under his hand to this effect, viz. that the devises to the male children were voyd, by reason that I had no \male/ child at my father's death; and so the power of J[ohn] Lewis was an appendix, and fell of it selfe (as he told mee), and his power must be prevented by a suit in Chancery; and the personall estate may be made pay the debts.

I feared it could not be true, for I overheard one say to Mr North, the [sic] he sett his hand to an impertinent busines etc., but sure he meant it because

---

[172] It was proved on 16th September, 1670 (Appendix 1).

[173] Sir Francis North (1637–85), later Lord Guilford, solicitor-general, 1671, chief justice of the Common Pleas, 1675 and Lord Keeper of the Great Seal, 1682. His legal career is detailed in Foss, *Judges of England*, 483–6.

the will was ill penned. However, I shew it to the judge, and he wholly approved of it

147/1671

wishing mee to use Mr North, as the ablest and honestest man that he knew. Soon after I seized on all, and warned the tenants from paying rent to J[ohn] Lewis etc., not thinking they would pay mee till my title was cleare. This did startle my mother, and she made light of it, and threatned to spend out of the estate against mee etc., and to arrest the tenants, so as I tooke order with an attorney to manage all for them on my score.

All this while J[ohn] Lewis had not acted, being sickly, as God would have it, and unfitt for busines. He only wrote to the tenants to pay him the rent. In Easter weeke I went to Dedham (as well as my ague left mee) and found not my mother at home; she was at London about her son George, who was frantick at that time J[ohn] Lewis came over to my house that day I went to see him, and because that I lay by the way, I mett not with him. I came home the next day and found him at 1st resolute to spend I know not what rather then I should putt him by etc. I had prayed God, the God of peace, in wisdome to order it so that we might not contend in law. We went to my father in law who made him understand the case, so that he promised to advise about what Mr North said, and soon after wrote to mee that if he could legally be discharged he would; and would advise with a minister as to conscience etc., and would send mee word.

My uncles encouraged mee in the busines, only were against our going to law; I was resolved to stand out as long as I could, for I thought they would not venture in a doubtfull case, for feare of bearing their owne charges, and my mother loved money, and had great losses by law already.

I besought God to give mee what, in nature, belonged to mee, and promised to honour him with my substance. I find that an estate will make a great impression upon the mind; and heighten the heart when had, or sinke it when 'tis lost.

148/1671

In Whitson weeke I went into Essex, and beyond what I looked for, the tenants owned mee; one paid me rent, the other promised it before witnes. I offered the rent to my mother, and she would not take it, for she knew not her son's mind; but was civill, and come of from that fiercenes she had showne before, and willing to agree, wheras before she said if J[ohn] Lewis would not act another should, and the will should be fulfilled to an heire etc.

I suppose her care was to secure the debts due to her; I offered bond, and to tie the land for them, as my uncle advised mee; and I told her the will would ensure the debts whether I would or not. I offered her the personall estate (coming to £180, wherof I and my girle have about £60 made sure), though Mr North said it might helpe pay the debts, if she and J[ohn] Lewis would leave their claime. This wrought with both, for in August last I had notice to meet him, and his mother. I went August 1, and found him sickly, not able to follow his calling; which was a great cause of our agreement, as God wonderfully ordered it for mee, whom I have much seen in all this busines.

He had taken advise with one Mr Hill, who owned that the estate was mine before my last girle was borne, and if I had sold it, there was no remedy: this I heard before, but did not intend to doe so. But he told him that now I had a child his trust was good, if he would act in it; and that his warning the tenants was an entring on his office, and he could not be discharged from it, as to the children, but by a release out of Chancery. J[ohn] Lewis was willing to take this release, if I would; and I deferre it till I speake with Sir Francis North; so as one way or other we shall agree all of us. Amen!

September 23. I went to Sir Francis North to Catlidge,[174] and shew him what he had written; he had not understood mee rightly about my 2d child, for he thought it borne before

149/1671

my father died, and so had written that the devise to the next eldest child would be good; but the other void, because I had no sonns at that time. Now I thought that reason would serve as well to null the other, for I had no child at all then. Upon this he reviewed the will, and blotted out that clause, and that about J[ohn] Lewis his power; which now he said was void, being an appendix of the other. And thus all the devises being void, Lewis his office failed; but still he confirmed that the personall estate might pay the debts. And wrote that 'twas J[ohn] Lewis's best way to sitt still; that he needed no release, and could not assigne his place, it being void: J[ohn] Lewis promised to stand to this judgment, and so I hope all is at an end.

What a remarkable providence is this! I shall never forget it; that God should let me see what my disobedience had deserved by suffering such a will to be made; and then, upon my repentance, should order it so as to give mee the estate, and that by taking away my child so deare to mee (yet had she lived, I had not had it) and by giving mee another, and that after my father's death (for other wise I had bin barred of it) and that so lusty, and so healthfull a girle etc., a large amends for my losse etc., this was wonderfull. That my wife should not come sooner; and that she should be neer her time when my father died (which was the reason he tarried, and did not alter his will) and that my father's death was so sodaine, and not feared till the last, so as he did not mind altering the will etc., this was very remarkable. That from so small beginnings (for I gave all over) I should come to know my title; that my mother's unkindnes should make mee inquire, and doe what I never

150/1671

intended in the least, this was wonderfull. For she told mee I should have a share out of it, seing her son was trustee etc., but when I moved it afterwards, she told mee she could make no debts; neither would she pay mee what my father ought mee; but putt mee in the inventory as owing my father somwhat, which was not so; and other things which I will not mention; and thus God made use of our clashings for my good, and from such beginnings I went on; the wider our breach, the more I gained; the Lord pardon all passion in the case, and teach mee to use my estate to his glory. Amen!

---

[174] Probably Kirtling, Cambs., where Lord North had a residence.

September 29. When I came last to Chippenham (of which, see p.130),[175] I thought to have setled there. But the shortnes of my allowance, and difficulty of getting it; inconvenience of dwelling (the house exposed to wind much, and all out houses being wanting etc.) distance from my estate; and a difference with one who abused mee when I reproved him mildly, and secretly etc., whose mother soon after ran out of her witts, for the losse of a daughter etc. but is now well, blessed be God! and other things were the outward motives to setle somwhere else neerer my estate. But the maine reason was a being wary of seing and hearing what I mett with; and the rudenes of the towne, being overrun with grooms and racehorses, and too neer the court somtimes; *exeat aula qui volet esse pius* etc.[176]

I longed for a retiring settlement; and to be at leisure to serve God thankfully all my dayes. I was about a place, but it could not be had, for the Patronesse changed her mind. On February 14, 1670, I went to see Dr Herbert,[177] a friend of our's; but he was at Wheltham the great (3 miles of Bury) with Mr Gyps,[178] the chiefe man. When I came, the 1st thing Mr Gyps said to me, calling me aside, was 'can ye helpe us to an honest man for our curate heer?' I said, 'what if I come my selfe?' 'Then', said he, 'wee will looke

151/1671

no farther.' I was almost a stranger, only he had heard of mee: thus God ordered it for mee, for the busines I had with Dr Herbert was about that place, the living being his, and his curate removing at Michaelmas next, and he having the next advowsion in his gift etc. I was to buy the next advowsion of him, and serve his cure in the meane time, and so 'twould be mine at last. It pleased mee that Mr Gyps should aske mee, to whom the Dr had granted to chuse a curate; and so our bargaine was soon concluded to my content.

September 27. The weather being wett, and uncertaine we removed, and came in safety through the good hand of God upon us. October 5. Our goods came safely, though the weather had bin wett before, and was wett after our removing.

October 7. I had sett the lid of a great chest open with a boord, and my girle was playing at one end of it, when on the sodaine the lid fell downe, and hurt her forehead, and lay on her wrist and hand; but by a mercy of God the boord in part kept of the blow, and little hurt was done. How if her head, or hand had bin bruised! 'Twas God that delivered her for our comfort! Blessed be his name Amen!

October 9. Now I hope I am setled; and shall sett my mind at rest, and follow my studies. We live in a little village, yet hard by Bury; so that I may retire, or goe into the world as I please. I have a very convenient house, and gleabe lying within it selfe; the aire is good, the towne on an hill chiefly, and I desired privacy, and God hath given it.

October 26. My wife and I dined with Mr Gyps and he spoke hotly about family duties; bringing his owne practise as an example, for he lives privately,

[175] See the entry for 24 June, 1670.
[176] *Exeat aula qui volet esse pius*: 'let him who wishes to be virtuous leave the court.'
[177] William Herbert, D.D., rector of Great Whelnetham, 1646–80, *Al. Cantab*.
[178] John Gipps, gent. of Great Whelnetham.

and reads the word morning and evening, and prayes with his family; he complained of the great neglect of ministers

152/1671

in duties, chiefly morning prayers; observing that the bishops etc. had prayers constantly, to the disgrace of others etc., with much to that effect. When I first kept house I had the word read, and did pray every evening with my family. I had an house so open that on mornings we could not be free from distractions (though closet duties I omitted not), and so had no prayers; and I had a base bashfulnes, by reason of the impediment etc., and could not pray so fluently as others, my speech being somwhat stammering.

There is also surely a shame of goodnes, and a feare of reproach for Christ in my heart in some measure, though I see it not, but palliate it with thinking 'tis from a loathnes to appeare religious to the world more then I must publickly etc., that makes mee so loath to duty in family. When I went to Chipnam, I was more private, and did pray on Lord's day mornings with my family. But upon this discourse of Mr Gyps, I putt in practise what I formerly resolved, viz. when I lived privately I would have prayers in mornings.

Blessed be God for this providence; I argued that 'twas commendable, but no indispensable duty; that the service was the only allowed forme to be in houses; that other sober men omitted it etc. Yet Mr Gyps his words stuck with mee that 'twas a shame; and that servants would blame it, though they minded little good; that ministers should sett a good example, or else how could they urge such things upon others? and much to that purpose. He was melancholick, and so was the more earnest; though I know much came from his temper, yet God directed it to mee, and I putt the duty in practise next morning; and shall doe by God's assistance. Yet must I not expose holy things to scorne, but shall be cautious whom I admitt into my society then,

153/1671

as my father's manner was. Those that will reverently joyne, viz. of strangers, may with all freedome; but if any like not these strict wayes of worship, let them seeke other friends, for I am a companion of them that feare the Lord; they have bin, and shall be my delight; and I thanke God I can live plentifully of my selfe, and so have not the necessities of complying which some have. The Lord give mee zeale, boldnes, and courage for that which is good, and cure that cowardlines for the truth that is in mee! See how I should be valiant for the truth, Jeremiah 9:3.

January 16. I found much sweetnes, and comfort by practising duties with my family, and chiefly by my selfe in evenings before supper; recollecting the passages of the day; and bewailing sin, or blessing God for keeping mee from it, as occasion served. My wife was hearty to mee in such things; and after the sacrament told with teares how great good she had found within a yeare; and that she looked upon her selfe with another eye then she used to doe. I suffered reproach from neighbour ministers for my preaching in afternoons, because their people would come somtimes. But this I value not; our bishop approveth of it; and 'twas used before I came. I could wish for good acquaintance, but if they cannot be had, God is my friend.

March 18. I tooke a journey to London to compose the busines with my mother, and brother. My uncles were hearty to mee; and, to please them, I yielded more then I might have done, to satisfy my mother's covetousnes, which they could observe as well as I. We agreed that she

154/1671–2

should have a mortgage for the debts, which were £250, and more; besides £100 Lewis should have a release out of Chancery (whether needfull or not) at my charges.

June 1. My wife was newly with child when we came from Chipnam: and had many paines for a weeke, and we had the midwife with us, because we live in a solitary place. This night, at 10 of the clock, she was delivered of a boy, lusty and large, but leane: this was the eve of Trinity Sonday, and, as we had counted, the time was just come about. Thus in each of my removes I have had a child; and when I was eager of a son, the Lord denied it, and now I was indifferent, God sent one; the God of my father's make him his by adoption! and give mee grace to educate him well!

June 13. My wife fell grievously sick, and faint by reason of some noxious and venomous impurities that nature should have cleansed her of: she had the very agonies of death, as she thought, and was seized all over with intolerable paine, and possessed with a persuasion she should die that night. Her father and mother were with her, and we all had griefe enough; I besought God to have mercy on mee, and my litle children, and to restore her; and by degrees her fitts went away, and nature did it's office, without any other physick, except herbs boiled for such an use. I pray God none of us may forget this new life given to her, Amen! I named the child of my father's name, in honour of his memory; when my wife recovered, he sucked and mends upon it every day, and gather's flesh. Now I have two children to stand up in my stead; I desire to weane my affections from worldly things, having one to continue my name, and to have what I leave.

155/1672

July 24. I heard that the decree in Chancery was ready, only more money must be sent, or the matter would not be finished till next terme. So I sent £5, and hope all will be ended at last. Amen!

August 4. I was seized with a sadnes of spirit, and great discouragment as to my worke of the ministry, and that day I preached about the enmity that Satan hath to God's people, and the reasons of it, one of which was because he knew that the saints should judge him at last etc., which I urged with more vehemency then usuall, and so my discouragment went quite of. I believe that the devil doth what he can to dishearten men, who by Christ are sett on worke to pull downe his kingdome, and so might fill mee with sad thoughts, and make mee loath to duty etc., as once at Chipnam 1665 I was to reprove some sins, and my heart went as a beare to the stake, and yet there \was/ some good done for present.

I thought of what Dr Harris used to say, that nothing was too hard for him but discouragement, which was the child of pride, and unbeliefe; and others have bin disheartned as well as I, as my father was very much etc. One said the devil either made him omitt duties, or would disturbe him in them. But that comforted mee which Luther wrote to G[eorge] Spalatinus, who was tempted to lay downe his ministry (as I have bin often etc.) 'either overcome, or slight such thoughts', saith he; 'Christ hath called thee, obey him; 'tis a temptation, and why it comes thou knowest not, but maist heerafter; we who looke on can see better; 'tis a sure signe thy ministry pleaseth God, and is usefull to men, that thou art tempted to leave it; for the devil makes thee weary of it, wheras, if it did not please God, thou wouldst eagerly continue in it, as they doe who run before they are sent etc., and so he was comforted, Mel. Adam p.100.[179]

156/1672

And againe, si aliqui audiunt, non est cessandum; alioquin et ego, in tanto verbi contemptu, iamdudum tacuissem; aliena iniquitas non est satis, ut propter eam locum deseras.[180] Now though some give not attention to mee, through drowsines, yet others doe; and many resort from other townes, I hope for a good end. So that I have overcome thoughts of leaving of ministry, and endeavour to grieve at people's neglect, as a sin to God, and not in respect to my selfe, who am nothing.

October 3. I tooke up my land at Bently;[181] and the fine was sett £15, which, as to the present rent, is too much; yet my father had £14 sett 19 yeares agoe, when he bought it, and mine was a yeare and halfe, and so I surrendred it to the use of my will, as I did that at Fordham.[182] Upon this I made my will etc.

October 6. My wife was much troubled at the sodaine death of her elder sister; I was sent for, and was much affected, and her father much more; the Lord doe all of us good by it, and prepare us also for a change! Amen. My father Peachy promised that if he lived he would double my wive's portion, for God did blesse him, and he abounded, and would lay up for his children. And this he may doe for his living is amended; and though I was by his promise to have my wive's land presently, during his life, and after her mother's death wholly; yet I freely yielded that he should have it, because God encreased my meanes: now he may spare, although then it was not so well with him, and he had spent much in education of his children etc.

December 23. Now I am 31 yeares old; and must say that much of the last 10 yeares hath bin spent idly enough. I followed not my studies so closely as at Cambridge, though now it is with more judgment.

---

[179] Melchior Adam, Vitae Germanorum Theologorum (Heidelberg, 1620).

[180] The passage translates as: 'One should not cease [preaching] if anyone at all is listening. Otherwise I would have long ago been silent on account of the great contempt for the Word. Unless you have some other reason which burdens your conscience, the wickedness and malice [of men] is not a sufficient reason for deserting your place and vocation . . .' Luther to George Spalatin, November 30th, 1524, in Luthers Works, 49, 91–3, ed. and trans. by Gottfried G. Krodel (55 vols., Philadelphia, 1972). Also in Melchior Adam, op. cit.

[181] Bentley, Essex, which lies to the east of Colchester. Archer is here discussing the level of his entry fine for his copyhold land.

[182] Fordham, Essex, which lies to the west of Colchester. Not to be confused with Fordham, Cambs.

157/1672

Against the sacrament I reflect, and am ashamed for my litle growth in goodnes, and that I have not gone on with that courage which should have answered my setting out. I resolve to grow better, and begg that God would seale pardon, peace, and all good things to mee! God hath in a great measure blessed mee since last sacrament, for which I offer praise, and promise obedience. He gave me a son, and delivered my wife from extreame danger; and wheras the child was very sickly, and voided blood, as in a fluxe, since Michaelmas he is very healthfull etc. Our health, and peace are lengthned out, blessed be God, and my condition is suited to my mind; only I find that I am apt to disquiet my selfe in vaine.

I tooke a young schollar to read service for mee. I found my selfe unfit, and was much discouraged in God's service by reason of it. 'Tis a great ease and comfort to mee, if God enable mee to maintaine it, and it may take away all exceptions against mee etc. Providence hath alotted mee a man sober, peaceable, and good natured; a comfort to us in this solitary place. This last yeare was bad to farmers, and so to mee: I was forced to borrow money for stock, and towards house keeping till the profits came in; but I hope by God's blessing upon my diligence to gett all cleare. Amen!

January 14. My wive's younger brother, and their man having had the small poxe (which also was at a neighbour's of our's), I sent for her mother and litle sister to be with us. And this very morning the girle had red spotts coming out, which we feared would prove the poxe; yet was she not sick, as is usuall in such a case. However that day we sought to remove for a time; we looked that Mr Gypps would

158/1672

have received us, because his house was large, and he was with us the night afore, and saw how well the child was, and might well know that there could be no danger in us, (for my mother was 3 dayes with my brother after they came out, and gott no hurt) and I sent twice, though not to aske directly, and he never invited us, nor sent to know how all was, till we were come againe. This I tooke unkindly from one that professed so great kindnes.

I tried other places, and they either denied us, or gave such limitations, that it would have proved a prison to us. At last we tooke a roome (in which we gott cold) and the man gave us all freedome etc., but before I went, I said I could not thinke our good God would bring so much evill on us, to suffer by those whom we had, in duty and hospitality, succoured. And God ordered it so, that next morning we were delivered from our feares: it not proving the poxe, but measles, or the nettle springe; so the day after we returned; and our hearts were full of joy, and thanks. And I blesse my God, and my faith in him is by this confirmed, to him be glory, Amen!

By this providence I tried my neighbours; and I thinke it an uncomfortable, helples, and desolate place to be sick in; my health hath bin continued hitherto, but who knoweth how long it may hold! My wife is seldome well heer.

159/1672

The 1st yeare I thought 'twas breeding, but stil 'tis the same. I have no relations, nor intimate friends in thees parts; my wive's are mine, and they would have us neerer, especially since this hapned: so that could I gett a place more convenient, I could remove, now my estate in Essex is, I hope, setled; which was a great motive to my coming neerer it then afore. So Ile wait upon God's providence!

My girle is forward in witt, and active beyond any that I can heare of; and so getts many falls; I can only take what care I am able, and committ her to God's care, whom I desire to keepe her from all evill, and to whose protection I leave her.

January 29. Mr L. preacht on Psalm 50:21, a good searching sermon which affected mee, and shamed mee for my secret faults, which I hope will not be sett in order before mee! Amen.

February 5. Mr C. preach't on 2 Corinthians 5:20, and did show us our duty to deport our selves so as it becomes ambassadours, seing God chose us rather then angells in the matter of reconciling sinners etc., and there came a sodaine thought into my mind how base it was for an ambassadour to be false to his prince! And how would God take it if I were treacherous to him! The Lord confirme mee in his faith, and encourage mee in his service!

See p.150.[183] That man at Chipnam, who had abused mee etc. had his stables, barnes, corne, and two houses burnt, to his great losse. I am sorry for it, yet I take notice of God's hand in it, and wish he may for his good. And his mother is still more distracted, as I heare then afore.

160/1672

February 18. I went to Mr Warren,[184] who had asked mee to take Frecknam (whose rectory he then newly had) and dwell in a convenient house, with ground to it to the value of £20 a yeare, which he then had bought of Mr Alders[185] his executors etc. My father Peachy had wished mee to that house before, but then I did not much mind it. But being very lonesome, and having litle comfort from my relations at this distance, in case of sicknes, counsell etc., I inclined to the motion. I desired respite for an answer; but the day before I went, Mr Warren had promised the vicaridge to one, who indeed supplanted mee, though he knew I was about it. So he told mee 'twas too late, and that he thought I would not have taken the place. When I knew he meant I should have taken that small vicaridge etc., I was not sorry for the disappointment, for I would not have done it. However, I was for his farme, and would supply Chipnam, which is close by, and somtimes my owne at Wheltham, and my cousin Goodwin be there. I had articles, and they were to hold till broke by mutuall consent. This I did to provide for my wife and children a setlement in case I die before her; for ministers widowes are putt to much confusion other-wise, as I had observed this yeare, wherin many ministers died, and one next mee for whom I preached etc.

I know by this I shall be thought fickle; and therfore I putt my selfe into a settlement, not to cease but by the leave of my friend. Some inconveniences I

---

183 See the entry for 29 September, 1671.

184 Erasmus Warren, rector of Worlington, Suff., 1666–1718, rector of Freckenham, 1672; son of George, formerly vicar of Chippenham, 1642–50, Al. Cantab.

185 John Alders, vicar of Freckenham, 1651, Al. Cantab.

must meet with where ever I am; but my temper is too apt to make mee droope (as my fathers was) and be discouraged, if I have not friends to relieve mee, and who so fitt as those that study my good, as my wifes friends doe? her father being wise, and able to counsell mee, for he is cordiall to mee: and if I should be sick he is a physician faithfull, and skilfull: then for neighbourhood, 'tis neer Isleham, Chipnam and Barton etc. where I have lived: wheras

161/1672–3

heer the ministers are not sociable, or not of a straine safe for mee to converse with, who am thought a fanatick, as they say, because my father was knowne at Bury: then the gentry carry all so highly, that such as I are but so many eyesores, and silent reprovers of their evill wayes, and as for religion they are heer more ignorant and sottish etc. then where I have lived formerly; and very untractable, and clownish, which is the lesse to be noted because so common. Therfore, providence making a way, I hope I may follow, especially being not able to brook that solitude into which my temper rather then my reason brought mee.

March 30. Against this sacrament I had many things to thanke my God for: the continuance of mercies to mee, and the delivering my family from the small pox, when I had reason to feare it etc., which I did as I could. I also beggd strength against my corruptions, and that I might not suffer wrath or revenge to breake out into words, much lesse into actions: but that I might be a pattern of meeknes, and putt up wrongs, and hard usage from some who had no such cause given them. And this I wait for, and hope God will heare mee in it, for I love peace, and unity, and shall study to give no offence.

The king had suspended penall lawes against Papists, and Nonconformists; the lasting of it but a yeare (for 'twas voted illegall by the parliament, and the king confessed his mistake etc.) made many rejoyce. With us it signified nothing, for none forsook the public; but if 'twas dangerous as to the growth of Popery, I am glad 'tis at end, though I could wish indulgence to sober, and peaceable men. 'Twas because of a warre with Holland that 'twas granted; and as the king said, it kept peace at home. What the limitations will be I know not, but somthing is promised by the parliament by way of comprehension. However, I am more satisfied in the Church of England then ever.

162/1673

May 26. I went to London to meet mother, and brother. The decretall order had bin passed June 29 last yeare; and they had putt in some things to my prejudice, as that J[ohn] Lewis should have 50s a yeare for his life, and that Bernards, being a lease for 1000 yeares, was my mothers wholly. Whether 'twas their doing, or the lawyers I know not; but providence ordered it so that my lawyer would not consent to the enrolling it, (though I hastned him, not suspecting such dealings) till I came up. They at last disowned those things, which were contrary to our agreement last yeare: and Bernards falling to my mother, as the rest fell to mee, viz. for want of a child at my fathers death, she setled it on mee (for else it should have bin towards the payment of debts) and so she had the personall estate, £80 as she saith, though 'twas more; and J[ohn] Lewis was decreed, by my consent, the arreares of 50s since my father died; and

£10 which he swore he spent, and so he transferrs his trust on mee, if any such were good in law by the will, the court leaving that undecided, as I was desirous it should be; and so the decree is. My uncles told mee plainly they saw my mother had a designe upon the estate, and to wrong mee, from her marriage all along; and disowne her in it, though one of their way etc. I was glad others saw it at last, for I thought so before.

163/1673

The court decreed that I should have the writings, and so I have, all but the last deed of the will, and meadow, which are mortgaged to my mother. The decree orders mee to pay the £100 contingent, and so the house was not at all mortgaged. We gave generall releases, and I am to pay £40 a yeare, besides use, til all be paid; and the 1st pay must be May 29 1674. And thus I made as good an end as I could, which I did the rather because, if we had gone to law, the rents must have bin to pay both sides etc., blessed be God! Amen.

August 3. I am apt to grieve, and disquiet my selfe that others are not so good as I would have them, of my parish and family etc., but this stayeth my heart, viz. 'tis God's will that there should be a mixture in the church, as 1 Corinthians 5:10, and where 'tis said there are tares as well as wheat. My soule hath a mixture, yea there is flesh in the best Christians etc., so that I will beare up as cheerfully as I can. It was said of the Puritans that they were fitt only to dwell in a wildernes; I suppose 'twas because they were weary of wicked company, and would complaine etc. I honour such as were so called then: but whether should a man goe? New England, whether they withdrew, abounds now with ill company: so that I must converse with such, and not follow their wayes, and so God will take it the better. Heaven is a kingdome of holy ones, and not earth.

164/1673

August 27. Going to Bury, and galloping that I might be at the sermon soon enough, my horse gave a sodaine stop, and threw mee over his head. It was my fault to ride hard in a narrow path, where the horse could not goe aside, as is usuall in starting; but blessed be my God I gott no hurt at all; see p.117 of this booke, another escape.[186] And this minds mee of another in 1667, when my wife was behind mee, in the way to Rougham from Bury; 'twas a steep way, and also there was but one path. A cart followed us so fast (the driver being in beer) that I could not turne my horse out; so I forced him to climbe a side hill (as there was on both the sides of the way) and he was beat along by the cart, which then came up, on one side, and my wife came of, and the wheele went over her safeguard whilst she plucked her feet away; but we gott no hurt, blessed be God. But this last escape I shall remember because 'twas distinguishing mercy: for when I came to Bury I found a friend of Isleham who had broke his legg with a fall from his horse as he came to Bury the weeke before. The Lord keepe mee!

August 19. I was sent for to bury the old Lady Russell; and I preached on Ecclesiastes 7:1 at midnight, and exhorted her relations to follow her example,

---

[186] See the entry for 5 February, 1666–7.

for she minded good things. I was much affected with the solemnities there etc. The last June, my uncle Peachy died, and left all he had, viz. about £30 a yeare, and stock, to my father; wheras my wife expected some etc. When my father urged my wive's father to move my uncle to promise her some of his

165/1673

estate, he offered to make it up, if her uncle did not give her as much as the rest; and he giving none of them, 'tis fulfilled: but yet I thinke her father foretold the thing as it happened; and promised to make it good himselfe, which I may well expect, and I am glad the estate is in so good hands.

September 30. We removed to Frecknam, and he that should have had the vicaridge fell short of his designe; for when Mr Warren understood that I had rather have employment neer hand, then farther of, he came of with the other as well as he could, and the towne were for mee. Now because my hiring the farme was the occasion of this breach, which I could not forsee, nor did I designe it, I offered the curate to serve for mee at Wheltham, and I give him the keeping a horse more then I have allowed. So I am rent free and have the small tithes besides; and I keepe the other farme, having my man there, and one stock of horses may doe the worke of both places.

November 14. The Parliament was prorogued in discontent; and the reason was because they desired the King to stopp the Duke of Yorke's match with a popish lady, allied to Rome etc., and now the Lord \Chancellour/ is putt out, and people are in great feares. The last 5th of November was kept with unusuall zeale in the city etc. Pray God all things may worke for the best! Amen. And confound the plotts against the Protesant [sic] religion! We may feare troublesome times.

December 5. My girle fell into the fire, and we were all sitting by: what made her fall we know not. Her face gott no hurt at all, blessed be God, but both her hands were burnt, especially her right. Last yeare her left arme was burnt, when we were at Bury; now I was just come from Mildenhall (where I had not bin since I removed) and had sate with vaine persons, and was vaine my selfe, and

166/1673

have reason, by this providence, to check my selfe, and be more grave in my conversation, which God grant I may be! Amen! 'Tis seldome I goe in to mixt company, but when I doe, God meets with mee; and I begg that I may make good use of all his dealings.

December 7. My wife was brought safely to bed of a girle, fatt, and lustier then usuall; 'twas borne about 12 of clock at noon, being the Lord's day. She was delivered in about 4 howres time, and thus the Lord followes us with mercies, blessed be his name! And thus have I children which are a gift from God, and happy is he that hath his quiver full of them![187]

February 21. I had written to my uncle Francis twice, and could heare nothing; and this day my cousin, his only son, wrote mee word he died October

[187] Psalm 127:5.

14 of a sore in his cheeke, which I suppose was a cancer, which began last May, and had almost eaten his whole cheeke away. He died well, and was a good man; my father was an instrument to convert him, and I have many savoury letters of his, written when he was young. My aunt died halfe a yeare before him; and my cousin married soon after his fathers death. He left £30 as a legacy, which I expected not. This comes well to helpe to pay my mother, and I see God making this way for mee, in some sort, out of my straits, whose name I prayse.

We had now peace with Holland, and hopes the times will mend as to farming, which I wish.

March 10. The old maid who lived \with/ mee 3 yeares and an halfe died just on her birthday, being 64 yeares old. Her sicknes was but short, her death strong. It grieved mee to see her lie so, and she called on Christ to the last, and Satan was not busy at all. She expressed much sense of Gods mercy, and is now in rest.

167/1673-4

When I took her to keepe, I did it purely because that I thought her God's servant, and a fitt object of charity; and I question not but she was good: but I undertooke what was beyond my ability, yet held out to the last, and would have done more, had she lived. I find however a great inconvenience in binding my selfe to such waies of charity, and shall heerafter bestow mine in other waies etc. She was of a very discontented nature (that I say no worse) and my servants and she could not agree, and so my quiet was interrupted: but God, in wisdome, and for her good, hath translated her where [deletion] all is content; and so I rest in that will of him who orders all things for good to mee.

April 19. At the sacrament, among other things, I besought the Lord, as Jacob, that if he would give mee bread to eat, and raiment to putt on, he should be my God.[188] I was much straitned since I undertooke to pay my fathers debts; times were hard, rent came slowly, repaires encreased, and I was to pay more yearly then I had from the farmes, considering all things. The house at Colchester had cost mee £18 in lesse then 4 yeares, which was almost halfe the rent; so that I was willing to sell it.

Some offers had bin made by Ro. Calfe, who now dwells in it, the last yeare, either to change for house and land in Suffolke, or to buy it out wholly. My uncles valued it at £240, wheras the rent is but £10 a yeare, and it cost my father but £200, which was too much; the man owed him £100, and he had no other way to gett it. 'Twas built since the siege [of] 1648; and is but weake timbred: I asked a lawyer what 'twas worth, and he told mee 16 yeares purchase; I thought that other houses were sold at 10, or 12 yeare's purchase; but thought that mine was fitt for a baymaker,[189] for I had laid out money to that end etc. I lived 30 miles of; and was forced to abate

---

188 Genesis 28:20.
189 Baymaking refers to the cloth-making industry centred around Colchester.

168/1674

10s a yeare for the chimnies.[190]

May 19. I took a journey into Essex to provide money against the 29th, when my mother was to have £60 of mee; my uncles legacy would have helped, but I could not heare from my cousin, and London journies I have found chargeable: so I tooke a writing with mee, to borrow the money upon a mortgage at Colchester, neer where the land was. But see how God ordered it! I thought not of selling the house, thinking the man would take advantage at my straits, and bidd mee litle; but being lated that night, I lay at Bures; and going towards Colchester in the morning I mett this very man that would buy the house, and he was more eager then ever because he was setled, and had laid out in cleansing the grounds of rubbish etc. a good deale, and so was loath to goe out, in case another bought it; and so I told him he should have the refusall, but was glad he was willing to pay for his convenience etc. I asked but £180, and he offers £150 which would bring, he told mee, £9 a yeare without any charges. Thus it rested; and I gott him to see if he could procure £60 upon my mortgage; but he could not; we went to another, but the time was too short; a 3d liked not the rent, viz. £6 a yeare, as too litle, but offered to lend mee it upon the house, which he knew; or would buy it of mee gladly. I saw other wayes stopped; and my mother would have the money; and concluded 'twas God's will I should sell the house, especially now two had a mind to it, which would make it goe of the dearer. Mr Calfe, seing this, offers mee £160, and after much higling for his owne convenience, and that he might not remove, was willing to give £170, which I tooke as a good offer; and so we agreed that

169/1674

he should pay my mother the £60 the next weeke, and the rest in 2 yeare's time, as I was to doe, and use for it, as I did. And thus I shall have my rents for my family for 2 yeares more; and who knoweth what enlargement may come to mee in that time! However, God hath answered my prayer, blessed be his name! Amen.

September 13. Now my time runns on swiftly, because we dwell contentedly, neer our friends, and relations: but God putts some stopp, least I should forgett him. My wife by suckling was insensibly fallen into a dropsie at Midsummer last; the child was weaned, and she used meanes of her fathers directing, and is now recovered almost. Had I lived at Wheltham, she might have died for want of looking to, for we imagined no such thing; but heer I find Gods providence for good to us, blessed be his name!

A poore maid at Chipnam had laine sick of a dropsy some time, and this day desired our prayers at church. I was carried out to recommend her case more particularly, and earnestly to God then usually; and when I had done sermon I went to see her, and she was newly dead; and they told mee she desired that I might be spoken to to pray earnestly for her, which was not told mee then, and yet I did it, and knew not why, but God did, and sett it upon my heart, and I

[190] A reference to the Hearth Tax of 1674/5 which levied a charge of 5s on every hearth in a property, twice a year.

hope answered my prayer. I desire to doe Gods will, and to eye his providence in all my affaires, as well as those of my calling.

And I cannot but note how things come about for good, beyond my hopes, or designes. I had lett a lease of Chipnam to Mr Sheriffe, whose son should officiate, and whose father in law, old Mr Fairclough, with him, should have lived in the vicaridge. I repaired it, and removed Mr Goodwin, who had

170/1674

proved ungratefull to mee, and was so violent against Nonconformists (as Mr Fairclough was) that they would not come to Chipnam til he was gone.

At Lady Day they should have come, but somwhat or other stil hindred; they gott mee to supply the place til Michaelmas, which, having a reader I might the easier doe. Before this I repented that I had disposed of Chipnam cure, meerly to gratify my friends, because of Mr Warren's imperious humour, who would prescribe to us what we should doe, as if the rubrick was not enough; and I thought it was the more because he saw my hands tied etc., wherfore I praied that God would so order it that I might not want employment. However, I did \not/ care to be ordered by Mr Warren, a man younger then my selfe etc., so I was resolved only to preach out the yeare, for which I hired the small tithes; and going to acquaint him, he prevented mee by offering mee the vicaridge, which when I refused he said he was resolved to putt in a vicar, and so the care of soules should be upon him.

Now when things were at this passe, and Mr Sheriffe had removed, only staid to meet some friends, there happened a sodaine change in affaires, and they were invited to dwell neer Norfolke, among relations, and so God opened mee a way, and I thinke it his will that I should doe him service at Chipnam; it being the 3d time I have bin strangely brought thither. The maintenance is now setled, and somwhat I shall save out of my farme heer, I hope; and somwhat out of Wheltham, for I pay but £75, and 'tis worth £100, charges paid, and hath bin lett for more; and this the rather because corne is now deare.

November 22. My youngest girle was sick as we thought, to death. I earnestly begged it's life, and God heard mee, blessed be his name! He is indeed a God hearing prayers.

171/1674

January 1. Since I left preaching at Freckenham at Michaelmas last, a vicar was inquired after, and desired much: at length one would take it, but must have some time to consider of it, and at last refused it. I recommended him that should have had it before, who now was at Wheltham; he was approved of, and my aime was to putt my reader to Wheltham, and the new vicar would read for mee at Chipnam, besides serving his owne cure, and I was to allow £12 per annum. But my reader would not goe unles he might have just the stipend the other had, whom I gave more then ordinary because of his disappointment, and so the matter rested. 'Twas well for my interest that this happened, for when the vicar was instituted he began to find the charges great, and was loath to leave Wheltham, so that Frecknam was much neglected etc., and in the upshot he was willing to stay, and that I should supply Frecknam, from Christmas, and the charges were to be borne out of the last quarter. Thus there was a vicar putt in. To satisfy Mr Warren, the vicar staies at Wheltham, to his and the townes content; and I that not long since did not know whether I should have employment at all, now have both Chipnam and this, and may the better allow to keepe a reader, who may helpe mee. Circumstances are such that I cannot but take notice of a strange overruling providence, that brought about what I never designed, or looked for, to the helping mee in an outward way. Blessed be my good God!

Dr Herbert very unkindly calls for his £100, which at 1st he was willing I should keepe for the good of his children: and now I am in a strait how to borrow this money, because my mother hath a mortgage of my best estate etc., but I will stil wait upon the providence of the all wise God.

172/1675

At the sacrament at Christmas last I begged of God health for my wife, who hath bin sickly since Midsummer. God doth not yet fully answer my prayer, so I wait stil; I doubt not but the sacrament is such that I may begg temporall things at it, but all must be conditionally.

April 4. At Easter, besides spirituall blessings, I besought God to deliver mee out of my straits in which Dr Herbert had putt mee. I could not prescribe a way, but begged earnestly that he would in providence order things so that I might procure the money, and not be forced to sell the presentation (as the designe against mee was) because of my layings out there etc. It troubled mee more then it ought to have done, and I putt it to this issue, that if God brought it about, as in the case of Abrahams servant, Genesis 24, I would look on it as a token for good that I had a share in Gods speciall providence, and that he had pleasure in the prosperity of his servant, Psalm 35:27. But if he stopped the meanes, I would submitt to his will, and be content.

So April 12 I went, having wrote before about it, but the letter was never delivered, and so 'twas full of hazard etc. I found Mr Calfe at home, and he was willing to have the house sold him right out, and pay mee the money downe, which was better then borrowing it. Now the difficulty was for him to borrow the money; he was willing to mortgage the house, and the writing was made, but that broke of; and I thought my hopes gone, when so neer accomplishment. At last they tooke his bond, and mine; and I have his to secure mee, and I had all my money, which paid Dr Herbert, and more etc., so that I have cause to blesse God for it, and that I was delivered from perills of robbing etc.

173/1675

I had tried heer to borrow the money, but was strangely disappointed by my lawyer; so that it seems 'twas Gods will I should pay it right out and pay my mother out of the rents. By employing £100 in this busines, I am to seeke how to pay my mother; she hath made a lease to a man who will not signe it except I joyne with her: perhaps this may cause her to forbeare mee one yeare, and she have use in a proportion; however, if she should be rigorous, Mr Gipps of his owne accord offered mee money to pay her, and so I wait Gods providence in it.

May 1. This day I had a letter from J[ohn] Lewis that my mother was willing the payment of the money should be omitted this yeare, and would be allowed for the time, which I had desired. And so God is pleased to grant mee another answer of prayer in kind, for which I praise his name. And I see that God was wise in disappointing mee heer, as to the money, for 'tis much better as he hath ordered it for mee. Now God hath granted mee the thing that I desired, I am confirmed in my faith, and trust in him, and he shall be my God, and I desire that I may amend in all respects. Amen.

May 12. There came the maid out of Norway to which my father had given £100 as a legacy;[191] and though in rigour I needed not have paid it til the debts were paid, yet considering that it was given Mr Cotton 18 yeares since, and by my father almost 5 yeares agoe; and also that I might take care of my father's good name, though he made not me executour, upon my brother Lewis his coming to mee, and offering to disburse the money etc.,

174/1675

I gave him 2 bonds, to be paid in 2 yeares; and he promised to defer the other debts til this money was paid, I allowing interest, and paying it in order, according to our agreement. I hope God will blesse mee the more for considering the poore orphan, as Mrs Cotton, they say, is! Amen!

August 7. My wife expected to have gone longer, but at 3 of clock in the afternoone, on Satterday, was delivered of a boy; her paines were but short, yet sharpe. She began on Friday morning, but had great intermission til about an houre afore deliverance. Blessed be my God that he hath sent mee a 2d son to beare my name, and stand up in my stead! I desire to bring all mine up in God's feare, to his glory, Amen.

August 20. My boy Will was taken very sick of a feaver of wormes, very dangerous to children; my wife had bin very sick, which made us putt of the baptisme of the little one; and now Will's sicknes made her worse, and 'twas stil putt of. I wrestled with God with much earnestnes for the child's life, so as I never was in such anguish before; by the skill of my father Peachy, and God's blessing, at the 5th day he began to cheer, after a great agony, wherin we all looked for death; he voided a great, and long worme, and vomited, and so revived. But my wife continued ill, because of the great love she had for it, and when, upon his mending, she began to be better, behold a sodaine change!

August 25. In the night the little one died, which was the same day my father died 5 yeare's since. I had taken a nurse into the house to suckle it because my wife was not able, as having suckled the last too long. The woman knew of it's ilnes, and yet told us not of it, so that it died

175/[1675]

whilst she slept, and unbaptized, which I could not in the least helpe, as knowing nothing of it's ilnes. I know God is a God of the faithfull, and their seed, and baptisme is a signe of it; and I no more question the child's happines

---

[191] A reference to 'the child of Robert Cotton', son of William Archer's second wife, Helen Godscall. She was bequeathed £100 under the terms of William Archer's will. See Appendix 1.

(what ever St Austin thought)[192] then that of the Jewish children who died before the 8th day. I take God to witnes I doe not, did not despise the sacrament; but now 'tis fallen out so, not through the fault of the infant, or our wilfull neglect, but through an unavoidable necessity, because of God's hand in Will's sicknes; and my not knowing 'twas ill etc. I comfort my selfe with hopes that God, who is not tied to meanes, hath washed it's soule in Christ's blood!

My wife was not as she used to be 8 weeks before, and that morning she cried out; the child was small, and came to it's favour too soone, so that many said it would not live, though it suck't heartily etc. Some said it could not be but my wife, or the child should die; which comforts mee somwhat, because God might have taken wife, or the other son, or all of them etc., and hath taken the poore babe only. He is pleased thus to make a breach upon mee; the Lord grant mee patience, and faith to trust in him, though he slay mee! I laid it in Freckenham chancell neer my seat; and I expect to meet it at the resurrection of the just, Amen!

October 30th. My son Will at the month's end began to come to his stomach; but vomited most of what he tooke. From October 3 his vomiting stopped, and he gatt strength, but no flesh, so that what he tooke nourished not. On Tuesday last he had a relapse, and suddainly lost his strength, and stomach. I sent to Cambridge for a doctor, that my father Peachy and he might discourse etc. He came not that day; and to day the child grew worse, and worse etc. The passages could not be opened, and so he wasted to skin and bones, and about 8 of clock October 31 he died! at night.

176/1675

How am I a man of sorrowes! My troubles are multiplied upon mee! God hath written bitter things against mee, the poyson of his arrowes is ready to drinke up my blood, and spirit! Job 6:4. I prayed night and day with teares that the sentence might be reversed; I was in bitternes as for an only son, Zechariah 12:10. I examined my heart, and confessed, and vowed against such sinns, and miscarriages as I was guilty of, as judging this stroake for my sake, as David's case was. I had bin unthankfull, and carried my selfe unworthily when God sent my last child, and now he meets with mee! The Lord knew how to strike to the heart, by taking away my joy, strength, builder of my house, and by casting my crowne to the ground! He tooke from my father wife and 2 children in a small time: I am deprived of 2 sonns! I wish I emprove this to his glory! Oh that my confidence were more in God! and that I may so live as to meet my 3 babes, sent to heaven before mee, in the joyfull resurrection! the Lord make up my losses, and comfort my poore wife, who had too much sett her heart on this lovely, manly boy! The Lord give us another in his stead! Amen!

November 1. My boy had a convulsion at times for 36 houres before he died, which made him senseles all the time; and this was a mercy to him, and to us because he felt nothing, as the doctor told us. I prayed that God would release him, for feare he should have come to himselfe, and felt those paines which,

---

[192] Augustine taught that unbaptized infants were condemned to a purgatorial state. See *De peccatorum meritis et remissione et de baptismo paruulum ad Marcellinum*, I, 55.

with griefe, we saw: though the convulsions were favourable. I blesse God that he spared him at 1st, when my wife lay in; for she could not have borne it, and hardly can now, the Lord be her support! I will be better to her, by God's grace, then ever. I thanke

177/1675

God that the child was so patient, seldome complayning, and having little violent paines that we knew of etc. He was restles, and we humoured him in all his desires which I now am glad of. He is at rest now, and hath shott the gulfe of death, and conquered it! I buried him November 2, by his sister Mary, on the south side of her, in Isleham church, in confidence of resurrection to life. Amen!

November 20. At Michaelmas last (that we may see the uncertainty of humane affaires) the vicar of Freckenham would not stay at Wheltham except I augmented his stipend; taking advantage because of the benefit I had heer. I would not doe it, and so he came to his owne, to his losse. I was glad at the occasion, for my supplying 2 places raised a clamour, and the benefit was not worth the while, so I was well pleased. I putt of my reader, and the maintenance at Chipnam is now setled, and the occasion of murmuring is taken away, and I doe not in the least remitt of my paines.

December 15. My wive's younger brother, after much lingring, died of a consumption in the 28th yeare of his age: and thus her sorrowes came one upon another. The Lord grant her patience under all her burdens! Amen! My boy was in a consumption, and fared much like his uncle; and we were satisfied as to the cause of his death, and that it was neither fruit, nor wormes, but an ill habit of body, which turned to a consumption, because the obstructions could not be removed etc.

December 25. At the sacrament I confessed my miscarriages, and promised reformation, which God grant! Also I begged that God would make up my losses. Amen.

178/1675

February 29th. My wive's elder brother was stabbed, at 3 of the clock in the morning, in Gray's inne (where he was entred) by Mr Hatton, a barrester of that house, his friend, and companion.[193] They had quarrelled before, and he and his foot boy sett upon him basely, and gave him not time to draw his sword etc. He was brought up at Cambridge, but went from home 5 yeares agoe, and lived after an higher rate then could be allowed, and run into debt, hindring the rest etc., and many did feare a wofull end. I wish this may doe good to all such! and that his parents may see the folly of indulgence to their children! and that I may restraine mine betimes, which I feare was wanting heer!

March 16. My uncle Charles Woolnough, whom I had not seen in 12 yeares last past, was taken ill with a nummpalsie last September, and sent for mee to acquaint mee that he had by will made mee his heir, and executour. I

---

[193] A monument erected to the memory of Roger Peachy in the north aisle of Isleham church also records this sad incident. Possibly William Hatton who entered Gray's Inn in 1634, Foster, p. 205.

acknowledged God's providence, and thanked him that he thought of mee unsought to, and though he had a brother in the same towne, who laboured to supplant mee etc. I prayed with him, and instructed him what I could, and he was very tender-hearted. Pray God he may bring forth fruit in old age! Amen!

When I came from Wheltham my income was so small, and my family great, and corne cheape, that I could not pay my rent that yeare, but gave Dr Herbert bond for it. He called it in, as if he had a mind to straiten mee, being vexed at my going away, as being wearied out by him, and made to keepe a reader (for it seems otherwise he would have complained of mee) but God ordered the matter so that a neighbour offered to

179/1676
lend it mee, upon my single bond, and so at Lady Day I paid it in. The Lord looke upon my straits, and find out waies farther yet out of them all! Amen!

April 25. My wife was with child, it seems, and had gone about 3 months, and, upon no occasion, miscarried. I impute it to her griefe, and ilnes; for the fruit was corrupted, it seems, and so 'twas well it came away. She was very sick, and, which I never saw in her, had a convulsion fitt. But the Lord, whose mercy we have experienced now in this sixth trouble, delivered her out of her affliction, for which his name be praised! Amen.

August 22. My wife miscarried againe, through a sodaine fright, upon an unhappy occasion, which I will not record, because 'twas beyond the intention of him that occasioned it.

November 1. I went to see my uncle Charles; and found him hearty to mee, only his brother, for whom he hath done much to no purpose, would be getting all.

To satisfy the world that my father's giving the estate from mee was for my conforming, and the consequences of it, and not at all in respect of my marriage, as he would have it thought, I have two things to say. First he told Mr Poole, a conformist, my mother's brother, more then 3 yeares before I knew my wife, that he was resolved to give his land from mee. And then when last with my uncle I understood from Mr Barry, a great friend of my father's, who told it my uncle, that my father offered £1000 with my sister Mary to marry his eldest son,[194] and a £1000 more at his death; and the young man knew mee then (being of the same colledge) and very generously denied, because he knew it could not be without disinheriting mee, which he scorned etc.; had I knowne this sooner I might have had what to answer in that case etc., but let it rest with the dead; I am satisfied since providence gives mee the estate, beyond my father's mind.

180/1676–7
<Dec.> January 10. My wife was taken with a tertian ague, with much violence, and had 5 fitts. I begged of Christ, who had diseases under his command, as the centurion, Matthew 8:9, to rebuke the distemper, and so he did; I

---

[194] Probably Thomas Barry, son of Anthony of Syleham, Suff., who was admitted to Trinity College in 1656–7, Al. Cantab.

hope her health will be the better for this, and that she will not forgett God's mercy to her!

April 25. I gott cold after a journey, and fell into a violent feaver; I had a doctor at my house then, who directed mee in the use of such meanes as did mee good. I rested not for 4 nights, and in the depth of my disquietment I called upon God for sleepe, and he gave it mee before I used meanes, that it might be his act. Blessed be God who hath raised mee up to praise him! The living shall doe it! He tooke away one younger then I in the time of my sicknes, Oh distinguishing love to mee! Oh that this feaver would burne up all the rubbish of sin! and that in this furnace God would purify my soule more then ever! Amen!

But I must not thus passe this mercy over; for the providence of God was remarkeably seen in that I should find a doctor at my house unexpectedly; otherwise I valued my ilnes so little (because I was not heartsick), that I should not have sought out for helpe til I might have bin past helpe. I understand now that my feaver was such as a 3d part of those that have died this yeare were taken with, the nature of which is not to make the patient sick but to kill suddainly.

Now because I was not sick, nor felt paine, only for want of sleepe, and by drought, I feared nothing, yet my pulse was so bad that the doctor told my friends if I mended not in a day or two I would die. He tooke his leave of mee without prescribing any thing; but unexpectedly came back, and found mee worse, and

181/1677

then gave order for a powder which made mee sweat, and breake out with heat, which was a good signe, and so that night I had sweet sleepe, only was troubled in my fancy, and with dreames. I knew not my danger til I was well, and so the Lord's mercy is the more to be regarded, and I owe him the more praise. I was much affected with it, and the rather because I was then upon Psalm 84:4, and tooke notice of how God was pleased with praise, which is all the creature can give. I thought upon Psalm 116:8, and it affected mee much. The Lord grant that I may never forgett the loving kindnes of the Lord.

June 10. At the sacrament I did, among other things, solemnly blesse God for my recovery from that dangerous feaver; and desire to walke more closely with him, and serve him under a sense of his goodnes, emproving my health to his glory. Amen.

My wife is now with child, and we hope past the danger of miscarrying, having bin lett blood twice,[195] and making use of suitable meanes to prevent it. I know not how God will deale with mee; but I have in an earnest manner begged a son of prayer, as the case of Abraham, and Hannah was,[196] and expect an answer, for my good, though it should not be in kind; my losse is great, and the Lord make it up againe!

September 1. There came last Lady Day a worthy gentleman to dwell at

---

[195] Blood letting: the therapeutic removal of a quantity of blood, now referred to as phlebotomy, once used as a panacea.
[196] On Abraham, see Genesis 15:2–3; on Hannah, see 1 Samuel 1:11–12, 27.

Chipnam Hall, who tooke such notice of mee that, without my asking, he promised to gett preferment for mee; and wished mee to sell the next advowsion of Wheltham, in confidence of providence, and what he would doe for mee. Accordingly I have done it, having my £100, and interest for 5 yeares, and £6 more if it falls within 2 yeares. And so I keepe the lease, and have lett it so as to have £20 a yeare

182/1677

towards taxes, repaires, tenths etc., and may save somwhat to make up my losses at Wheltham.

October 6. About 4 of the clock in the afternoon my wife was delivered, 2 months before her reckoning, and of a girle, which came wrong, and stuck so long with the head in the birth, that it was dead when fully borne, though alive in the time of travaile. and so next day 'twas buried in Frecknam chancell, on the north side of the little boy, under a stone. My wife was in danger of miscarrying often, and was not well, or as she used to be, severall times, especially a weeke before her delivery. I thanke God she is hearty, and I hope may be healthfull in time, after so much cleansing etc. Amen!

I see now that God stopps his eare to us as to this; he may deny in mercy, and grant in judgment; the time, it may be, is not come; perhaps I am not worthy of a son etc. I resolve all into God's unsearcheable will, and pleasure! The losse is the lesse because 'twas a girle, though we could have wished the life of it. God's will be done! and the Lord make my losses furtherances to mee!

December 27. That weeke I sold the presentation of Wheltham, there fell a living which was in the Deane of Canterbury's gift, who was much obliged to my friend Mr Atkyns;[197] and I thought providence seemed to make a way because I was putt upon this busines etc.; but it was in the gift of the prebends with the deane, and my interest was sure, if unexpectedly one of the prebends had not appeared for his brother, who also was nephew to two more of them. I never stirred for this place, and had no great mind to it, only for the present, and so am satisfied with the disappointment.

183/1678

June 26. I had borrowed £50 to pay Mrs Cotton, and surrendred my copyhold at Fordham, which the lord would have taken advantage from; but I went over to disappoint him, and by good providence dispatched my busines with successe, upon no motive altering my mind, and going on to Colchester where I found the party accidentally, who lived some miles of, and so in little time I finished all. Thus I desire to read lines of God's love to mee even in outward things! The last month my wife and I were at London, and saw our relations, who made us welcome, but I find a kind of reservednes towards mee because they differ in judgment. I heard Mr Baxter[198] with great delight, and satisfaction etc.

---

[197] Edward Atkyns, brother of the judge Sir Robert. His association with Chippenham may have originated with the loan of £3500 to Lady Frances Russell in 1676, CRO, R55/7/7/19.

[198] Presumably the famous nonconformist divine Richard Baxter (1615–91); his *Saints Everlasting Rest* was greatly admired by Archer.

August 10. My eldest girle fell sick of the new distemper, and on the 12 day my youngest; and my wife for a good while had not bin well. This was a sad case, but on the 14 day my youngest was taken with a fitt of fainting (whilst I was gone for my father Peachy). My wife could not helpe her through griefe, but crying out, the servants came, and called a neighbour who laboured with her a good while, and at last perceived some life. I had 2 messengers came to tell mee the child was dying, which filled mee with griefe, and I cryed to God for it, and pleaded, and asked if his mercies were quite gone! and begged that he would shew wonders, and recover the child etc. And when I came, I gave her some bitter potion, which made her struggle, and at last came to life, but had no senses; and so continued fainting from 3 til midnight, in a violent sweat; when that began to weare of, she spoke, and said the fitt was not of yet. But in the meane time the eldest was as bad, and as neer death, as my father thought, for a while, but vomiting did her some good. Thus they both lay sick of a pestilent feaver, having little intermission: but God heard our prayers, and at 3 weeks end they mended sensibly.

184/1678

Upon this occasion I considered that children were not capable of emproving afflictions; that they were chastnings sent by God for the good of parents, as in David's case,[199] and therfore I examined my life, and found that I had failed in all duties, and relations, and so promised amendment, by the grace of God. For if God tooke my child away I would conclude that 'twas a stroake for somwhat amisse in mee, and so I would reforme: if he spared it, I would take it as a token that he had accepted my vowes of new obedience; and therefore I resolve to amend my carriage, especially in one particular, in which I most failed for some time, and which might most reflect, which God enable mee to doe! Amen. I begged their recovery night and day, praying to Christ, who had diseases at his command, and who, in this case, did rebuke the fever in Peter's wive's mother, and it left her, Luke 4:38, that he would doe so heer, and 'tis done. How should my faith be confirmed in this saviour! And how should I love him who delivers from death! Amen!

No sooner had I made these resolutions, but in the beginning of September a letter came from my uncle Theophilus to know what I [deletion] \owed/, with a promise to pay the money, upon my bond, and to take no use of mee. This was a providence without my seeking, and beyond my hopes, for I looked for nothing til his death etc., but God would shew mercy in judgment, and move his heart to confirme mee in my purposes of reformation! So I accepted of his offer, and Michaelmas day he paid £100 to my mother, and sent mee the receit, and I sent him my bond, which he had drawne so that 'tis only to himselfe, not his executours, and I suppose he will give it mee at his death.[200] This token of God's love I will record with thankfulnes; he doth by sweetnes as well as severity draw mee after him! God grant I may follow him fully! Amen.

---

[199] See for example the death of David's son Absolom in 2 Samuel 15.
[200] Archer was indeed given the money at his uncle's death in 1680. See PRO, PCC, 1680, f. 75: will of Theophilus Archer.

January 14. My children had agues, and were often ill, so I stil urged God to cure them, and now I hope they are both sound.

185/1678

I had bin troubled with rhewme,[201] and toothach since September, but gott ridd of the toothach soon; but a salt rhewme did so discompose mee, that my rest was little, and I could eat nothing but spoon meat, and that increased it. I saw God chastning mee in my children, and now in my owne body! How small a distemper will make mee useles when armed by God! I was like an old man for tendernes, and could scarce study, or preach but with paine. At last by keeping my selfe warme, and prayer to God, and quickning my selfe in former resolutions, in performing which I had bin too slack, by degrees I grew well, so as to eat without paine, and goe to church, though I am tender stil. I find that I am wonderfully weaned from that wherin I had offended, and that God doth assist mee in conquering the inward corruption, which I thought would hardly be, praised be his name! I desire a full victory, and that I may be dead to that wherin I delighted! Amen. The feares of Popery, and massacre, with which the land was alarmed, made mee serious, and my heart was enlarged to plead for the poore nation fervently. I hope the same spirit is in all good men, that so the Lord may once more spare us, Amen!

February 14. Since God tooke away my two boyes I ceased not privately to pray for another to make up my losse. My wife miscarried twice, and then had a girle dead; and now after all God's time is come, although we used no meanes to prevent miscarrying as before, and she is gone her time, and this day at 3 of the clock in the morning is delivered of a son, for whom we both prayed. But my wife indured much, being in travaile a weeke, at times; and at the extremity of all God gave her courage, and patience, though the arme of the child was tied to the head by the navell string yet she endured those great paines, and that without faintings as formerly.

186/1678-9

My joy however was somwhat damped when the women thought the child would not live because it changed colour, and froathed at the mouth, but I urged God that he had created it, and brought it into the world, which were great things, and therfore desired preservation of it; and I had learned that I must expect a returne of prayer, and use it as a meanes as well as a duty, and so I waited, and doe stil, and I hope all our feares are over, February 18.

I sent to see my old uncle Woolnough, and he is yet living, but his brother George had bin dead a month before I sent; he was much younger then his brother. God secures mee by this providence from such attempts as once he made, to putt mee by the inheritance by ill meanes.

February 27. The child thrived, and this day was baptized, and my name was given it for the same reason that I was so called. I was a child of prayer, as well as the patriarch, and so was this. God built up my father's house by my birth, and made him glad, although 'twas a troublesome time in the nation; the same

---

[201] A cold.

may I say now, the dayes are evill, yet God builds mee an house by giving mee a son, as the word in the Hebrew signifieth,[202] and so hath made mee glad!

May 25. My youngest daughter had the measles, which were dangerous this yeare, but God heard mee, and restored her, blessed be his name! My eldest I had putt out, a little before, to schoole at Bury, where I trust God's providence will be specially over her, Amen!

June 8. At sacrament I renewed former promises, and begged strength to performe them; I found my selfe much enlarged in my affections to God, both before, and on that day. I desire more of it!

June 11. About 9 of clock in the morning my uncle died. He had bin ill 11 weeks, and sore with lying. I had a letter, which lay a good while at Bury, and in it he desired to see mee; hitherto for above a yeare he had excused mee, it being so far, and I having bin ill. Now I was resolved to goe when the sacrament was over at Whit Sonday, for I did

187/[1679]

not heare of his great ilnes til he was dead; so I went halfe way June 10, but was taken ill by the way, the riding in the heat, and wind and dust discomposed mee that I dared not goe on, but sent my man. He found him speechles, and senseles (so that I could have done no good). He came next day to mee, and he died halfe an houre \after/ he came out, but I knew it not. I sent from Bury, where I lay, a letter by him that if I could come soon enough to bury him I would, but he had bin dead above 24 houres when he came, and my aunt and he, by my order buried him June 17, very decently.

Thus God hath made a way for mee to gett out of debt; I must see his hand in it, for 'twas unasked, as also that my other uncle did for mee last yeare, and it falls at a time when I have most needs. I should last May 29 have paid my mother all, and my brother Lewis was to meet mee with the writings, and I was to borrow the overplus etc., but he failing mee, and I trying in vaine to borrow the money, I was confident providence would find out some other way, as I had prayed, and this is that way by which God hath enlarged mee, blessed be his name! Amen!

June 23. I went over to my aunt, who had bin in a sickly condition ever since my uncle died. She was vexed that he gave not her all, and so froward that she would not let the goods be prized, and seing her so wilfull I gott two men to prize those few that belonged to mee (for all the household goods, and stock were given her, and most were her's before marriage) which with two bonds, viz. £40, and £10, made about £80. He paid £30 to his brother, who died before, and so the £10 remainder is mine; and £5 to my cousin Judeth Harrison, who also died before him; and the rest I am to pay a yeare after his death. The land is lett for £16 a yeare; he told mee 'twas £19 a yeare some yeares since. 'Tis well wooded, and only a barne upon it. The tenant bid mee £300 for it at 1st word, which will pay legacies, and all my debts, and more.

---

[202] See note 11 above.

188/1679

June 11. When providence brought mee back to Bury, next day Mr W. happened to preach from Matthew 25, and it came home to mee, and confirmed mee in the waies of God. He said that how low a rate soever grace was prized at now, time would come when the market would rise etc., and when all would wish they had bin good, and like them they now despise, and many things that affected mee.

July 16. My litle boy was ill, as we thought, of teeth; but the 21 [July] he had an ague, and feaver, and every day til the 29 [July], such as the girles had last yeare. We both had a kind of perswasion that he would live with us, because he was obtained by prayer, after often miscarriages, and was lusty, and thriving, only a cough from the moment of his birth, which at times continued to the last. But God saw good to take him away at 3 of the clock, July 29 in the afternoon, in a fitt, and with out any pangs of death, only groaned as he used some daies before, through wind, as we thought.

Thus my confidence was dashed, and God is unaccountable for what he doth; my son of prayer, desire, and hopes is taken away! I forfeited him by sin, and uneven carriage Godward, or presumption that he would not die, because preservation is better then creation. I reckoned my case like Abraham's, and Hannah's, and the Shunamites,[203] only God doth call my sins to remembrance, and will not restore my son, as he did her's. God stopped his eares, my pleadings were ineffectuall, which prevailed to have him, and to have my 2 girles restored last yeare. Yet the child had some inward decay, as my eldest, as he was very like her etc., but meanes are ordered by God. God may answer prayer in anger, and deny in mercy; and I will love God stil, who loves those he rebukes, Revelation 3:19, and I hope this will be so to us. In his sicknes I tried my waies, humbled my selfe, and solemnly promised better obedience etc.

189/1679

as last yeare; but how weake am I to promise any thing, who can doe nothing of my selfe! If I know my heart, I was sinceer, but God knowes mee better then my selfe, and would not trust such a blessing with mee, blessed be his name who gave to shew what he could doe for mee, and tooke away to shew his soveraignty! Perhaps we loved it too well, and so lost it! The Lord comfort my poore wife who laieth it to heart more then I could wish! Amen! The child was a fine, promising child, featured like my eldest; and lies in Frecknam chancell next the last girle! Heer is a succession of mercy and judgment to us all along, but under various providences I will love God alike, for I know that all shall be well if I doe so.

August 1. But God hath not yet done with mee! This day my deare wife through griefe fell sick of a feaver and ague, but was much worse one day then another. On the 7th day my youngest girle had an ague; every fit I noted a trembling, in the mouth especially, but we were so taken up with my wife that we saw no danger in the child, for she could rise, and eat and drinke, only it came every day. Next night my wife was taken senseles in the fitt, had cold

---

[203] For Abraham see Genesis 22:9–14; for Hannah see 1 Samuel 1:11–12,27; on the Shunamite woman see 2 Kings 4:8–37.

clammy sweats, oppressions that stopped her. At midnight her father and mother thought her drawing on, and we were trying the last remedies when God gave us some hopes. The next fitt, August 10, we feared she would die, but God heard my prayers, for though she lay drowsy, and almost without sense from 3 in the afternoon til 9 at night, yet then she came to her selfe. The next fit was lesse, and she was in a fine way of recovery, but the fitts of the child grew worse, which grieved my wife, and sett her back. This was Tuesday August 12, the very day she fell sick last yeare.

At 9 at night I observed she shaked her head and left arme, which proved a convulsive motion; then it went farther, and both armes were seized, but gently, the mouth was well, the senses were entire. The child that was naturally patient yet could

190/1679

could [sic] not forbeare shrieking most of the night, saying she had the crampe, and alas a day I know not what to doe, not I; this was all her note. My father Peachy came in the night, and used all the meanes he could. My wife being sick in bed in the same roome was much grieved, and I sate by it, and helpt it all night. In the morning the fitts went of, and she slept with my arme under her more then halfe an houre, and we had some hopes, for the head was well; but the fitts returned stronger, yet she made no noise, as in the night which was a comfort, and did eat severall times, and talked with us, complayning of her head, and the crampe. She was willing to say her catechisme, upon my asking her, and told mee who made her; but speaking was painfull, and so I asked her if she would goe to God; she look't earnestly on mee, but said nothing. My wife was up, and came to kisse her, and she lifted up her selfe to meet her and looked earnestly to see her mother cry. I told her she was going to heaven to her brothers and sisters, and that we should all meet againe etc. About 4 in the afternoon I sate at some distance, and asked her if I should come to her (as I was alwaies almost by her, and could quiet her best); she said 'yes if you please', speaking with difficulty, but shewing her selfe dutifull, as all her life long so, to the last.

She was soon after in a great heat, and did not complaine etc. She was patient, as last yeare she said I would beare it if I could etc., only asked for beer. At six her senses went away, and the convulsions tooke her mouth. My father told mee she felt nothing now, but 'twas the last agony, so I was comforted. I prayed for her, and urged the mercies of last yeare to her when we judged her dead, and renewed promises, but God had but lent us her last yeare, and would not be entreated! Her drawing on was long, and the fitts held strong, and at two next morning she died, the very 14 of August that her agony was last yeare. I will hold my tongue, and say nothing, oh Lord, for 'tis thy doing! She was almost 6 yeares old, a good natured, mild, harmles child as ever man had! beloved of all much, and lamented more. Thus I have lost, as to us, two in a small space, as once before!

191/1679

The Lord comfort mee, and my wife! I hope the sword of the Lord is sheathed, and will devoure no more! I feared my wife, the child is gone in her roome, whom of the two I could best spare! My father lost wife, son, and daughter in a moneth's time, I hope I shall loose no more! My father Peachy hath buried 16 out of 18; we are not alone, there is no hatred but love in correction, if we make use of it. I hope God by sicknes prepares my wife for her losse, she hath enough to beare her owne burden. Had she bin well the double stroake might have killed her! The Lord give her strong consolation! My child would not keepe, and so we buried her at night in Isleham church on the south side of her brother, to whom she was like in life, and death, and manner of it, in hopes of a resurrection! What a mixture of judgment and mercy have I had for some yeares! I desire to blesse God for all, and to walke better with him!

The child said to two neighbours that she should be sick as she was last yeare, some time before she was ill, and her complexion was changed, and her face leaner etc., but the boy's sicknes, and ilnes of my wife, tooke us up so that we feared not danger; and my father made light of it, for \she/ rose every day, and came downe, and dined with us the day that the convulsions came. On the Munday she looked sharpe, and had somwhat of convulsions, but we were not apprehensive of them.

September 9. My wife continuing ill, I fetched my girle from Bury; her mother was afraid to have her home for feare of the disease that was so common, but I found that she had it at schoole, and they dared not send us word, this was August 21 and she was ill a weeke of the feaver. Blessed be God for his watchfull providence over her! I did daily recommend her to him, but knew not her case; she is now our comfort at home, in stead of all the rest. 'Twas well she came home, for she was swelled after the feaver, and they said 'twas fat, but she fell away at home, upon taking physick; she had the scurvy in an high degree so that she was lame, but that went of, but she was ill to October 18 when, after some fitts of a

192/1679

tertian, she fell into a quartane, which she beares well, and is hearty, and hath a good stomach. I hope this will carry of all <all> former ilnes!

November 22. Upon the 25 of September in the night I had an hott fitt of an ague: and on the 28 [September], but not so bad; and on October 1 worse; but October 4 in the afternoone I was taken with a terrible shaking, and so the fitt held most part of the night. I had it every day til Thursday October 9 and it missed that night, but came on Friday like a tertian. Then it missed Saterday and Sunday, and on Munday discovered it selfe a quartane, which continues stil, and so doth the child's. At 1st, for a fortnight, 'twas tedious, but I went to Isleham, and tooke physick, and then it shortned, and now I can beare it, only I am not able to preach etc. The Lord sanctify it to mee, and remove it in his time, that is, when I have gotten that good that he intends for mee!

December 25. I ventured to preach, and so onwards.

February 12. I have the ague stil, only on January 1 it changed the day by anticipation, and for some time I had it double, but since it is more favourable, especially since my 2d taking of Physick. My mind is more cheerly, and I gett strength, and stomach mends, and I can officiate, only I goe but once a day.

March 10. I tooke a small journey, and came home wett, upon which my ague came that night, wheras the next day was the day; I had relicks of the other for a good while. I ventured to preach twice for about a month, but gatt hurt, and my speech was difficult, and my breath shorter then ever I knew it: at last providence brought againe him that had supplied my place before, and he not being willing only to read I agreed to preach only in afternoons and he should doe the rest, otherwise I might have gotten much hurt.

My daughter's ague left her February 12 but she was ill, and had little stomach, and much troubled with the spleen. I heartily blessed God for it, that he had heard my prayers for her, though not for my selfe, for she was afflicted, I thought, for my faults.

193/1680

April 8. My child's ague came againe, though not so bad; she is light headed, but cheerly, and we hope in no danger.

April 11. On this day I received the sacrament, and was inlarged much. I begged health for mee and my child, and more strength against inward lusts, and corruptions which had troubled mee, and for giving way to which I judged my selfe afflicted. I grew weary of farming, and outward cares, and longed that providence would make a way for mee to be out of the occasions of vanity, and folly which too oft I mett with heer.

April 20. At Isleham the child missed her ague, but next fitt at home it came againe.

April 29. I missed my ague, having never missed a fitt since it tooke mee. The humour dispersed, and upon the ague nights I was hott, and could not sleepe so well, butt better then all this while, in which I seldome could sleepe til past midnight, the spleen and scurvy keeping mee awake.

May 11. My child's ague left her; and mine returnes no more, and I am better upon taking some physick, and those heats are almost gone, and my sleepe mended. I am somwhat hotter those nights then ordinary, which is all the signe I have had the ague.

May 30. I received the sacrament, and did in a solemne manner blesse God for the health restored to mee, and my child, which is all that I can doe. I was much affected the day before, and then. I resolved upon an unblameable conversation more and more, and to deny my selfe in some lawfull things, so to gett an habit of goodnes, and vertue. I argued my selfe into a liking of meeknes, and temperance as to passions, and doe find great satisfaction in the practise of them. I find sinns doe weaken, and effeminate the soule, and that pleasure is of an unsatisfying nature, and hath more sting then content. I purpose to be more studious, and diligent, which will keepe out idle thoughts; and to be grave, remembring my calling, and giving a good example to others.

A neighbour of Chippenham came and hired my farme of mee of his owne accord, upon the same termes I have it, only I reserve some rooms til I can provide better.

194/1680

June 7. My ague was gone so that I knew not the day, and am well as to sleepe, the Lord be praised! I hope I have gotten good by so long an affliction.

June 14. I had a letter that my uncle Theophilus died on the 4th day of June, after 7 months ilnes, and a gangrene in his leggs. He gave mee the £100 I borrowed in 1678, without taking use, and £100 more, and £10 to my children. My cousin the merchant is his executour, who buried him at St Margrets, neer to Hodsden, as he desired.[204] I praise God for this providence! and that my uncle kept the faith to the end!

July 20. I went up to London, and paid my mother all, and tooke in my writings. I have paid about £440, with use, which I could not have done if my uncle had not helped mee. Now I hope I shall live more without care (which debts bring on any one) and serve God the better!

September 1. I removed to a convenient house at Mildenhall, a market towne, for health, and to be free from worldly and other cares, and distractions etc. The curate of Freckenham is resident at Chipnam, and doth offices for mee in my absence, and the inconvenience is only going 4 miles on a Lord's day morning, which may be for my health. Before it was the same considering I went twice in a day. The house I left, they tell mee now, was never healthfull to those that lived in it; I lost 5 children in it; my wife had 2 sicknesses, and I my rhewmatisme in '78, and ague '79; and my girle the ague and two sicknesses. I live heer pleasantly, and my wife hath good friends of her old acquaintance, and I hope God will blesse mee, according to my sincere purposes of avoyding sin etc. I follow my studies better, having not such occasions of spending time idly, as I did too much before.

September 28. Upon overheating my selfe I fell ill of that distemper that is so rife, and generall this yeare. I was a month before I had strength to preach, but God hath once more restored mee.

195/1680–1

Two dayes after mee my wife was taken worse then I, and October 19 miscarried, when she reckoned she had gone about 18 weeks; but she is getting up. We never were sick so both at a time before, the Lord sanctify it to us! God is good to us in that my child holds well in a sickly time. I had a relapse, and was worse then before, but I desired to accept of my punishment, as Leviticus 26:41. I knew God had enough against mee, and wished that all this might weane mee from former vanities! Then I had, after getting up, 3 fitts of an ague, but November 1 it went away. I gett up but slowly, but went to preach, when scarce able to goe, my health being chiefly to serve God in. I desire it for that end, confessing how much I have abused it.

March 5. Upon my going to Cambridge I gott another ague, but had only 3 fitts; otherwise I have held well, and am growne hardy. I had from Easter last til Michaelmas an assistant to read, and preach in the mornings. And since that I had one to live with mee, and goe with mee etc. but his friends, being for more maintenance, take him away at Easter. I shall have the former man, with whom the parish was pleased, in case I could not doe all; and so is to reside there, read and preach once a day: providence ordering it that he is out of employment just when the other is to leave mee, so I shall be partly eased.

April 3. At sacrament I gave thanks for our health restored, and other mercies: resolved against all sinns, and to be more tender over my wife, she

---

[204] PRO, PCC, 1680, f. 75: will of Theophilus Archer (1680).

highly deserving it, and not to be so seveer, or harsh as I had bin. I begged a son, of God, in stead of those I lost! Amen! and desired a greater freedome from vaine thoughts etc.

May 22. At sacrament I promised as before, and upon preparing found my heart enlarged. I tooke delight to meditate in a garden I had the use of, and was seriously taken up in reading some sermons of my father's: that upon Isaiah 26:3 affected mee much,

196/1681

for I have a restles mind, and see the way to fixe it is by staying it upon God, Psalm 94:19. I must exercise my selfe unto godlines, and so I shall be cured of vaine thoughts, and muzings: I begged to have them rooted out, or that I may wholly disallow them! I am uneasy under them.

July 14. My wife was ill, we went to her father's; on the 23 [July] I was just come home, and word was brought that she was in danger of miscarrying, for she was quick; 'twas late, and Satterday night, so I went not, but was in great affliction, and prayed with many teares, in bitternes of spirit, that God would spare mother, and child etc., urged God that he was creatour, and father of spirits, who formes the spirit, Zecharaiah 12:1, and preserver of his creatures; and therfore begged that he would preserve the fruit of the wombe, now curiously wrought etc. I loved my wife most tenderly now in danger, and promised to be kinder then ever, and not so angry with her as had bin, and to governe my selfe better in my carriage etc.

I went next morning, and found that after two houres paines of travell, the very time that I was so taken up, all went over: so that I hope this is a token for good that God heares my prayers, and accepts of my promises! And I begg his grace that I may not forfeit his mercies! Amen! I find God nurturing mee, and reclayming mee from sinfull courses by his providences, which I desire to read, understand, and treasure up! Amen.

August 9. My wife was ill, and we thought she would have miscarried, but did not, only went on ill, and the child wasted, as we concluded. She went on in that case til the month came about, August 20, and next morning about 4 of clock was delivered of a girle;

197/1681

after 3 houres sharpe paines, she came wrong, and was wasted; it lived halfe an houre, and died. I buried it at Frecknam by Isaac, in hopes of resurrection! I see God is soveraigne; I dare not murmure, he would not heare mee in this case, I hope for my good! My wife may be the better, the distemper she had (which she had 3 summers besides this) caused her coming 8 weeks before her reckoning. I begg of God health for her! Amen. I have too eagerly desired children, I suppose, by God's dealings with mee; I may be a signe, and wonder, as my father was in such a case! But I desire to blesse God, and to be more obedient to him and more tender of my wife who endured all this. As for children I shall be lesse solicitous.

August 26. My daughter was taken with a feaver, which made us afraid, and sett my wife back in health, and getting up. I besought God not to adde sorrow to sorrow! and he heard mee in mercy, for she was ill almost a fortnight, and then grew well. I feare we love her too well, and so may offend God; every litle ilnes makes us feare the worst, having had so many instances of God's severity. She is towardly, and listens to good things, with teares somtimes; I desire her eternall welfare! Amen.

February 23. Upon getting cold, I suppose, I was strangely seized with a numbnes in my left hipp. My wife was scared (being from mee at Isleham) and her father judged it worse then it proved, fearing a palsie if it had gone higher, or death, had it taken my head; for I was taken so sick in my stomach, and with cold sweats, that I could not stand, or goe, or lie but in paine, as I wrote to him, with much difficulty. 'Tis now 2 months since, and is not quite gone, what ever 'tis: I take notice what a litle matter may disorder mee, and make mee useles! and therfore I should spend time well. Amen!

198/1682
March 25. I sold my land at Denton for £300; it was inconvenient being so far of, and the tenant would not hold it, so that I am glad 'tis sold so well.

April 16. At this sacrament I thanked God for all former mercies, health restored to mee, continued to wife, more then usually, and to child; for methods of providence to weane mee from sin etc. I gave the sacrament, which I did not last yeare, and so could not just at the time meditate as before; but before, and after I found enlarged affections, and hope that, being busied for the good of others, God will not impute sin to mee. My wife is quick, and I begged of God, after all the breaches made upon us, a child to live with mee! and I will hearken for an answer. I thanke God I was more tender over my wife then when I had more cares, and vexations upon mee; we now have litle of the worldly busines upon our hands, and have both more leisure for heavenly things, and I desire to be exemplary to her, and encourage goodnes in her, which she minds much, as I see with joy. I found, for a good while, a great freedome from thoughts, that used to haunt mee. I preached much from Jeremiah 4:14, and now am upon Romans 6:21 which I studied for selfe, who have enough to be ashamed of! Amen![205]

September 3. My wife, after ilnes at times 7 weeks together, was delivered of a lusty girle, fatter, and larger then any yet, for she had her \health/ well, and a good stomach. She was in extremity from 1 to 4 in the morning, being the Lord's day, when, after great danger, God heard us, and she \was/ delivered. I blesse God that we have a living child; I never so much as asked of God a son, though we thought it would have bin one by all signes; God saw it not good for mee, to weane mee from my eagernes! His will be done, Amen! I take this as a making up my last losse, which lay so heavy upon both of us, and desire to emprove it so. And September 16 we had it baptized by the name of Frances in remembrance of that deare child, whom God tooke away so suddenly, and putt her to nurse.

---

[205] Romans 6:21: 'What fruit did you have then in the things of which you are now ashamed? For the end of those things is death.'

199/1682

November 3. Ever since May last my curate hath bin gone, and I preach twice, and read my selfe, and find my breath and speech better; the people are better pleased, and my charge is encreased now, so that I am willing to take more paines, if God enables mee. I have used my selfe to meditation, and private prayer, with more freedome then in family, on evenings; since I came hither I am more constant, and find my heart affected, but not alwaies alike. I find greater freedome from vaine thoughts then for many yeares I have done, for which I adore God's infinite wisdome, who by wonderfull methods of providence hath weaned mee! It had bin better if I had left them sooner, and I struggled, as he knowes, but for the most part they were too hard for mee, and would returne, though I wished a totall riddance, and can say they were a burden to my soule. But blessed be his name, he vouchsafeth to receive mee when I come, let it be from feare, or other principles then love to him, which had bin most ingenuous! The Lord goe on to weane mee from sin of all sorts! Amen!

December 10. We were frighted betimes in the morning with the sad newes of my litle girle's death. She was well the night before, and never sick in it's life, only came out with heat, and had a cough, which yet was gone, and thrived to admiration. She had a tender hearted nurse, but we feare 'twas overlaid, as many that saw it did positively say. That side it died on was red at plotts from the eare to the foot, and swelled on the out side of the thigh, and flank on the left side; but the face was well, and no signes of vomiting. The nurse wisht her owne child had died in the roome of it, and appealed to God that she found it dead on the pillow, at distance from her, with the thumbs closed, as if it were in a convulsion fitt. But she might lie on the side of it, and breake the rimme of the body, when she turned to quiet her

200/1682–3

owne child, as she did, there being 4 in the bed; and this she might not know, and yet stopp the breath as soon as overlaying, as my father Peachy told us. One thing more was a signe of violent death, viz. the not purging at all, though full bodied; and the jaw did not fall, nore were the eyes open, wheras they say they need closing where the death is naturall. However God's hand is in it, though not so immediate in suffering it, as doing it by his owne stroake, as I feared! I know not what to thinke! or how to interpret God's waies! They are past finding out![206] 'Tis a time for mee to search, and try my waies! The word pronounceth those blessed that endure chastning! Hebrews 12:6 etc., and all things fall alike to all! Remember Job's case! David's case, 2 Samuel 12, I am told was extraordinary![207] The Lord shew mee what my provocations now were to make him my adversary, as my guilty heart may make mee thinke! I have bin guilty of disobedience to my father, unkindnes to my wife, negligence in my calling, and many frailties; but had reformed (thoughts I could not governe) in

[206] Cf. Romans 11:32.

[207] 2 Samuel 12 relates the story of the death of David's son, the product of his adulterous relationship with Bathsheba, wife of Uriah. The prophet Nathan foretold of its death as God's judgement for David's sin.

some measure, what I thought provoked him in such cases; and yet he writes bitter things against mee! Am I like to Pharaoh, that God plagueth mee![208] But where is such a message that I have hardned my heart against: or doth the Lord vouchsafe to try mee, like Job, to see my patience and constancy! The Lord teach mee his meaning! O my soule, hope in God, for I shall yet praise him! I hope my latter end will be more blessed! Amen!

April 8. I had spent some time in preparing for the sacrament, and found my selfe affected especially before the ordinance; the very searching our selves doth good in it's owne nature, how much more when 'tis for such an end as the supper is! I begged pardon, and strength, blessing God for freedome, in great measure, from distractions, and that my mind was more fixed, so that I could buckle to my worke more cheerfully.

I sett upon expounding the Creed, besides preaching; and that

201/1683

because I lived from my people, and could not doe them that good I might otherwise; I am not satisfied, and wish that God would, in providence, find out a way more for his glory! In the meane time I shall take paines in my calling, which I pray God prosper! Amen.

My numbnes held a yeare, but with litle trouble, and my father directed to a plaister of bay berries, which at first dispersed the humour all over my legg, as if it had bin asleepe, so that I went lame til I gott the same plaister, made up by another apothecary, and upon a daie's triall I was cured of my limping; and by degrees my sense came into that part which was numbe, so that May 5 'tis almost well. I praise God for this providence towards mee.

May 11. I read the lives of some moderne divines, and I was ashamed to find how short I came of such examples for zeale, and diligence. In Mr Stockton's life,[209] whom I knew, I found that being soberly brought up he found not that change, which others, who were wicked, found at their conversion, which was a trouble to him, as if he had not bin humbled enough for sin. But afterwards he was comforted by hearing Mr Vines, and compared his case with the word from whence he gathered signes. I have also bin often troubled upon the same account: but I read in Dr Sibbs[210] that that sorrow (more or lesse, it matters not) was sufficient which brought mee to Christ, and this is that I would labour after. I now have leisure for my soule, and my studies, which I have followed more then some yeares, the Lord blesse mee in them! We have health in a sickly time, and place, I desire that we may emprove it, for the account else will be the more heavy! I am encouraged to meditate by the good examples I read, and I doe think that an heavenly conversation may be had on earth! I am ashamed that I have given God so litle of my time, and sin and vanity so much! Oh that I may now redeeme it! Amen!

---

[208] See Exodus 7:14 – 12:30.

[209] Owen Stockton (1630–80), Lecturer at St Andrew's, Cambridge, 1656; town lecturer at Colchester, 1657. His 'life' is to be found in Samuel Clarke, *The Lives of Sundry Eminent Persons* (1683).

[210] Richard Sibbe's *Bruised Reed and Smoking Flax* (1630), to which Archer later refers; see note 210 below.

May 15. Looking casually on some letters to my father, I found one from Mr Fulham who comforted him when he suspected himselfe not sound, and which may be a direction to mee, as it was a reviving upon the reading it.[211] He saith the heart is darke through the veile of ignorance; 'tis so in naturall things, Ecclesiastes 11:5, John 3:8. The acts of God on the soule are secret; the refexe [*sic*] acts of the soule are more secret.

202/1683

'Tis harder to know, I believe, then to believe; yea a stander by may see what we cannot in our selves, for he sees grace singly, without corruption, but we doe not; the light of grace convinceth him, but we need also the light of the spirit to make us see grace.[212] The veile of infidelity is hard to be knowne, and hinders us so that we may have all grace, and yet see none, so that we must fetch our signes of grace out of the word, otherwise in temptation they will faile; and having cleared them from doubts, we must not *petere principium*,[213] or question our estate any more. We must try our chiefest grace often, and marke the chiefest turnings of life, upon which syncerity depends, and provide there. By this I find that a man may have much grace, so as others may see it, and yet he may want assurance. Moreover my father, in his latter sermons, told the people that living by faith was best, and signes were uncertaine, yet not to be rejected; but if not had, we should the rather rest on the promise, as I would. Mr Fulham built grace upon poore feelings, and knew not what Christ meant; and found it as easy to make worlds as to cast away performances, which yet must be, or there is no grace. He tried by fasting, prayer etc. to worke himselfe out of misery, but could not, til God inclined him. He warnes us of rash entring upon duties, and of limiting God when, and where, to make use of us, which I am prone to; wheras we should leave all to his wisdome! He knowes best, and will not lead us *in praecipitium*.[214]

May 19. I heard that my tenant at Bently was dead, who owes mee more then 2 yeare's rent. I spared him because his last landlord sued him etc., and my rent went to pay him; and now he began to recover himselfe, God tooke him away. I found a saying in a letter, that our good God could not doe evill to us, which I thought on. I had desired God to order all, that I might not fare the worse for my forbearing poore men etc., and I hope he will make up my losses some other way!

203/1683

I thought of Christ's saying that our life consists \not/ in abundance, that I ought to be content with such things as I have,[215] and in every estate, and should know how to want. The last summer I preached against taking thought from Luke 12:22, and now I would practise it. Last yeare my tenant, being a widow, would needs goe on, when her husband was dead, and by sicknes and other waies left my farme to mee, where more then £40 was owing; her stock I

---

211 In margin: i.
212 In margin: 2.
213 *Petere principium*: 'keep striving after beginnings'.
214 *In praecipitium*: 'into the pit'.
215 Hebrews 13:5.

sold, and what I shall loose I know not yet. I prayed God that in wisdome and providence he would find out a way for mee: and at last Lady [Day], a time unusuall, a man newly married, and meeting with unkindnes from friends, beyond his intention, enquired after, and hired my farme, which is a satisfaction to mee in some measure, and now this is come to passe, I begg the same blessing from my good God! As also that, seing he visits mee in this manner by losses (which are fruits of sin, as I learned in Perkins his catechisme,[216] at schoole, and now remember), he would sanctify all to mee, and give mee his loving kindnes which is better then life,[217] or the increase of corne etc., Amen!

May 27. Being at Isleham I could not examine against the sacrament so orderly as before, though I spent more time, and did not find my selfe so enlarged in prayer, and sermon as last time: this troubled mee, and I mourned over it, grieving that I made it not so solemne, and serious as I ought, and my heart was more tender afterwards then usually. I must trust in God, and use meanes, but not depend upon them! and live by faith, when I have not sensible enlargements! Amen.

July 2. That gentleman mentioned p.181 who now is a judge, went from Chippenham Michaelmas 1680, yet was mindfull of mee. Coming to Barton on Easter Tuesday last I supped with him, and speaking of Waltham, in his brother Sir Robert Atkyns[218] his gift, he wrote for mee, and did not question but he should obtaine it: I sought God to blesse, and facilitate meanes that I might see it his doing, and honour him accordingly, or to give mee patience to be disappointed. I heare now that he was pre engaged (though the present minister is yet living) and so my busines could not possibly be done; but the judge promiseth to doe for mee, when he hath opportunity. God is wise, and doth all for the best, and yet I know

204/1683

not how to take this: the place was so suited to my circumstances, as to the way of maintenance, being a stipend of £100 a yeare, no tithes, or trouble; a great place, in which I might have done good, as the judge told mee. But let God dispose of my paines! I have all from him, and must labour where he pleaseth! I hope to see the reason of this stopp of providence! Amen.

August 14. I had read Mr Whately of the new birth,[219] and it affected mee exceedingly, and putt mee upon prayer, and search of my selfe; and was troubled that he makes the knowing my selfe to be regenerate an effect of it, so common, and sensible, as to know we live, and breath etc. But I find others making an high degree of grace needfull to the knowing our state, and so may be answered, but not satisfied til I come to that knowledge of state etc.

August 19. My father Peachy was sick to death, as we thought, and made his will to my content,[220] yea and beyond expectation: for though he was obliged to

---

[216] W. Perkins, *The Foundation of Christian Religion, Gathered into Six Principles* (London, 1642).
[217] Psalm 63:3.
[218] Sir Robert Atkyns, of Sapperton, Glos., a justice of the Common Pleas and later Chief Baron of the Exchequer, 1689. See Foss, *Judges of England*, 24–6.
[219] William Whateley, *The New Birth* (1618).
[220] PRO, PCC, 1684, f. 152: will of Roger Peachy, clerk, of Isleham (1684).

nothing, he gave my wife halfe his estate; the copyhold presently, the free at her mother's death: by which God's providence is seen, so that my owne father might have bin satisfied, had he lived; and I desire to see, and owne his hand in all, and honour him the more.

January 25. My father gott a relapse, and died the 31th [*January*], in the 63 yeare of his age: and to adde to my sorrow, (for he was my only friend to advise with) my wife, having bin with child about 8 weeks, miscarried, so that God mingles my griefs and comforts together! For just at the time I heard of a living void, in the gift of Sir Robert Atkyns, and I am sent for about it. There was no question made, but whether I would goe so far as Glocestershire, where it was. I went up to London, and should have gone with the Baron in his circuit without charge. I beggd of God that his hand might be seen in all! and to incline my mind to that which was best, for his glory and my good. But when I saw Sir Robert's letters, and the terms

205/[1683–4]

upon which the incumbent was to come, as to live in the great family (whether Sir R[*obert*] intended to come, and to live with his son) and read service morning and evening etc., I that am used to ease, and liberty, and not to a forme in my house, was not willing *aliena vivere quadra* etc.,[221] but understanding from the baron how contrary the humours, judgments, and waies of the father and son (as appeared by the letter wherin he saith his son was eager for a prebend etc., but he would choose for himselfe, and expected one that for conformity, and moderation etc. was such as I was, [*deletion*] so that 'twas said that none would suit him better etc.) were, I laid hold of that argument to wave it, saying, I would not for all the profit, come to a living against the mind of the young patron, which he approved of.

Then I gott him to write to Sir R[*obert*] that I was come up in order to the living, but because of the distance, and other reasons did wave it; and desired \him/ to thinke of mee for Waltham, which is not promised, as I thought, but he will not engage him selfe during the minister's life, who is 80 yeares old. And so I wait the issue, and leave it to God's disposing, who hath the hearts of all in his hands. My wife, and friends are glad; and I should have made little of my estate, if I had gone so far of. God order all for good! Amen!

March 30. Against this Easter sacrament I had many things to examine, and thinke on. I did meditate on some passages in my father Peachy's sicknes, and death; and found that I had not that tendernes which so good a friend deserved at my hands. I thought of my wife's miscarriage, which was a great trouble to mee, but I know not God's mind in it. I remembred my old vanities, and my small growth in goodnes. I begged a place more to God's glory, his churche's, and my good, though I tooke more paines, and wasted my selfe, for I could not serve a better master. I begged a child if God saw good, but not to have it in anger. I asked of God counsell in my outward affaires, and to incline mee to the best, as to selling that at Bently, which my brother Williams offered to buy, when I was at London.

---

221 *Aliena vivere quadra*: 'to live from another's table (as a parasite)', Juvenal, V, 2.

206/1684–5

I recollected severall providences of God towards mee! and I was affected before the sacrament. I begged pardon of all sinns, strength of grace against corruption, peace of conscience, government of tongue, and passions, a quiet and meeke spirit, fitt to be lived withall, now I had two families lived with mee; all these I wait for. Amen! The next day I had a letter that my brother Williams would give mee my price for Bently, so that much of my care will be at an end. He gives mee £225 for it; the greater halfe is copyhold, and all out of repaire, so that he intends to lay out £100 about it. I could not gett a tenant that would give above £12 a yeare for it; my father was overreached in the purchase much etc.

April 3. To day I heare that Sir Robert Atkyns wrote to the Baron that I should have had the living, if I had come, and is engaged to give mee Waltham, which is more then I looked for! Blessed be my God!

July 23. My wife miscarried, having gone about 10 weekes, without any apparent cause; the losse to mee is very unkind! but God's will be done!

February 6. The king died of an apoplexy to the great griefe of all. Our feares for religion were great too, and the first thing that came into my mind was that of Joshua, 'what wilt thou to thy great name', *cap.* 7:9, yet we were comforted upon the promise the new king made in councill not to alter the goverment in church, or state, which God confirme! Amen!

April 19. Against this sacrament I found my selfe, upon triall, a masse of inward sin. I was convinced that my musings and thoughts were but vaine, and impertinent, and unworthy a reasonable soule! Have not I spirituall objects to settle my mind upon? I am vexed, and ashamed at it! I found envy, thoughts of revenge, a turbulent and unquiet temper that needs healing.

207/1685

I had grieved my wife, and others with unkind words, and strangenes in my behaviour: my passions were not mastered, old vaine imaginations lodged, at least given way to: I was slothfull in God's service, and negligent in visiting my flock, though I preached constantly. I was affected before, and after; God is not tied to the very moment of receiving, yet then I was composed, and more distinct in my thoughts then I usually have bin. I begged pardon, and strength, wisdome, and Christ's meeknes, settlement of the gospell and for my selfe, with submission to God's will; as also a child, though I deserve to be bereaved wholly.

May 3. I found a case putt in Mr A's *Vindiciae Pietatis*,[222] about a violent inclination from naturall temper (which suits mee), wherin he saith there is to be a disowning, and resisting, and if we find we can refraine occasions etc., 'tis a comfortable signe. Soon after in Dr Sibbs his *Bruised Reed*,[223] I found that resisting sin was one degree of victory, so that if I cannot root out ill thoughts, I will resit [sic] them, by God's helpe, and, as Satan, they must flee.

---

[222] Richard Alleine, *Vindiciae pietatis* (1664). Alleine (1611–81), was a moderate nonconformist, ejected from his living in 1662, but continued to preach in his native Somerset. His theological output was focused mainly on aspects of practical divinity, *BDBR*, I, 8–9.
[223] See note 200 above.

May 12. My boorders went away, by which meanes my wife is ridd of much trouble, and some inconveniences: we have more time to serve God, and have fewer to please. I am also much weaned from some things I delighted in formerly, choosing, I hope, that better part that will not be taken away.

December 25. I gave notice of a sacrament, which for some yeares I had omitted: surely that ordinance is the most spirituall because my heart is so backward to it, more then to the rest. But I strive against that sluggishnes so naturall to mee! Why should I be sadd at a time of joy, except for sin? And yet this is the best remedy against it, even Christ's blood! Amen.

208/1686

April 4. Our new bishop[224] had sent strict orders about the sacrament: I gave my parish notice a month before, and expounded on Lord's dayes, and privately instructed the younger sort, finding them very serious, so that I hope my paines will not be in vaine!

At my first coming hither I was wished to deale for the advowson, and my friend, the incumbent, promised mee the refusall, but broke his word, and sold it to another, who came between etc. But now I find it a good providence that I missed it, there being such a flaw as I would not willingly meet withall. I see God is wiser then I, and putts stopps for good reasons, though I see them not then! Let him provide for mee!

December 25. I had somwhat before, by accident, chosen a booke to read, which I had long by mee, but never did read it. 'Twas upon Ephesians 3:19, which did much affect mee, and some short hints of it I used in my sermon before the sacrament, and then I was much moved with a sense of Christ's love, and could \scarce/ forbeare weeping. These passions are not so frequent with mee; when I have them, I am glad: but will endeavour to have an high esteeme for Christ in my judgment, which may last when passions doe not stirre mee.

The estate at Chippenham is seized on,[225] and I know not how my allowance will be paid, but I goe on in my duty, leaving all to providence; I beare the hardest I meet with, knowing I serve a good master. I am not satisfied in my nonresidency, but my maintenance is so uncertaine that I dare not settle among them, the heir having not confirmed it. I have begged of God to be my counsellour in all! 1684, in summer a young maid at my parish hanged her selfe, because of her hard service as was said; I desire to record this! who makes mee to differ! All praise be to my preserver! Amen.

The yeare before, in the beginning of summer, a good man, and eminent professour in my parish, was overtaken with covetousnes (as he told mee) and sold some

---

224 William Lloyd (1637–1710), bishop of Norwich 1685–90, when he was deprived as a non-juror, *DNB*.

225 The Russells' Chippenham estate began to run into trouble in the mid-1660s. Its future became increasingly uncertain as the Russells failed to meet repayments on money borrowed over a ten-year period, and creditors threatened to seize the estate. This made Archer's position as incumbent an extremely precarious one, as the prospect of new, and possibly hostile, patrons grew. The fortunes of the estate may be traced through a series of mortgage agreements which survived from the mid-1670s, CRO R55/7/7/18–38.

209/1686–7

goods by fraud; the man found him out, and spoke reflectingly upon his profession. This so troubled his conscience, that he cast himselfe into the water to drowne himselfe, but, it not being deepe, he came out in somwhat a better mind. I was sent for, it was on a Lord's day morning, and he confessed all, and despaired, as one that had sinned to death. He said the enemy came betwixt God and him in all duties, and applied all in my sermons against himselfe; at last he died without comfort. I preacht to vindicate religion in that case, and shewed he might be happy notwithstanding etc., but God keepe mee from dallying with sin! Amen.

March 27. My wife last yeare, in April, was taken, as she went to see her mother, with a kind of vertigo, and fell downe dead for a litle space, but it went over. On the 9th of this month, when newly in bed, she had a kind of palsy in the tongue, so that her speech faltred, but in lesse then halfe an howre she came to her selfe. I sent for a doctor, who applied what was proper: but my heart and eyes were towards God. At this sacrament I begged her life, as also the preservation of religion, now toleration is let loose. I desired direction, and a prosperous issue about an affaire which for some time, I had in hand! The Lord answer all! I instance in what I begg at such occasions more then in an ordinary way, for pardon, and strength are alwaies wanting, but God allowes to aske outward mercies.

April 15. My wife is getting up, I blesse God, and I am in a way of setling, I hope, as much as can be expected in an unsetled world: but when present want of money might have hindred it, this day, I heare, my aunt in Norfolke died suddenly, and of no great age, so that I shall have the £200 of Mr Vynne, the use wherof was paid to her since my uncle died.

About January last, when my affaires at Chippenham were at the worst, and I never had such cares as to my ministry (this winter, though not sharpe yet making mee more tender, and inclined to rhewms then before)

210/1687

or a settlement (my land lord breaking his bargaine), it pleased God that, without my seeking, an offer was made of the perpetuall advousion of Mildenhall, with assurance that the title now was cleare. I did wave the offer in '81, expecting preferment from Baron Atkins etc., and for that whole summer slipt my time, and when 'twas too late repented mee.

My hands were tied so that I could not putt in for it; and my not resolving, and not making an interest in the townesmen (who knew not, but that I was upon even ground with the other man), putt them upon choosing this stranger, who promised to live heer, the great thing they looked at, though he never did. The former patron was the chiefe, who, with some few, went to Bury, and, after some contest with the incumbent, who stood up for mee, they owned they had nothing to except against mee (concealing then the reason), they forced him to a worse bargaine, as now he ownes, then would have bin with mee. He wrote to mee of it, and wondred at it; and because they made him believe none were for mee, that there would be a flame if any but this man was putt in, and would have him, and none else etc., I told Mr

W[arner][226] of it, who, though the incumbent was imposed on by their ambiguous words, thus explained them. That the flame feared was in respect of curates to be imposed on them, and not reflecting on mee, and so was saying he or none. That saying none were for mee, was meant none spoke for mee in the vestry, which I had forbid indeed. He professed, and assured mee that, had I signified my mind to the towne, I might have had it from any; but thought my not doing so, seing the choyce was in them, which then I knew not, so great a slight that they did what they did. This I did acquaint the incumbent with, who saw the mistake etc.

However he promised mee that if ever twas sold, I should have it, and thought my waving it was in hopes of other preferment, and that I would have left them, and hath bin kind ever since. Now being wary of waiting, and finding men of high degree but vanity, and God, by sending sicknes to this man, after 5 yeares having it, making way for mee: after seeking counsell from God in these dangerous daies, and begging that he would facilitate meanes, and turne all to the best, by Mr W[arner]'s letters my offers were accepted to my content.

211/1687

I was with the incumbent May 2, and told him how things were, and he might see now whether any were for mee by this that 'twas taken for granted, as Mr W[arner] managed it without making it a vestry busines, as before. He was glad of it, and offered to beare the name stil, giving mee a letter of attorney, and promising *verbo sacerdotis*[227] to resigne when ever I required it of him.

September 2. I had bin grievously and causlesly defamed by one from whom I deserved it not; this day he came to quarrell with mee, and I used bitter expressions to him, which I offended in, and was sorry for: but see a providence to humble mee! I had lent a booke which was newly come home; before I sett it up I opened it up by chance, not knowing there was anything of that nature, and found the beginning of Bishop Hall's sermon upon Ephesians 4:30, who tooke notice that by the connexion of the text 'twas evident that sinns of tongue did unkindly grieve God's Spirit. This struck mee with griefe, and shame, resolving to be more watchfull heerafter, which God grant! Next day I went to Chippenham to preach, and the second lesson was Matthew 5, in reading which I resolved to offer to be reconciled, as I did by a friend to us both. I desire such providences may be recorded with thankfulnes. Amen!

September. I promised Sir William Russell to resigne Chippenham, upon taking this: but the curate here not being provided for, I putt him in there for a while, and at New Yeare he was offered a living in his owne country, whether he went. My not resigning was taken ill: but in the meane time I had writings from London, making out my cleare right to tithes kept from mee to the value of almost £400, for 25 yeares. I wrote to Sir William Russell offering to remitt

---

[226] Henry Warner, owner of the advowson of Mildenhall before Archer. See SRO(B), E18/420/21. Warner had inherited the Manor of Wamhil (lying between Mildenhall and West Row) in 1644. His extravagance led him to sell the manor piecemeal.

[227] *Verbo sacerdotis*: 'on the word of a priest'.

all, if he would settle it heerafter. In stead of an answer, one of his uncles, whom I had no variance with, stomaching that I should charge his family with sacrilegious detaining my dues, threatned to create mee trouble here with the High Commissioners, who suspended the bishop of London, and fellowes of Magdalen in Oxford.[228]

212/1687-8

He could fasten nothing on mee, but would question Dr B[urrell]'s title,[229] because of pretended simony, and gett the king's title, right or wrong, and putt mee by. I knew that a court whose power was questioned would favour any that would owne it, and I being sent for to Sir William Russell, who was selling the estate, and offered to secure mee against all trouble, if I would resigne, that he might putt in his friend, whom I had disappointed a while. I promised to doe it, which I did March 21 and the rather because, upon advice in that whole case, I had a right, but 'twas my part to find out those lands, which I could not doe, after 40 yeares discontinuance. However, to right the church, I left my writing with the bishop of Norwich.

April 4. I tooke institution to Mildenhall vicaridge, upon Dr B[urrell]'s free resignation, as he wrote to the bishop. The malice of Mr G[erard] R[ussell][230] was such that he had told my lord strange things, which I cleared by telling him the ground of all, viz. my stickling in the churches cause etc.

April 12. On Maundy Thursday, I was inducted etc. God blesse mee, and give an heart to doe good! Amen!

April 29. I read service, the 39 articles, and tooke the sacrament from another minister, in order to the Test,[231] which next day I tooke at the sessions at Bury. I begged God's blessing upon mee in my new office, and that he would continue mee in it to his glory; and promised to lay out my selfe in serving him, and the people in this place now committed to mee. I asked pardon for any neglect in my other place, and desired that God would not require the blood of soules of mee![232] Also I prayed for the peace of our Jerusalem. Amen!

At Whit Sunday last I begged a respite of those dangers which hung over our heads for not reading the king's declaration for liberty,[233] as was required. The archbishop, and 6 more petitioned against it, and were putt in the Tower, 'til

228 On this incident, see G.V. Bennett, 'Loyalist Oxford and the Revolution', in L.S. Sutherland and L.G. Mitchell (eds), *The History of the University of Oxford, V, The Eighteenth Century* (Oxford, 1986).

229 Nathaniel Burrell, brother of Christopher whom Archer had already met at All Saints, Sudbury; Nathaniel moved there after resigning from Mildenhall, being vicar from 1687–1710, *Al. Cantab.*

230 Probably Gerard Russell, younger brother of Sir John, 3rd baronet, who was party to several of the later negotiations to secure the Chippenham estate against collapse.

231 The Test Act of 1678 which required anyone intending to hold office in Church or State to be a communicating member of the Church of England, and to subscribe to the Oath of Allegiance.

232 See Ezekiel 3:16–21.

233 James II's Declaration of Indulgence of April 1687, which suspended all penal laws and the Test Act for dissenters and Roman Catholics. The majority of clergy were prevailed upon not to read it, on the grounds that it had not received parliamentary approval, the king having prorogued parliament.

they were acquitted by the jury,[234] to the joy of all but the Papists; and so, for present, there is a stopp putt, and harvest ended! I did

213/1688-9

intend, long since, to have a sacrament the first Sunday in September, which is to morrow; and it falls out well as a feast of ingathering, that I may thanke my God that I am yet in his service, who expected to be putt out. I never saw such a need of prayer, and living by faith, as now; I reckoned all gone, and was prepared for it, and now at a prospect of some hope I rejoyce with feare.

September 2. Besides what I used to aske at the sacrament, as pardon, and strength, and growth etc., I begged a settlement in church, and state, a continuance of us in the ministry; and that God would keepe my people in the unity of the faith, now seducers are let loose upon us, and give mee wisdome to carry my selfe, in my place, as I ought to all.

December 25. At this sacrament I had matter of praise; we were in danger of slavery, and Popery, if God had \not/ sent the Prince of Orange on November 5 who, without any blood shed, hath, in some measure, setled us. The King is gone, and a Convention[235] is to be on January 22, and because he may strirre up the French, I begged that the Lord would repell forraine force, and setle us: I putt my trust in him, what time I am afraid. Amen!

March 31. I had more matter of praise that God hath setled us in a new and wonderfull way, by the Prince of Oranges being made King. The government is new, and as a tender plant, I desired that God would send downe on it the dew of heaven!

May 26. I earnestly begged that God would relieve the Protestants in Ireland, whither the late king is gone, and which is said to be given up to the French: that he would give victory to the man of his right hand, and make him strong for himselfe, and for us. I begged wisdome, and meekness to order my selfe in my calling ! Amen.

214/1689-90

My wive's mother lived with mee from Michaelmas last; and my sister coming of age we divided the estate, and I am building mee an house, in which I hope I shall be setled.

The troubles of the kingdome, and some private ones, were an occasion of putting mee upon a farther pitch of devotion by my selfe; and I find comfort in it! *si nil curarem, nil orarem* said one.[236] I find it represseth cares of all sorts to have a God to tell my mind to; and am abundantly satisfied that he answers prayers.

---

[234] The seven were the Archbishop of Canterbury, the bishops of Bath and Wells, Bristol, St Asaph, Chichester, Ely and Peterborough. They were summoned before the Privy Council on 8 June for publishing seditious libel. They were tried on 29 June but were found not guilty of conspiring to challenge the power of the crown.

[235] The Convention Parliament which sat to decide the terms of William of Orange's assumption of the crown. See the discusion in W.A. Speck, *Reluctant Revolutionaries* (Oxford, 1988), 92–114.

[236] *Si nil curarem, nil orarem*: 'If I had not cared, I would not have prayed'. Source unidentified.

March 12. We kept a fast for reducing Ireland; which is to continue til the warre be ended; and the Lord heare us, and putt an end to troubles!

April 20. At this sacrament I begged of God deliverance of this church and nation from warres and dangers! and that we may be a praise in the earth! that he would heare his people's cries, and Christ's intercession for us in this day of distresse! Amen!

This yeare I went on in my worke of the ministry; but at Midsummer my reader left mee, and the whole burden lies on mee. By use I find it easier, and my speaking much better. The people are not so mindfull in matters of religion as I could wish, and as I found in other places; but I pray for them. Drinking reigns much, as in all places else.[237] I am apt to despond at it somtimes, but I encourage my selfe in the Lord, and begg a spirit above these things, and have it. I serve a good master, who will reward my zeale, and fervency in his service! Amen. I went into debt by building; but hope I shall recover my selfe, and pray to God for that end.

215/1690–1

At the beginning of this yeare I had a match offered mee for my daughter, now about 20 years of age. The man is minister of the next parish, and of an excellent temper, and sober, and serious, which was a great motive to us all; yet he hath an estate in reversion of £100 a yeare, a colledge lease, besides about £40 a yeare present, made sure to my child upon marriage, which was October 21. They are yet with mee, and God hath blessed her with conception; I pray for her daily, as is my duty.

I am now going upon the 50th yeare of my age; the first climactericall is past with mee, I thanke God, in whose hands my times are: I shall thinke of loosening my selfe from the world, and prepare for that state which will certainly come upon mee.

April 12. This Easter, at the sacrament, I did begg, as for my selfe, and mine so, a blessing upon the church, and kingdome, and an happy end to the warres. Some by their base ingratitude refuse to be healed, and so hinder much good; the Lord turne them!

August 31. My daughter had bin very well, all the time of gestation; and this day was safely delivered of a girle, about 12 of clock; she had a good time, and short. God heard mee, and answered mee, as many times before, upon the like occasions, for my wife: but I was now in greater feare then ever, it being the first child, and she of no strong nature; therfore in bitternes of spirit, and many teares I recommended her to my God, whose name be praised.

September 10. She had an ague, and feaver, which surprised mee anew; but I betooke my selfe to

216/1691–2

my good God by prayer, and have hopes of her! I minded her of her soule, and chiefly begged that God would save her, however he dealt otherwise with her; and the feaver is rebuked, as I prayed.

---

237 William Coe, our other diarist, was a frequenter of Mildenhall's inns, especially the Cock and the White Hart.

From August last I had a reader: and upon the fast day I went, with the officers to search the alehouses, which did exasperate some of them against mee; they will not be reformed in that sin.

At Christmas, my reader went to Bury, so that the burden lies on mee, but God enables mee. November '92. My son mett with trouble from his aunt, whose life he had bought for £700 etc. and, through his brother's neglect, who lives in the estate, was behind in the rent charge; but upon my bond, though a stranger, she stayed til she was paid, and the mortgage transferred. I lived comfortably, having joy of my daughter, and the child, who is forward in knowledge, and speech. We had fast dayes this yeare, and my heart was much taken up for the church beyond the seas, which endures much, though all be quiet at home, which is a mercy I would be more sensible of .

I have at sacraments interceded with God to see to his owne cause, and make good his promises to his people, and confound the devices of the enemy: that he would heare the cries of his servants, and Christ's intercession for us in this day of distresse: but the Lord suffers the way of the wicked to prosper! They lay wast his heritage! and I feare our sins make the French strong, and us weake! The Lord putt a stopp to the oppresion of the innocent! Places are taken by treachery, and the confederates are outwitted in many instances.

217/1693

November 27, '92. I had a curate to read, and take the schoole, vacant by the remove of the other: to encourage him I make up what it wants of £25 a yeare; and so liveth with mee: but I find him disorderly, though I solemnly warned him against it.

August 12. It being a sickly time, I who have bin so well for almost 13 yeares had somwhat of the feaver, which ended in two fitts of a tertian ague; the heat came out in great twiddles with a great itching, and so went away, blessed be my God! It was a good time with mee, and I was serious; I would take notice of every warning to take mee of from the world, and prepare mee for heaven.

My son went to London, and staid about 18 weeks; to abscond, as it appeared afterwards, and give some creditours, to whom he was bound with, and for his brother, occasion of seizing for above £400. They did so; and he, having concealed from us where he lodged for feare of being taken, although he wrote weekly, at last came home, upon my sending a man for him; to all our comforts, chiefly my daughter's, who was bigg with child; but we were kind to her, or she had sunk under triall. We forgave him for her sake: but I find his brother ought him for rent almost £500; and he is bound with his brother for £300; besides his owne debts, upon that occasion. All men cry out at it; but his carriage deceived all his friends; only his aunt was partly in the right. About Christmas his brother died of griefe: he tooke letters of administration; so that the overplus of the

218/1693

inventory will be his, towards the payment of his debts. I was bound with him for some money: and the first thing I did, after his coming home, was to secure my selfe.

He confessed a judgment to mee: I gott a sale of his goods; and a sequestration of his living til I be paid. So they all live with mee. I blesse God that I prevented others from seizing! He heard my prayers, and salvaged mee! I will trust in him at all times!

January 20. My daughter was delivered of a girle about 4 in the afternoone, and had a good time, the child likely to live, though the mother went through so much sorrow; and a fright December 5 when the bailiffes rudely arrested her husband: I gave bond for his appearance, January 25, and she was brought to bed just soon enough to have him with her, which she much desired. He appeared, and was putt in the Fleet; but removed himself to the King's Bench, til he can pay his debts.[238] I told my daughter 'twas good to beare the yoake in her youth, whilst I was living to doe for her: God gave her patience; but her husband's absence she could not beare: she forgave his disappointing her, as to estate; because in every thing else he is a singular good husband; and alwaies wrote to her with all the kindnes, that could be. She was afraid I should be angry at her unfortunate match; but I told \her/ 'twas with our consent; she was obedient in all; and every one hereabouts thought her happily married, til this broke out, which none suspected, and which I could not foresee: though he \did/ ill to all of us, in concealing it.

219/1694

March 23. My eldest grandchild had an ague, almost 12 weeks; I prayed earnestly for her recovery, and God hath heard, and answered mee! blessed be my God! My wife was ill, but it went of with an ague at Easter; and was more healthfull then of many yeares. She hath dimnes of sight stil; which did begin about 6 yeares since, so that she can neither read, nor worke; yet God gives her patience, and she is cheerly under it.

My son came downe in vacation time; but found the marshall very exacting, contrary to promise. In November execution came; and he concealing himselfe angred the marshall, so that upon appearing he confined him from December 13 to January 31, when I undertooke for the debt, and he is with an uncle of his in the Mint, and cannot come downe without danger. I was bound for chamber rent, rule money, and to answer all escapes; the not yeilding himselfe was judged one; so that it was cheaper to pay the debt then to maintaine him there: I owne a speciall providence and answer of prayer that not one in all that time of danger, putt in a declaration against him; for then he had never come out. Pray God sanctify this amazing providence to all of us! I am ashamed that I should be so overseen in the disposall of my child, and cannot forgive my selfe, yet hope God will not long punish the innocent with the guilty, or let my daughter, and her children suffer for my son's basenes!

220/1694

God is righteous in all, Jeremiah 13:1, yet I have pleaded with him; the great judge will, I hope, in his time turne our captivity. Amen! I was upright in my ends, and just in my dealings with my son; but he had mortgaged before what he setled upon my daughter; yea, and soon after borrowed money upon that

---

[238] Both the Marshalsea of the Court of King's Bench and the Fleet were prisons for debtors in London.

estate which I gave her! Let God judge in that case! I am a signe, and a wonder to others! The Lord discover for my good, why he contends thus with mee, as in Job's case *cap.* 10:2. Not that I would justify my selfe, but reforme what is amisse, upon my knowing Gods meaning in this dispensation towards my family. I found good by all, as to my soule; I was putt upon prayer; God prepares the heart to pray, and hearkens thereto, Psalm 10:17.

I have read that God bespeaks the hearts of his servants to aske what \he/ intends to give them, so that I hope for enlargement some way or other: I have had experience of God's deliverance formerly, in many instances; I will trust in him.

December 16. I having a reader began to supply Eriswell in the afternoons; and they are content: I shall earne somwhat to maintaine my daughter, and her children; my living fell short of what I used to have, so that I had much adoe to keepe house, as formerly; but I relieved as many poore as before my new charge came upon mee, and shall not omitt that charity; God may deliver mee the sooner. Amen.

221/1694–8

We were much troubled at my son's absence, but it cannot be helped: I begg that God would support my daughter, and be all in all to her. She desires to goe to him, but the small pox is much in the city, which pacifyes her for the present.

January 3. He came home to serve his cure; for somtime before he had a protection from the Earl of Sandwich, so that he is safe by priveledge of parliament, most part of the yeare, 'twas in '95.

August '96. My reader went away; but I had another offered mee; the bishop would not ordaine him, being not old enough; but winkes at his reading service for a time.

October 12. My daughter had a son, whom I baptized William, on the 29th day, '96.

My mother Peachy came to live with mee, [*deletion*] July 14, '98, and died September 1, 73 yeares old. And I must owne God's providence in it to enlarge mee, an estate coming to mee; but wheras all her care was for my sister, giving her all she had, though my wife was most dutifull, and she had a designe to gett my aunt's estate for her, being about £40 a yeare, and gott her to live with her at Bury, and concealed all from us; yet they could not agree, my aunt went from them in great anger, would not bury her, as she had promised; so that probably she may now give my wife somthing, who never angred her.

My wife hath bin almost blind severall yeares; and of late hath bin very ill by obstructions which brought a dropsie on her.

222/1697–8

She hath bin under care 3 months; and God endueth her with patience, and is in a good mind.

Last yeare I was much straitned for my son's debts to his aunt: he was to pay her £150, with use, if she lived 7 yeares after he bought her out, which the Chancery charged the estate with, after her decease: she would not part with her title except I would be bound for it, as I was: at Our Lady Day '97 the 7 yeares were out, and she called for the money. I had many feares of being arrested; and had no way but to buy my mother Archer out of Pooles,[239] she being 85 yeares \old/, and had let it run to ruine many yeares: I found her willing to take £15 a yeare cleare, only would have the farme tied for security, which would spoile my designe: I was perplext, and begged of God to find out a way for mee; and my mothers agent prevailed with her, upon my writing, to take bond for the security: and so I tooke the money, and paid it; and if my son live, the sequestration will pay it.

I adore God's wisdome in the whole affaire; 'twas hard to be bound for so much money; but if I had not bin bound, what title could I have had to the living? And if another had seized (as I heare was one judgement, which I paid, and 2 outlawries, and a statute staple etc.),[240] how should they all have bin maintained for these 5 yeares? so that things have bin ordered for the best! blessed be God! Amen!

223/1698

August 14. My wife with much paine gott to church (for religion was her busines) and, as God ordered it, I preacht on Psalm 145:19, shewing that hearty desires should be fulfilled etc. She was setled in her mind by this, and doubted not of her case God-ward. This was the last sermon she heard; for on the 16th she kept her chamber, and came downe no more. She hath bin sickly 23 yeares, and grieving for her children's deaths brought her to all her ilnes, and blindnes, as she thought, and repented it too late.

About the midst of June she went to Mr Mansell, who told her all her inwards were obstructed, but putt us in hopes of cure. She tooke pills, and dropps, having confidence in him, and would heare of no other meanes. Some good she found at first and the humours came downwards, so that she could scarce goe. He made light of all, not questioning the removing them; but when his [illeg.]-drinke did no good, and cordialls could not heat [?] her then he said all her inwards were unsound. and she past cure, and so it proved: for September 23 she lost her stomach, and had cold sweats; her hands were cold etc., but would rise daily: grieving that she could not kneele to pray in her closet, and that she could doe no more, but said Christ had done all for her; I told her God \did/ not require it of her now.

September 25. I lay from her at her request, being watcht with, and I weary: but next night she would have mee lie with her, and none [?] sittinge, and so I did. She was full of paine, crying out 'sick heart', but tooke some rest as formerly: at two in the morning I rose to feede her.

---

239 Pooles: land in Fordham and West Bergholt, Essex, which Archer eventually left, in trust, to his grandson Isaac. See Appendix 2.

240 According to J.H. Baker, a statute staple was a form of security 'whereby the borrower could by means of a registered contract charge his lands and goods without giving up possession; if he failed to pay, the lender became a tenant of the land until satisfied . . .', *An Introduction to English Legal History* (3rd ed., Edinburgh, 1990), 354.

224/1698

I called the servant, and my daughter, who was great with child, came to her. We tooke each an hand, which was cold, and held it; she would have risen, but we disswaded her. She cried often 'sick to death, let mee die! what shall I doe? what course shall I take?' She had heavenly discourse with mee; I told her this was the last enemy, and that Christ would give her victory! I bidd her trust in God, though he killed her! and remember that, as Hezekiah, she had walked uprightly with God many yeares etc. At 4 in the morning she seemed asleep, but died without noise, groane, or sobb, yielding up her righteous soule to God, to our great griefe but her joy, and infinite advantage. Righteous art thou, O Lord!

She feared some disease in the head, having had a continuall paine there, and desired to be kept as long as we could, for feare of coming to life in her cofin; but all passages were stopped, and the water sewed[?] out of the cofin, and I buried her September 29, Thursday, in the chancell, causing the grave to be deeper by 2 foot then usually, in a rocky[?] soile that I may have roome there. How is my crowne fallen to the ground! For such she was to mee! and a gift from the Lord, lent mee almost 31 yeares. Proverbs 12:4, Proverbs 19:14. She had the ornament of a quiet spirit! suitable to mee, and bearing with mee, and hiding my failings; I never was from her above 8 dayes, and that but once, in Lincolnshire, 1670. We prayed in my study in the mornings, and since her blindnes I read to her; as I did formerly on Lord's days over and above. She had a deepe sense of religion, and gott good at my ministry, as she owned.

225/1698

I ledd her to church some yeares, and we went to the house of God as friends: since her blindnes I was tender over her, and pitied her. I begged her pardon for former unkind words, when she would be controlling mee; but now I am satisfied she did it out of great love; and have with teares begged that God would pardon all! Mr W. preacht from Revelation 14:13, and gave her an eminent character for Christian vertues; the poore will want her, for she was charitable beyond her ability, and loved, and lamented by rich and poore. I desire that my daughter and I may follow her example, and that her memory may be alwaies deare, and precious to us! I know I shall value her by the want of her every way. But I have great reason to blesse God, and to adore his wisdome that, as she desired, at her best, that I might outlive her, so God hath ended a sickly, dying life with eternall glory: Amen. She knew the welfare of the family depended on mee; and how shiftles she would have bin without mee, though I had given her all for her life, and so God answered her desires.

We had levied a fine to lead to such uses as vertue[?] should declare; and accordingly, to prevent creditours coming in after our deaths, we setled the estate on Mr Pamplyn for my daughters use; and then to goe to the boy. This was signed that morning she died.[241]

I used in my private retirements, twice a day to pray for my wife, among other petitions, that God would continue her a comfort, and blessing to mee;

[241] For these deeds, see SRO(B), E18/420/22.

that I might be kindly affectioned to her, and tender over her; and since her blindnes I begged that God would restore her to her health, and sight, and comfort her on every side. Now I am apt to pray for her stil etc., but I thinke I may pray, as I doe, that I may follow her example, and with her enjoy an happy resurrection. Amen.

226/1698

October 9. Having staid at home one Lord's day, which I had scarce in my whole ministry done, but in sicknes, I did preach twice on Phillipians 1:27 with much sorrow; at last I wisht all, as Hebrews 6:12, to follow her example, for whose sake I had studied those sermons. This I did out of respect to her memory!

October 10. Upon this sad occasion I looked over some writings of my father's, and found him worse, at the death of my mother, as to some circumstances then I am. My mother was healthfull, and he sickly, and yet taken of at the first sicknes; he had not bin married quite 9 yeares; and I almost 31 to a sickly woman many yeares, and I very healthy. But we both lost suitable wives every way, and eminent for piety! The Lord be my helper! Amen.

November 23. My daughter was delivered of a boy, and wanted not her mother, as she feared, but had the best lying in that ever she had; the Lord make us thankfull for so signall a mercy!

December 13. It was baptized by my name Isaac. I found it not good to be alone; my daughter and her family were some diversion to mee; but the winter was tedious, and the nights long: I could not sleepe, as formerly.

I had thoughts of changing my condition; not but I could have lived single as to fleshly concernes; but I wanted society for religion and other affaires. I had bin healthy beyond most men, but I knew not but a time of sicknes might come; and therefore, that I might not want a carefull nurse in my old age, I thought it best to take one

227/1699

young in yeares, but religious, and suitable to mee upon all occasions, though not my equall, for none such would venture on mee, considering my circumstances with my daughter etc.

In order to this I was to settle my son in his house at Eriswell, which could not be without compounding his debts; we agreed with the greatest creditors for 10s in the pound; so I sold my advowson of Mildenhall for £600, halfe of which was to compound withall. I bought cowes, and other stock, and goods which they wanted; I keepe the eldest girle, whom I answered for; so about Midsummer they removed; and I married a neighbour's daughter, with the ill will of those that envied her etc.

As I lookt at suitablenes in religion chiefly, so I found it abundantly in one so young; she was serious beyond her yeares, a diligent hearer of mee, in the hardest weather, at Eriswell, so that God hath made up my breach in some degree.

October 30. My uncle's legacy of £80 was not demanded by any of the sonns til '89. When Thomas came, and demanded £40, I ask't counsell and was advised to offer [£]20, as my uncle did meane; but he went into Ireland, and was killed in the army; John went to Barbadoes, and is reported to be dead. Upon which the sister tooke letters of administration, and never gave mee notice but by a subpoena in Chancery, in '95. I demurred upon the bill, but was overruled: I then answered the bill, and after many delayes we

228/1699–1700

came to an hearing in '99, and the whole £80 was given with interest from the demand for £40, and from the commencing the suit for the whole: but their attorney dying at the time, who had sett them against mee, they compounded for lesse, and I paid it.

I know my uncle's mind was otherwise, for two died before him; and he thought their shares would have come to mee; and wrote that he would not make a new will, but wisht mee to give it among the rest that were living. I thought I needed not doe it, and so concealed it from them: but God is righteous in making mee willing to fulfill my uncle's desire at least; for he never intended it for mee.

March 31. At the sacrament the maine outward blessing which I begged was my daughter's safe delivery; and God heard mee for April 4 she had a girle, after two howres travell, blessed be our good God! Amen.

[*facing inside back cover*]

My children are:

Mary, borne April 3, 1669, Saturday. Died March 30, 1670.
Anne, borne November 27, 1670, Sunday.
William, borne June 1, 1672, Saturday. Died October 31, 1675.
Frances, borne December 7, 1673, Sunday. Died August 14, 1679.
Anonymus, borne August 7, 1675, Saturday. Died August 25, 1675.
Anonyma, borne October 6, 1677, \Saturday./ Buried next day.
Isaac, borne February 14, 1678, \Friday./ Buried July 29, 1679.
Anonyma, borne August 21, 1681. Buried same day, Sunday.
Frances, borne September 3, 1682, Sunday. Died December 10, '82, Sunday.

[*Inside back cover*]
My great grandfather died 1569 at Epping.
My grandfather was borne 1561 at Epping, and there he died \December/ 1636, *œtatis suœ* 75. He gave order that no funerall sermon should be had, least the minister should speake too well of him. He was buried on a L[*ord's*] day, and Mr Jeremiah Dike[242] preached in his ordinary [*damaged*], and at last said 'my heart would serve mee to speake much of him before us, but I make conscience of fulfilling the will of the dead.' 1639 Mr Dike, Mr Whately, and Dr Stoughton died, the last for griefe at the times etc.

---

[242] Possibly the Jeremiah Dyke who held the living of Epping from 1609 until his death in 1620. However, Archer states that he died in 1639. The *DNB* notes this confusion and cites another Jeremiah Dyke who appeared in Epping in 1623.

My father married December 1, 1640.
I was borne December 23, 1641, Thursday, 8 of the clock in the morning.
My mother died September 23, 1649.
My grandmother died at Arnhem, October 7, 1643.
My Uncle John, 1639.
\Theophilus died June 4, 1680, 80 yeares old./
My uncle Edward, 1633.
My aunt {Frances, 1638
        {Elizabeth.
Henry, January 1675.
My sister Mary, April 28, 1664.
My father, August 25, 1670; had married 1661.
My girle died March 30, 1670. \Borne April 3, 1669, at Barton Mills. Mary./
My sister Betty died, 1649.
Hannah died, 1657, September 5.
Will died, 1649.
Uncle Francis, 1673, \October 14/.
My son Issac borne February 14, 1678. Died July 29, '79.
My mother-in-law died 1657; married 7 yeares.
My girle Frances borne December 7, 1673, at Freckenham. \Died '79./
Mistress Anne Peachy of Isleham in Cambridgeshire, my wife. Borne 1643, the first Tuesday in March at Aye.
My 2d girle \Anne/, borne November 27, 1670, Sunday, 11 [o']clock [at] night, at Chippenham in Cambridgshire.
My son William borne June 1, 1672, at 10 of clock at night, at Wheltham Magna in Suffolke. It was in Whitson weeke, Trinity eve. \Died October 31, 1675./

Appendix 1
Will of William Archer, 1670

[PRO, PROB 11 333, 114]

In the name of God Amen. I, William Archer of Dedham in the county of Essex clarke, being in perfecte health and memory, thankes be given to God for the same, doe make and ordayne this my laste will and testament in manner and forme following. First and principally I commend my soule to God my Creator that gave it, and my body to the earth out of which it was formed, trusting in the resurrection of the just through the merritts of Jesus Christ, my only and alone Saviour. And as touching those worldly goods which it hath pleased God to bestowe on mee, I give and bequeath the same in manner and forme following.

Imprimis, I give and bequeath unto Grace my loving wife all that tenement called Pooles with the appurtenances scituate, lying and being in the parishes of Fordam and Westbergholt in the county of Essex, to hold to her the said Grace for and dureing the terme of her naturall life. And after her decease I give the same to the heire male of the body of my sonne Isaac Archer clarke to be begotten, at the age of one and twenty yeares. And for want of such issue male, then I will the same to the issue female of my said sonne and the heires of such issue female to be begotten.

Item, I give unto my sonne Isaac Archer my messuage called Grayes Frith with the appurtenances in Fordham in the county of Essex, to hold to him the said Isaac Archer and his heires forever. More, I give to my said sonne all my bookes and alsoe two chaires and foure stooles and a picture.

Item, I give unto my grandchild Mary Archer, daughter of the said Isaac my sonne, a tenement called Barnards and two closes of land and a wood with the appurtenances which I late purchased of Nathaniell Gibson, together alsoe with that meadow and nyne acres of land which I late purchased of William Abell lying in Fordham, to hold to her the said Mary and the heires of her body lawfully to be begotten. And for want of such issue, I give the same to the next eldest child of my said sonne, be it male or female, and to the heires of the body begotten forever of such child, bee it male or female.

Item, I give to the second sonne of my sonne Isaac, if any such bee, my messuage, mill and lands called Cookes Mill in Fordham and Westbergholt with the appurtenances in the occupacion of one Robert Seamer, to hold the same to such issue male and his heires begotten lawfully of such issue male. But if in case such issue male happen to dye without issue, then I give the same to the third sonne of my said sonne and the heires of his body lawfully to be begotten. And for want of such issue, to the fourth sonne of my said sonne and the heires of his body lawfully to be begotten. And for want of such issue then to the daughters of my said sonne and to the heires of their bodies lawfully to be begotten, and for want of such issue to the right heires of my said sonne for ever.

More, I give to my said grandchild Mary a trunck marked with M.A. with all the money, plate and other things in it at my decease, being in the house wherein I now live. Alsoe a greene rugge and the curtaines there to belonging with a coverlett, alsoe a blankett, a looking glasse, three bedds and three bolsters and three pillowes. But if in case my said sonne shall have more daughters, then my will and mynd is that all the said goods here in before bequeathed to the said grandchild Mary shalbe equally devided amongst my female grandchildren, parte and parte alike at their ages of one and twenty yeares or day of marriage, which shall first happen.

And my will and mynd further is that the rents and proffitts of all my lands and tenements herein before given, excepting of those lands called Pooles which I have herein given to Grace my wife for life, shalbe towards the payment of all such debts which shalbe oweing by me at the tyme of my decease, and for the discharge of my funerall, untill all of them be paid and discharged. And then afterwards I will the same shalbe enjoyed in such manner as is before herein beqeathed. And my will and mynd further is, and I doe hereby give and bequeath all that my messuage or tenement scituate in Ladder Lane in the parish of St Giles in Colchester, and alsoe all those my freeholde messuages, lands and tenements in Much Bently to the youngest sonne of my said sonne Isaac at his age of one and twenty yeares, to hold the same to him and his heires for ever.

And my will and meaning further is, and I doe appointe my loving friend John Lewis of London silke man to be my trustee to see this my will performed in all things. And I doe will and doe appointe him to take and receive all the rents and proffitts of my said lands herein before given to my grandchildren from and after my decease, and to improve them to the best advantage for the benefitt of my said grandchildren, and to pay what rents, sommes of money and proffitts shalbe raised of the same, to be paid at their severall ages of one and twenty yeares, and at this age of one and twenty yeares or dayes of marriage of my female grandchildren. And for the paines and care of my said trustee herein, I give unto him fiftie shillings a yeare untill my said grandchildren shall come of age.

And my will and mind further is that if it shall happen that the child of Robert Cotton sonne of my late wife Helen Archer deceased, living in Norway, be it sonne or daughter, shall come over into England, and shall demand of myne executor one hundred pounds, then my will and mynd further is that that [sic] the said one hundred pounds shalbe forthwith paid to him out of the rents and proffitts of my said lands, to be raised by the said John Lewes my said trustee.

Alsoe I doe hereto will and declare that my said trustee shall lett and demise my said lands by lease or otherwise, as to him shall seeme meete for the best advantage that can be made of the same, with covenants of repaires and of re-entry for not payment of rent. And I desire my loveing cousin John Archer to bee counselling and assistant to him and my executrix hereafter named in the performance and execucion of this my will in all things. And for his paines therein, I doe give him twenty pounds.

And all the rest of my goods herein not formerly bequeathed, I doe give unto Grace my loving wife, whome I make sole executrix of this my last will and testament. And revokeing all other wills by me made, I doe ordayne this to be my last will and testament. In witnes whereof I now to each sheete of paper conteyning three in number, sett to my hand and seale to a labend [sic] with which the same are affixed on the toppe, and published the same to be my last will and testament, this seaventeenth day of June Anno Domini One Thousand and Six Hundred, Sixtie Nyne, in the yeare one and twentieth of the raigne of King Charles the second of England etc., William Archer. Sealed, published and delivered in the presence of us, Thomas Lucas, John Lucas, Abraham Bradway.

[Proved 16 Sept. 1670 at London]

Appendix 2
Will of Isaac Archer, 1700

[PRO, PROB 11 457, 110]

In the name of God, Amen. I, Isaac Archer, vicar of Mildenhall in the county of Suffolke, being in good health and of sound memory, upon the consideration of the uncertainty of my life, doe make this my last will and testament in manner and forme following. I committ my soule to God my creator, trusting for pardon through the only meritts of Jesus Christ my redeemer, whose unworthy minister I have bin many yeares. I leave my body to be buried in the chancell of Mildenhall in the grave of my late wife, by the care of my executrix hereafter to be named, and as for the estate God hath entrusted me with, I thus dispose of it.

Imprimis, I give and bequeath to my deare wife Elizabeth my nine acres of meadow lying in Fordham and West Bergholt in Essex, during her life, and to the heyres of our bodyes to be begotten, and for want of such heyres to my honoured friend, John Pamplyn esquire, in trust for my daughter Foorth, during her coverture. But in case she be a widow, then I give the aforesaid meadow with the appurtenances to her for her life, and after her death to my grandchild Mary Foorth and her heyres for ever.

In the same manner and under the same trust, I doe assigne and sett over my lease lands, wood and tenement called Bernards, lying in Fordham: only after my daughter's death I assigne it to my grandchild Anne Foorth and her assignes for the terme of years unexpired.

Item, in case I have issue by my wife Elizabeth, I give to such child my messuage and tenement, lands and meadows called Poolts with the appurtenances lying in Fordham and West Bergholt, and to the heyres of such child for ever. But for want of such issue, I give the said Poolts with the appurtenances, immediately after my death to Mr Pamplyn, under the same trust and in the same manner as before, only after my daughter's death I give it to my grandson Isaac Foorth and his heyres for ever.

Item, I give my daughter Foorth my copyhold lands and tenement called Gray's Frith in Fordham for her life, \and/ if I leave noe issue after her death, I give it to my grandchild Anne Foorth and her heyres for ever. In the same manner, my twelve acres of copyhold wood lying in Cozford in Essex. As also, though I should leave issue, my six acres of land lying in Mildenhall, being copyhold, as alsoe a tenement in the West End called Kidd's House, which were my former wive's.

Item, I give and bequeath to my daughter Foorth my copyhold close called Boxes' Lane or Yard, as also my Freshwater Close with their appurtenances during her life, and after her decease I give them to my grandchild Mary Foorth and her heyres for ever.

Item, I give to Mr Pamplyn the sequestration of Eriswell parsonage and the proffitts of it, til the summe charged upon it be satisfyed in trust, to cleare all my bonds due at my death, except that to my mother, and pay of a mortgage of £300 borrowed by me of Mr Shute, and paid as parte of my sonn Foorth's debt, for which I was bound as farr as it will extend, his charges allowed.

Item, I give my daughter Foorth the cows and other stock, living and dead, and goods that are of mine at Eriswell. I alsoe give her the silver tankard, the pictures (except my own) I have in the parlour, my weather glass, the best paire of brass cobirons, the hangings of the parlour and the two chambers which I would have goe with the house, for the advancing the rent, if she thinks good.

Item, whereas my mother was to have [*illeg.*] for life and I bought her out, giving bond to pay her fifteene pounds a yeare, my will is that it be paid out of the rents, and I give it upon that condition.

Item, I give my wife Elizabeth all my debts and goods and chattells unbe-queathed, perticularly a bond of £100 due at the death of Aunt Harvey of East Bergholt in Suffolk, without interest (now or lately in the hands of Mr Percivall, whom I make sole executrix of this my last will).

Lastly, I give to the poor of Chippingham forty shillings. To the poor of Great Wheltham twenty shillings, to be paid within a yeare after my death. And I give to the poor of Mildenhall five pounds, to be put out by the towne churchwardens, the interest to be paid by them to such poor as shall be present at the sermon on Mundays and Thursdays for ever. To this my last will, I have sett my hand and seale. Isaac Archer.

Published, signed and sealed, January 19, 1699 [1700] in the presence of William Foorthe; the marke \of/ Thomas Parson, Mar' Abre.
[*Proved 3 Aug.*, 1700]

Index of Names

NB All page numbers refer to Archer's own pagination.
Names in italics refer to persons from Biblical or classical literature.

Index of Places

NB All page numbers refer to Archer's own pagination.

Index of Scriptural References
in Archer's Diary

Index of Subjects

THE DIARY OF
WILLIAM COE
1693–1729

Cambridge University Library
Additional Manuscript 6843

[*Inside front cover*]
A penitentiall litany. Rule of Holy Living, page 373.
A form of Thanksgiveing, page 378.
On the passion of our Saviour etc, page <391> 317.

There is more merit in Christ Jesus, the sonn of God, to procure our pardon
and reconcile us to God, than there is guilt in us to merit condemnation etc.
See Mr Craddock's book of *Knowledge and Practice*[1] of faith, part 2, chapter 3,
page 39. Hallelujah.[2]

Our light afflictions which are but for a moment <work for> work for us a farr
more exceeding and eternall weight of Glory.

'Keep innocency and take heed unto the thing that is right for that shall bring a
man peace att the Last.' Psalm 37, verse 38.

[Diary of Mr Coe who resided at West Row, Mildenhall, 1693 to 1729.][3]

fol. 1r
My accomptall[4]

'Judge thy selfe and thou shalt not be judged.'[5]
God's mercyes are greater than our iniquityes, his clemency exceedeth our
malice, and he can forgive more than wee can sinn.
We cannot doubt of God's willingness to forgive the sinns of the penitent,
when the forgiveness of sinns is one of the articles of our (Creed) Christian
faith.

fol. 1v
Damna fleo rerum; sed plus fleo damna dierum.[6]
Romans 6:21. 'What fruit had I of those things (sins) whereof I am now
ashamed, for the end of these things is death.' <*Damna fleo rerum; sed plus fleo
damna dierum*> *Vide*: supplement to *Knowledge and Practice*, page 382.

'What thou hast neglected bewail with contrition. What thou hast repented,
forsake with resolution. What thou hast resolved, strengthen with devotion.'
Boanerges and Barnabas, page 88.[7]

fol. 2r
I confess unto thee, O Almighty God, the sins and offences of my youth and

---

1 Samuel Cradock, *Knowledge and Practice* (1659).
2 Written in Hebrew characters.
3 This entry is written in a later hand, on the following inserted sheet.
4 'My accomptall' is written twice in different hands.
5 Matthew 7:1.
6 *Damna fleo rerum; sed plus fleo damna dierum*: 'I weep for the loss of [material] things, but I
   weep more for the loss of time'.
7 Francis Quarles, *Barnabas and Boanerges* (1644).

riper yeares, and I hope through the merits and mediation of our saviour Jesus Christ to have forgiveness of them all, if forsakeing and amendment followes my <repentance> confession, or else I'm sure my <repentance> confession will proffit me nothing.

<I wronged my grandmother of severall small sumes of money when I was an idle schoolboy, and when she charged me with it I denyed> it with severall lyes, so I chose rather to sinn against God then to have the \shame/, rebuke or correction of this world.[8]

When I went to school at Bardwell I ledd a poor blind man out of his way into the water at Bardwell. [deletion]

fol. 2v

I have loved and delighted in filthy songs and discourses, and have been guilty of the same myselfe.

I have sett up severall whole nights att play and idleness, whereas I never spent one part of \a/ night in prayer.

I have drank severall tymes to the abuse of the creature and \to the offending/ of my Creator.

I have been the occasion of much sweareing and curseing, and had once gott an habitt and custome of it my selfe \att Beccles/.

[deletion]

I \have/ wished the death of those whom I have thought to be mine enemies, contrary to that commandment 'bless them that curse you.'[9]

I have severall tymes been irreverent in God's house and indevout in my prayers there, and neglected to come att all upon wicked <pretences> or slight pretences.

fol. 3r

I have not observed the holy times, as the feasts and fasts of the Church.

I often hear good sermons but seldome or never think of them after.

I have often broken the solemn vowes which I make before the holy sacrament, and have been too cold in my devotion there and also att my private devotions.

I have too long neglected the duty of repentance and have not called my selfe to dayly, weekly, nor monthly account for my sinns.

I have been apt to be puft up with too great a conceit of my selfe by beleiving the vain praises of those as miserable as my selfe, \this when I was young, active, and strong/.

I have endeavoured to sett men to quarrelling and fighting (calling it good sport).

I have used arts and wayes to [deletion] deceive the buyer in selling horses etc, and in buying I have exacted upon the necessity of the seller. But it so happened that I lost one tyme considerably by it. Many acts of wickedness severall wayes have I been guilty of in the whole course of my life, which [deletion]

---

8   This paragraph has been partially deleted in the original.
9   Matthew 5:44; Luke 6:28.

fol. 3v

cannot possibly now be remembred by me, [*deletion*] being long since committed <past>.

And many a night and day have I spent in nothing but idleness and play, and that after I have severall tymes received the holy sacrament, perticularly November 23, 1693 I sett up 'till 2 a clock in the morneing att play.

[*deletion*] So that my sinns of all sorts presumpt sinns, \(viz.)/ sinns against my owne conscience, ignorant sinnes, youthfull sins, sinnes of my riper yeares, those which I have so long endeavoured to hide from others, that I have now hid them from my owne memory, and that I cannot now call to mind. Good Lord forgive them all and grant that I may come holy to thy table, and for the future I will keep a watch over my words and actions that I offend not, but \when/ (for who can say he is without sin) I doe relaps, I intend (thy speciall grace assisting me) to note it in my book and sett imediatly to sorroweing and repentance for them.

Turn over to page 9.[10]

fol. 4r

Mercyes received.

In the hard winter in the year 1683 I lay sick of the small pox, and tho' I had but a very indifferent nurse \(not to say a very bad one)/ yett by God's mercy I was restored to my former health. Turn over.

I have heard of an ancient prophecy which say[11] when our Lord falls on our Ladyes lapp, then lett England beware of a clapp. That is when Easter day falls on Lady Day,[12] as it will

In the year of our Lord 1722

And in the year of our Lord 1733

And in the year 1744

And as it \did/ in the year 1638.

3 years after, (the Civil Warr and murther of the best of kings) the troubles in England began, and continued for about 20 years. I pray God prevent the like, or any troubles to follow.

fol. 4v

1692/3. Mercyes received.

June the 5th, 1680. I fell of an horse att Bury and was taken up dead by one Clim. Simpson. \I was then a school boy./

I was <struck> once struck with a coach horse upon the verge of my hatt with both his hinder heeles, but by God's mercyes he missed my head and face; this happened when I was about 15 or 16 year old. About the same time also I twice escaped the losse of one of my eyes [*deletion*]. Once it had like to have been struck out by a cudgell: and another time by the winch of a well, run full into it.

---

[10] See f. 5r.

[11] 'Which say': Suffolk dialect for 'which says'.

[12] Lady Day: the feast of the Annunciation of the Virgin Mary, 25 March.

March 31, 1692. My daughter Anne escaped the danger of being choaked with a pinn in her throat.

January 9, 1692/3. My daughter Judith escaped a great mischiefe by the fall of a spitt which narrowly escaped her head, \she was then a little above 5 yeares of age./

See Mr Cradock, book of *Knowledge and Practice*, 2 part, 19 chapter, 106 page. Blessed be the Lord, in all my life I never broke a bone, never fell into the hands etc. See page 137, 138 of this book.[13]

fol. 5r

25th of December, 1693. I received the blessed sacrament and renewed my covenant with my God in my Saviour's blood. The Lord give me grace to keep it.

Tuesday 26. I omitted prayers in my family.

27. Omitted prayers again and was guilty of idle discourse that day, when I know that for every idle word I must give an account att the Day of Judgment.

28. Neglected publick prayers again and my owne private devotions for forenoon and afternoon.

29. I was the occasion of another's sweareing and cursing.

31, Sunday. Spent most of this day in vain and idle discourse. Lord be merciful to me etc.

January 1st. Stayed out 'till midnight and then neglected prayers in my family.

3. Mispending my pretious time att play att Mr Bradbury's.

7. Being Sunday, spent all that afternoon in vain and fruitless discourse and visits.

fol. 5v

1693/4. Mercyes received.

February 11th, 1693. My \daughter/ Betty escaped choakeing, by a pinn in her victualls, the Lord make me truely thankful for this and all other his mercyes.[14]

April 1st, 1694. My wife received no hurt by a fall, tho' great with child within about a fortnight of her tyme.

May 24. I escaped the danger of being hurt, being kicked att, in the dark, by my sorrell mare, which rubbed past my clothes without hurt.

December 6, 1694. My wife <and myselfe escaped [*illeg.*]> swooned in the night comeing home on a blind horse I had of R. Bugg.

20, '94. I gott a fall off my horse goeing to Bury but received no hurt, I thank God.

March 16th, 1694/5. My sonn William escaped the danger of being choaked with a peice of apple (being not a yeare old).

---

[13] See ff. 70v, 71v.

[14] The frequency with which Coe refers to swallowing pins (or nearly so) in his victuals, suggests the trussing of meat, although on one occasion he refers to a pin in his bread. See ff. 8v, 32v (bread), 55v, 58v, 67v, 81v (meat), 82v.

17. A fire had liked to have broke out in the kitchin chamber but was happily discovered and prevented.

fol. 6r

January 10th, 1693/4. Sett up 'till midnight att play att Bury.

14, being Sunday. I was idle att church, and full of wandring thoughts.

15. Sett up 'till midnight att play at Mr Fisk's.

17. Sett up 'till midnight att play.

19. Sett up 'till past midnight att play.

24. Sett up 'till midnight att play att Bury.

26. Neglected prayers with my family.

31. Spent all that day in play.

February 12. Played 'till 11 a clock.

23. Sett up 'till 3 a clock att Barton Mills. Many failings and infirmityes from February 23 to

March 11th, being Sunday. Sleeping at church, and idlely spending the rest of the day.

20. Drinking too much att Swafham.

1694, April 1st. Sleeping att church and mispending most part of that day.

<May 6. Sleeping att church and discoursing of bargaines.>

fol. 6v

1695–7. Mercyes received.

<July> 1695, June 12. My grey horse fell downe with me comeing from Royston, and I gott no hurt.

July 2. He fell downe againe with me [deletion] and did fling me over his head, and I gott no hurt.

July 3. He fell downe againe with me and I escaped any hurt, I thank God.

October 7th. My son William escaped choaking with a pinn at dinner.

1696, December 6. He escaped burneing, his capp on his head being sett on fire by a candle.

November 28. My wife gott safe to Tilney.

December 21. She came safe home which, as the weather was then, was a dangerous journey.

1697, March 30. I went into a little stable of Mr Seyliard's not expecting any danger, and was struck att severall times by a mischieffull horse and had scarce room enough to shift for my selfe, yett by God's great mercye I gott no hurt, tho' his heeles touched my coat. <and did mee no hurt>

fol. 7r

April 8th, '94, Easter Day. I received the blessed sacrament of the body and blood of our Saviour Jesus Christ, God give me grace to live more circumspectly for the future and to keep a strickt watch over all my words and actions.

April 29, Sunday. Idley spending all that day.

May 6. Sleeping att church and discoursing of bargaines and worldly buisiness most part of the day.

207

13. I spent all the afternoon in <lewd> wicked and profane discourse, not spending one moment in reading or other good exercise.

May 16. Sett up 'till 2 a clock in the morning att play att Bury.

17, being Ascension day. Spent all that day att play 'till 4 a clock in th' afternoon.

April 3, 1693. Drank too much att Barton with uncle St Gens. This should have been placed 2 or 3 pages before, but I had scarce then begann to keep account of my tyme.

fol. 7v

1697/8. Mercies received.

January 29. My wife should have gone to Lynn by the stage coach, but (God be thanked) there was noe roome, for it was overthrown in <in> the water att Barton and the passengers very narrowly escaped drowning, the water then being very high, a great flood.

August 14. I escaped an hurt on mine eye, a springell struck in just att the corner of mine eye, and did me no other hurt. *Deo gratias.*

October 25. I had a dangerous fall off my yellow mare comeing from Newmarkett and gott noe hurt.

26. I had a fall from my bay colt by rideing over a steep bank in the dark att Mildenhall Towne's end, \neat-way/, comeing from Bury, and gott noe hurt, I thanke God.

February 13. My house was in danger of being burned, the chimney in the great parlour chamber being on fire, but by God's good providence did noe damage. I was then att Downham Markett.

fol. 8r

May 27, Whitsunday, 1694. I received the blessed sacrament and renewed my covenant again with Almighty God in my Saviour's blood. Lord give me grace to amend my life for the future and to spend every day as if it were to be my last.

June the 3, being Sunday. I slept att church.

10th. Talked of worldly buisiness so soon as I came from church.

24. I slept att church and talked of my worldly buisiness, Lord be mercifull etc.

25. Spent all that day at play.

July 29, Sunday. Idlely spending all that day and talking of worldly buisiness.

November 22. Sett up 'till 1 a clock att play att \our/ court.[15]

30. Sett up 'till 3 a clock att play.

December 10. Spent all that day in play att Wammell.

12. Sett up 'till 4 a clock att play att Unley.[16]

22. I fasted, being to receive the blessed sacrament of Christ's body and blood on Christmas day next, and on examination I found my selfe guilty of this catalogue of sinns following viz. Turne over.

---

[15] One of the manorial courts of Mildenhall.
[16] Undley, in the parish of Lakenheath, Suff.

fol. 8v

1699. Mercyes received.

May 3. My daughter Sarah escaped choacking with a pinn in her victualls.

June 5. I had like to have swallowed a large spider in my beer, and what effect it would have had upon me, God \onely/ knowes.

I likewise <received a singular mercy> \escaped another great danger/ this very day 19 yeares, as may appear 4 leaves back in this book,[17] (viz.) I gott a dangerous fall of an horse att Bury and was taken up dead.

July 15. Wee went safe to Groton.

19. Wee returned safe and found all well at home, God be praysed.

September 11. I escaped the danger of falling into a deep pitt, being just upon the brink of it in a dark night. God be thanked for these and all other his mercyes. Turn over.

fol. 9r

1694. Sinns against the 1st Commandment.

I have been often guilty of feareing men more than God, by telling lyes and equivocating to shunn and avoid some outward shame or sufferings from them. 2nd Commandment.

I have been guilty of irreverent behaviour in the church and att other holy duties, often idley and prophanely spending the Lord's day talkeing of worldly buisiness. I have \often/ omitted publick and private prayers upon \slight/ pretences [deletion], and when I have been present att them, my thoughts are always wandring, and am guilty of too much dulness, deadness, and distraction, that tho' I draw \nigh/ unto God with my lipps, my heart is too often wandring and farr from him. 3rd Commandment.

I have been guilty of rash vowes and protestations, to confirm what I have said, when I have not been beleived upon my bare word, notwithstanding the truth.

I have not seriously considered and bewailed my frequent and dangerous violations of that great and solemn vow made att \my/ baptism, neither have I observed as I ought the holy vowes and purposes of ammendment.

fol. 9v

1699/1700. Mercyes received.

February 26. I escaped a great danger. It was God's great mercy that my hand was not rent off or spoiled by my horsemill, and it onely rent a little of the flesh.

March 27. My wife very narrowly escaped choking haveing a pinn in her mouth which by drawing her breath sliped in to her throat, but by God's great mercy it came up again.

April 22. A fire had like to have broken out through the carelessness of Oliver Brand's family, carrying fire out in their ashes into yards amongst the straw, but was happily discovered and prevented, this the 2d time in less than a fortnight.

---

[17] See f. 4v.

May 12. My sonn William fell into ye crick up to the knee and nobody with him. It was through God's great mercy he did not fall over head and ears, and be drowned [deletion]. He was then a little above 6 year old.

fol. 10r
Amendment which I am apt to make in adversity and alwayes before the sacrament.

I have drawn others into sinn \and idleness/ by my wicked example, counsell and advice.

4th Commandment.

I have not so stricktly observed the holy feasts and fasts of the Church as I ought, but have spent them cheifly in vain and idle recreations, \often/ neglecting the prayers of the Church, [deletion] appointed for such dayes.

I have profaned the Lord's Supper, 1st by comeing ignorantly to it and without strict examination and contrition, 2dly without devotion and spirituall affection, my mind and heart being full of wandring and worldly thoughts, and 3dly by often breaking my vowes and purposes of amendment, and leading a new life. I have not been carefull to call my selfe to a strickt account for my sinns, and to act revenge upon my selfe by fasting or other acts of mortification.

6[th Commandment]. I have wished the death of those who in their life time have been froward and troublesome to me.

fol. 10v

1700. Mercyes Received.

June 1st. I ventured to shoot as I sett upon horse back, and the horse started and threw me downe, and by God's great mercy I gott not the least hurt.

December 25. My daughter Elizabeth had a hurt by a stone cast accidentally \into the chariot/ as she was comeing from church, which might have proved a greater mischiefe. God be praised it was noe worse.

April 18, 1701. My daughter Susan was almost choaked with a pinn in her throat as she was layd in bedd.

July 26. My sonn William gott a fall off Mr Meadowes' mare with Thomas Meadows, and she did tread upon his thigh and made it black and blew. But (God be thanked) gott no further hurt.

[folio removed][18]

fol. 11r
I have used arts to deceive the buyer and have been guilty of lyeing and equivocating to put off horses and other things I had to sell, and in buying \I have/ exacted upon the necessity of the seller.

---

[18] This missing folio will have contained more confessions relating to the 6th–8th Commandments, and probably more 'Mercies Received'. Part of this missing information is recorded in A. Simpson's *History of Mildenhall* (1901), p. 28. It accounts for the local tradition that 'Squire Coe of fair West Row cut off the hair of his three eldest daughters in order to have a wig made for himself by Mr Eldred of Bury St Edmunds'. (See Introduction, pp. 35–36)

9[*th*] Commandment.

I have been too forward to believe ill reports of my neighbour.

10[*th*] Commandment.

I have had secret covetings of the goods and delights of my neighbour.

I have threatened revenge and hurt to him for some small trouble or inconveniencye done to me.

I have been often guilty \by my provocation/ of another's sweareing and cursing and was guilty of it my selfe att Beccles.

I have spent whole nights and dayes att play, whereas I scarce ever spent one hour <att prayers> together att prayer.

I have often drank too much to some degree of drunkenness, [*deletion*][19] but I repent, oh my God, I repent, I accuse, and judge, and condemn my self for all these my misdoeings. Lord be mercifull to me a sinner.

fol.11v

Cito praeterit quod delectat, ad permanet sine fine quod cruciat, St Augustine.[20] That is, 'the pleasure of a sinn is soon over, but the sting and bitterness remaineth for ever.'

There is more meritt in \Jesus Christ/ the sonne of God to procure our pardon, and reconcile us to God, then there is guilt in us, to merit condemnation.

Let every one think thus with himself, I must shortly dye, and though sinn seem now sweet, and delightfull, it will at the hour of death be as gall and wormwood. Therefore let me not allow in my selfe anything now, that will be bitterness to me at my latter end. Mercyes received. Turn over.

fol.12r

December 25, 1694. I received the blessed sacrament of Christ's body and blood, and renewed my covenant with Almighty God (in my Saviour's blood) which I have so often and greviously broken; I beseech God to enable me to keep it better for the future. Lord be mercifull to me a sinner.

28. Sett up 'till 1 a clock att play att Wammell.

29. Sett up 'till 11 (being Saturday night) att play att Mr Seyliard's.

30, Sunday. Vain and idle discourse goeing to church, [*deletion*] irreverent behaviour and wandring thoughts there.

31. Sett up 'till 3 a clock \at play/ att Wammell.

January 1. Sett up too late att Barton takeing delight in filthy and wanton discourse and unchast songs.

3. Sett up 'till after 2 a clock att play att Wammell. Severall times runn after worldly vanityes and neglected the main buisiness of my life, that one thing necessary.

20. Being Sunday, I spent most part of that day in idle and vain discourses.

---

[19] Some of the words are legible: '. . . with . . . often att Bent[..] . . .'

[20] The full quotation runs: '*nimium miseranda conditio est, ubi cito praeterit quod delectat, et per diabolum in cruce manet sine fine qoud cruciat,*' Sermon, 250, de temp. cap. 3, tom. 10.

fol. 12v

1702/3. Mercyes received.

May 1. A fire kindled in my yard near the stable muckhill (where lay a great deal of dry litter and straw), through the carelessness of \some of/ my servants carrying out ashes with fire in them, which had done me very great damage \but/ was hapily prevented, being discovered so soon as it began to blaze. The Lord be praised for this and all other his mercies continually bestowed upon us.

November 3. My son William had a dangerous blow upon his eye with the end of an oaken rail, but God be praysed it did not perish his eye. It was att Tuddenham.

February 27. My horse colt struck att me as I stood behind him in the stable, but by God's great mercy missed me. For this and all other thy continued mercyes to me and mine, my soul doth magnifye thee, O Lord.

fol. 13r

January '94/5.

21. Too many idle and rash words att Bury and giveing idle names to persons.

22. Filthy and obsceene discourse att Mr Bradburye's.

March 8, Lent. Sett up 'till 11 a clock att play.

13. Drank too much att Mr Challings' (which was the occasion of a week's sickness) in that solemn time of Lent, but I believe I was imposed upon, by them putting some strong spiritts into my drink, unknown to me.

March 24, 1694/5, being Easter day. I received the blessed sacrament of Christ's body and blood, and renewed my vowes <and purposes> of forsakeing my sinns and amending my life, with full purpose to live more circumspectly for the future, God's grace assisting me.

April 5. Stayd out att play 'till past 9 a clock and neglected prayers in my family and my owne private devotions for the afternoon.

Also, the 3 Aprill, spent all the afternoon att play, att Bury.

fol. 13v

1703. Mercyes Received.

June 4. I stood near a lyon (which came about for a sight) with my back to him, and he rose up (as I was told by some that called to me) to mischief me, and I stept forward the same moment \out of his reach/ and God knowes what the event might have been.

November 26 att night and [Nov.] 27 in the morning, was a very high wind and blew downe severall houses and trees and killed severall persons,[21] but blessed be God who spared our lives and limbs, and though I sustained a considerable loss and damage \my cowlodge was blown down and killed 3 cows,/ yet if God's great mercy had not intervened, it had proved a great deal worse.

February 15. I escaped a mischief which I was in danger of by running in the dark, and stumbled upon a mapp stick that was in my way, and had like to have

---

[21] The great hurricane of 26 Nov. 1703; see Daniel Defoe, *The Storm* (1704), p. 338.

broke my finger, my hand happening between 2 pales as I was falling, but I thank God onely bruised my little finger.

fol. 14r

April 28, 1695, Sunday. Spent most part of that day idley, in vain and fruitless discourse.

May 7. Spent all this forenoon att play (*domi*).[22]

8. Spent great part of that day att play att Bury.

May 12, Whitsunday. I received the blessed sacrament of the body and blood of my Saviour Jesus Christ and renewed my vowes and purposes of forsakeing all my sinns and amending [*deletion*] my life. Lord give me grace to keep them.

15. I told a lye about my old mault att Royston.

19. Talked of worldly buisiness most part of that day, being Sunday.

31. Sett up 'till 12 a clock att play att White Hart.

June 2, Sunday. I slept att church.

23, Sunday. Slept att church.

27. Spent all that afternoon att play (*domi*).

July 9. Spent all that forenoon att play.

21, being Sunday, I [*deletion*] spent all that day idley and profanely. Lord be mercifull, etc.

22. Vainly spending all that day att Barton Mills.

fol. 14v

1703. Mercyes Received.

February 16. As I was goeing to Bury my horse stumbled by reason of my galloping in a deep narrow road, and runn a good way upon his knees, and had much adoe to recover himself that I was in great danger of falling, but (God be praised) I kept his back, so gott no hurt.

22. I had almost rode over a little child att Newmarket and did not see him. But (God be thanked) he escaped. Young Christopher Clemens, at the White Horse.

July 29, 1704. My horse started in Jos. Ellington's lane and threw me, but I thank God I gott noe hurt.

August 9. Towards night I was taken ill and it proceeded to a fever, and I was very ill so that all about me feared I should have dyed; this sickness produced such effects that I reckon it amongst God's mercyes, and doe say it was good for me that I was <in trouble> afflicted. I was ill about 10 dayes.

fol. 15r

July 26, 1695. Sett up 'till midnight att play att the Cock att Mildenhall with uncle Chambers.

August 17. Spent all that day att play.

September 7. Spent most part of that day att play, and I was the occasion of another's sweareing (viz.) cozin W. Heron.

15. Spent most of that day in vain and idle discourse, being Sunday.

---

[22] *Domi*: 'at home'.

December 23. I fasted, being to receive the blessed sacrament of Christ's body and blood on Christmas day next, and bewailed \all/ my former breaches \of/ vowes and purposes of forsakeing my sinns and amending my life, with a more stedfast resolution for the future \to live more circumspectly,/ Lord give me grace to keep them and be mercifull to me for what is past. Amen, Amen.

January 26, being Sunday. Talked of idleness just as I entred the church.

February 3. I laughed and was pleased att leud and profane sweareing, and filthy talking and unchast songs att Cambridge, comeing from Bicklesworth fair.[23]

fol. 15v

1704. Mercyes Received.

November 12. My horse started and flung me downe as I was comeing from church in the afternoon, but blessed be God I gott not the least hurt.

February 9. My horse started and did throw me down in Milden town[24] almost by the slough-pond as I came from Lynn mart, in a very dirty place. But I thank God I gatt noe hurt.

April 12, 1705. My great bitch Surly which I had from London, flew upon my daughter Sarah and bitt a a [sic] hole under her right eye, but I thank God she had no further mischief.

June 3. The same bitch snapped att my daughter Barbara and bitt her under her left eye a little hole, but God be praised she had noe further damage.

fol. 16r

March 9th. Sett up 'till 1 a clock att play.

April 12, 1696, being Easter day. I received the blessed sacrament of Christ's body [and] blood, with full and stedfast resolution to amend my life and live more curcumspectly for the future (God's grace assisting me).

24. I sett up 'till 11 a clock att play.

May 10, Sunday. Slept att church forenoon and afternoon and spent the rest of that day idley.

31. Slept att church again forenoon and afternoon.

June 7, Trinity Sunday. I received the blessed sacrament of Christ's body and blood, Lord give me grace to keep my vowes and purposes of amending my life and fosaking my sinns better than I have hitherto done.

July 17. Sett up all night att tables att the Whitehart.

August 9, Sunday. I vainly spent all that day.

fol. 16v

1705. Mercyes received.

July 7. A fire had like to have broken out att John Compton's by the carelesness of \his/ daughter carrying out ashes, but was in time happily discovered; the wind lay to bring it towards my house.

[23] Bicklesworth: Biggleswade, Beds.

[24] Coe frequently refers to Mildenhall as 'Milden' or 'Milden town'. This has no connection with the parish of Milden in south Suffolk.

September 30, 1705. My little bay mare fell downe with me as I was goeing to church and did throw me over her head, but I thank God I gott not the least hurt.

October 12. The same mare started with me att Georg Clift's muckhill as I was goeing to Milden and threw me down, but God be praised I gott noe harm. Turn over.

fol. 17r

September 7, 1696. Sett up 'till 1 a clock att play.

October 17. Spent all that day att play, *domi*.

19. Spent all that day att play, *domi*.

November 13. Sett up 'till 1 a clock att play.

December 19, being Saturday. Sett up 'till almost midnight att play att Wammell.

27. Received the blessed sacrament of the body and blood of our Lord and Saviour Jesus Christ and renewed my vowes and purposes of leading a new life, which I have before so often and so greviously broken. O Lord, create in me a new heart that I may live more circumspectly for the future.

1696/7. January 11. Sett up 'till 4 a clock att Wammell.

17, Sunday. Vainly spent all the afternoon.

22. Sett up 'till midnight and *fere aebrius*.[25] Att J. Ralph's.

fol. 17v

1706. Mercyes received.

October 18. My wife went to Milden in the coach upon a visit, and as she came home the horses were frighted att \a/ flock of sheep that came running by them, that they began to run away, and my wife jumpt out of the coach and my daughter Sarah. My wife gott a fall and hurt her breast, and gott a great cold with comeing home on foot in the evening, and was very much out of order for 3 or 4 dayes, but thanks be to God she recovered. She was blooded the next day.

This should come in 3 <4> leaves forward, on the backside of page 41.

fol. 18r

February 1, 1696. Slept att church.

12. Sett up 'till past midnight at play. Talking of idle and worldly business almost every Lord's day, both before and after church. Causlessly thought ill of Mr Archer my minister.[26]

April 4, 1697, being Easter day. I received the blessed sacrament of Christ's body and blood wherein I renewed my vowes of better obedience to God's holy will and commandments. Lord give me grace to keep them better than I have hitherto done.

Sunday. Neglected my owne private devotions.

12. Vainly spent all that afternoon.

---

[25] *Fere aebrius*: 'for the most part/entirely drunk.'

[26] Isaac Archer, vicar of Mildenhall, 1688–1700, whose diary appears in this volume.

May 8. Idlely spent all that day.

11. Spent all that day att play.

23, Whitsunday. Drank too much that afternoon att Barton Bull[27] and Mr Hanmer's, he being to goe to London the next day. And omitted the sacrament.

fol.18v

1705/6. Mercyes received.

July 7. Oliver Brand's house was burned down and did noe other harm. It was very calm weather, I thank God, or else it might have done me and others great damage.

February 12. My bay horse called Duke fell down with me as I came from Newmarkett, but I thank \God/ I gott not the least hurt.

March 2. My house escaped burning by a boyler of fatt hanged over the fire and was forgott, but my wife happily saw it just as it began to boyl over, and with hastily takeing it off. As it boyled over and flamed up into chimney, some spilled upon my son Henry's frock as he satt by the fire, but by God's mercy did not scald him, so wee escaped two great dangers.

fol. 19r

July 29, 1697. Spent all that whole day att play att the Cock.

September 9. Spent all that day att play, *domi.*

December 19, 1697, being the <first> second day of the 36th yeare of my age, I made a solemn resolution between God and my selfe, \that/ as I have (by God's great mercyes) begann a new yeare, so to beginn a new course of life, God's speciall grace assisting me.

'What fruit had I of those things whereof I am now ashamed, for the end of those things is death.'[28]

December 26, 1697. I received the blessed sacrament of Christ's body and blood and thereby have confirmed those good resolutions above said. Lord give me grace to keep them to my life's end.

fol. 19v

1706. Mercyes received.

May 4. I received 2 young colts from Leicester Fair and put them <in> to the coach to try them, and they gatt away from the men that ledd them and rann towards the river and stoppd att Thomas Bovell's ditch and did noe harm. The men were thrown down but gott noe mischief, thanks be to God who continually preserves us \in and/ from dangers.

May 26 being Sunday. My brown mare fell down with me as I came from church, but God be thanked I gott not the least hurt. Once before (viz.)

April 22. She fell down with me upon Ely cawsway as I was goeing to March, and I thank God I gott noe harm.

July 7. I told Thomas Spencer that Mildich Close was not tyth free but belonged to the church, if sowed with corn, and only tyth free when layd for grass.

---

27 The Bull Inn, Barton Mills, Suff., which still stands today.
28 Romans 6:21.

fol. 20r

December 30, 1697. Sett up 'till 1 a clock att play att Wammell.

July 1st, Saturday. Sett up 'till 10 a clock att Mr Glascock's.

3. Sett up 'till 3 a clock att play att Wammell.

And here I have made a solemn resolution that I will never play more after 9 a clock att night out of my owne house \or lodgings/. The Lord be mercifull to me for what is past. Amen. Amen.

April 24, 1698, being Easter day. I received the blessed sacrament of Christ's body and blood, wherein I renewed my vowes and purposes of amendment of life and of better obedience to God's holy will and comandments. God give me grace to continue in the same to my live's end. Amen. Amen.

fol. 20v

1706. Mercyes received.

July 11. About midnight my wife had a false conception came from her, and was in great danger, but I thank God she grew very well in a few dayes

23. Wee were att Wammell with the young colts in the coach, and \when/ wee were ready to come home they took some [*deletion*] distast and rann about the colt yard, and then again they rann away and stopped att their field gate, and then rann again 'till the corn in the field shackled them. And att last wee were forced to have two men come leading them all the way home. All this time I thank God there was noe mischief done.

fol. 21r

May 22, 1698, Sunday. Vainly spent all that day, tho' I was \att/ church both forenoon and afternoon, yett even then my thoughts were wandring and my devotions cold.

June 5. I mispent the Lord's day being sleepy att church, and cold and careless in my devotions, and idlely spending the remaineing part of the day \without/ reading or meditation.

12, Whitsunday. I received the blessed sacrament of Christ's body and blood and made new resolucions and vows of better obedience to God's holy will and commandments. Lord give me grace to keep those resolutions and vowes better than I have hitherto done.

November 16. Spent all that day att play.

17. Playd with Mr Glascock att home from noon 'till almost midnight.
Turn over.

fol. 21v

1706/7. Mercyes received.

July 29. I struck a mole lyne into my face a little way, near my right eye and by God's great mercy it escaped my eye.

May 23, 1707. My young bay mare being smooth shodd, and just after a rain, slipt up with me just before my door and threw me. My foot had like to have \hung/ in the stirrup but I shaked it out of the stirrup before she gott up again, and I thank God I gott not the least hurt.

June 16. I went to Icklingham to have my bay filly covered by Francis

Barkham['s] horse, and I stood carelesly behind her and she kicked me on my thigh a little above my knee, but I thank God she did me noe harm.

fol. 22r

December 25, 1698. I received the blessed sacrament of Christ's body and blood and and [sic] renewed my resolutions and vowes of forsakeing my sinns and amending my life. I pray God forgive all the breaches of my former vowes and assist me with his speciall grace to observe and keep them better for the future.

Aprill 9th, 1699. I received the blessed sacrament of Christ's body and blood and renewed my former vows and resolutions of forsakeing my sinns and amending my life. Lord assist me with thy grace to observe and keep them to my life's end. I have been cold and indevout in my prayers.

April 23, Sunday. Idley spent all that day. I have spoken uncharitably of my neighbours for any little injury done to me, perticularly Mr Edmund Young.

fol. 22v

1707. Mercyes Received.

November 11. My bay mare started \as I was goeing to Newmarkett/ att a lock of hay that lay in the road and threw me down, but I thank God I gott not the least hurt.

December 25. My sonn Thomas gott a sharp aul which I happened to leave about the house, and was playing with it and att last runn it att my daughter Barbara, and thrust it into her arm, but I thank God did himselfe nor her noe further harm. It was God's great mercy he did not thrust it into his own eyes or body, or her's.

February 22. My bay colt called Darling threw me as I came from church, but blessed be God (whose providence continually preserveth us) I gott noe hurt. The first time I rode upon him.

fol. 23r

May 21, 1699, Sunday. I slept att church and was dull and heavy att my devotions.

May 28. I received the blessed sacrament of the body and blood of my Saviour Jesus Christ, wherein I renewed all my former vowes and purposes of forsakeing my sinns and amending my life. Lord assist me with thy speciall grace to keep and observe them to my live's end.

June 14. Spent all that day att play with Mr Glascok junior, at home.

August 6, being Sunday. I bought a cow but it was fully against my will. I did it to save the best cow I had, which I had changed away for this I bought. Many sinnes and infirmityes committed and many good dutyes omitted.

fol. 23v

1708. Mercyes received.

September 24. My bay mare started att a calf that stood close under Thomas Mallabar's wall \neer Butts Green/ and threw me down, but blessed be God I received little or noe hurt. I fell upon head and shoulders, jarrd them a little for the present.

December 23. I went into my cart-horse stable and nigh my Darby colt, to put his shackle upon his fetlock, and when I was stooping he bitt att my head, and if my hat had not been on he might have done me a great mischief, or if he had gott hold of my arm or shoulder. But I thank \God/ who continually preserves us, I gott noe hurt.

January 7. My Duke horse fell down with me and Mr Robert Wilkin behind me, and threw us both down in the snow, but blessed be God wee gott noe hurt. Turn over 9 leaves.

fol. 24r

December 25, 1699. I received the blessed sacrament of Christ's body and blood and made new vowes of better obedience to God's holy will and commandments. Lord assist me by thy speciall grace to keep and observe them to my live's end. Amen. Amen. Amen.

March 9. Spent almost all day att play att home.

24. Slept att church forenoon and afternoon, and dull and heavy att my devotions.

March 31, 1700, being Easter day. I received the holy sacrament and renewed my former vowes and resolucions of forsakeing my sinns and amending my life. Lord assist me with thy grace to keep them to my life's end.

> Thou can'st not tell what strength
> Thy God may give thee att the length:
> Renew thy vowes, and if thou keep the last
> Thy God will pardon all that's past,
> Vow whilst thou can'st: while thou <can> \can'st/ a vow
> thou may'st,
> Perhaps perform it, when thou thinkest least.

Turn over.

fol. 24v

> Thy God hath not deny'd thee all,
> Whilst he permitts thee but to call:
> Call to thy God for grace to keep
> Thy vows, and if thou break them weep,
> Weep for thy broken vows, and vow again:
> Vowes made with tears cannot be still in vain.
> Then once again
> I vow to mend my waies
> Lord, say Amen, Amen[29]
> And thine be all the praise.
> Halelujah, Halelujah.[30]
> Halelujah.

Let them who are tempted to dispair of their salvation, consider how much

---

[29] The second 'Amen' is written in Hebrew characters.
[30] 'Hallelujah, Hallelujah' is written in Hebrew characters.

Christ suffered to redeem us from sinn, and its eternall punishment. And he that considers this, must needs believe that the desires which God had to save us were not less than infinite, and therefore not easily to be satisfyed without it.

fol. 25r
April 6, 1700. I spent almost the whole day att play att the Ferry.[31]

May 12, Sunday. Idley spent that afternoon in drinking att my house. Natt. \Howler/, Francis J. Shafton, T.S.[32]

21. Neglected prayers in my family att night.

24, Fryday. Spent all that day att play att home with Mr Phillips, tho' utterly against my will (being to receive the blessed sacrament on Sunday following, being Trinity Sunday). I intended not to have gone to the markett that day but to have spent it wholly att my devotion, if he had not prevented me. I was too easyly <to be> perswaded by him.

26. I received the blessed sacrament of Christ's body and blood and renewed my former resolucions of forsakeing my sinns and amending my life, with full purpose (God's grace assisting me) to perform them better then I have hitherto done.

July 7, Sunday. Spent the whole day idley, though I was att church 'fore and afternoon.

September 1, Sunday. Spent the whole day vainly and idlely, though att church twice.

fol. 25v
October 20, 1700. I received the blessed sacrament of the body and blood of our dear redeemer, wherein I again renewed my vowes and purposes of obedience to God's holy will and commandments. I pray God give me his grace to walk in the same all the days of my life.

26. Spent all that afternoon att play. T. N.[33]

December 25. I received the holy sacrament of the body and blood of our blessed Saviour, Lord grant to me the benefitts of his death and passion and assist \me/ with thy Holy Spirit to amend my life and to perform the covenant made att my baptism <of obed.>

January 9. Spent almost the whole day att play att home from 11 a clock in the forenoon 'till almost midnight, with company that dined here.

fol. 26r
April 5, 1701. Spent all that day att play att the Ferry with Mr Ley, an excise man.

13, Sunday. Vainly and idley spent the whole day, though att <the> church twice, listless and dull att my devotions there.

20, Easter day. I received the blessed sacrament of the body and blood of my dear redeemer, and renewed my former vowes and purposes of forsakeing my

---

[31] The Ferry Inn at West Row in the parish of Mildenhall, lies on the north bank of the River Lark; also known as Jude's Ferry.

[32] T.S.: Thomas Spencer (see f. 19v).

[33] It is not known to whom 'T.N.' refers.

sinns and amending my life. Lord assist me with thy grace to keep them to my life's end.

May 18, Sunday. Vainly spent all the afternoon.

June 2. Spent all the afternoon att play att home with Mr Ley.

3. Spent all the afternoon att play and idleness att the Ferry.

<Whitsunday> 8.

fol. 26v

June 8, 1701, Whitsunday. I received the blessed sacrament of Christ's body and blood and made new vowes and resolutions of better obedience to God's holy will and comandments, his grace assisting me.

22. Slept att church forenoon and afternoon.

24. Intemperance or inordinate use of lawfull things. \I have forgot what it was. 1726./

August 10. Slept att church.

December 13. I spent all the afternoon att play 'till almost Sunday morninge, domi.

24. Upon examination of my selfe and looking over the accounts of my later years in this book, I find sleeping att church and mispending the Lord's day, talking of worldly[34] buisiness, and neglecting reading and meditations comes in very often and swells the catalogue of my sinns. I doe now resolve (God's speciall grace assisting me) upon a stricter observation of that day.

fol. 27r

1701. And also not to lett idleness and gameing take and steal away so much of my precious time as it has formerly done.

December 25. I received the blessed sacrament and begged of God to strengthen these good resolutions I now made, begging pardon and forgiveness (for all former breaches of my vowes and resolutions) in and through the meritts and intercession of Jesus Christ my dear redeemer.

1702. January 8. Sett up 'till 1 clock att play att home.

April 12. I received the Holy Comunion and renewed my former vowes and resolucions of leading a new life. Lord grant me grace to perform them to my live's end. Amen.

May 22. I talked a little wantonly and idlely. T.N.

24, being Whitsunday. I received the blessed <the blessed> sacrament and am steddfastly purposed to lead a new life, God's grace assisting me.

31. I spent all the afternoon vainly and idlely (talking of and doeing worldly business) upon the Lord's day.

fol. 27v

June 21, 1702. Sunday. I slept att church forenoon and afternoon and spent the rest of \the/ <whole> day vainly and idley.

28, Sunday. I spent the whole day vainly and unprofitably, tho' att church

---

[34] 'Worldly' is underlined.

twice, but I repent, O my God, I repent of these my misdoeings. Lord be mercifull to me a sinner.

August .27. I was guilty of too much vain and idle discourse att Mr Casbourne's wedding \with Mrs Mary Glascock/.

30, Sunday. I was att church twice but spent the rest of the day idley.

Could the eyes of my sense behold the least \glimps/ of that glory that beholds me, it would make me ashamed of my purest actions, says good Judge Hales, page 272. The least glimps of that glory that beholds me etc.

fol. 28r

December 25. I received the blessed sacrament of the body and blood of Jesus Christ my dear redeemer, wherein I renewed my former vowes and purposes of leading a new life. And whereas the mispending the Lord's day and consumeing my precious time att play and idleness are two sinns which I am very often guilty of, I doe now stedfastly purpose (God's grace assisting me) to observe the sabbath more strictly and to spend my time more prudently, remembring the great account I must one day make of these and all other my misdoeings; and doe purpose to sett apart one day in every week to examine my selfe how I have spent my time, and for what I have done amiss in thought, word, or deed, imediately to begg God's pardon for Christ Jesus his sake.

March 21. I was att church twice but slept [deletion] there in the afternoon and spent the rest of the day idley.

fol. 28v

March 28, 1703, being Easter day. I received the blessed sacrament of the body and blood of Jesus Christ my dear redeemer and renewed my former resolucions of forsakeing my sinns and amending my life. Lord assist by thy grace to perform them to my life's end. Amen.

April 11. Att church twice but spent the rest of the day idley and vainly.

May 2. Att church twice but spent the rest of the day idley.

16, Whitsunday. I was att church the forenoon. Slept there and spent the rest of the day idley. Omitted the sacrament.

23, Trinity Sunday. Omitted the sacrament again and missed church the forenoon.

30. I was att church twice but spent the afternoon idley with Mr Ley, Nat. and Fra. and T. Sp., domi.[35]

June 24. I spent the whole day att play with Mr Bradbury att T.N's.

July 11. I was att church twice, but spent the rest of the day idley att N. Howlers[?], and talked of worldly buisiness with John Cornwall after I came home about hireing him for a servant.

fol. 29r

July 25, 1703. I was att church twice, then went to Widow Bolden's and spent the rest of the day idley, tho' I have severall times resolved with my selfe to spend the sabbath more strictly and holily.

[35] 'Nat. and Fra. and T. Sp.', would seem to refer to his friends Nat. Howler (see f. 25r), Francis Shafton (see f. 25r), and Thomas Spencer (see f. 19v).

August 1. I was att church twice but spent the rest of the day idley.

October 10. I received the blessed sacrament of Christ's body and blood and renewed my former vowes and resolucions of leading a new life, and not to mispend the Lord's day as I have often done. God Almighty grant me his speciall grace to perform those good resolutions to my life's end. Amen.

16. [deletion] * 36

December 12, being Sunday. Talked of worldly and idle buisiness and appointed a meeting of idleness and play, that is to spend a day <idley> or part of it <play> att play.

fol. 29v

December 25, 1703. I received the blessed sacrament of Christ's body and blood and renewed my former vows and resolucions of forsakeing my sinns and amending my life. I pray God assist me with his speciall grace to keep them better than I have hitherto done, Amen. Amen.

28. I was too vain and idle att Barton and comeing home.

January 2, being Sunday. Talked of the preeceding day's idleness and vanity, and wrangled with H. Morley as soon as I came out of church in the afternoon, and sleepy and drowsy att church.

April 16, 1704, Easter day. I received the holy sacrament and renewed my former vowes and resolucions of forsakeing my sinns and amending my life. I pray God assist me with the grace of his Holy Spirit to enable me to keep them to my life's end. Amen. Amen. Lord be mercifull to me a sinner.

fol. 30r

May 14, 1704. I slept att church.

21. I was att church twice but drowsy and sleepy there, and spent the rest of the day idley and vainly.

August 21 or 22 [deletion] *

September 10. I was att church twice but spent the rest of the day idley.

November 26. I made a rash vow att Richard Wright's that I would not goe home with my wife 'till her hollow tooth was out (thinking to perswade her not to be fearfull of haveing it drawn) and att last was forced to break my vow. Lord pardon all my sinns, my light and rash words.

December 25, 1704. I received the blessed sacrament of Christ's body and blood and made new resolucions of better obedience to God's holy will and commandments. The Lord give me grace to keep them to my life's end. Amen. Amen.

fol. 30v

January 14, 1704/5. I was not att church the forenoon. I deferred trimming[37] 'till the Sunday morning, and before I had done it was too late to goe to church.

March 25, 1705. I slept att church.

April 1. I slept again and was dull and listless all church time.

---

36 First occurrence of Coe's 'shameful practices'. See Introduction, pp. 34–35.
37 Either refers to shaving, or cutting the hair.

8, being Easter day. I received the holy sacrament and renewed my resol-ucions and vowes of leading a new life. The Lord give me grace to perform them better than I have hitherto done.

June 3, being Trinity Sunday. I received the blessed sacrament and renewed my baptismall vow with a steadfast purpose and resolucion \to/ amend my life and live more circumspectly for the future. *Jesu! tuam opem.*[38]

fol. 31r
June 10, 1705. I was att church twice but spent the rest of the day in vain and wanton talk att Mr Abbott's.

17. I was att church twice but spent the rest of the \day/ idlely (and slept att church) in preparing for a journey to Holm the next day.

26. *Unnat. . . poll. . .*

30. I spent the whole afternoon att cards with Doctor Wallis etc. att Milden-Cock, he being to goe away.

July 7. I spent the whole afternoon idley att cards att Matthew Jerrold's with Mr Bradbury etc. 9 of us dined there.

Also [*deletion*] *unnat. pol.* And 24 [*July*].

29, Sunday. Stayd att home the afternoon and slept in the little cellar chamber, mispending the whole afternoon.[39]

October 14. I was att church twice but spent the rest of the day idley.

fol. 31v
December 25, 1705. I received the blessed sacrament of the body and blood of our dear redeemer and renewed my former purposes and resolutions of forsa-keing my sinns and amending my life. Lord give me grace to performe them to my life's end.

<March 19. *Unnat. . . poll. . .* error I think>

March 24, 1705, Easter day. I received the holy sacrament of Christ's body and blood and made new vowes and resolutions of leading a new life, God's grace assisting me. *Jesu! tuam opem.*

31. I was very dull and heavy att church and slept forenoon and afternoon.

April 14. I slept and was very drowsey and heavy att church.

28. I was att church twice but slept forenoon and afternoon. Lord be merci-full to me a sinner.

fol. 32r
May 6, 1706. I was att church twice but spent the rest of the day vainly.

December 25. I received the blessed sacrament of the body and blood of our dear redeemer and renewed my former vowes and resolucions of forsakeing my sinns and amending my life. Lord give me grace to keep and observe them better than I have hitherto done.

March 14. * [*deletion*]

---

[38] *Jesu! tuam opem:* 'O Jesus, by your power'.
[39] In margin: *unnat. . . pol. . .* (see Introduction, pp. 34–35).

April 6, 1707. I was att church twice but was drowsy and sleepy and dull forenoon and afternoon.

13, Easter day. I received the blessed sacrament of Christ's body and blood and made stedfast resolucions of amending my life. Lord assist me with the grace of thy Holy Spirit to keep them to my life's end. Amen. Amen.

fol. 32v

1708/9. Mercyes received.

February 18. As I was att dinner and put a peice of bread in my mouth, there was a pinn which, by God's great mercy, I felt in my mouth before I swallowed the bread I was chewing and so escaped choaking, for which, and all other mercyes, my soul doth magnifie thee, O Lord.

July 7. My sonn Tommy \did/ hang by the neck in the hall window endeavouring to gett out there, being left alone in the house, and it was God's great mercy he was not killed, for there was nobody near to save \or/ help him if he had not scrambled in again of himselfe, being then between 4 and 5 yeares of age.

Turn over 5 leaves.

fol. 33r

May 1, 1707. A thanksgiving day by a proclamacion from the Queen for the union with Scotland.[40] I was att church but spent the rest of the \day/ idlely att Milden Cock.

May 25. I was att church twice but was very drowsie and sleepy.

June 1, Whitsunday. I received the blessed sacrament and made new vowes of better obedience and amending my life, God's grace assisting me.

September 29. I told a lye that my \wife/ might not be uneasye; it was noe advantage to me nor disadvantage to anybody, so I hope the sinn was not so great.

1716. I have quite forgot now what it was about.[41]

fol. 33v

December 25, 1707. I received the blessed sacrament of the body and blood of Jesus Christ my dear redeemer, and renewed my former vowes and resolutions of forsakeing my sinns and amending my life. Lord assist me with thy grace to keep and observe them better than I have hitherto done.

And I doe resolve to sett apart \some part of/ Saturday in every week to call my selfe to account how I have spent the preceeding week, and to begg God's pardon \for Jesus' sake/ for my sinns committed and good dutyes omitted. And if any necessary buisiness hinders me upon any Saturday I will sett some other time imediately after, resolving to lett noe week slipp without strict examination of my selfe and my waies, and where anything extraordinary happens to note it in my book.

---

40 The 1707 Act of Union which established the new political entity of Great Britain under a single Parliament, Scotland being represented by forty-five MPs.

41 This entry is a later insertion.

fol. 34r

January 6, 1707/8. \Wee dined att Tuddenham and/ it was about 2 a clock in the morn before wee gott home. Omitted prayers in my family that night.

22. I playd att cards att my owne house 'till past 2 a clock in the morning and omitted prayers in my family.

27. *

29. Omitted prayers in my family.

February, *inter* 18, 19. *

March, *inter* 30, 31. *

April 2, 1708, being Good Fryday. I fasted being to receive the blessed sacrament of Christ's body and blood, and upon examination <of my selfe> I found my selfe guilty of these sinns following.

I have often talked of worldly buisiness and used other vain discourse on Sundayes, and when I have been att church my mind and thoughts have been too often wandring, and I have not been so devout and intent in what I was about as I ought to have been, or as I purpose to be for the future, God's grace assisting me.

fol. 34v

I have spent too much time in play and idleness since my last receiving the holy sacrament and omitted prayers severall tymes in my family.

I have not, so strictly as I ought, kept to that promise I made between God and my selfe of setting apart Saturday in every week to examine my selfe how I have spent the preceeding week, and in what I have done amiss imediately to begg pardon for Jesus Christ's sake.

I have often since disturbed my mind with anger and peevishness upon small provocations, which I purpose to avoid for the future.

I have not so strictly as I ought kept those solemn vowes and resolutions of amendment of life as I am apt to make in adversity, and alwaies before the sacrament.

I have often mispent my pretious time and have drawn others into the same idleness by my perswasions and example.

I have profaned the holy sacrament, 1st by comeing ignorantly to it without strick examination and contrition, 2dly without devotion and spirituall affection my mind being

fol. 35r

full of wandring \and worldly/ <idle> thoughts, and 3dly by often breaking my vowes and purposes of forsakeing my sinns and amending my life.

I have been too forward to beleive \and set forth/ ill reports of others which is seldom minded by the generality of men, but is a sin of a very uncharitable nature.

April 4, 1708, Easter day. I received the blessed sacrament of Christ's body and blood and made new vows and resolutions of leading a new life. Lord assist me by the grace of thy Holy Spirit to keep and observe them better than I have hitherto done.

11. I was not at church this day. I took physick on Saturday and was not very well on Sunday forenoon, and Nurse Kent dineing here with the child, the

coach did not goe 'till night, and I was afraid of getting cold to ride \to church/ on horseback. I bestowed all the forenoon in my closett, but spent the after-noon in vain and fruitless discourse with them.

fol. 35v
April 1708, *inter* 16, 17, * 1708.

May 2. I was att church twice but spent the rest of the day vainly, and was sleepy and drowsy att church. Lord be mercifull to me a miserable sinner.

16. I was att church twice but was drowsy and slept forenoon and afternoon, and spent but a very little time in private.

23, Whitsunday. I received the blessed sacrament of the body and blood of Jesus Christ my dear redeemer, and renewed my former vows and resolutions of forsakeing my sinns and amending my life. Lord assist me by the grace of thy Holy Spirit to keep them better than I have hitherto done.

August 15. I was att church twice but spent the rest of the day idley talking of worldly buisiness about hireing servants and land.

22. I was drowsy and sleepy att church forenoon and afternoon.

fol. 36r
August 29, 1708. I was att church twice but spent the rest of the day idley, ordering my worldly buisiness for the next day.

<September> October 10. I received the blessed sacrament of the body and blood of my dear redeemer and renewed my former vowes and resolutions of forsakeing my sinns and amending my life. Lord assist me with the grace of thy Holy Spirit to keep and observe them better than I have hitherto done.

October 27. I was att the Cock with Sir Thomas Hanmer,[42] Sir Henry Bunbury[43] \and others/, where there was a great bowl of punch, and though I had my freedom to drink ale and drank but one glass of punch, and severall full glasses of ale, yett I was very ill for a little time and almost fudled, worse than I had been for many yeares before. But I repent, oh my God, I repent \I accuse and judge and condemn my self for it/. Lord be mercifull to me a most miserable sinner.

fol. 36v
December 11, 1708, Saturday. I spent all the afternoon <idly> \att cards and tables/ att the Ferry with Mr Bradbury, Thomas Bird, Mr Wilkin, Mr Bugg.

26. I received the blessed sacrament of the body and blood of my dear redemer and renewed my former vows and resolucions of forsakeing my sinns and amending my life. Lord assist me with the grace of thy Holy Spirit to keep and observe them to my live's end. Amen.

January 24. Omitted prayers in my family and talked idley att Doctor Wallis's house.

---

[42] Sir Thomas Hanmer (1677–1746), Speaker of the House of Commons; only surviving son of William Hanmer and Peregrina, daughter of Sir Henry North of Mildenhall. He married Isabella, widow of Henry Fitzroy, 1st Duke of Grafton. His estate passed to his nephew Sir William Bunbury, Bart., *DNB*.

[43] Sir Henry Bunbury was 3rd baronet.

February 17. Omitted prayers in my family, staying att Milden 'till \most of/ my family were <most> in bed.

27, being Sunday. One Mr Underhill of Cambridge, surgeon, came to see my bay mare, (which being gone) he looked of my other horses and wee talked of prices and other worldly matters.

fol. 37r

March 3, 1708/9. Wee dined att Tuddenham, came home about midnight and omitted prayers in my family.

April 17, Sunday.[44] I was att church twice but was sleepy and drowsie forenoon and afternoon.

24, Easter day. I received the blessed sacrament of Christ's body and blood and renewed my former vowes and resolutions which I have so often and so greviously broken. I beseech God to enable me to keep them to my life's end. *Jesu! tuam opem.*

May 1, Sunday. I was att church the forenoon but spent most part of the afternoon idley.

June 12, Whitsunday. I omitted the sacrament haveing disturbed my selfe about James Clift's getting a bastard child, and forceing the woman to swear who was the true father, which caused Clift and I to have words so that I could not think my selfe in true charity with him, or he with me.

<Idley> I was att church twice but sleepy and drowsy forenoon and afternoon. Lord be mercifull.

fol. 37v

1710. Mercyes received.

April 10. Wee dined at Tuddenham, and as my wife and daughters came home in the coach the footboard fell down just att the new river bridge att Barton Mills and <scared> frighted the horses, who runn away over the white bridge and through the little bridge water (the man all this tyme hanging upon the pole), but the water stopped their speed so that the man recovered himselfe (tho' almost stifled in the water) and gott better hold of the reines and stopped them so soon as they came out of the water, and by God's great mercy there was noe mischief done. In the coach were my wife, my daughters Judith, Anne, and Sarah, and Mr Thompson; they all came walking from that place to Milden, this was about 9 a clock att night. Mr Thompson creeped out att one of the foreglasses and gott hold of the reines which helped to stopp the horses.
Turn over 2 leaves.

fol. 38r

September 10, 1709, Saturday. I spent all the afternoon att play att Matthew Jerrold's att the Chequer and omitted prayers in my family, it being past 10 of the clock and the family in bed.

---

[44] Coe often abbreviates 'Sunday' by using a symbol which looks like a capital 'o' with a dot within, meaning 'sun', followed by 'day'.

November 28. I spent all the afternoon att play att the Ferry and omitted prayers in my family, again.

December 17, Saturday I spent part of the forenoon and all the afternoon att the Ferry with Thomas Cheston and Durg. [sic] Robert Cheston, neither have I so carefully as I ought sett apart Saturday in every week for calling my selfe to account how I have spent the foregoeing week according to a <promise> vow made between God and my [deletion] owne soul on Christmas day 1707, but I doe purpose to observe it for the future. Jesu! tuam opem. Could the eyes of my sense behold the least of that glory that beholds me, it would make me ashamed of my purest actions. Judge Hales, page 272.

fol. 38v

December 25, 1709. I received the blessed sacrament of the body and blood <for> of Jesus Christ my dear redeemer and made new resolutions of forsakeing my sinns and amending my life which I stedfastly purpose to keep and observe, God's special grace assisting me. Jesu! tuam opem.

January 2. I began to play within a minuit of 9 of the clock.

April 9, 1710, Easter Day. I received the blessed sacrament of the body and blood of Jesus Christ my dear redeemer and renewed my former vowes and resolutions of leading a new life, which I purpose to keep and observe better than I have hitherto done, God's speciall grace assisting me.

May 14. I was att church twice but spent the rest of the day vainly and idley. Lord be mercifull to me a sinner.

fol. 39r

June 25, Sunday, I was very drowsy and sleepy att church.

July 9. I was att church twice but very drowsy and sleepy fore and afternoon.

26. Omitted prayers in my family.

September 24. I was att church twice but was guilty of speaking and hearing idle discourse with Mr Seyliard and Mr Bradbury, who walked with me as far as Wammel hedge, after church.

October, inter 13 and 14. * *

November 30. I spent the whole afternoon att play att the Ferry and neglected my own private devotions for the afternoon.

December 25, 1710. I received the blessed sacrament of Christ's body and blood and renewed my vowes of forsakeing my sinns and amending my life (which I have so often and greviously broken) with full purposes to live more circumspectly for the future, God's grace assisting me. Amen. Jesu! tuam opem.

fol. 39v

1710/11. Mercyes received.

November 8. My son Thomas fell backwards into a kettle of scalding water and scalded all his back; it put him into a high fever so that wee thought he would have dyed, but blessed be God he grew well again and his back healed in less than a month.

May 21, Monday in Whitsun-week. My son William, who lived then in Wisbich, was rideing before a coach and being upon a young horse, by some accident the horse he was upon gott his flanck over the pole, and the hook att the pole's end rent the horse's flank and body, and with striveing threw him amongs the coach horses and they trode upon his clothes and held him down when he was riseing, but I thank God he gott no harm.

fol. 40r

January 11, 1710/11. Wee dined att Tuddenham; it was about 3 a clock in the morning when wee gott home, so omitted prayers in my family.

January 12. I was att Milden Cock att play and forgott to look on my watch (as I used to doe), and playd \one sett att cards/ after 9 contrary to my resolution made January 3, 1697, twenty leaves backward.[45] But I repent, oh my God, I repent. I accuse and judg and condemn my selfe for it. Lord be mercifull to me a most miserable sinner.

April 1, 1711, Easter day. I received the blessed sacrament and renewed my covenant again with Almighty God in the blood of Jesus Christ my dear redeemer. Lord give me grace to keep and observe it and to spend every day as if it were to be my last. *Jesu! tuam opem.*

Inter 21, 22. *

fol. 40v

1711. Mercyes received.

December 10. My two little boyes Henry and Thomas was att play in the cowyard, and Thomas was reaching into a cow bing, and a cow on the other side of the bing runn her horn into his mouth and <rent> ranched the inside of his right cheek, and did him no further hurt. For this and all other thy mercyes to me and mine, my soul doth magnifie thee O Lord.

March 20. I was att Bury, being the assize tyme, and came home by Worlington; it was 8 a clock when I got thither, and dark and cloudy and rained a little about 6 or 7. I lost my way between Worlington and the Ferry and turned back <again> to goe to Worlington again, but could not find it and wandred about the fields, I know not where, for about halfe an hour, *verte* [continued on fol.41v].

fol. 41r

May 6, 1711, Sunday. I slept att church the afternoon and spent the rest of the day idley. Came home by Munns to see my wheat and rie there.

10, being Assension Day. I spent great part of the day reading an idle jest-book.[46]

Inter 13, 14. * 18. *

20, Whitsunday. I received the holy sacrament and renewed my vowes and resolutions of leading a new life, God's grace assisting me.

---

[45] See f. 20r.

[46] Jest books were common and cheap in the period, and were usually distributed by pedlars; their humour was frequently scatological. For a wide-ranging treatment of the subject, see Margaret Spufford, *Small Books and Pleasant Histories* (Cambridge, 1981).

June 4. I spent all the afternoon att play with Doctor Wallis and Mr Burgis.
10, being Sunday. I was very dull and sleepy att church 'fore and after noon.
15. I perswaded and enticed men to play att the Crown.
August *inter* 6, 7. *

fol. 41v
1711/12. Mercyes received.

and when I could not tell where I was nor which way to turn, I lett my horse
have his head to goe which way he would, and he found the road and carryed
\me/ safe to the Ferry, the Lord be praysed.

April 11, 1712. My sonn James went into cart horse stable and playing too
near the horses, the Delph horse struck him and broke his thumb. It was God's
great mercy he did not strike him on the body or head.

March 23, 1711/12. My sonn Thomas was taken sick, and the next day the
small pox begann to appear, and it went through my family, 8 children and 3
servants had it,[47] and through God's great mercy and goodness every one of
them gott up again. For these and all other thy great mercyes to me and mine,
my soul doth magnifie thee, O Lord.[48]

fol. 42r
October 14, 1711. I received the blessed sacrament of Christ's body and blood
and renewed my vowes and purposes of forsakeing my sinns and amending my
life. Lord assist me with the grace of thy Holy Spirit to keep and observe them
better than I have hitherto done.

21. I was att church twice but spent the rest of the day idley, talking of
worldly buisiness comeing home from church forenoon and afternoon.

November 4, Sunday. I was \too late att/ church in the forenoon, dined att
Sir T[homas] H[anmer's], stayd there 'till about 4, then sent for by one Mr
Vincent to the Cock, talked of worldly buisiness. And after wee came home,
too buisie about preparing for our Lincolnshire journey the next day, so not one
of my family, nor scarce myself, spent any part of the day in reading or private
devotion.

fol. 42v
1712. Mercyes received.

July 13. My 2 little boyes Henry and Thommy \on the little hobby/ came
galloping into yard as they came from church, and rode against a ladder that
stood up against the malthouse (as the thatchers left it) and were both thrown
down, but by God's great mercy they gott noe harm.

July 15. I rode on the said hobby to Newmarket and she fell down with mee,
and in falling I wrinched my right thumb, but I thank God got no further hurt.

August 26. The same hobby fell down again with me goeing to Newmarket. I
fell upon my face and beat the skin off my forehead and nose, but God be
praised got noe further hurt.

---

[47] The fact that Coe had at least three servants is another indicator of his status as a gentleman.
[48] In margin: 'See the Almanack 1712. March, April, <and May> how they fell down.'

1714 mercys received

Der: 10. My 2 little boy of Henry
& Thomas was att play in ye Cow
=yard, & Thomas was reaching
into a Cow bing & a cow on ye
other side of the bing runn
her horn into his mouth &
rauushd the inside of
his right Cheek & did him no
further hurt, for this & all
other thy mercys to me &
mine my soull doth magnifie
thee O Lord.

Mar: 20. I was att Bury being the
assize tyme, & came home by
Worlington it was 8 a Clock
when I got thither & dark &
Clondy & rained a little ab't 6 or
7. I lost my way between Worling
=ton & the ferry & turned back
again to goo to Worlington again
but would not find it & wandred ab't
the fields I know not where for
ab't half an hour = verte

William Coe's Diary,

1711 4 (83

May 6. Sunday I slept at Church the —
afternoon & spent ye rest of the day
Idley. came home by Murrey to see my
wheat & [illegible] there.

 10 being Ascension day I spent great
 part of ye day reading an idle jest=
 book.

mt 13.14.tt. 18 tt.

 20 Whitsunday I receid the Holy
 Sacramt & renewed my vowes &
 resolutions of leading a new life
 Gods great assisting me.

Juñe 4. I spent all the afternoon att
 play wth Dror Walley & mr Burgiss.
  10. being Sunday I was very dull
  & sleepy att Church fore & afternoon
  15 I perswaded & enticed men to
   play. att ye Crown.
Aug. mt 6.7. tt

Folios 40v–41r

fol. 43r

November 11, 1711, Sunday. I stayd att home the forenoon and was very drowsy and sleepy in the afternoon.

December 25. I received the blessed sacrament of the body and blood of my dear redeemer and renewed my former \vowes/ and resolutions of forsakeing my sinns and amending my life. Lord assist me with thy grace to observe and keep them better than I have hitherto done. *Jesu! tuam opem.*

February 16, 1711, \Saturday/. I spent most of the afternoon att play att George Fisher's of Worlington, contrary to my resolution mentioned on the 68th page of this book.[49]

June 8, 1712, Whit Sunday. I received the blessed sacrament of the body and blood of our Saviour Jesus Christ, renewed my vowes and purposes of forsakeing my sinns and amending my life with a steadfast resolution to observe the same, God's grace assisting me.

fol. 43v

1712. Mercyes received.

October 2, Thursday. My sonn William was carrying Mrs Banyer,[50] his mistress, from Wisbich to Long Sutton, and rideing near severall wind mills which stand upon the bank as they goe, the horse started and threw them both down the steep banck into the river, which is a little arm of the sea. Mrs Banyer fell quite in, and the horse lay upon my sonn a little while \on the sands/, and after he got up he went upto the wast to help his mistress out. This was a very steep and dangerous fall, and if the tyde had been up they would not have escaped drowning, but God be praysed they got noe hurt.

fol. 44r

July 11, 1712, Fryday. Began a new sett at cards within 5 minutes of 9, so 'twas past 10 before I got home, and omitted prayers in my family.

August 2, \Saturday/. I went to Milden <about> about 3 to agree about my sons Henry and Thomy's board \with Mr Thetford/, and schooling with Mr Pawlet, without any designe or intent to play, but when company came together I was very easily perswaded to play and mispend my tyme 'till 8 a clock att night, contrary to a former resolucion herein mentioned, page 68.[51]

29, Fryday. I began a set of cards within 7 or 8 minuits of 9 and it held 'till about 10, and before I got home most of my family were in bedd, so I omitted prayers with my family.

fol. 44v

1712. Mercyes received.

November 19. As I was comeing from Bury upon my horse called Swallow, I met severall waggons loaded (for the fair next day), att which my horse started and was afraid att noise of the bells, and with my holding him <he> he arose up

---

[49] See f. 33v.

[50] Mr Bangor, an apothecary of Wisbech, Cambs., to whom William was apprenticed.

[51] See f. 33v, above.

with his fore feet and fell down on his side, being gagged with the curb. I cleared the stirrups and gott noe hurt, I thank God.

23. My 2 sonns Henry and Thomas fell off the hobby as they came from church, but by God's great mercy they got noe hurt.

December 15. I lent our coach without the doors to carry Goody Hibble to be buried, and my 2 sonns Henry and Thomas came home \in/ it, and because it jolted goeing over wheat ridges Henry jumped out, and by God's great mercy gott noe hurt. If he had jumped short or his clothes had hung on any thing, the wheel had gone over him.

fol. 45r
December 25, 1712. I received the blessed sacrament of Christ's body and blood and renewed my vowes and resolucions of forsakeing my sins and amend-ing my life, God's grace assisting me. Lord assist me by the grace of thy Holy Spirit to observe and perform them better than I have hitherto done. Amen. *Jesu! tuam opem.*

28. I was att church the forenoon, but spent almost all the afternoon in vain and fruitless talking with one of my neighbours that came in. *Domi* Clift.[52]

January 29. I sett up 'till 4 of the clock next morning att play att home, with some friends that came to dinner with me, and omitted prayers in my family.

31, Saturday. I spent most part of the day idley att the Ferry with Mr Wilkin; wee met there about some small buisiness between Simon Jude and John Hopkin, about Hopkin's hireing the ferry-house.

fol. 45v
1712. Mercyes received.

December 16. I was goeing to Bury upon the same horse mentioned page 90,[53] and as he served me there so he served me again, starting att an empty waggon; but he did not rise up with me, but slipping into a deep cart rake with his hinder leggs, fell down <of> on his side. I cleared the stirrups and got noe hurt, I thank God.

June 9, 1713. As I was comeing from Newmarket upon my Delph horse he fell down with me. I fell upon my right elbow and jarrd my head and bones for the present, but praysed be God who preserves us in all dangers, I gott noe further harm. I felt of this jarr 3 or 4 dayes in my right breast.

fol. 46r
April 5, 1713, Easter Sunday. I received the blessed sacrament of the body and blood of my dearest Saviour and renewed my vowes and resolucions of forsa-keing my sinns and amending my life. Lord assist me with thy grace to keep and observe them to my life's end.

8. 10. 14. *

18, Saturday. I spent all the afternoon att play with Thomas Spencer, who

---

[52] *Domi* Clift: at the house of Clift.
[53] See f. 44v.

came to buy some chaff of me, see page 68,[54] contrary to my good resolution there mentioned.

In the first life \or thoughts/ of any action or intention, let me bring them to the rule of God's word, to the rule of my own conscience, and to the rule of God's presence, and impartially measure them thereby; and if they will not abide that examination, let me reject them without any more reasonings or disputings.

fol. 46v

1713. Merceys received.

June 23. I was rideing with Mr John Fenn of Wisbich in Cambridg street, goeing to Hasleingfield, and Mr Fenn's horse stood still at something and jostled against mine (which was the horse I call Delph), and thrust him against a low peice of dirt wall, and he fell over it with me upon his back. I fell against a window with my elbow and broke as much glass as I paid 6d for, <and fell> but I thank Almighty God, who dayly preserves us, that I gott not the least harm. It was God's great mercy he did not fall upon my legg or chrush me against <the> the house side. For <this> this and all other thy great mercyes towards me and mine, my soul doth magnifie thee O Lord.

fol. 47r

December 25, 1713. I received the blessed sacrament of the body and blood of Jesus Christ my dear Redeemer and renewed my former vowes and resolutions of leading a new life. Lord assist me with the grace of thy Holy Spirit to keep and observe them to my life's end. *Jesu! tuam opem.*

March 28, 1714, Easter Sunday. I received the blessed sacrament of the body and blood of Jesus Christ my dear redeemer and renewed my vowes and purposes of leading a new life, remembring the great account I must one day make. Grant me, O Lord, the assistance of thy Holy Spirit that I may alwaies be prepared for that great audit. 'Turn thy face from my sinns and put out all my misdeeds', Psalm 51.

fol. 47v

1713. Mercyes received.

December 26. My sonn Thomas had a desire to goe with my man to the wheelwright's to fetch home 2 carts that were there to mend, and they were tyed one to the other and my sonn in the foremost. It was night before the man could get away, and my sonn being cold sayd he would get down and walk. That \man/ bad him not come down, \but/ by God's good providence the boy would get down, for the cart very soon after overturned, and there was an old wheel in the buck of each cart and that might in all likelyhood have killed him, or done him some great mischief. For this and all other thy mercyes, my soul doth magnifie thee O Lord.

---

[54] See f. 33v, above.

fol. 48r

May 16, 1714, Whitsunday. I received the blessed sacrament of the body and blood of my dear redeemer and renewed my vowes and purposes of forsakeing my sinns and amending my life. Lord give me grace to keep and observe them to my live's end.

11. *

June 13, Sunday. I was at church twice, but spent all the afternoon vainly and idley, with Symon Jude comeing hither and appointing company to meet at his house to play.

July 11. Att church twice, but very drowsy and sleepy there.

August 8. Att church twice, but slept there att the forenoon sermon.

fol. 48v

1713/4. Mercyes received.

January 27. My 2 sonns Henry and Thomas were goeing to school rideing on the little hobby, and she started att a woman who stood behind a tree at Wammel-hedge and threw them both down, but God be praised they got noe great hurt. Henry beat the skin off his legg, and Thomas fell upon his face and onely made his nose bleed.

February 13. My 2 sonns abovesaid were comeing from school on the same hobby, and she fell down with them and lay with her neck double, and upon Thomas's legg, 'till a man that was att plough near them came and released him.

August 17. My 3 eldest daughters walked to Milden, and att night I sent our coach to meet them and put my son James into it, and in the Church lane it overturned, and God be praised he got no harm.

fol. 49r

September 10, 1714. I received the blessed sacrament of the body and blood of Jesus Christ my dear and onely Saviour, and renewed my vowes and purposes of forsakeing my sinns and amending my life. Lord assist me with the grace of thy Holy Spirit to keep and observe \them/ better than I have hitherto done. *Jesu! tuam opem.*

He that hath created our souls after his own image, and redeemed them with his own blood, will not refuse them when they are commended, and given up \un/to him.

December 18, Saturday. Spent the afternoon att play at the Ferry from about 4 'till 9, contrary to my former purpose and resolution mentioned, page 68.[55] Every breach of that resolution is an high agravation.

fol. 49v

1714/15. Mercyes received.

December 26. My sonn James fell down the kitchin staires, made his nose bleed and swelled his cheek a little, but God be praised got noe further harm. He was then about 5 years old.

---

[55] See f. 33v, above.

April 13. I hired Gates's mare to Bury; she carryed me well thither, but fell down twice with me comeing home, and the last time she threw me over her head and my forehead came first at the ground, but by God's great mercy and providence I got noe harm. The first fall was \soon after I got/ out at the little gate on this side of the hide, the other in Mr Glascock's close called Hencroft. I omitted my double guard that day through forgetfulness.

fol. 50r

December 25, 1714. I received the blessed sacrament of the body and blood of Jesus Christ my dear redeemer. God Almighty assist me with his speciall grace to live more circumspectly for the future, and to keep a strict and constant watch over all my words and actions.

January 13, 1714. I set up 'till about 3 of the clock next morning with some friends that came to dine with me, and omitted prayers in my family. Lord be mercifull to me a miserable sinner. *Damna fleo rerum, sed plus fleo damna dierum.* See <Mr> Dr Cradock's book of *Knowledge and Practice*, chapter 19, page 89. The directions there mentioned may also be of great use to all persons who desire at any tyme more solemnly to humble themselves before the Lord, for the sinns of their past lives, and especially before the sacrament.

fol. 50v

1715. Mercyes received.

May 3. Wee set out for Long Sutton in Lincolnshire, got safe thither next day.

14. We got safe home, and found all well. God be praised whose providence preserved us in our goeings out and comeing home.

August 23. My sonn James, being a little above 5 yeares old, runn between the waggon wheeles to get some barly off it, as it came past our door with a load of barly, but by God's providence our cowyard gate was shut and the horses stood still 'till the man went to open the gate, else the hinder wheel had in all likely hood gone over him. For this and all other thy great mercyes, my soul doth magnifie thee O Lord.

Turn over.

fol. 51r

March 13, 1714/15, Sunday, I was att church twice, but talked of worldly buisiness (of letting, hireing, and exchangeing of land) with Robert Rolfe goeing \to/ and comeing fro church, and with Richard Clift of buying of land.

March 1715, *inter* 29, 30. *

April 2, * 3. *

April 17, 1715, Easter Sunday. I received the blessed sacrament of \the body and blood of/ Jesus Christ my blessed Saviour and redeemer, and by the \assistance of the/ grace of Almighty God resolve and purpose to live in stedfast union and conformity to all his holy commandments, for there is noe satisfaction but in a quiet conscience, noe solid pleasure but in religion, noe true joy but in God, so said the royall prophet, 'In thy presence is fullness of joy and att thy right hand there is pleasure for evermore,' Psalm 16:12.

fol. 51v

1715. Mercyes received.

November 17. As I came from the Ferry about 9 at night, comeing over the stile into my croft, my foot slipped off the stepp when I was stradlings [sic] over the stile, and I jolted down on my members (being cross the stile), and bruised my selfe and might have spoyled me. I felt at <times> tymes uneasy for some <years> \monthes/ after, blessed be God it proved noe worse.

December 16. I set up my foot on the ladder as it lay in my stable at Milden town to feel on my legg, which was hurt about a week before with my pattin (as I was then telling my brother Davies), and as I was setting my foot down my heel stuck on the end of one of the broad staves of the ladder. I could not recover my selfe, but fell down with my head and shoulders first to the ground, but God be praised got noe harm.

fol. 52r

May 15, 1715, Sunday. I was very drowsey and sleepy at church the afternoon.

June, inter 4, 5.

June 5, Whitsunday. I received the blessed sacrament of the body and blood of Jesus Christ my dear redeemer and renewed my former purposes and resolutions of forsakeing my sinns and leading a new life, God's grace assisting me. Jesu! tuam opem.

Inter 8, 9 * July. Inter 15, 16 August. *

October 16. I received the blessed sacrament of Christ's body and blood and renewed my covenant with Almighty God in my Saviour's blood, which I have so often and so greviously broken. I implore the divine assistance of his Holy Spirit to enable me to observe and keep it to my life's end. Let the light of thy Holy Spirit alwaies direct and guide me. Amen. Amen.

fol. 52v

1716. Mercyes received.

June 18. My son Henry stood by the river side to see the water horses draw, and the haleing line took him and threw him into river, but God be praysed he got noe harm.

July 17. My son Thomas fell into a quagmire in Frecknam Fenn up to the wast, but God be thanked got noe harm.

January 29. I fell from the topp of our kitchin staires to the bottom; my heels slipt up and I slidd down on my back, and praised be God I got noe hurt.

fol. 53r

December 25, 1715. I received the blessed sacrament of the body and blood of Jesus Christ my dear redeemer and renewed my vowes and resolucions of better obedience to God's holy will and commandments. Lord give me grace to keep and observe them to my life's end. Amen. Amen.

January, inter 25, 26.

February 2. Set up 'till 4 a clock at play at home, and <neglected> omitted prayers in my family.

April 1, 1716, Easter Sunday. I received the holy sacrament of the body and blood of my Saviour Jesus. I acknowledge and believe thy blood, O Holy Jesus, to have been shedd for my sinns, let it rest on me for the remission of them, and therein let all my sinns be washed away, and sprinkled from all evil conscience. Amen. Amen.

fol. 53v

1716/17. Mercyes received.

March 13. I was at Bury, and when I came home between 9 and 10 at night (haveing stayed and supped at Tuddenham), and goeing to alight off my horse, my foot hung a little in the stirrup which made me fall backward and jarrd my head against the ground, but blessed be God I got noe greater hurt.

April 21, Easter Sunday. As I came from church the afternoon upon my little grey hobby, she fell down and threw me over her head. I pitched upon my head, but God be praysed I got noe hurt.

April 22. The same hobby fell down with my sonn Henry and 2b[*ushels*] of wheat, and threw him over her head, but blessed by God he got noe hurt; he was goeing to mill.

fol. 54r

April 8, 1716, being Sunday, I gave directions to my men about their next day's work (before I considered the day), which might without damage \have been deferred/ 'till the next morning.

May 20, Whit Sunday. I received the holy sacrament of Christ's body and blood, and renewed my former vows and resolucions of forsakeing my sinns and amending my life, bewailing the loss of those pretious hours which I have spent in play and idleness, stedfastly resolving, God's grace assisting me, to live more circumspectly for the future.

> Thy God hath not denied thee <all> all
> Whilst he permits thee but to call,
> Call to thy God for grace, to keep
> Thy vows, and if thou break them weep,
> Weep for thy broken vowes, and vow again,
> Vows made in tears, cannot be still in vain.
> Then once again
> I vow to mend my wayes,
> Lord say Amen
> And thine be all the praise.

fol. 54v

1717. Mercyes received.

December 8. I was at my sonn's at Mildenhall to meet <my brother> Mr Delamore there, and comeing out of the kitchen through the hall to goe into the parlour, I mistook the door being in the dark, and the cellar door being open I stepped one stepp down, and it was through God's great mercy I did not fall headlong downe; it was very deep and steep. For this and all other thy providentiall mercyes to me, and mine, my soul doth magnifie thee O Lord.

January 7. I cocked my abbot gunn to put some oyl under the cock, and forgot to let it down, but charged it so, and did not discover the danger I was in all the tyme I was charging it, 'till I had layd it up, and then I was surprized and frighted to see what a danger I escaped. For this and all other mercyes my soul doth magnifie thee O Lord.

fol. 55r

July 1, 1716, Sunday. I went into corn chambers to get a sample of old and new wheat to send by Mr Norman to Huntington.

8. At church twice, but drowsey and sleepy forenoon and afternoon.

29. I was not at church the forenoon, it being too late before I got ready. I lay in bedd too long, being somewhat tired with my journey from Sutton the day before, and midnight before I gott to bedd.

August 4. Mr John Bradbury and Mr Wilkin came to my house about 8 at night, and wee playd at all 4s 'till about 10, being Saturday.

September 7. I was the occasion of meeting together to play at cards. I came away about 9, but they stayd and mispent their precious tyme, whereof I was the chief cause, but I repent, O my God, I repent, Lord be mercifull to me a sinner.

'Ο μισεις μηδενι ποιησεις.[56] Job 4:15.

Hic est apex summae sapientiae, ea viventem facere, quae morienti essent appetenda. Great Exemplar, page 172, margin.[57]

fol. 55v

1717/18. Mercyes received.

March 14. As I was goeing into Mr William Warren's house, I stumbled over a board sett to \keep/ the child from goeing out, and might have gott some great mischief with the force I fell down, but praysed be God I gott noe harm.

September 7. My son William narrowly escaped drowning on the Wash, goeing from Lynn to Long Sutton.

28. My sonn Thomas narrowly escaped choaking with a pinn or needle in his victualls at supper; he felt it prick his throat as he was reddy to swallow it down, and so by God's great mercy raised it up.

fol. 56r

December 25, 1716. I received the blessed sacrament of the body and blood of Jesus Christ my dear Saviour and redeemer, with an hearty sorrow for my past sinns, and a sincere resolution to live the rest of my dayes more circumspectly <for the future>, God's speciall grace assisting me.

February 16, Saturday. I spent all the afternoon from 3 'till 9 at play att the Ferry, contrary to my resolution mentioned, page 68,[58] which I purpose to keep and observe for the future, God's grace assisting me.

---

[56] 'Ο μισεις μηδενι ποιησεις: 'you hate nothing you make.'

[57] Hic est apex summae sapientiae, ea viventum facere, quae morienti essent appetenda: 'this is the highest point of wisdom: to do those things as a living person, which would be desired by the dying'. . . Jeremy Taylor, The Great Exemplar of Sanctity (1678).

[58] See f. 33v, above.

March 25, 1717. I spent part of the afternoon at play at home with Mr John Bradbury, Mr Shield, Mr Love, Mr John Delamore and my son.

April, *inter* 16, 17 * and 22. *

fol. 56v

De Contemptu Seculi

O that men would be wise \to know,/ understand, and foresee.
Be wise, to <understand> know 3 things:

1. The multitude of those that are to be damned.
2. The small number of them that are to be saved.
3. The vanity of transitory things.

Be wise to understand 3 things:

1. The multitude of sinns.
2. The omission of good things.
3. The loss of tyme.

Be wise to foresee 3 things:

1. The danger of death.
2. The Last Judgment.
3. Eternall punishment.

But there are but few soe wise as to consider these things.

fol. 57r

April 21, 1717, Easter Sunday. I received the blessed sacrament and made new resolutions of better obedience to God's holy will and commandments, for upon examination of my past life, I find to my great grief that mispending the Lord's day, drowsiness and dullness at church, and mispending my pretious tyme in play and idleness, and neglecting to set apart Saturday in every week to examine how I have spent the preceeding week, according to my former resolution page 68,[59] swells the catalogue of my sinns, being committed against so many resolutions to the contrary and after so many tymes receiveing the holy sacrament, which are great and high aggravations. But I repent, O my God, I repent. I return with grief and affliction of spirit, that I have so notoriously and highly offended thee, detesting the thoughts of doeing the like again, and resolving to live more carefully and circumspectly for the tyme to come.

fol. 57v

1718/19. Mercyes received.

February 2. Wee supped at my sonn's with Captain Pamplyn and others, and stayd 'till near 11; and as I came home, my horse started at something, I know not what, and threw me down, but God be praised I got not the least hurt. For this and all other thy wonderfull mercyes to me and mine, my soul doth magnifie thee, O Lord.

March 24. My son Thomas was comeing off the corn chamber next the coal

---

[59] See f. 33v, above.

house, and layd hold on the key to lock the door and to stay himself, and the key came out before he was aware of it and he fell from the topp of those steep staires to the bottom, and through God's great mercy got noe great hurt.

fol. 58r
June 9, 1717, Whit Sunday. I received the blessed sacrament of the body and blood of Jesus Christ my dear redeemer and renewed my former vowes and resolutions of forsakeing my sinns and amending my life, bewailing and lamenting all former breaches of them, resolving God's grace assisting me to live more circumspectly for the tyme to come.

25. *[unknown symbol][60]. August 1. *
October 20. I received the holy sacrament, and renewed my covenant with Almighty God in my Saviour's blood, which I have so often and so grievously broken. I beseech God to enable me to keep and observe it to my life's end. Amen.

25. I was too earnest and forward to get company to play. I followed Mr Wilkin to the Crown, thence I went to the Whitehart and sent for him thither, and playd with John Mainprise 'till 9.

And all this so soon after the sacrament, before which I resolved with my selfe not to [be] a ringleader or promoter of idleness and mispending of tyme.

fol. 58v
                    1719. Mercyes received.

May 4. I was at Reach Fair and was struck by an horse on my legg, but the blow happened slenting so that by God's great mercy I got noe hurt.

June 28. My sonn James escaped the danger of being choaked with a pinn in his victualls at dinner; it run into the roof of his mouth as he chewed.

December 28. As my son Thomas and I came from Tuddenham about 7 a clock at night, and he upon my buck horse I had of Mr Wilkin, which started at something and set a running and plunging and threw him down, but through God's great mercy and providence he got noe harm.

fol. 59r
November 8th, 1717. I was guilty again of the same fault as is mentioned on page 117th[61] on October 25, (viz.) tempting others to play, and went to Milden the day before (viz.) 7th on the same intent, but failed. So that I not only mispend my pretious tyme my selfe, which I must give an account of, but am too much like the tempter in perswadeing and enticeing others into the same sinn. I doe resolve, God's grace assisting me, to doe so noe more.

Decemeber 25. I received the blessed sacrament of the body and blood of my dearest Saviour and renewed my vows and resolucions of forsakeing my sinns and amending my life. Lord assist me with the grace of thy Holy Spirit to keep and observe them to my life's end. Amen. *Jesu tuam opem.*

January 4, Saturday. Brother and sister Davies and my sonn Coe's family

---

[60] Another symbol is used, similar to an inverted triangle, whose meaning is unknown.
[61] See f. 58r.

dined and supped here, so that I could not spend much of that day by my selfe, as I purposed, page 68.[62]

fol. 59v

1719/20. Mercyes received.

March 7. I rode my Bacon colt[63] to Milden and back again, he was not 3 years old and he carryed me very gently, I got noe harm the first tyme that ever I rode him.

April 6. My son James was at harrows with the Bacon mare which is very gentle, and I thank God she was so, for as she was goeing he stept over one of the trayse and put his arms about her hinder leggs to stopp her, and by God Almightye's good providence she stood still, else the harrows must have gone over him. For this and all other thy mercyes, my soul doth magnifie thee, O Lord.

Turn over [*to fol. 60v*].

fol. 60r

Fryday January 17, 1717/18. I went to call both the Mr Bradburyes out to play, contrary to my resolution mentioned page 119th.[64]

April 13, 1718, Easter Sunday. I received the blessed sacrament of the body and blood of Jesus Christ my dear redeemer and made new resolutions of forsakeing my sinns and amending my life. Lord assist me by thy grace to keep and observe them to my life's end.

18. I was comeing home from Milden market in good tyme, but saw Mr Wilkin near the White Hart, and did not resist the temptation but went to him and presently agreed to goe to the Cock, and there playd 'till 9.

June 1. I was drowsey and sleepy at church (and examined my selfe), and at other tymes at church and \at/ my owne private devotions I have been guilty of coldness and dulness and full of wandring thoughts, though I strive what I can against it. I have not so strictly observed my good resolution of calling myself weekly to account for my sinns and failings as I resolved page 68,[65] or as I purpose to doe for the future.

fol. 60v

1720. Mercyes received.

The same day my son James escaped (viz.) April 6. Thomas Challis and my sonn Thomas was goeing for a little hay to the barn in the close with onely a filler in the cart, who ran away and overturned the cart upon Thomas Challis who was taken up dead for the present; but blessed be God he came to himselfe in a short tyme, tho' very much bruised: if my son Thomas had not shrieked out and called help, which happend to be near hand, he must have dyed on the spot.

---

[62] See f. 33v, above.

[63] The 'Bacon colt' and 'Bacon mare' to which Coe refers were presumably animals which he had purchased from a person called Bacon (see also ff. 61v, 72v).

[64] See f. 59r.

[65] See f. 33v, above.

May 26. Mr John Seyliard and Mr Francis Howlet came past my house with a gunn and shot at the rooks and the paper fell upon the mault house, Turn over [*to fol. 61v*].

fol. 61r

1718. I have often pleased my selfe with impure fancyes and thoughts and [*deletion*] and in unchast songs and filthy and obscene talking, but I thank God not these many years, but still I cannot forget it when I examine myselfe. I have often resolved against my mispending my pretious tyme, yet the next slender temptation has overcome me.

June 8, Trinity Sunday. I received the blessed sacrament of the body and blood of Jesus Christ my dear redeemer and made new vowes of better obe-dience, resolving hereafter to be more watchfull, more diligent, more zealous in the performance of my duty and to walk more circumspectly, and to make it my delight to doe thy will, O God. I have sworn and am stedfastly purposed to keep thy righteous precepts, thy speciall grace assisting me.

July 8. * *bist. del.*[?][66]

14. Playd at cards at my own house with Mr William Warren, Mr Baldwyn and Mr Ralph, junior, 'till past midnight, and omitted prayers in my family. I was the occasion, and perswaded them to stay.

fol. 61v

and began to smoke and blaze, but, by God's great mercy and providence my sonns and 2 or 3 other boyes had got a ladder on that side of the house goeing to get a rook's nest, and so rann up and pulled down the fire, in all likelyhood it would have done a mischief before a ladder could have been fetched. For this and all other thy great mercyes, my soul doth magnifie thee, O Lord.

June 3. I rode to Milden on my Bacon colt (3 years old). He started at something in the Church Lane and I was very near falling off his back, but I thank God I recovered my self and kept his back.

fol. 62r

Inter 20, 21. * 27, 28. *

October 19, 1718. I received the blessed sacrament of Christ's body and blood and renewed my vowes and purposes of leading a new life which I have so often and so greviously broken. Lord give me grace to keep them to my live's end.

November 13. My son and daughters and some others dined here and playd at cards, and I set up 'till <past> near 2 in the morning at play.

28, Fryday. I went to \the/ Cock on purpose (after I had done my market buisiness) to get Mr Wilkin to play at cards with me, and I would have got others, but the rest of our company was gone to \take/ leave of Mr Glascock goeing to London.

December 6, Saturday. I spent some part of the afternoon idley, see page 68.[67]

25. I received the blessed sacrament, and renewed my covenant with

---

66 These abbreviations have so far defied interpretation.
67 See f. 33v, above.

Almighty God in my dear Saviour's blood. The Lord of his great mercye grant me grace to keep it to my life's end. Amen. *Jesu! tuam opem.*

fol. 62v

1720. Mercyes received.

July 1. Thomas Challis was goeing with the cart to Charles's Close for hay, he lead the horses all the tyme I saw him, but when I parted from him in our lane (being goeing to Milden) he got up to ride. My sonn \James/ and he was then in the cart together, but <before> they had gone but a little way before, the horses turned back and rann home and overthrew the cart in our yard, and through God's wonderfull providence they got noe harm. When I saw the cart goeing out of the yard with my son James in it, I rode up our lane with him, and bad him have a care, and if the horses rann away I bad him fall down into the buck of the cart, which they both did and saved themselves, <tho'> because Thomas Challis had like to have been killed before, as on page 122.[68]
Turn over 5 leaves.[69]

fol. 63r

March 29, 1719, Easter Sunday. I received the blessed sacrament of the body and blood of Jesus Christ my dear redeemer and renewed my vowes and purposes of leading a new life, remembring the great account I must one day give. Lord assist me with the grace of thy Holy Spirit to observe and keep them to my life's end. Amen.

April 20. I tempted Mr Wilkin and Mr William Warren to play. Wee begann for a pint of wine. I left them at 9 a clock.

May 15. Upon examination I find my selfe guilty of these following sinns and failings:

I have not so strictly as I ought observed my <promise> vows and resolution of setting apart Saturday in every week for examination of my selfe how I spent the preceeding week, as I purposed when I made that

fol. 63v

good resolution as is mentioned in this book, page 68.[70]

I have been drowsy and sleepy at church and often talking of worldly and other buisiness at other tymes of the Lord's day.

I have not so seriously considered and bewailed my frequent and dangerous violations of that great and solemn vow which was made for me in my baptism, as also the breach of many other religious and deliberate vows and promises made in any tyme of adversity, and alwayes before the holy sacrament.

I have \often/ mispent my pretious tyme in play and idleness, and have drawn others into the same sinn by my example and importunity.

But I repent, O my God, I repent, I accuse, and judg, and condemn my selfe for it. Lord be thou mercifull to me a most miserable sinner.

---

[68] See f. 60v.
[69] See f. 67v.
[70] See f. 33v, above.

fol. 64r

May 24, 1719, Trinity Sunday. I received the blessed sacrament of the body and blood of Jesus Christ my dear redeemer and made new vowes and resolutions (of leading a new life) which I intend and purpose, God's Holy Spirit assisting me, to observe to my live's end. Amen. Amen.

There are noe joyes like to the joyes of God, noe pleasures comparable to those of Christian piety. All thy commandments are sweeter than the honey and the honey comb, and in keeping them there is great reward. 'In thy presence is the fullness of joy, and att thy right hand there is pleasure for ever more.' So sayd holy David, the man after God's own heart.[71]

fol. 64v

A good conscience never wanteth joy; but an evil conscience is its own proper torment.

Study alwaies to doe well, and thou shalt never want a sweet tranquillity of mind.

A good conscience is the best pillow to sleep on, the best dish to feed on, nay it is a feast, a continual feast. Wouldest thou fare diliciously every day? Keep a good conscience.

Of the folly and mischief of sinn: it is a most unprofitable and foolish thing; the content that is in it is but imaginary, and dyes in the compass of a thought; the expectation of it, or from it, is nothing but disappointment, and the fruition of it does perish in a moment.

fol. 65r

June 1, 1719, Monday. Mr Wilkin, Mr Mano and Mr Ralph senior came to my house about 5, and I playd at all 4s with Mr Wilkin 'till near 11 at night and neglected prayers in my family that night.

6, Saturday. Wee were forced to brew small beer haveing a great many workmen, and tunned on Sunday morning. The Lord forgive us. I thought it would have been fit to have tunned on Saturday night. I will never order to brew again on Saturday. Our small beer was just out, we were forced to drink new as soon as it was tunned.

14, Sunday. I was drowsy and sleepy at church the forenoon, at home the afternoon and spent but little of that tyme in my closet.

fol. 65v

July 7, 1719. I went to Bremell Fair[72] on purpose to look <enqu> after a saddle I lost the 29 of November last, (because I knew all sorts of people resorted thither and I was in hopes of finding it), and stayd at Mr Clark's at Brandon with Mr Wilkin, Mr Ralph junior and Robert Snare 'till past 9. Got home about 12 and neglected prayers in my family.

9. I spent the whole day at play at the Ferry with Mr Wilkin and Doctor Wallis from 11 'till past 8. I resolve never to \doe/ so again. The Lord of his

[71] Psalm 16:12.
[72] This is almost certainly Bromehill Fair in the parish of Weeting, Norfolk. See William Owen's *New Book of Fairs* (1816), 48.

infinite mercy forgive me for what is past. Wee cannot doubt of God's willingness to forgive the sinns of the penitent, when forgiveness of sinns is one of the
articles of our Christian faith. Why then art thou so vexed,

fol. 66r
O my soul, and why art thou so disquieted within me? O put thy trust in God
who never faileth to help and comfort them, that with hearty repentance and
true faith seek unto him.

October 11, 1719. I received the holy sacrament of the body and blood of
Jesus Christ my onely Saviour and redeemer and made new vowes and resolutions of leading a new life and of not spending so much of my precious time in
play as I have formerly done. Lord assist me with the grace of thy Holy Spirit to
keep and observe them to my life's end. Amen.

Inter December[73] v, vi. * <being the>

December 11. I was the chief instrument to get company together to play
and loose our tymes, though I have formerly resolved against \being so./

fol. 66v
December 25, 1719. I received the blessed sacrament and renewed my covenant with Almighty God in my dear Saviour's blood. The Lord of his mercy
give me grace to keep it to my life's end. Amen.

April, 1720. *Inter* xiii and xiiii. *

April 17, Easter Sunday. I received the blessed sacrament of the body and
blood of Jesus Christ my dear redeemer and renewed my vows and resolutions
of better obedience to God's holy will and commandments. Lord give me grace
to keep and observe them all my dayes.

June 5, Whit Sunday. I received the blessed sacrament of the body and blood
of my dear redeemer wherein I again renewed my vows and purposes of better
obedience to God's holy will and commandments. Lord assist me with thy Holy
Spirit.

fol. 67r
July 3, 1720. I was drowsy and sleepy at church.

September 23. I went to the Cock to ask Mr Wilkin to play, but did not like
the cold new room he was in, so I did not stay, tho' my will was good, but I
resolve for the future not to be a promoter to it.

November 7, *diluc* * 13, *idem.* [74]

December, *inter* 11, 12.

December 25. I received the holy sacrament of the body and blood of Jesus
Christ my dear redeemer and renewed my vows and resolutions of better
obedience, God's grace assisting me. I have sworn and am stedfastly purposed to
keep his righteous precepts.

There is more merit in the Sonn of God to procure our pardon, and reconcile

---

[73] Coe writes 'Xber', meaning December (see also f. 85r).

[74] The meaning of *diluc.* is uncertain (see also f. 87r), but may be an abbreviation of *diluculo*: 'at
daybreak', referring to the time of day when Coe's indiscretion was commited.

us to God, than there is guilt in us to merit condemnation; the satisfaction made by him is of infinite value, and so abundantly sufficient.

fol. 67v

1720. Mercyes received.

August 3. I had a pinn in my victualls at dinner, and by God's great mercy I felt it in my mouth before I swallowed.

\September 24. I forgot to enter this mercy so soon as I recovered./[75] I fell sick, but not unto death.

November 10. As I was walking through the court at Sir Thomas Hanmer's in the dark, I did not think of the stepps in the freestone walk, but walked hastily on and stepped them all at once. I did not fall down, but wringed my heel and might accidentally have broke my legg or hurt my selfe by a fall, but I thank God I did not feel the wrinch but just at the present.

15. My black mare fell down with me comeing from Newmarket (the first tyme), but I thank God I got noe hurt.

17. I was at Henry Plumpton's to have some small irons made for the great chariot, and I was strikeing to cut off a peice; it flew up and hit my forehead \without/ hurting or burning me. *Deo gratias.*

fol. 68r

January 12, 1720/21. I asked Henry Morly to goe to John Stead's to play, contrary to my resolution mentioned page 134,[76] for I resolved never to be a promoter to idleness and play. I pray God to give me his grace to keep that my resolution better for the future.

February 26, Sunday. I talked with Robert Rolfe as soon as wee came out of church about seed tear, and changeing some seed barly, which I ought to have put off 'till another day.

April 7, 1721, Good Fryday, about 5 m.

9, Easter Sunday. I received the \blessed/ sacrament of Christ's body and blood, and renewed my vows and resolutions of leading a new life and not to mispend my pretious tyme as I have too often done. Lord give me grace to observe and keep them to my life's end. Amen.

fol. 68v

1720/1. Mercyes received.

December 9. As I was bringing my wife home behind me (and goeing through the church yard in at the little gate by Mr Howlet's), her petticoats or gown hung upon the post and pulled \her/ down from behind me, but God be praysed she got noe hurt.

February 10. My black mare fell down with me as I came from Milden and threw me over her head. I beat the skin off my forehead and nose, but I thank God I got noe more harm; it was a very hard frost, and the grownd very hard.

---

[75] This part of the entry occurs in the margin, marked by two pointing hands.
[76] See f. 67v.

March 31. I gave my son Thomas a sword to carry up into mault chamber,[77] to kill some ratts if he could happen of any in the thatch, and as he was giveing me the candle out of the lanthorn, he held the sword in the same hand and the poynt touched
Turn over.

fol. 69r
April 30, 1721, Sunday. I was drowsy and sleepy att church, tho' I endeavourd against it.

May 14, Sunday. I was again sleepy at church.

28, Whitsunday. I received the blessed sacrament of the body and blood of Jesus Christ my dear redeemer with a full and stedfast resolution to lead a new life, God's speciall grace assisting me.

July 14. I begann a set at cards within 7 minutes of 9 a clock as I thought, but when I came home I found my watch to be about 5 minutes slow by my clock, so it wanted but 2 minutes of 9, which I am hearty sorry for and will never doe so again.

August 29.

October 15. I received the blessed sacrament of the body and blood of Jesus Christ my onely Saviour, and resolved with my selfe God's grace assisting me to live more circumspectly for the future.

fol. 69v

1721. Mercyes received.

my cheek, and very narrowly escaped <my fa> running into my face or eyes, but God be praysed it missed both.

May 24th. My black mare fell down and threw me over \her/ head, but God be praysed I got not the least harm. I rode a slow trott reading the Northampton news paper,[78] but I could not stop my selfe but tumbled easily over her head. I held the bridle in my hands, she pulled to get away and sladed me a little before I could get up; it was upon Bury heath.

June 19. My daughter Sarah comeing from Watton upon my grey hobby, she fell down with her upon Brand[on] heath and threw her over her head, but God be praysed she got noe hurt.

fol. 70r
Doctor Cumber's Companion to the Altar, page 337, edition 4.[79] Nothing is more bruitish, than to lose peace of conscience, the love of God, and the hopes of heaven, for the short and miserable pleasures of sinn.

December 25, 1721. I received the blessed sacrament of the body and blood of Jesus Christ my dear redeemer, and resolved with my selfe, God's speciall

---

[77] A reference to Coe's interests in malt production, some of which he used for brewing. He had at least two maltings, one in West Row, Mildenhall, and one in Royston, Herts.
[78] The Northampton Mercury was founded in 1720; G.A. Cranfield, The Development of the Provincial Newspaper, 1700–60 (1962), 19.
[79] Thomas Comber, A Companion to the Altar (1675).

grace assisting me, to lead a new life, and not to mispend my precious hours as I have too often done, to my great sorrow and grief.

January, *inter* 14, 15. *

He that would dye holily and happily must in this world love tears, humilyty, solitude, and repentance, sayes Doctor Jeremy Tayler. *Mors tua, mors Christi, trans mundi, gloria coeli, et dolor inferni, sunt meditanda tibi.*[80]

fol. 70v

1721. Mercyes received.

August 24. My sonn Thomas was driveing barly cart from the 2a. 2r.[81] next the street, and comeing with an empty cart in at the gate over against Thomas Hynard's, a girl scared the horses so that they turned short and took the post and overthrew. Thomy was in the cart, but by God's great providence he got noe hurt.

September 5. I was taken sick, 2 or 3 dayes after my wife was so, and \about that tyme/ 4 of my children, Sarah and Barbara, Thomas and Nanny, but I thank God \all/ recovered.

See Doctor Cradock's book of *Knowledg and Practice*, 2 part, 19 chapter, page 106, at directions for the sick, the mercyes there mentioned I can truly apply to my selfe, and say as it is there.

Turn over.

fol. 71r

October 15, 1721. I received the blessed sacrament of the body and blood of Jesus Christ my dear and onely Saviour, and made new vows and resolucions of forsakeing my sinns and amending my life, God's grace assisting me.

March 25, 1722, Easter Day and Lady Day.[82] I received the holy sacrament of the body and blood of Jesus Christ my dear redeemer and renewed my vows and purposes of leading a new life. Lord assist me with the grace of thy Holy Spirit to observe and perform them to my life's end.

March 29. I voted against Sir Robert Clark[83] at Cambridge election, after I had told his servant that I would not vote against him, intending not to goe at all, because I was unwilling to vote against \him/ as a neighbour, nor for him, because I thought him too much of the Court party. \I am heartily sorry for breaking my promise. I was too easily perswaded./[84]

fol. 71v

1721. Mercyes received.

Blessed be \the/ Lord in all my life tyme I never broke a bone, never fell into

---

80 *Mors tua, mors Christi, trans mundi, gloria coeli, et dolor inferni, sunt meditanda tibi*: 'Your death, the death of Christ, the glory of heaven, and the anguish of hell, are things worth your consideration.'

81 2 acres, 2 roods.

82 See his reference to a current saying concerning the conjunction of the two days, f. 4r.

83 Sir Robert Clark of Snailwell was a Whig candidate in the Cambridgeshire county election of March 1722. Coe clearly had a vote in that shire as a 40 shilling freeholder. In the Suffolk county elections of 1705 and 1710, Coe voted solidly Tory.

84 This insertion was added in the margin.

the hands of robbers, never into publick shame, or noisome diseases, I have not begged my bread; God gave mee a right shape of body, the right use of my understanding, carefull and pious parents, good and bountifull friends, a religious education; delivered me, and by his Almighty providence preserved me in and from a great many dangers, heard my prayers in many particular pressures of spirit, and in tyme of need. Oh! what shall I render to the Lord for all his benefitts towards me: Oh! grant me grace to be alwaies truly thankfull.

> Plerique, ut accipiant, importuni,
> Donec acceperint, inquieti
> Quando acceperint, ingrati
> [deletion]

St Bernard[85]

Turn over.

fol. 72r

Doctor Comber's short discourse upon the whole Common Prayer designed to inform the judgment, and excite the devotion, of such as dayly use the same, page 51.[86]

'Tis the wisest thing in the world to be a good man.

May 13, 1722, Whit Sunday. I received the blessed sacrament of the body and blood of Jesus Christ my Saviour, and therein renewed my vows and resolucions of leading a new life, God's speciall grace assisting me.

In the commission of evil, fear no man so much as thy own selfe. Another is but one witnes against thee: thou art a thousand; another thou mayst avoid, but thy selfe thou canst not, wickedness is its own punishment.

July 22, Sunday. I was drowsy and sleepy at church.

fol. 72v

1721. Mercyes received.

December 18. My man Henry Rickard was at plough with a colt not 3 years old and the other Bacon colt not 5, and they broke away from him and rann away with the plough twice, and threw the man down when he had hold of one of their heads, and the plough had like to have gone over him, but God be praysed neither horses nor man got any hurt. The plough ear broke so they left the plough behind 'em.

The English of the foregoeing Latin.[87] 'Many men (says St Bernard) are importunate in begging mercyes, and impatient 'till they receive them, and then unthankfull when they have them.'

February 10. Henry Rickard above said had a kick on his right legg by one of my horses, as he was upon another leading him, it was God's great mercy it was not broke.

---

[85] Coe supplies the translation on f. 72v.
[86] Thomas Comber, A discourse concerning the daily frequenting the Common Prayer (1687).
[87] See f. 71v.

fol. 73r

St. Matthew 11 v. 30. 'My yoke is easy, and my burden is light.' These are the words of our Saviour. Virtue hath more pleasure in it than vice, and to live according to the laws of Jesus is in some things most naturall and proportionable to the desires and first intentions of nature. And there is in it less trouble than in sinn and it conduces infinitely to the content of our lives, and is a means to preserve our temporall lives long and healthy, and is most reasonable; and he onely is prudent who does so, and he a fool that does not. Therefore to live according to the laws of the Holy Jesus is the onely way to bring us to a glorious and happy eternity. *Great Exemplar*, page 415.[88]

This is the victory that overcometh the world; even our faith, that is our belief of God's promises, the promise of the Spirit for present aid and the promise of heaven for the future reward is strength enough to overcome \all/ the world. *Ibid*.

fol. 73v

1722. Mercyes received.

April 30. My daughter Graves and daughter Barbara very narrowly escaped drowning, goeing over a deep dike at Long Sutton upon a plank. They were goeing over together, but there happened by God's providence a small gale of wind which made them a little afraid so that they would not goe over together (as they did over another dike just before hold\ing/ one the other by the hands) but called at an house just by, and a maid came and took Barbara by the hand to lead her over first, and when they came in the middle, the plank broke and they both fell in. The maid pitched on her feet and was up to the shoulders, but Barbara fell down all along <if> and the maid was forced to lift and hold her up 'till others came to draw her out. In all likelyhood if both my daughters had ventured <alone> together they <might> had been drowned. For this and all other thy mercyes to me and mine, my soul doth magnifie thee O Lord.

fol. 74r

Methinks it should be a most transporting delight to us to be employed in the praise of that great and glorious God, by whose inexhaustible fountain of goodness wee enjoy all the blessings of life, and by whose omnipotent agency, wee are preserved from sinking into our originall nothing. The mercyes bestowed upon all the world in one day, (says an eminent writer) are above human arithmetick, and the blessings which one single man enjoys in the whole course of his life, doe transcend the bounds of numeration; what an amazing summ therefore would all the mercyes make, which all men in all ages have received!

The infinite and inconceivable myriads command us into silence, and adoration, and it is the employment of angels and glorifyed souls to enumerate them in the regions of eternity; yea and heaven it selfe seems to be designed on purpose, that wee might supply the defect of our imperfect earthly prayers, Turn over.

---

[88] Jeremy Taylor, *The Great Exemplar of Sanctity* (1678).

fol. 74v

1722. Mercyes received.

and fully give glory to God for all the acts of his goodness, which will require an everlasting duration to recount.

August 7. My sonn Thomas, goeing into fenn upon a fenn waggon, went to set down upon the side of it and the horses trotted at the same tyme, and hee fell backward and between the wheeles, but by God's great mercy the wheeles missed him and he got noe harm.

November 2. My wife very narrowly escaped being seized on by a <fierce> fierce mastiffe at Mr Foorth's,[89] if his servant had not at the very instant came and rebuked him. He used to be kept chained, and then happened to be loose. My wife was goeing into the yard not knowing the danger.

fol. 75r

October 14, 1722. I received the blessed sacrament of the body and blood of Jesus Christ my dear redeemer and renewed my former vows and resolutions of leading a new life. Lord assist me with the grace of thy Holy Spirit to observe and keep them to my life's end.

November 1. * 2. *

December 18, 1722. 60 years of age.

December 30. I received the holy sacrament of the body and blood of Jesus Christ my onely Lord and Saviour and made new vowes and resolucions of leading a new life, and of spending the short remainder of my days more warily and circumspectly than ever yet I have done, God's speciall grace assisting me.

God hath promised pardon to him that repenteth, but he has \not/ promised repentance to him that sinneth.

fol. 75v

1722. Mercyes received.

November 12. My black mare fell down with me at Fornham comeing from the Lady Castleton's[90] about 8 or 9 of the clock at night, within a little of her gate, but God be praysed I got not the least hurt. I fell over her head.

January 8. My black mare jumping out of the boat when I came from Newmarket, before I could get out of her way, struck me on my right ancle, made it very sore and swelled. If my boot had not been on, she might have done me a greater mischief. I thank God it was noe worse.

February 15. I was at the Duchess of Grafton's funerall at Euston church, and as \I was/ goeing over the vault (where all that family are deposited)[91]
Turn over (to f. 76v).

---

89 Probably a son of William Foorth, rector of Eriswell, and husband of Isaac Archer's daughter, Anne. He had died in 1715. Coe may, however, be referring simply to the household formerly headed by Foorth.

90 Probably the widow of Sir John Castleton of Stuston, Suffolk, who died 1705; by 1722 she was apparently living in the Bury area.

91 Isabella, Duchess of Grafton, was daughter of Henry Bennet, Earl of Arlington. Her husband was Henry Fitzroy, 1st Duke of Grafton (1663–90), 2nd son of Charles II and his mistress Barbara Villiers, Countess of Castlemaine. The Duchess of Grafton later married Sir Thomas Hanmer of Mildenhall.

fol. 76r

May 2, 1723, Whitsunday. I received the blessed sacrament of the body and blood of Jesus Christ my onely Saviour and redeemer with stedfast purposes and resolutions of forsakeing my sinns and leading a new life, God's grace assisting me.

July 7. I was drowsy and slept at church.

October 13, 1723. I received the holy sacrament and renewed my covenant with Almighty God in my Saviour's blood, which I have so often and so greviously broken, and earnestly implore the divine assistance \to enable me/ to keep and observe it to my life's end. Amen.

December 19. Being the second day of the sixty first year of my age I examined my self, being to receive the holy sacrament on Christmas day next: and as I have through God's great mercy begann a new year, so I intend God's grace assisting me to lead a new life. *Jesu! tuam opem.* Amen. Amen.

fol. 76v

1722/3. Mercyes received.

to read the Lord Arlington's inscription on white marble against the wall, the corner of a seat catched my clothes and put me suddenly back, and if I had \not/ catched hold of the seat I had fallen backward down the vault (a great steep), which must inevitably \have/ done me a great mischeif, but blessed by God I saved my selfe as above said. Mr Thomas Baldwyn of Worlington was then near me and saw it.

Lord give me grace in all my wants and necessityes to fly to thee by prayer, and in all my supplyes and deliverances to return unto thee with thanksgiveing.

October 7. My daughter Barbara hurt her breast against the waggon, what the issue will be God knows.

fol. 77r

December 25. I received the blessed sacrament of the body and blood of my Lord and Saviour Jesus Christ, and renewed my vows and purposes of leading a new life, God's speciall grace assisting me. Amen. Amen.

January 16. L. G. . . *[92]

When death comes, the most comfortable hours that can return to our memories, will be those wee spent in improveing the true and experimentall and practicall knowledge of Christ Jesus, and him crucifyed.

April 5, 1724, Easter Sunday. I received the blessed sacrament of the body and blood of Jesus Christ my dear redeemer with a stedfast resolution to live more circumspectly for the future, God's speciall grace assisting me. *Jesu! tuam opem.*

fol. 77v

1723/4. Mercyes received.

November 19. My wife got a fall at Mrs Foorth's and jarrd her right arm; it was God's great mercy her arm was not broke. She felt a weakness and pain a great while.

[92] This entry is partially erased and its meaning obscured.

January 15. My wife <narrowly missed> escaped a great mischief by the fall of an heavy chopping board off the high shelf in the outward pantry, which very narrowly missed her head, she was but just passed from under it when it fell down. For this and all other thy great mercyes to me and mine, my soul doth magnifie thee, O Lord.

March 28. My men were at plow with 3 ploughs sowing barly in Mildich, most of them young colts. One of them took some distaste and rann away and all the others followed. One pair came running home, jumped over Mr Thurston's pightle gate, the other were stopped, and I thank God all this tyme noe mischief done.

fol. 78r

May 24, 1724, Whitsunday. I received the holy sacrament of the body and blood of Jesus Christ my dear and onely Saviour with a stedfast resolucion of forsakeing my sinns and amending my life, God's speciall grace assisting me. Amen. Amen.

5. *Inter* 20, 21. *. vi, mo. 1.*[93]

October 18. I received the blessed sacrament of the body and blood of Jesus Christ my dear redeemer, stedfastly purposeing, God's speciall grace assisting \me/, to spend the short remainder of my dayes more circumspectly and warily than I have hitherto done. *Jesu! tuam opem.*

Judg Hales's book, page 208. Meditations upon the Lord's Prayer.[94] Thus hath it, viz. the misery from which wee are redeemed is so great; the prise by which wee are redeemed so invaluable; the glory and blessedness to which wee are redeemed so full; and all these appearing so to the soul by faith, that the soul Turn over [*to fol. 79r*].

fol. 78v

1724. Mercyes received.

March 29. As I was rideing to church on my black mare, she fell down with me and threw me. I hurt my left buttock which was painfull for a few dayes.

April 23. My sister Davies and daughter Ann returned from Holm, and as they came about Wangford Grang they were persued by a foot-padd and were forced to gallop almost to Eriswel to escape. Sister Davies was behind her man, and daughter Nanny single, and nobody else to assist them. He persued them 'till they came near 2 sheepherds, they had been robbed if not strippd or murthered.

June 24. My son Thomas and John Rooks were goeing in the cart to the 16 acres for tears, and the filler went too near a wall, and the wheel rann up against the wall and overturned with them in the cart, but God be praysed they got no harm.

fol. 79r

cann think nothing too much to return, to that God that hath so freely done so much for it. Thus faith worketh by love.

---

[93] This entry is again obscure. The 5 may refer to the month, i.e. May.

[94] No work of this title seems to have been written by Sir Matthew Hale.

December 27, 1724. I received the blessed sacrament of the body and blood of Jesus Christ my dear and onely Lord and Saviour and thereby have confirmed my good resolutions and purposes, God's speciall grace assisting me, to spend the short remainder of my dayes more carefully and warily than I have hitherto done.

Lord give me grace in all my wants and necessityes to fly to thee by prayer, and in all my supplyes and deliverances to return unto thee with thanksgiving.

July 11, 1725. I was very sleepy and drowsy at church, the Lord forgive me.

Ante senectutem curandum est ut homo bene vivat; in senectute autem ut bene moriatur. Seneca.[95]

fol. 79v

1724. Mercyes received.

July 29. My son Thomas fell off a stool at Wammel with a sack of wheat on his back, but God be praysed he got noe mischief. He stepped on to the stool, and then goeing to stepp on to the cart the stool kicked up, and he fell backward.

October 20, Tuesday. My daughter Barbara slipt upon our kitchin staires with her legg double under her, and wrinched and streined her foot, but God be praised got noe further harm.

December 7. My house very narrowly escaped burning, our kitchin chamber chimney being on fire and blazed out at the topp, but was happyly discovered and prevented by fireing off severall gunns which brought down the fire. For this and all other thy former mercyes, my soul doth magnifie thee, O Lord.

fol. 80r

March 28, 1725, Easter Sunday. I received the blessed sacrament of the pretious body and blood of Jesus Christ my dear and onely Saviour and redeemer, and am stedfastly purposed, God's grace assisting me, to spend the rest of my dayes more circumspectly than I have formerly done.

April, *inter* 22, 23. *

May 9. I was drowsy and sleepy at church.

16, Whitsunday. I received the holy sacrament of the body and blood of my Saviour Jesus Christ and renewed my vows and purposes of leading a new life, God's Holy Spirit assisting me.

June 27. I was drowsy and slept at church.

July 18. Sleepy at church th'afternoon.

October xii. *

October 17. I received the blessed sacrament of the body and blood of my dearest Saviour and made new resolutions of better obedience to God's holy will and commandments, his speciall grace assisting me. *Jesu! tuam opem.*

---

[95] The actual quotation is *ante senectutem curavi, ut bene viverem, in senectute, ut bene moriar.* Seneca, *Ad Lucilium Epistularum Moralium quae supersunt*, LXI, 2, 5: 'Before I became old, I tried to live well; now that I am old, I shall try to die well.'

fol. 80v

1725. Mercyes received.

March 30. My wife rode single with me to Tuddenham, and as wee came home her horse plunged and playd the jade that she very narrowly escaped falling off, but God be praysed noe mischief happened.

June 1st. My wife narrowly escaped chokeing with a mackeril bone in her throat, but by God's great mercy she pulled it up with her finger.

July 14. As I was comeing from the Ferry home by the creek, wherein the boats goe to bring clunch, just after a rain it was slippery, and my heels slippd up and I fell just up \on/ the edge of the creek and very narrowly escaped falling in. For this and all other thy mercyes to me and mine, my soul doth praise and magnifie the, O Lord.

fol. 81r
1725.

> Let above all, religion be your care,
> And all your actions must be cent'red there;
> It must not be with a light air received,
> For then as lightly, it will be believed.
> To love your neighbours, and the poor relieve,
> To doe noe wrong, nor any wrong conceive,
> And all the wrong that's done you to forgive:
> Is sure the best and safest way to live.

He that is not content and patient in affronts, hath not yet learned humility of the holy Jesus. *Great Exemplar*, page 514, line 27.

December 5. I was at church twice but spent all the evening in vain and fruitless discourse at Mr Rolfe's; wee all supped there.

December 26. I received the holy sacrament of the body and blood \of/ my dear redeemer Jesus Christ, with a stedfast purpose and resolution to spend the short remainder of my dayes more warily and circumspectly, God's Holy Spirit assisting me.

fol. 81v

1725. Mercyes received.

July 17. As I was getting on horseback by my door, the horse began to goe before my legg was quite over, and I fell back again and ranched my legg on the topp of the pales and fell to the ground, but God be praised I gott noe further hurt.

18, Sunday. As I was getting up on this same horse to come \home/ after church <in> the afternoon, he moved on again before I was quite up and I fell back again on my left buttock and bruised a little, but I thank God I got noe further hurt.

19. My wife, as she was at supper put a peice of meat in her mouth wherein was a pinn. She felt it in her mouth before she swallowed it, God be praysed for all his mercyes.

August 26. I struck my legg unaware against a fork, and onely rent an hole in my stocking, but I thank God did not hurt my legg.

fol. 82r

April 10, 1726. Easter Sunday.

April 17. I received the holy sacrament of the body and blood of Jesus Christ my dear and only Saviour and renewed my vows and resolutions of better obedience to God's holy will and commandments all the days of my life. *Jesu! tuam opem.*

24. I was sleepy and drowsy at church.

May 29. Whitsunday. I received the blessed sacrament of the body and blood of Jesus Christ my dear redeemer with a stedfast purpose and resolution to spend the short remainder of my dayes more circumspectly and warily, God's speciall grace assisting me.

Mo[nth] 5th. 3. *

October 9. I was sleepy, and slept at church.

16. I received the blessed sacrament of the body and blood of Jesus Christ my dear redeemer and made new vows of better obedience to God's holy will [and] commandments. I beseech God to give me his grace to keep them to my life's end. Amen.

fol. 82v

1725/6. Mercyes received.

February 25. As I was at dinner I felt a pinn in my mouth which was in the victualls, but God be praised I felt it before I swallowed.

August 11. As my son Thomas was driveing an empty cart into field, the horses rann away with him in the cart, up our lane and round the pitt at the lane's end and through the field gate and over some meers' head, and I thank \God/ noe mischief done. They escaped very narrowly overturning into the pitt.

September 3. My black mare fell down and threw me over her head upon Milden Warren as I came from Wrettham, but God be praysed, I got not the least hurt. I think her foot slipt into a rabbit hole that was covered with sand.

fol. 83r

Often call to mind these excellent words of St. Austin (viz.)

Love the good things which Christ Jesus promises you; fear the evil wherewith he threatens you, and then you will slight as well the promises as threatnings of this world.

Ex hoc momento pendet aeternitas.[96] This life is but a moment if it be compared with eternity, and eternity depends upon it. Wisdom then it will be so to improve every moment of this life, that it may be a foundation for eternity, for from this moment of our lives depend our eternity, either of bliss or woe.

Decemeber 25, 1726. I received the blessed sacrament of the body and blood of my dear redeemer Jesus Christ and made new resolutions of better obedience to God's holy will and commandments. O that the short remainder of my dayes may be the better for this day. Amen.

---

[96] *Ex hoc momento pendet æternitas*: 'upon this moment, eternity hangs'.

fol. 83v

1726–8. Mercyes received.

December 14. My foot slipped when I was got cross a stile, and I jolted down, but by God's good providence I did not hurt my self, but escaped very narrowly. See November 17, 1715.[97]

Many mercyes received within this space of tyme. Every day's health and every night's rest and every hour free from pain is a mercy.

May 11, 1728. A very great tempest of thunder, hail and lightning began about 7 at night and very terrible in the night, tho' blessed be God we neither heard it nor felt it; but the hail destroyed a great many acres of rie in and about Exning and Newmarket, and shattered a great many glass windows and other great damages wherever it went.[98]

fol. 84r

This world would be an image of heaven if all men were charitable, peaceable, just, and loveing. *Great Exemplar*, page 421.

March, *inter* 14, 15. *

April 2, 1727, Easter Sunday. I received the blessed sacrament of the body and blood of Jesus Christ my dear and only Saviour and redeemer, and made new vows of better obedience to God's holy will and commandments, Lord grant me grace to keep and observe them better than I have hitherto done. *Jesu! tuam opem.*

May 28, Trinity Sunday. I received the holy sacrament of the body and blood of my Saviour Jesus Christ and renewed my former vows of forsakeing my sinns and amending my life. Lord assist me with thy Holy Spirit to keep and observe them to my life's end. Amen.

September, *inter* 12, 13. *

fol. 84v

Let us every day think upon our last day; let us in tyme think upon eternity; let us every minute wee have to live, so live, as if wee lived in fear of everlasting torments; that so by the mercy of God in Jesus Christ wee may for ever escape them. Alas! how unlike are the houses of eternity, one of them wee must inhabit, wee must either for ever rejoyce in heaven, or for ever burn in hell.

St. Matthew 16: 26 'What is a man profited if he shall gain the whole world and lose his own soul.'

Therefore, O man, though thou losest every thing thou hast in the world, have a care to keep thy soul. Let Christ be thine end and thou shall reign with Christ without end.

fol. 85r

September 24, 1727. I received the blessed the holy sacrament [*sic*] and renewed my covenant with Almighty God in my Saviour's blood. Lord grant

[97] See f. 51v.
[98] Cf. hurricane of 1703, note 21.

me grace to amend my life and to spend the short remainder of my life, as if every day were to be my last.

December,[99] *inter 2, 3.* *

O all ye holy angels behold and wonder, wretched man hath sinned against God, and God himself hath suffered the sinner's punishment. Christ was crucifyed.

December 25.[100] I received the holy sacrament of the body and blood of our Saviour Jesus Christ and renewed my vows and resolutions of obediently keeping God's holy will and commandments, his speciall grace assisting me. *Jesu! tuam opem.*

fol. 85v

1728/9. Mercyes received.

January 28. As I was goeing into Charles's barn which Thomas Clark hire[101] of me, I stumbled over the high threshold and fell down upon my breast, so that I could scarce fetch my breath for the present and bruised my right legg; my breast was sore a good while.

May 20. A great tempest of thunder and lightning at night, but God be praised wee received noe hurt.

fol. 86r

April 21, 1728, Easter Sunday. Haveing then renewed my covenant with Almighty God in my dear Saviour's blood at his holy table, I doe with all devotion of my heart and soul entirely surrender up my self and all that is mine to his service and glory, vowing all fidelity and obedience to him, and resolving that he shall have the full guiding, governing and disposeing of me and mine, God's grace assisting me.

Noe labour must seem hard, noe time must seem long, all the while wee are seeking after eternall glory.

June 16, Trinity Sunday. I received the holy sacrament and made new promises and resolutions of better obedience to God's holy will and commandments. Lord give me grace to keep and observe them to my life's end.

fol. 86v.[102]

fol. 87r

June 30, 1728. I was drowsie and slept at church.

September 8. I was very sleepy at church.

October 27. I received the blessed sacrament of the body and blood of Jesus Christ my dear redeemer, and renewed my vows and purposes of better

---

[99] 'Xber', as f. 66r, note 72.
[100] 'Xber', as f. 66r, note 72.
[101] 'Hire': Suffolk dialect for 'hires'.
[102] This folio is blank except for an entry in a later hand which reads: 'Extract from Mildenhall parish register book. Burialls, September 1729. 3rd. William Coe, gent.'

obedience to God's to God's [*sic*] holy will and commandments, God's grace assisting me.

December 29. I received the blessed sacrament and made new vows of better obedience to God's holy will and commandments. Lord give me grace to keep and observe them to my life's end.

January 1. *diluc.* * [103]

April 13, 1729. I received the holy sacrament and renewed my vows and resolutions of leading a new life, God's Holy Spirit assisting me.

May 25, Whit Sunday. I received the blessed sacrament of the body and blood of my dear redeemer and renewed my vows and resolucions of better obedience to God's holy will and commandments which I purpose to keep and observe the short remainder of my life, God's speciall grace assisting me.

fols. 87v–100r. [104]

[*Inside back cover*]
True Repentance is a motion of the heart, kindled by the Holy Ghost, by which a man comeing to the knowledge of his sinns and the wrath of God, doth earnestly grieve; and by faith in Christ, who made satisfaction for his sinnes, is again raised up, being certainly perswaded that for Christ his sake his sinnes are forgiven.

The doctrine of \the/ Law and the Gospel, hath each of them its proper and peculiar effect in the conversion of man. The Law striketh fear and terrour, whilest it manifesteth sinnes, and the wrath of God against them. The Gospel giveth comfort, whilest it setts before the man that is contrite Christ the mediatour, that Lamb of God which taketh away the sinnes of the world.

fol. 100r[105]
Issue by Sarah Hatfield my second wife. William Coe was borne April 19th 1694, half an houre after 6 att night, baptized May 8th *per* Mr Powell.

<St Bernard's Consideration (*viz.*)>
I consider three things in which all my hope consisteth; (*viz.*) 1st God's love in my adoption, 2dly the truth of his promise, and 3dly his power of performance. Therefore lett my foolish cogitation murmur as long as it list, saying who art thou? and what is that glory? or by what merits dost thou hope to attain it? for I can answere with sure confidence. I know on whom I have beleived and I am certain that in his love he adopted me; that he is true in his promises, and that he is able to perform them. This is the 3-fold cord which is not easily broken which God letteth down from heaven unto us into this prison, which I pray God we may apprehend and firmly hold, that it may raise us up and draw us

fol. 100v
to the sight of the great God of glory. Mr Cradock's *Knowledge and Practice*, 2d part, chapter 19, page 107, lines 22, 23:

[103] See note 73 (f. 67r).
[104] These folios form the section of the manuscript book remaining at Coe's death.
[105] F. 100r is the first of a new sequence of numbers, working back from the back cover.

> God is so just he is not to be questioned,
> so good he is not to be suspected,
> and so strong he is not to be resisted.

Let above all, religion be your care: and all your actions must be centered there.

> It must \not/ be with a light air received,
> For then as lightly it will be beleived,
> To doe noe wrong, nor any wrong conceive,
> And all the wrong that's done you, to forgive,
> Is sure the best, and safest way to live.

A good life makes a good name. And he that governs himself ill, need not complain if he lose his good name.
Turn over 2 leaves.

fol. 101r
An account of what money I have laid out. *Imprimis* paid Mr William Clark of Sechy Bridge £59 10s 0d. Item, paid Mr John Clark. Edward <Davies>

Mr Archer dyed April 24, 1700.[106]
The texts or subjects which Mr Payn preached upon after Mr Archer dyed:
    April 28. I forgott to sett downe
    May 5. Mr Newson
    May 12 forenoon, 1 Thessalonians, chapter 4, verse 1.
    Afternoon, Haggai, chapter 1, verse 7.
    Whitsunday 19. St John, chapter 14, verse 16. And I will pray etc.
    2 Corinthians, chapter 6, verse 1. We then etc.
    26. Psalm 34, verse 17. The righteous cry etc.
    Proverbs 14, verse 12. There is a way etc.
    June 2. Proverbs 3, verse 17. Her wayes are wayes etc.
    John 13, verse 34. A new comandment I give etc.
    9. Job 11, verse 11. For he knoweth vain etc.
    Colossians 3, verse 2. Sett your affections on things etc.
Turn over.

fol. 101v
1700. Mr Pain's subjects since he came to Mildenhall:
    June 16. St Luke 10, verse 28. And he sayd unto etc.
    Jeremiah 8, verse 6, part of the verse. No man repented him of his wickedness etc.
    23. Mr Badcock preached. Mr Pain sick.
    30. Hebrews 12, verse 12. Wherefore lift up the etc. The same in the afternoon.
    July 7. Ecclesiastes, 11 verse 8. But if any man live etc.
    Jeremiah 13, verse 23. Can the Ethiopian etc.

---

[106] Isaac Archer, vicar of Mildenhall, 1688–1700. The Mildenhall parish register also has 24 April as Archer's date of death.

14. 1 Corinthians 10, verse 12. Wherefore lett him that etc.
abfuit pomeridiano tempore.[107]
21. I was att Tilney church in Marshland.
28. 2 Timothy 6, verse 17, 18, 19. Charge them that etc.
The same in th' afternoon.
August 4. Amos 3, verse 2. You only have I known etc.
Ephesians 5, verse 4. Neither filthiness, nor etc.
11. Job 14, verse 1, 2. Man that is born of a etc.
1 Corinthians 15, verse 19. If in this life onely etc.
18. St Luke 16, verse 9. Make to your selves friends.
St Mark 11, verse 24. What things soever etc.

fol. 102r
Jonas Hubbart's accounts.[108]

1688. An account of what mony I lay out of my portion.

	£	s	d
Imprimis. Paid Mr Clarke senior of Sechy bridge for a gray horse I bought of him.	4	0	0
Item, paid Mr Clark junior of Sechy bridge for 15 bullocks bought att Sechy.	49	10	0
Item, paid my brother Coe[109] for 2 mares and a filly I bought of him.	10	0	0
Item, paid Goodman Lister for making and stacking hay.	1	1	0

1688. Jonas Hubbart's accounts.
This was my brother Jonas Hubbart's book and here he begann to keep account, how he disposed of [£]300 his father gave in money by will.

fol. 102v
One would wonder, how men cann indulge their mirth to so extravagant a degree, when the miseries of this life and the sinns wee have to account for, are so many and so great, that a man who seriously considers the danger his soul is in, can very hardly be merry att all, without some sudden damp upon his spirits. It is from the levity of our own unthinking minds, a stupid forgetfulness of our sinfull condition and a continueing insensible of those sorrows which ought most tenderly to affect us, that wee so often indulge the excesses of laughter and gayety, when sighs and tears would much better become us.

fol. 103r
A prayer for any time of the day when a person has leisure to retire, taken out of a book called Dr Patrick's *Devotions*, or *The Devout Christian*.[110]
 O Lord, the great creatour and governour of all things; I prostrate my selfe

---

[107] *Abfuit pomeridiano tempore*: 'He [Mr Pain] was absent in the afternoon'.
[108] This line is written in a different hand.
[109] 'My brother Coe', i.e. William Coe the present diarist.
[110] Symon Patrick, *The Devout Christian instructed* (1673).

before thee, in the humblest adoration of thy incomprehensible majestie: aknowledging [sic] that I depend entirely upon thee, praiseing and magnifying thy most glorious power, wisdom, and goodness, which are conspicuous every where and rendring unto thee my most hearty thanks for all the benefits which thou hast so freely and underservedly conferred on me. Thou art bountifull to the whole world: all thy works praise thee; and we the children of men ought more particularly to bless thee, and speak good of thy name, who have received singular marks and tokens of thy favour and grace, above all the rest of our fellow creatures. Thou hast made us after thine own image, and indued us with reasonable and immortall spirits; and given us a capacity to reflect on

fol. 103v

thee the author of our being, and to be like unto thee in wisdom, holiness, goodness and truth. But above all I ought to remember continually that great demonstration of thy love, in sending thy dear Son to live among us, to dye for us, and to give us an assured hope of immortall life. I love thee, O Lord, I renew the obligation which I have often made of my soul and body to thee. I wait upon thee still for what thou seest good for both. I hope in thy everlasting mercies, that thou wilt pardon all my forgetfullness of thee, and ingratitude unto thee. And I most earnestly implore the grace of thy Holy Spirit, to preserve in my mind a powerfull sence of thee; an ardent love to thee; and an holy care to please and obey thee in all things. That the very same mind and spirit may be in me which was in Christ Jesus our Lord; the spirit of wisdome and understanding, and the fear of thee, the spirit of meekness, humility, purity and charity: and that I may doe thy will with such chearfulness, zeal, constancy, patience and perseverance as he did.

fol. 104r

I thank thee, O Lord, for all helps and assistances of that good spirit, which thou hast already favoured me with all, that thou hast so frequently made good motions to my soul; inspired me with holy thoughts, and devout affections; and inclined and disposed my will, many wayes, to the choice of that which is good. I thank thee for the many seasonable admonitions which thou hast given me, for the hapy [sic] opportunityes which have been afforded me, for wisdome and vertue; for a good education, pious examples, faithfull friends, and all other furtherances in the way of salvation.

I remember likewise, with my most gratefull acknowledgements, what abundance of good things thou hast bestowed on me, from time to time, for my better accommodation in this present life. Blessed be thy name for my continued health and food and rayment. Blessed be thy name that my bones are not broken, that I am not groaning under the sorest pains; that I dwell in safety night and day; and that I still see my friends and acquaintance, and many other comforts round about me.

fol. 104v

I thank thee, O Lord, for these, and all blessings whatsoever, that thou hast conveyed to me by the ministry of thy holy angells; unto whom thou hast given the charge of me. O bless the Lord, together with me, ye his angels which excell in strength, that doe his commandments, hearkening to the voice of his word. And enable me every day, I most humbly beseech thee, O Father of mercyes, to bless thee better, with a purer heart, and a more lively sense of all thy love, and a greater delight in thy devine service, and a forwardness to every good work. And as thou hast preserved me hitherto this day: so bless me the remaining part of it, that endeavouring sincerely in all my designes, words, desires and actions to approve my selfe to thee, as thy good and faithfull servant, I may with a good conscience present my selfe before thee in the conclusion of it: and with the greater confidence of thy gracious acceptance renew my prayers and acknowledgments, and commend my selfe to thy blessing, and hope for the continued protection of thy holy angels, through Christ Jesus, to whom be glory for ever, Amen, and in whose name etc.

fol. 105r

A shorter to the same purpose.

I prostrate my selfe before thee, O Lord of heaven and earth, in all humility of soul and body. I acknowledge my dependence upon thee, and thy constant care and providence over me ever since I was born: particularly this day, in keeping me hitherto from many dangers, and providing for me many good things; as well for the comfort and pleasure, as for the necessary support of this present life. Especially I thank thee for thy exceeding great love in the Lord Jesus; through whom thou hast given me good hope of better enjoyments in the life to come, by following that blessed example which he hath sett us, of well doeing and contented suffering.

It is all reason, O Lord, that I should love thee, and entirely trust in thee, and most willingly serve and obey thee. Accordingly I here again dedicate my selfe both soul and body to thee. I vow my selfe ever to thy service. I hope still in thy great mercyes, which have been so tender and so abundant towards me. I depend upon thee, for what thou seest to be profitable for me. I refer my selfe absolutely to thy divine will, resolving to rest contented and satisfyed in that condition wherein thou placest me. I believe thou orderest all things in heaven and in earth; and takest the

fol. 105v

greatest care of those that wait upon thee, and commit themselves unto thee, as I now doe, in confidence of thy goodness, and submission to thy pleasure. Especially I relye upon thee, for thy Holy Spirit, to preserve me continually with good thoughts, and stirr up in me heavenly affections, and increase and strengthen my faith and hope in thee, and assist my endeavours to doe according to my pious resolutions.

Blessed be thy great goodness for what I have felt already; I thank thee for thy many illuminations from above; for thy grace so early preventing me; for the assistance and furtherance thou hast given me; and the happy opportunityes I have mett withall of improveing my selfe in true wisdom and goodness. It is the earnest desire of my soul to grow more in both, and to be made perfectly like to my blessed Lord and Saviour, by whom all honour and glory be given to thee, O Father Almighty, world without end. Amen.

fol. 106r

Good rules to be observed.

Sett a part one day in a \week or/ month att least, for meditation and prayer to Almighty God. And then call to mind:
1. All the great and shamefull sinns you have committed.
2. All the excellent or greater acts of pyety which by God's grace you have performed.
3. All the great blessings you have att any time received.
4. All the dangers and great sicknesses you have att any time escaped.

And then lett them produce these good acts in you:
1. Repentance and prayers for pardon.
2. Resolutions to proceed and increase in good works.
3. Thangsgiving [sic] to Almighty God.
4. Fear, and watchfullness <least> lest you fall into worse as a punishment for your sinns.

fol. 106v

A prayer to be said at the bed side just before you stepp into bedd.

Good Lord, pardon \all/ my sinns against thy love: let me lye down this night reconciled to thee my God, and in <peace> peace and charity with all the world. Amen.

Another prayer to be sayd just att getting out of bedd.

To thee, my most adorable preserver, I humbly offer up my preserved self: my body, my soul, my members, my senses, my facultyes, my thoughts, my words, my desires, my inclinations, my affections, my actions, to be governed, guided and sanctifyed by thee and to be made conformable to thy holy will this day and alwaies. Amen.

fol. 107r

A short prayer to be said at any time of the day.

O my God, to thee I humbly offer up myself, accept of me graciously to be thine in thy dear son. Thou hast made me what I am, and given me what I have. I live by thee, O that I may live to thee, by thee I am this moving body, and this thinking soul. O that both may pay homage to thee; thou upholdest and sustainest me every moment, I am a liveing monument of thy mercy, O that I may be a liveing monument of thy praise: Glory be to thee, O Lord most high. Amen.

As mankind is never out of the reach of God Almighty's power to afflict and correct, so it is never out of the reach of his power to relieve and recover.

fol. 107v

A short prayer for my children.

O Almighty, and most mercifull Father, who hast promised children as a reward to the righteous, and hast given to me as a testimony of thy mercy, and an encouragement of my duty; be pleased to be a father unto them, and give them healthfull bodyes, understanding souls, and sanctifyed spirits, that they may be thy servants and thy children all their dayes.

Let a great mercy and providence lead them through the dangers and temptations and ignorances of their youth, that they may never runn into folly, and the evils of an unbridled appetite.

fol. 108r
So order the accidents of their lives, that by good education, carefull tutors, holy examples, innocent company, prudent councell, and thy restraining grace, their duty to thee may be secured in the midst of a crooked and untoward generation: and if it seem good in thy eyes, let me be enabled to provide conveniently for the support of their persons, that they may not be destitute or miserable in my death; or if thou shalt call me off from this world by a more tymely summons, let their portion be, thy care, mercy, and providence over their bodyes and souls: and may they never live vicious lives, nor dye violent or untimely deaths; but let them glorifie thee here with a free obedience,

fol. 108v
and the dutyes of an holy life; that when they have served thee in their generations, and have profited the Christian common wealth, they may be co-heires with Jesus in the glories of thy eternall kingdom, through the same our Lord Jesus Christ. Amen. Amen.

Doctor Tayler, page 181:
Take notice that all things that befall thee, come from the most wise and just hand of God; therefore in all thy blessings acknowledge his justice and his wisdom; and labour to find out the cause, and give him the glory.

fol. 109r
A prayer for a contented spirit and the grace of moderation and patience.

O Almighty God, Father and Lord of all the creatures, who hast disposed all things and all chances so as may best glorifie thy wisdom, and serve the ends of thy justice and magnifie thy mercy, thy secret and undiscernable ways bringing good out of evil; I most humbly beseech thee to give me wisdom from above, that I may adore thee and admire thy ways and footsteps, which are in the great deep and not to be searched out: teach me to submit to thy providence in all things, to be content in all changes of person and condition, to be temperate in prosperity, and to read my duty in the lines of thy mercy, and in adversity to be meek, patient, and resigned, and to look through the cloud, that I may wait for the consolation of the Lord, and the day of redemption; in the mean tyme doeing my duty with an unwearied diligence, and an undisturbed resolution, haveing noe fondness for the vanities or possessions of this world, but laying up my hopes in heaven and the rewards of holy liveing, and being strengthned with the spirit of the inner man, through Jesus etc.

fol. 109v
An holy and pious ejaculation to be used at any tyme.

Preserve in me, O Lord, such a serious and deep sense of the worth of my soul, of the weight of all eternity, of the certainty and greatness of the glory that shall be revealed, that they prevail more with me then all the honours and riches, and pleasures of this <life> short and transitory life. Amen. Amen.

fol. 110r

Consideration against anger.

It is good to mark and observe those that are stirred up with passionate anger, beholding their countenance, how unseemly and disfigured it is; how rude their actions are; how absurd <the> their words; how base and contemptible all their behaviour is: and the sight of this in another will be some means to make him loath it in himselfe.

fol. 110v

A short prayer to be said by any pious person as soon as soon as [sic] they are up.

Most holy and eternall God, Lord and sovereign of all the creatures, I humbly present to thy divine majesty my selfe, my soul and body, my thoughts, and my words, my actions and intentions, my passions and my sufferings, to be disposed by thee to thy glory, to be blessed by thy providence, to be guided by thy councell, to be sanctifyed by thy Spirit, and afterwards that my soul and body my [sic] be received into glory; for nothing can perish which is under thy custody, and the enemy of souls cannot devour what is thy portion, nor take it out of thy hands. This day O Lord, and all the dayes of my life, I dedicate to thine honour, and the actions of my calling to the uses of grace, and the religion of all my dayes

fol. 111r
to be united to the merits and intercession of my holy Saviour Jesus, that in him and for him I may be pardoned and accepted. Amen. Amen. Amen.[111]

---

[111] The last 'Amen' is written in Hebrew characters.

Appendix 3
Will of William Coe, 1729

[PRO, PROB 11 635, 32]

In the name of God, Amen. I, William Coe of Mildenhall in the County of Suffolk, gentleman, being in health and in sound and perfect mind and memory, God be praised, but considering the frailty of human nature and uncertainty of this life, do make and ordain this my last will and testament in manner and form following. First, I bequeath my soul into the hands of Almighty God who gave it, trusting in the alone merits and mediacion of Jesus Christ my Lord and my Saviour and Redeemer for my salvacion, and my body to Christian burial at the discretion of my executors hereafter named. And as to my worldly estate wherewith it hath pleased God to bless me, I give and dispose thereof as followeth.

Imprimis, I give to my two daughters which I had by Elizabeth my first wife, Judith the wife of William Graves of Long Sutton in the county of Lincoln, gentleman, and Anne the wife of Ralph Cole of Sudbury in the said county of Suffolk, gentleman, the sume of five pounds apeice to buy them mourning, if they shall be liveing at the time of my decease.

Item, I give and bequeath unto my said two daughters my close of pasture lyeing on the east side of my now dwelling house, which my father purchased of Mr Richard Clift, and called or known by the name of the Whom Close, containing by estimacion one acre and two roods, be the same more or less, and holdeth of the mannor of Aspalls. And also all that part of my orchard which my said father purchased of Robert Hynard and holdeth also of the said mannor of Aspalls, both which I give and bequeath to my said two daughters and their heirs, according to the uses mencioned in and by their mother's joynture, and whereof I passed a surrender to the use of my will in the year of our Lord one thousand, seven hundred and sixteen.

Item, I give \and bequeath/ unto my sister Bickerstaffe the sume of ten pounds to be paid her by my executors within six months after my decease, if she shall be then liveing.

Item, I give and bequeath unto the poor of the parish of Mildenhall aforesaid the sume of five pounds, to be paid by my executors within one month after my decease in manner following, that is to say: to the poor of Westrow the sume of forty shillings, \and/ to the poor of the High Town, Beckrow and Hallywellrow, to each watch the sume of twenty shillings, to be distributed amongst them at the discrecion of the minister and churchwardens then being.

Item, I will and order that the executors of this my will, or the survivor or survivors of them and their heirs, shall with all possible speed after my decease expose to sale to such person or persons and to his, her or their heirs as they shall see fitt, for such price as they can gett, all and every my coppyhold messuages or tenements, lands and hereditaments whatsoever and wheresoever with the appurtenances, not herein before disposed off. And the money ariseing upon such sale thereof I will shall be put out at interest from time to time dureing the terme of the natural life of Sarah my dear wife, so as she shall receive the interest, profitts and produce thereof to her own proper use. And after her decease I will that the principall money shall be disposed of to and amongst all my children borne of her body (excepting my son Henry who hath been paid or secured to be paid what he can expect from me) in equall shares and proporcions.

Item, I give and devise to my said beloved wife all my freehold messuages or tenements, lands, reall estates and hereditaments whatsoever and wheresoever with the appurtenances, dureing the term of her natural life. And after her decease I give and devise the same to my said executors, and the survivor or survivors of them and their heirs, upon this trust and confidence reposed in them: that as soon as conveniently may be after the decease of my said wife, they, or the survivors or survivor of them and the heirs of the survivor of them, shall expose all the same freehold premisses to sale for the best price they can gett, and shall pay and dispose of the money ariseing by the sale thereof to and amongst my children born of the body of the said Sarah my wife, except before excepted, in equall shares and proportions.

Item, I will that all my debts shall be honestly paid and discharged. And I do will and order that my said beloved wife shall take for her own use such part of my houshold stuff, plate or other goods of any kind whatsoever, as she shall think fit. And I will that all other my goods, chattles, cattle and personal estate shall be sold by my said executors, and the survivors or survivor of them. And then I order that the money ariseing upon the sale thereof shall be put out at interest, in trust for the benefit of my said wife and all her said children, except before excepted, in such manner as the money herein before mentioned is ordered to be put out at interest and applyed. And it is my mind and will notwithstanding anything herein before mentioned, that in case any of my said children shall happen to marry with the consent and good likeing of my said wife, then my said executors, or the survivors or survivor of them and their heirs, shall out of the money herein before mentioned or by sale of any part of my real estate, raise moneys and pay to such of them as shall so marry and not otherwise any sume of money not exceeding the sume of two hundred pounds, which I do hereby order to be paid accordingly. But my will and mind is that if any of my children shall happen to marry before mine and my wife's decease, then all such and so much money as they or any of them so marrying shall have and receive as his, her or their present portion shall be reckoned into his, her or their share, and shall be discounted by them and every of them so marrying proportionably, so that all my children by my present wife, except before excepted, shall all have and receive equall shares out of all my real and personal estate after mine and my said wife's decease, all my debts and legacys being first fully paid and satisfyed.

And whereas upon certain contingencies, I am entituled to the remainder in fee of and in all that messuage or tenement wherein I now dwell, called or known by the name of the Brewhouse, with the houses, outhouses, malthouses, yards, gardens, orchards, land, grounds, hereditaments and appurtenances in Mildenhall aforesaid, by vertue of a marriage settlement formerly made upon my deceased wife Elizabeth, formerly Elizabeth Hubbart, as in and by the said marriage settlement or joynture and a schedule thereunto annexed is at large mentioned and expressed, now I dispose of the said remainder in fee as followeth, that is to say: in case my said daughter Judith, the wife of William Grave of Long Sutton in the county of Lincoln, gentleman, and my grandson William Graves, and my said daughter Anne, the wife of Ralph Cole of Sudbury in the said county of Suffolk, gentleman, shall all dye without issue lawfully begotten, then I give all the said messuage or tenement, lands and premisses to be sold by my executors, and the survivors or survivor of them, for the best price which can be gott for the same, and as soon as conveniently may be after the said estate shall fall to me or my heirs. And I will that the money ariseing upon such sale shall be put out at interest from time to time during the term of the natural life of the said Sarah my dear wife, if she shall be then living, so as she shall receive the interest, profits and produce thereof to her own proper use and benefit. And I will also that she receive the rents and profits of the said estate to her own proper use till it can be sold, and after her decease, or if she shall happen to dye before such remainder in fee shall fall to me or my heirs, then I will that the money ariseing upon such sale be disposed of as followeth, that is to say I give and devise unto my said son Henry Coe, if he shall be then living, or to his lawfull issue if he shall leave any, the sume of fifty pounds of lawfull money of Great Britain. And all the rest of the said money ariseing upon such sale, I will shall be equally divided between all and every of the rest of my children who shall me and my said wife survive, share and share alike, and if any of them shall happen to dye before such remainder in fee shall happen to fall, then I will that his, her or their share so dying shall go to and amongst such lawfull issue as he, she or they so dying shall leave, share and share alike.

And lastly I do nominate and appoint the said Sarah my beloved wife and Sarah Coe my daughter and Thomas Coe my son, executors of this my will. In witness whereof I have to this my last will and testament contained in two sheets of paper set my hand and seal this first day of September in the year of our Lord, one thousand, seven hundred, twenty and five, 1725. William Coe. Signed, sealed, published and declared to be the last will and testament of the said William Coe, in the presence of us who at his request and in his presence subscribed our names as witnesses, Robert Wilkin, Adam Macro, James Steed.

[CODICIL]
I, William Coe of Mildenhall in the county of Suffolk, gentleman, do hereby order this present writing or codicil, to be deemed and taken as part of my last will and testament to which these presents are annexed, viz. I do hereby confirm the same will and do order the executors in the said will named, in case my nephew Coe Bickerstaffe is not now in England \or shall not returne to England/, to expose that peice or inclosure of ground lying near the the East-gate in Bury St Edmunds in the said county of Suffolk, mentioned in the last will and testament of my late sister Bickerstaffe deceased, to sale pursuant to the tenor of the said will, and to dispose of the money ariseing thereby according to the true intent and meaning thereof, witness my hand and seal this ninth day of December in the year of our Lord 1728. William Coe. Sealed and delivered in the presence of us, Robert Owers, Mary Owers, Mary Hinard.

[Proved 17 Feb. 1729/30 at London]

Index of Names

NB All numbers refer to the folios in Coe's Diary (see Introduction, p. 36).

Index of Places

Index of Subjects

NB All numbers refer to the folios in Coe's Diary.

Foliation and Pagination in Coe's Diary

Folio	Page	Folio	Page	Folio	Page
1r	1	16v	34	32v	66
1v	2	17r	35	33r	67
2r	3	17v	36	33v	68
2v	4	18r	37	34r	69
3r	5	18v	38	34v	70
3v	6	19r	39	35r	71
4r	7	19v	40	35v	72
4v	8	20r	41	36r	73
5r	9	20v	42	36v	74
5v	10	21r	43	37r	75
6r	11	21v	44	37v	76
6v	12	22r	45	38r	77
7r	13	22v	46	38v	78
7v	14	23r	47	39r	79
8r	15	23v	48	39v	80
8v	16	24r	49	40r	81
9r	17	24v	50	40v	82
9v	18	25r	51	41r	83
10r	19	25v	52	41v	84
10v	20	26r	53	42r	85
[page cut out]		26v	54	42v	86
11r	23	27r	55	43r	87
11v	24	27v	56	43v	88
12r	25	28r	57	44r	89
12v	26	28v	58	44v	90
13r	27	29r	59	45r	91
13v	28	29v	60	45v	92
14r	29	30r	61	46r	93
14v	30	30v	62	46v	94
15r	31	31r	63	47r	95
15v	32	31v	64	47v	96
16r	33	32r	65	48r	97

Folio	Page	Folio	Page	Folio	Page
48v	98	64v	130	83v	156
49r	99	66v	–	84r	157
49v	100	67r	134	84v	158
50r	101	67v	–	85r	159
67r	134	68r	135	85v	160
51r	103	68v	–	86r	161
51v	104	69	136	86v	162
52r	105	69v	–	87r	163
52v	106	70r	137	88v–100r blank.
53r	107	70v	–	No pagination
53v	108	71r	138	From back cover,
54r	109	71v	–	opposite direction
54v	110	72r	139	100r
55r	111	72v	–	100v
55v	112	73r	140	101r
56r	113	73v	–	101v
56v	114	74r	141	102r
57r	115	74v	–	102v
57v	116	75r	142	103r
58r	117	75v	–	103v
58v	118	76r	143	104r
59r	119	76v	–	104v	No
59v	120	77r	144	105r	pagination
60r	121	77v	–	105v
60v	122	78r	145	106r
61r	123	78v	146	106v
61v	124	79r	147	107r
62r	125	79v	148	107v
62v	126	80r	149	108r
63r	127	80v	150	108v
63v	128	81r	151	109r
64r	129	81v	152	109v
65r	131	82r	153	110r
65v	132	82v	154	110v
66r	133	83r	155	111r

Glossary of Terms Used in Both Diaries

abbot gunn	probably a corruption of 'hagbut' or 'arquebus', a portable gun with a stack, used for practical or sporting purposes.
Act of Uniformity	a decree requiring general conformity to the religious practices of the Church of England. A new act was issued in 1662 to revoke the relaxed church policies introduced during the Interregnum.
advowson	the right of presenting to a church living.
ague	a malarial fever with cold, hot and sweating stages. A tertian ague is a fever occurring every other or, by inclusive reckoning, third day. A quartane ague occurs every third or, by inclusive reckoning, fourth day.
All Fours	a card game, so called from its four points (high, low, jack and game).
apparitour	an officer of an ecclesiastical court, especially concerned with the delivering of summonses and decrees.
appropriation	an appropriated living; a vicarage, perpetual curacy or donative.
assize	a periodic sitting of senior judges in each county, to deal with criminal and civil actions.
augmentation	an increase in the value of a church living; a church living so treated.
aul	awl, a sharp tool used for piercing small holes.
avoydance	the next time a living is vacant or offered for sale.
bed-maker	a domestic servant at Cambridge University responsible for menial duties, including bed-making.
bedle	beadle, a university officer with largely ceremonial duties.
bishop's articles	injunctions and guidelines, usually issued by a new bishop, laying down the standards of discipline and liturgical responsibilities of the clergy in a diocese.
blood stones	precious stones worn as amulets to stop or prevent bleeding.
blooded	to undergo blood-letting; phlebotomy.
brasse money	coins of small denomination.
breeding	pregnant; the condition of pregnancy.
canons	the doctrines and regulations of the Church of England, passed in 1604.

catechizing	instructing in the Christian faith, by way of questions and answers learned by rote.
chirugergy/ chirurgeon	surgery/surgeon.
choller	choler; bile or other bodily secretion.
clunch	a harder form of chalk, used as a building material.
Common Prayer	a service according to the liturgy of the Church of England.
commonplaces	notable passages, often of scripture, frequently preached on, or entered into a book.
commons	daily fare, referring to common table at Cambridge University, enjoyed by junior members; as opposed to high table.
coverture	the legal condition of a married woman, under the authority and protection of her husband.
cow bing	a bin containing animal feed.
crick	creek (part of River Lark).
curb	a strap or chain attached to the bit and passing under the jaw of a horse.
dames	married women.
decretall order	a decree issued by a court of law.
double guard	some kind of protective clothing worn by horse-riders (*cf.* safeguard).
dropsy	accumulation of watery fluids in the human body.
dutyes	common religious practices or 'exercises', used habitually to reinforce faith, eg. prayer, reading the scriptures and reciting sermons.
fanatick	a perjorative term used by conformists to refer to a person staunchly committed to nonconformity.
fancy	easily attracted to whims and unsound opinions.
favour	'came to its favour too soone' appears to mean a premature childbirth.
filler	horse which is attached to the shaft or pole of a cart, wagon or other vehicle.
First Fruits	a payment equivalent to the first year's revenue made by each holder of a benefice to the crown.
fluxe	an excessive discharge of blood etc.
glebe	land attached to a church living and held by the incumbent.
Goody	Goodwife, a title given to the mistress of a house, usually of middling or lower social status.
green heads	callow, immature company.
haleing line	haling line, used for hauling boats.
haply	by chance.

hide	perhaps a version of 'hithe' or 'heath', both of which were features of the Breckland.
hobby	a small, working horse.
horsemill	a mill powered by a horse walking in a circle.
induction	officially placing a person into a church living; the final stage of appointing a new incumbent, after nomination and institution; usually done by an archdeacon.
ingathering	a period of harvesting; a harvest festival.
institution	admission of a new incumbent into the spiritual care of a parish; done by a bishop.
iznigglasse	isinglass, a gelatinous substance obtained from fish, used in cookery and to make glue.
jarres	quarrellings; discord.
joynture	estate settled on a married woman to support her after her husband's death.
labend	tongue or tag of a document, to which a seal was affixed.
Lady Day	the feast of the Annunciation of the Virgin Mary, 25 March; one of the four quarter days (q.v.).
laid downe	the relinquishing of a church living. Forced upon ministers refusing to conform to the Church of England by St Bartholomew's Day, 1662.
lascivious	used in the sense of wanton and unruly, not necessarily lustful.
learned/learning	often used to mean taught/ teaching.
Lecturer	a clerical appointment in which the main duties were to teach and preach, rather than to perform liturgical or sacramental tasks. Many lectureships were supported by voluntary contributions from a congregation or town corporation; they were effectively outlawed after 1662.
meers' head	meres were unploughed balks and tracks in open fields.
Michaelmas	the feast of St Michael the Archangel, 29 September; one of the four quarter days (q.v.).
mole line	moline or mill-rind; the iron centrepiece of a millstone, with spiked ends.
morall men	derogatory phrase used to mean those who placed great weight upon the outward performance of religion, eg. the Book of Common Prayer (q.v.).
neat-way	a track along which cattle were driven.
nettle spring	nettle rash, or urticaria, an irritative skin condition.
New England	English communities newly established on north-east coast of America.

nine pins	a game, a form of skittles.
nonconformist	a person refusing to conform to the Church of England, preferring to worship in voluntary assemblies.
nurse	'put to nurse' refers to the practice of wet nursing, whereby infants were suckled by women other than their natural mothers.
outlawries	deprivation of legal protection.
overlaid	smothered by lying on top of; Archer's youngest child was overlaid by her wet-nurse (*see* nurse).
Papist	a pejorative term used of Roman Catholics, or those suspected of collusion with them.
pattin	patten, an undershoe worn to raise ordinary shoes out of the mud or wet; generally of wood mounted on an iron ring.
plotts	spots or blotches on the body.
prized	appraised.
professour	one who strongly professes a religious creed, in this case puritanism.
providence	the actions of God, in practical terms, seen to work in the lives of all men. A belief that all things happened as a result of God's will in response to men's actions, and not by accident, furnished an entire theological and religious system for many in the 17th century; often referred to as 'providentialism'.
quartane	(*see* ague)
quarter day	one of four days in the year when rents were due: Lady Day, Midsummer Day, Michaelmas and Christmas.
quickning	the movement of a child in the womb.
rabated rapiers	blunted rapiers used in fencing.
rake	a wheel rut.
ranched	wrenched.
received	took Holy Communion.
reversion	the right to succeed to the title of land or a church living.
rhewme	rheum, a heavy cold, catarrh.
rule money	money paid for the issuing of a court order.
safeguard	a large, outer riding skirt worn by ladies (*cf.* double guard).
seed tear	tares or vetch grown for seed.
seniour	a senior fellow in a Cambridge college; seniors were of long standing and managed the affairs of the college.
sequestration	the temporary removal of property until debts are satisfied, or a court order complied with.
service book	the Book of Common Prayer.

sine-cure	an ecclesiastical living without regular duties.
sizar	a student at Cambridge who received an allowance from the college in return for certain menial duties.
skarre	scare.
sladed	slid.
slenting	slanting (blow on the leg).
small tithes	farming tithes taken on less important produce, as opposed to great tithes.
springell	rod used in thatching.
statute staple	a form of security whereby a borrower could charge his own lands without relinquishing possession.
stock	a block of wood.
stoppings	the stopping of normal bodily functions, such as constipation.
tables	the game of backgammon.
tears	(see seed tears)
term	a period of time during which a court of law conducts its business.
tertian	(see ague)
Test	the Test Act, which required all office holders in church and state to take Holy Communion according to the rites of the Church of England, and to subscribe to the Oath of Allegiance before they could take up office.
towne	often means township or parish.
travell	travail, especially referring to the pains of childbirth.
tunned	putting beer into barrels for storing.
twiddles	pimples (a Suffolk word, see J. O. Halliwell, Dictionary of Archaic and Provincial Words, 1847).
use	interest on money borrowed.
usher	an assistant to a schoolmaster; an under-master.
water horses	horses used to pull water-borne craft, on River Lark through Mildenhall.
wheat ridges	probably ridged lands in the open fields of Mildenhall, suitable for growing wheat.